LETTERS OF HELENA ROERICH

1929 - 1935

I

Portrait of Helena Roerich (1937), by Svetoslav Roerich.

LETTERS
of
HELENA ROERICH

1929-1935

VOLUME I

AGNI YOGA SOCIETY
2017

Agni Yoga Society
319 West 107th Street
New York NY 10025
www.agniyoga.org

© 1954 by Agni Yoga Society.
Published 1954.
Reprinted 2017.

FOREWORD

The original edition of this book was published in Russian in 1940 by the Latvian Roerich Society in Riga.

The publishers extend grateful acknowledgement to Mme. V. L. Dutko for her penetrative and sensitive work in rendering the first English translation. Without her devotion to this task the present publication would not have been possible.

Agni Yoga Society is honored to present the *Letters of Helena Roerich* as an integral part of The Teaching of Living Ethics.

PREFACE

"When the images of great historic figures reach us from remote antiquity they are somehow assimilated in consciousness more easily. Even if they are veiled in myths and legends, they are very convincing. With the passage of time, everything seems possible. Writers and artists of all ages dedicate their best inspirations to these distant images. Whole generations are inspired by these heroes and heroines. No one envies them, and no one ponders at what cost the achievements were performed. What is preserved is purely the record of glorious human ascent.

"It is not quite so with images from the recent past, to say nothing of the present time. Take, for instance, the biographical sketches of the great men of late. So much that is unessential, uncharacteristic, is mentioned regarding them! This only proves that the final essence of their lives has not yet been weighed and appreciated. The most doubtful, the least-proven details are invariably included; hence, the conclusions, if not altogether negative, tend to be depreciative.

"Of course, with passing ages the scales will be balanced. The justice of the people will remove much that obscured the eyes of contemporaries. The judgment of the ages does not necessarily have to demean. Even in the short span of a hundred years we see that a great deal has attained its own balance. The lengthy pages on which the great souls were disparaged have not yet disintegrated. Our grandfathers witnessed how cruel and unjust was the attitude of people toward certain manifestations which, in less than a century, were to become the pride of their country and even of the whole world. And we ourselves are now witnesses of the same. ...

"Beautiful images are passing before us of men and women who are the true creators of culture. And it would seem desirable to recognize them immediately rather than postpone unnecessarily. Why hide them in the archives and screen them from sight until they grow into a fantasy of the folk imagination?

"Here, we encounter a remarkable contemporary figure, an outstanding Russian woman. Revealing unusual qualities even in childhood, she is seen as a little girl secretly carrying away a heavy volume of Dore's Bible. Bending from its burdensome weight, hiding it from the grown-ups, she has taken the treasure in order to study the illustrations, and eventually (when she teaches herself to read) to study the Testaments.

"From her father's bookcase, at an unusually early age, she also took volumes on philosophy. Amidst the noisy, and it seems distracting, environment she was able to develop a profound contemplation of life, as if she had possessed it long ago. Honesty, justice, a constant search for Truth, and love for creative work—all this actually transformed the whole of life around the strong young spirit. And the whole house, the whole family, became directed by the same benevolent principles. All difficulties and dangers were endured under the same stoic leadership. The accumulated knowledge and striving to perfection brought a victorious solution of problems, and this led the surrounding people toward the luminous path. Ignorance, darkness, malice were always acutely sensed. Wherever it was possible, both physical and spiritual healing was performed. Life became full of true labor. From morning till night everything was performed for the benefit of humanity. The broadest correspondence was carried on; books were written; works of many volumes translated; and all this was done in an amazingly tireless spirit. Even the most difficult circumstances were conquered by true faith which became real straight-knowledge. Surely, wonderful accumulations are necessary for such knowledge! All young people should know of this tireless life as a vital example of austere achievements, benevolence, and constructiveness. When the difficulties of this inspirational work are known, it will be particularly helpful toward the realization that incessant advancement can be made. Often, one thinks that everything is hopeless, that good is defenseless against evil, so great are the delusions resulting from human despair. Therefore, real vital examples are indeed most important; and we may rejoice at the encouragement such an example as this provides for all beginners in constructive work." (Nicholas Roerich, *The Great Images*, in *The Invincible*.)

So speaks the authentic witness! We, friends and admirers of the works of Elena Ivanovna [Helena Roerich], can receive fiery flashes of her broad and wise contemplation from her letters, for is not her whole life imbued with fire? The Women's Movement, cosmological researches, the Living Ethics—all these can be found in her letters to friends. Elena Ivanovna was opposed to the publication of her letters, but, we, her numerous friends, have been exchanging copies of what were for us their most precious indications. Eventually we came to the conclusion that, considering the demand for these letters by an increasing number of friends and co-workers, it was necessary to publish them in book form. We applied to E.I. herself, and at last received her permission. Of course, the first volume consists only of a relatively small number of letters, or rather fragments of letters, which in most cases are just the answers to various questions of co-workers. The names of the co-workers and even their places of residence are not mentioned, as what is important is the subject dealt with. As to the correspondents, they themselves know whom the letters concern and on what occasions they were written.

Through the gradual publication of these letters, the breadth of thought of this remarkable Russian woman will be revealed. In Russia as well as abroad during their world travels, she always gave herself in service both to her own country and to humanity.

The Russians have contributed quite a number of remarkable women in various fields of life. One can think of the names of such heroines as Kovalevsky, Blavatsky, Dashkova, Volkonsky, Morozova and many others. From the remote past until now, they have served humanity with their unusual talents and knowledge. The activities of women have been recognized only recently, but already we can see the influence of woman in all spheres: art, literature, philosophy, medicine, education, industry, aviation—in short, wherever the new world is being built. Elena Ivanovna has always been hoping to publish a worthy book, a bibliographical work, dedicated to woman. Moreover, she has never had in view any estrangement from the world; on the contrary, she always thinks of the broadest, closest cooperation, which would forever remove the conventional limitations of ignorance.

Being privileged to present these thoughts of a wonderful woman thinker, the publishers take great pleasure in giving to all seekers of truth and culture the possibility of becoming acquainted with the profoundly penetrative letters of Elena Ivanovna Roerich.

Part I
LETTERS TO AMERICA
1929-1932

1

1929

MY YOUNG FRIENDS!

From far-off India, the country of beauty, of achievements of the spirit, and of great thought, I send to you who are gathered in the name of the great labor and structure of the future—greetings of the heart! I call you to self-perfection and unlimited attainment.

The book of new discoveries and the light of daring is open before humanity, and you have already heard about the approach of the New Era. Every epoch has its Call, and the calling foundation of the New Era will be the power of thought. That is why we call you to understand the great significance of creative thought, and the first step in this direction will be the *opening of consciousness*, freedom from all prejudices and from all tendentiousness and forced concepts.

Let us glance at the entire immensity of the night sky. In our thoughts let us fly over the innumerable worlds and the hidden depths of infinite space. Thought in its substance is infinite, and only our consciousness attempts to limit it. Therefore, without delay, let us start the next step—*broadening of consciousness*. The most ancient wisdom of India says: "Thought is the primary source of world creation." The Great Buddha pointed out the meaning of thought which builds our essence. He taught his pupils to broaden their consciousness. Lao Tze, Confucius, Christ—all Teachers of spirit and great thinkers taught the same thing.

The Great Plato said: "Thoughts rule the world." And modern scientists, as for instance Professor Compton, have expressed the probability of an active, rational force in every phenomenon of nature, and of the influence of thought upon matter. He concludes with the following remarkable words: "Possibly the thoughts of men are the most important factors in the world."

With such broad understanding let us become acquainted with the history of the development of thought. Putting aside all prejudices of place, time and nationality, we, like the bees, shall collect the precious honey of human creative thought!

After placing into the foundation the powerful achievements of those great creators who molded our consciousness, let us begin the third step—the *development* of our *own thought*, our own creativeness; and from the new combinations we shall hew sparks of the fire of thought, this crown of the Universe.

Let us remember that a thinking being is never lonely because thought is his greatest magnet and brings similar response from space. Therefore, if we want to receive a beautiful answer we should send into vibrating space our striving thoughts saturated with the pure fire of the heart; only the thought which is spiritualized by striving, nourished by the heart, can create and attract as a powerful magnet. Thought without the striving and flaming quality is sterile. Thus, let us long for knowledge, for broad thoughts, and in our striving we shall dare, as only daring thought molds new ways.

You, my young friends, who have approached art and creation, you should be able to utilize your gifts as a condensation of your forces; for sound and color, thought and rhythm are the foundations of the Universe and of our existence. Sound and color, knowledge and creation are the chalice of Amrita, the Chalice of Immortality!

Eternal, continuous creation of the universal Life surrounds us, and we, being part of this great creation, should create every moment of our life—create by thought, by word, by action.

My young friends, fill up the treasury of your spirit. Absorb all the sounds, all the colors, all the rhythms from the fathomless source of space. These finest vibrations, consciously absorbed, will refine your receptivity and your thought.

The refinement of receptivity will give you the possibility of penetrating into the Sanctuaries of Space, and will open the joyous path of achievement and continuous, endless ascent.

My friends, labor with all the tension of your forces because only by reaching the limit of your tension do new possibilities come to you. The laws are alike in everything. We know that sublime energies are born of the greatest efforts. Therefore, only increased activity and intensified strength will bring the achievement of beauty.

And I beg you, do not fear difficulties. Display readiness to meet all obstacles, for each obstacle strengthens you and leads you to the future victory. Try to love the difficulties, and say, "Blessed be the obstacles, through them we grow." Courageously, inspired by striving, realizing the majesty of the endless perfecting of creative life, strive toward the calling Infinity—infinity of lives, infinity of achievements, infinity of knowledge, infinity of construction, infinity of beauty!

My young friends, hearken to the Call of Creative Infinity!

2

1 March 1929

The approaching great epoch is closely connected with the ascendancy of woman. As in the best days of humanity, the future epoch will again offer woman her rightful place alongside her eternal fellow traveler and co-worker, man. You must remember that the grandeur of the Cosmos is built by the dual Origin. Is it possible, therefore, to belittle one Element of It?

All the present and coming miseries and the cosmic cataclysms to a great degree result from the subjugation and abasement of woman. The dreadful decline of morality, the diseases and degeneration of some nations are also the results of the slavish dependence of woman. Woman is deprived of the greatest human privilege—complete participation in creative thought and constructive work. She is deprived not only of equal rights but, in many countries, of equal education with man. She is not allowed to express her abilities in the building of social and government life, of which, by Cosmic Law and Right, she is a full-fledged member. But a woman slave can give to the world slaves only. The proverb "great mother, great son" has a cosmic, scientific foundation. As sons mostly take after their mothers, and daughters after fathers, great is cosmic justice! By humiliating woman, man humiliates himself! This explains today the paucity of man's genius.

Could the terrors and crimes of today be possible if both Origins had been balanced? In the hands of woman lies the salvation of humanity and of our planet. Woman must realize her significance, the great mission of the Mother of the World; she should be prepared to take responsibility for the destiny of humanity. Mother, the life-giver, has every right to direct the destiny of her children. The voice of woman, the mother, should be heard amongst the leaders of humanity. The mother suggests the first conscious thoughts to her child. She gives direction and quality to all his aspirations and abilities. But the mother who possesses no thought of culture can suggest only the lower expressions of human nature.

The woman who strives to knowledge and beauty, who realizes her lofty responsibility, will greatly uplift the whole level of life. There will be no place for disgusting vices which lead to the degeneration and destruction of whole countries.

But in her striving toward education, woman must remember that all educational systems are only the *means* for the development of a *higher* knowledge and culture. The true culture of thought is developed by the culture of *spirit* and *heart*. Only such a combination gives that great synthesis without which it is impossible to realize the real grandeur, diversity, and complexity of human life in its cosmic evolution. Therefore, while striving to knowledge, may woman remember the Source of Light and the Leaders of Spirit—those great Minds who, verily, created the consciousness of humanity. In approaching this Source, this leading Principle of Synthesis, humanity will find the way to real evolution.

And woman is the one who should know and proclaim this leading Principle because from the very beginning she was chosen to link the two worlds, visible and invisible. Woman possesses the power of the sacred life energy. The coming epoch brings knowledge about this great omnipresent energy, which is manifested in all immortal creations of human genius.

Western woman is awake and realizes her powers. Her cultural contributions are already evident. However, the majority of Western women—as with all beginners—start with imitation; whereas, it is in original self-expression that real beauty and harmony are found. Would we like to see man losing the beauty of manhood? The same is true about a man who has a sense of beauty. He certainly does not wish to see a woman imitating his habits and competing with his vices. Imitation always starts with the easiest. But we hope that this first step will soon be outlived and that woman will deepen her knowledge of Mother-Nature and will find true, original ways of self-expression.

The Cosmos manifests unity of law, but there is no repetition in its variety. Why then does humanity alone strive toward uniformity in everything, while at the same time it violates the fundamental unity of law? Uniformity of perception, uniformity of life, and especially uniformity of thought is cherished by man. It is forgotten that uniformity of expression leads toward stagnation and death. Life and its power are in perpetual change of form. It is necessary to apply this life-giving principle in all expressions of our life.

Let us collect the most beautiful, heroic images of all times and countries, and with creative imagination let us apply their achievements in our life, taking into consideration the peculiarities of our epoch. Only such imitation will give the correct foundation for further progress.

I shall finish my address to woman with a page from The Teaching of Life:

"When nations started disunity, the result was self-destruction. And only a return to balance can stop this self-destruction. Humanity does not apply the principles of creativeness in right proportion and thus violates the foundations of Being. When by the law of the Cosmic Magnet the lower forms are subordinated to the higher, this concerns only the energies which should be transmuted. But when the Origins are called to create and give life, it is impossible to remove one of the Origins without self-destruction. Therefore, humanity will start its real evolution only when both Origins are affirmed in life. All principles which do not include the understanding of the dual Origin can only increase the lack of balance. Humanity must understand the law of the Cosmic Magnet. Much can be done for evolution by the realization of the grandeur of the dual Origin which is the basis of Life."

Even this simple truth still does not find its place in the consciousness of man! Our scientists—biologists, chemists, physicists—should know the truth about the dual Element, or polarity, but they are silent. And such truth, in its most sacred and vital application, is scorned, and the rights of the strong selfishly dominate. The trouble is that the mind of man is disconnected from it source—the Cosmic Mind. Being part of the Cosmos, the human being yet does not see his solidarity, his unity with the Cosmos. And his observations of the manifestations of nature do not suggest to him any analogies. However, only in observations and comparisons with human nature is it possible to find the keys to all the mysteries of life, and therefore the solution to many problems of everyday life. People, like parrots, love to repeat the favorite ancient formula "Macrocosm is microcosm"! Much is said, much is repeated without the proper attention to its meaning! The enforced dogmas, human laws, and the standard of life have caused humanity to neglect the process of thinking; and the human mind, with rare exceptions, has become an automaton. Everybody is preaching various freedoms, but the most opposite schools of thought agree in one thing—they all are afraid of freedom of thought!

Therefore, woman must defend not only her own rights but the right of free thought for the whole of humanity! Through the development of thinking, our abilities will expand. Let us think with the broadest, the purest thoughts. It is said:

"The kingdom is not made up of royalties or of subjects, but is created by cosmic ideas. Let us create our own cities, our countries, our planets! But let such thought be created by the heart, as only thought born of the heart is vital. The heart is the greatest Cosmic Magnet. All cosmic energies are attracted to the heart, and the heart assimilates them. The heart manifests in life all aspirations. The fire of space is attracted to the heart and the whole cosmic process lies in this principle. Therefore, the Cosmos exists in the attraction of the heart. Only the energies which are based on the attraction of the heart are vital. Thus, infinitely, the chain of life is forged by the heart."

Have you listened to your heart? Does it beat in rhythm with the Perfect Heart which embraces all of you?

Thus, I shall finish with the words about the heart. Let woman affirm this great symbol, which can transfigure the whole of life. Let her strive to transmute the spiritual life of mankind.

The mother, the life-give, the life-protector—let her become also the Mother, the Leader, the *All*-Giver, the *All*-Receiver.

3

19 October 1929

Today, I write using the words of the Great Teacher about the Sacrament of Hierarchy. Truly, this is a sacrament because it is based upon the immutable and exact law of the Cosmic Magnet which leads all beings to perfection. It is necessary to realize the Hierarchy clearly, precisely, and broadly as the only way toward progress. We must realize the whole chain of Hierarchy, holding strongly to our nearest link. Woe to the one who tries to skip this link and thus loses his connection. It is impossible to catch up again, as the rhythm of the movement of the whole chain will carry away the saving link. Grave indeed is this error! How much time will be lost in trying to recover the vibrating link which responds to the call. But the new link will be different in sequence and tension because the previous one has been carried away in the rhythmic striving of the whole Hierarchical chain.

"Subordination of the lower to the higher represents the foundation of the whole Cosmos. Subordination of the lower to the higher will bring purification. But humanity subordinates to the lower that which should lead. When the higher leads, the transmutation of the lower occurs. This transmutation creates a valuable sequence which grows infinitely. By transmutation we mean the subordination of the lower to the higher, and we want to confirm the consciousness of mankind in the process of infinite progress."

Therefore, let us not delay the transmutation of our consciousness. Let us remember the leading Hierarch, and let us honor the nearest, the earthly Guru. "The earthly Guru is given for reverence, for progress, for unity, for construction." By neglecting the Guru, by depreciating the Guru, one neglects and demeans the Great Teacher who confirmed the Guru because the Guru is the representative of the Great Teacher. Let us remember how the Lords of Light hold sacred the Sacrament of Hierarchy. The Hierarch carries the Synthesis of the Chalice and, therefore, He holds both obedience and command. The one who does not know the art of obeying will not attain the art of commanding. Beautiful are these two concepts. Conscious subordination approaches command. After the firm realization of Hierarchy, we shall with all our heart begin a deeper understanding of the Teaching of Life. It hurts the heart to feel how little understood are those treasures which the Teacher bestows so generously. On these treasures will be founded the new race. Ponder over the majesty of what is given! I feel frightened when I think of the responsibility we take upon ourselves when we accept these treasures, knowing that among us are those who still fail to realize all their value for humanity. And what is given for distribution as the most essential food for starving souls, that which should lie in the foundation of the new evolution, remains with them without appreciation. Do feel the call of my spirit! Reread as often as possible your treasures; collect all the crumbs, and with all your being merge with them. They will give you such broad and clear understanding of the most complicated problems of existence. The only way will be by absorbing it, and the austere joy of infinite progress will fill your hearts. My heart longs to inspire you with the joy of majesty and beauty which the Teaching of Life opens to you. New souls are coming and will multiply. We must be able to hold them. It is necessary to give to everyone according to his mentality. Nothing attracts people so much as the necessary word which liberates their minds and gives them new possibilities. All beings are drawn toward Light. This is the first law of the Cosmos. The Teaching and the ability to give it in full commensurability is the magnet which attracts people and all possibilities. It is that armor which can withstand all attacks, that source which brings endless joy. But it should be accepted by the heart and not by the head alone.

Love each other, respect each other, but let the inner life of each one of you be his own Holy of Holies. You are united by the Teacher, the Teaching, and by actions; but you are not the judges of each other. The judge can easily become the judged one in the eyes of the Teacher. Their measures are not our earthly measurements. This we must always remember. And a stone thrown at one's brother will weigh one down like a heavy burden. After accepting the Hierarchy, absorb the Teaching; for the only indestructible joy is the joy of that broadening of our consciousness which forces us into the higher Sacrament of Being, where all our most sacred, most holy strivings find their materialization, as the Higher Reality is above all human imagination.

4

13 October 1929

Lately, I have been thinking a great deal about the members of your group. Once more, I am convinced that no one can be replaced and that everyone is needed. And how simple it is, in such circumstances, to achieve the complete harmony which guarantees victory in all directions. But my heart feels that there is something that prevents this unity. What is the remedy? Of course the only solution is comprehension of the Teacher and the Teaching by the heart and not by the head alone. Therefore, we must pay attention to the development of our heart, that amazing organ which includes in itself, in its numerous centers, all creativeness and psychic life. Without development of the centers of the heart we are sterile; there is no creation of psychic life; there is no life in the higher spheres; and the crown of the Arhat is unapproachable. Only with our heart are we able to approach the consciousness of the Arhat, of the Teacher, as his consciousness is in the heart. Humanity has an obscure understanding of the Arhat, but without this understanding it is impossible to advance.

In the book, *Hierarchy*, it is said:

"It is customary to think of an Arhat as a dweller of the clouds. The records of the drift of thought are dreadful and grotesque. Verily, We Brothers of Humanity do not recognize Ourselves in the concept of humanity. The images of Us are so fantastic! We deem that if people applied their fantasies precisely conversely Our Images would assume true form. ... Everything takes on a new scale. Everything becomes improbable. Everything becomes uncorrelated to reality. On the way to the higher worlds, let us say, 'an Arhat is without limits in all manifestations.' ... an Arhat proceeds carrying the power of the Cosmic Magnet in his heart!"

But let us see how this Image is expressed by the Higher Consciousness.

"The heart of an Arhat is like the heart of Cosmos. The heart of an Arhat is like the fire of the Sun. Eternity and the motion of Cosmos fill the heart of the Arhat. Maitreya is coming, radiant with all fires. His Heart flames with compassion for destitute humanity. His Heart flames with the affirmation of the new Covenants.

"Among people there exists the concept of benumbed Arhats, and poor yogis feed the imaginations of men with their own images. But when humanity realizes that the Arhat is the highest manifestation of Materia Lucida, it will be understood that there is no difference between Materia Lucida, which emits Light, and that matter of love enveloping all with Light. Humanity invests the Arhat with an austere image, but Materia Lucida radiates love. ... When will it be possible to enlighten man with Our Image?

"The mind with difficulty realizes the purity of the higher spheres. To him who is aware of the path to Us, let us say, 'Walk by the path of love. Walk by the path of labor. Walk by the path of the shield of faith!' To him who has found Our Image in his heart, We shall say, 'Walk by the way of the heart, and the Chalice will affirm the path!' To him who thinks he has attained the path through conceit, We shall say, 'Go and learn from the spirit who knows consummation.' Conceit stops all progress.

"All creation is contained in the call of the heart. The entire cosmic expanse is permeated with a call, and the heart of Cosmos and the heart of an Arhat are permeated with the call. The call and the answer comprise a combination of cosmic fires. ... The Heart of Our Brotherhood safeguards for humanity the path toward the General Good."

* * *

Each one must find the key to the Teaching in his own heart. The understanding of the Teaching of Life should inaugurate the creativeness of the spirit. The Image of the Teacher can give an enlightened path toward cosmic space. Thus, when we accept within our hearts the chosen Image, do not our hearts become aflame with love toward all beings? The creative Materia Lucida serves as embodiment for the high spirit, but this energy is attracted through love. The whole Cosmos is upheld by love. Love is the greatest magnet.

My love for all of you, and my eagerness about your progress, tells my heart to point out the necessity for improvement. ...

Now one general suggestion. In applying this suggestion, you must remember the ordainment of the Teacher: "Severity to yourself and an open heart for your brother. Only the benevolent eye can create." The Teacher always advises to apply the Teaching first of all to your own self; otherwise you will remain on the same step. "It is sad when the spirit, after making its life circle, returns to the same point. It is sad when the spirit sets for itself the same limits, and its brood, as faithful fellow travelers, await at the gates."

Above all, develop the sense of justice and co-measurement. Both these qualities are measured by the heart. Therefore, begin to think about the heart so that you can remember about it and then hearken to its call. The magnet of the heart grows with sincerity and striving. There is nothing abstract in this because all the finest cosmic energies pass through the heart—all the finest energies, the most powerful and creative ones. But in order to attract these creative energies one must kindle one's own fires.

Thus, build up all your fires! But do not mistake sentimentality, that weeping kindness, for the severe, wise manifestation of the heart. Remember what the Teaching says about compassion and pity. Love each other, take care of each other, and give joy to each other.

5

11 February 1929

Each of you is writing about his striving toward unity. What then prevents it, if you fully realize this necessity? I shall answer: lack of spiritual discipline, lack of ability to apply the Teaching, first of all, to your own self. When one needs to show tolerance, the old habit of uncontrollable antagonism, or not-outlived atavism, rises in all its strength, and then all the best intentions are immediately forgotten. Of course, it is difficult to eradicate all the bad habits at once. Therefore, let us start to rooting out with the most urgent—the driving away of intolerance. Let us write with fiery letters in our consciousness this testament of the Teaching, and let us remember it beginning and ending the day, at work and at rest.

Let us remember how the Lord Buddha taught his pupils, how He demanded that they should first of all learn how to control their temper. Only after the bridle of spirit restrained all the feelings of the pupil, only then did the Blessed One lift a little the veil of the sacred Teaching. The path of the Teaching is the same now as it was then. For coming closer and for the highest confidence, the very same foundations are necessary: reverence for the Hierarchy and the discipline of spirit.

By applying the gifts of indications and possibilities bestowed by the Generous Hand of the Teacher, we can build a great deal, elevating ourselves in the eyes of the world and in this life, completing the good karma by obedience to the guiding indications. But what will be put into our real treasury if we do not transmute our inner motives and feelings into the highest strivings? In spite of all our work in the direction pointed out by the Great Teacher, the Tower will remain inaccessible. All this sounds so complicated and difficult; and, at the same time, all is so easy and simple. If the heart burns with love and enthusiasm for the Teacher and for the beauty and breadth of the Teaching of Life, these sparks could so easily be fanned into the flame of unquenchable striving which carries us above all and everything. Strive, my friends! Is it so difficult if you have before you the Image of Beauty? Is it not the highest joy to bring every bit of yourself to the service of the General Good? The achievements are so beautiful, and there are no limits to them! But all the possibility, all the joy of it, is only in ourselves. No one can take more than he can contain—otherwise destruction will follow. The laws of Cosmos are exact and immutable. The highest joy for one may cause intense anguish in another, if assimilation is not there. Do understand this! The Rays sent to us by the Teacher in the greatest joy of his Spirit will call forth our anguish and may even ruin our organism if we are not prepared to receive them. Do understand this, my dear ones, and give access to the Rays of the Great Teacher. Each ray in Cosmos can be either creative or destructive. It all depends on correlation and assimilation, as "Man, being part of the Cosmos, is subject to all its laws."

Let me quote from the book, *Infinity*:

"The cosmic creation uses all vital impulses, tensing the levers of life. Of all the impulses the most powerful one is unity, which contains all the manifestations of life and by which are created the combinations of life. Why then not apply in life this principle? When unity struggles with differentiation, then comes a strong explosion and the fragments from the explosion are often blown far away and these particles lose their mutually attracting power. Thus, by rejecting the forces with which he is tied by karma, man causes a powerful explosion. The law can create only by unification. The element of attraction marks out the path for all the propelled energies. The Brothers of Humanity mark out the path for everything confirmed by evolution. So the force of attraction is meant to be the law of Existence. This cosmic power of unification confirms the power of Cosmic Mind."

* * *

Again let me quote:

"Let us consider the revolt of a pupil. When the pupil hides his revolt against the Giving Hand of the Teacher, it means he is hiding a handful of stones. We shall remind such a pupil that the anger will be turned back upon him. Let the pupil who is counting his offerings turn toward the Giving Hand—great will be his deficiency! The pupil who considers himself more important than the Guru breaks off connection with the Teacher. In enumerating his offerings the pupil is already rewarded. It is unworthy to affirm one's own importance. From his light-minded remarks one may assume that his listing is incomplete. If these debts are not out-lived, the journey will be long. Self-conceit is a plague! One can deplore one's own deficiency, but the revolt against the Giving Hand is similar to an arrow thrown against the Shield. The pillars of the Teaching uphold the actions! Thus let us remember."

Rightly is it said about the Hierarchy:

"Of course the spiral of life is built only by this principle. The creativeness of the Teacher is also manifested in eternal motion. Therefore, the saturation of a pupil must proceed through the creativeness of the Teacher. The pupil who is counting his achievements throws himself outside the boundaries of Truth. Thus, I shall say that the Hierarchy is the only Shield. Therefore, the pupil who considers his soft chair higher than the throne of his Guru, verily, must remember the Giving Hand. I grieve when the self-assertive pupil acts arrogantly. We consider arrogance against the Guru as the height of self-conceit. Thus let the pupil remember in all his steps."

Someone is wondering, "Are not the results counted first of all?" To this I shall answer, "Could this someone count them already?" The counting may not come up to expectations.

Carry the Treasures entrusted to you by the enlightened spirit and sow the seeds of spiritual creativeness, fully striving and realizing the significance of the great Gift. The result depends upon striving, which brings spiritual creativeness.

Someone is exasperated at the severity of the foregoing. But, may I ask, is it possible that this someone still remains on the first step of the call when so many pleasing things are given? Are we still at the stage of childhood when the salutary but bitter medicine is offered in chocolate-coated pills? Courage and patience must be found for throwing away the old shell to be reborn in joyful, luminous spirit. All of us have experienced the plungings of spirit. It is almost unavoidable, but it should be carefully watched because it is dangerous if the last plunge is deeper than the previous one. To rise again will be difficult, and much will be lost.

Let us hearken to the voice of our heart. Let the heart whisper what great, loving Hearts live in the Stronghold of Light, and how the inaccessibility is changed into the strongest magnet for the striving heart. Nothing can stop this attraction if the spirit has transmuted its inner fires.

You are all so dear to me, and I would like so much to have all of you around me, to whisper a gentle cheering word and, above all, to grow with all of you in the joy of understanding the infinite Teaching.

Often your calls reach me. I feel it is not easy for you, but so much bigger will be the victory. My heart often talks and calls, as the great labor is ahead of us. Let us make it easier by applying the ordainments of the Teaching. I know your firmness and devotion, but everything can be refined, and in this is the joy of our existence.

To the strong spirit the difficult time shows the shortest way. Let us welcome all the difficulties. The joy is destined, but it is necessary to withstand the attacks of the dark forces. We shall remember that "will and energy are the rulers of karma." Let us apply our will power to the transmutation of our fires. Let us attract the pure fire of space. All joy will come with pure fire. Let us remember that the essence of the pure intense fire contains the quality of unification. Therefore, where unification is not manifested, there is no pure fire. But only the pure fire leads to the Tower.

I am sending all my love and support in this difficult time of the struggles of the spirit. You are surrounded by constant care. Do not doubt it. Every pupil is dear to the Teacher. Every movement of your heart echoes to the Great Heart. Not always can the projected rays reach our physical consciousness; but every minute they dispel and annihilate so many hostile sparks around you. Help these invaluable messages by your striving and by your conscious, solicitous attitude toward them. They are sent by the Perfect Heart and the Perfect Mind.

* * *

Are you convinced of the complete insolvency and dubiousness of the manifestations of the "spiritual order" of the majority of mediums? Each one sees only in his own sphere, no more and no less. Are you going to look for knowledge from a person only because he knows the alphabet? Look for the accumulations of the Chalice or for the great Synthesis. You have the Highest. Do not overload your aura by contacting the imperfect spheres.

6

17 December 1929

I quote to you a page from the book, *Infinity*. This page, with its close analogy between the seven cosmic and human manifestations, will help you once more to ponder over the seriousness of events.

"Only in tension, only when all the strings are vibrating, can the cosmic task be realized. Only when the task assumes the tensive form may the predestined take place. When the foundations of Cosmos support the firmament by their attraction, the firmament can withstand. But when the foundations impede the mutual attraction, the dome is subject to unbalanced tremors; thus, the foundations can either affirm or destroy the work. The foundations can always unite the most diverse energies. Cosmos directs its energies according to polarity. Negative and positive give the manifestation of combinations."

Think over the depth of the above-mentioned, and do not impede your mutual attractions; do not evoke the shaking of the foundations. How can you estimate the results of tremors? In a partial explosion, a new foundation can be carefully built up, but often a single explosion, by the force of detonation, strikes the nearest hearths. Everywhere is the great law of analogy and similarity.

Also, you should remember to "avoid turning useful forces into a jar of scorpions." The possibility was foreseen a long time ago and warning was sent. Let us learn how to apply the indications. Let us be imbued with the seriousness of the present time. Each light-mindedness is on the borderland of crime.

When we shall replace the limiting concept of "I" with the powerful, creative and joyous "we," all the possibilities and wealth of the spirit will blossom immeasurably; our power will be increased exceedingly. People are afraid of the concept "we." "I" can always be checked, while "we" is unknown and therefore threatening.

The great time predicted long ago has come. Do you not feel it in all the tension of cosmic and human explosions? All the crust of the earth is aquiver, and a great change is approaching. This time it is not the comparatively harmless tail of a comet but our own emanations which, by their discord with the approaching higher fiery energies, may evoke—or rather will evoke—an unexpected change. It is good during such perturbations to be on the solid indicated rock, under the Umbrella of Dukkar. Our tasks will all have room under this cover! One more indication:

"When you create a new step, when Uranus is collecting the sixth race, then it is necessary to be imbued with the affirmed great time, and all the interfering worries should be discarded."

We must welcome all the dear ones, close in spirit; but all the destroying ones, those who bring division, must be either driven away or put in their places. We labor and create not for self-aggrandizement, not for individual personalities, but for the great General Good.

And so, remember the unprecedented, beautiful and threatening time. Not one minute should be lost! Do strengthen unity with all your forces of the spirit, and commit to strictest ostracism the petty concept of "I."

I send you all the strings of my heart; let each one of you find a resounding one.

7

11 September 1929

People will come to you with questions and indications about various psychic and mediumistic phenomena, considering them as manifestations of Agni Yoga. Therefore, I shall try to clarify this difference by quoting from the talks and books of the Teaching:

"The spirit of Agni Yoga links us with the higher spheres and connects us with the currents of the Cosmic Magnet. The quality of fire is confirmed by the tension of the magnet. The magnet of the spirit determines that step which can be manifested. The same principle guides the kindling of the centers.

"The spirit whose consciousness is on the lower planes cannot ignite the fires of the higher centers. Only the highest attracts the highest; therefore, where there is only physical striving there will be a corresponding receptivity and result. In the approaching epoch of Agni Yoga, it is necessary to know the principle of forcibly sent messages. In nature there is also direct accordance which has its limits. Only the finest can assimilate the finest, and this is the principle of the magnet. Just as the principle of the fine energies is characteristic of the highest

Agni Yogi, the physical receptivity determines corresponding manifestations. Everything that is forced, everything that is ostentatiously crude, everything that is physically manifested is inferior to the subtle principle.

"An Agni Yogi possesses the highest balance; the self-denying creativeness of his spirit leads to the balance of universal correlation, and thereupon the imbalance and disharmony of the centers ends in equilibrium. The Teaching refers often to these subtle differences. Therefore, in order to progress to the next degree, it is important to understand the imbalance of the lower manifestations and the beauty of the highest harmony. The nature of an Agni Yogi is so high that comparison with any mediumistic manifestation will be like a muddy drop of water in a fiery chalice. Therefore, I shall say that the understanding of the higher fires will bring one to the pure fiery heights. The Agni Yogi is the collector of a new race. He works in the higher spheres, gathering the spirits of a new race. The manifestation of the Agni Yogi's fire has its purpose on this Earth, just as in the higher spheres. Therefore, the Agni Yogi is the connecting link between the worlds.

"The exact differences in human instruments given for different aims and confirmed by the motive power of evolution should be assimilated by the consciousness of people. When we speak about the transmutation of the fires, the confirmation of the most tensive fire of the Cosmic Magnet should be accepted. When humanity understands all the creative power of the spirit of an Agni Yogi, only then can it be said that all his centers are vibrating, responding to cosmic events. The human instrument which is used for the simple visual impress could not possibly be compared with the manifestation which reflects every breath of Cosmos. Therefore, let all those who are striving toward Agni Yoga find the highest understanding of the opened centers.

"The medium, truly, has no opened centers, and the psychic eye is also not in contact with the higher worlds. Humanity has a false idea about the power of a medium, and often We are distressed seeing how people are deluded by psychic manifestations. Physical materializations attract as a magnet."

Thus, if it may be so expressed, it is usually the lowest centers of the medium that act by their primitive tension. Often it is a forced phenomenon, which does not lead to the opening of the centers but merely toward their temporary irritation. But the fires of the Agni Yogi are due to the kindling of the highest centers, which really are opened.

Strictly speaking, there are no lower centers, and the high Agni Yogi has his "lower" centers transmuted by the finest fires. But this transmutation takes place after the kindling of the highest centers, and then all the "lower" centers are subordinated to the solar plexus. We must also remember that the gradation of these fires, or rather their quality, is infinitely perfected, just as everything else in the Cosmos. But one principle is beyond doubt in determining the Agni Yogi—it is the principle of synthesis. To kindle the fires without the Synthesis of the Chalice is impossible. By this principle you can already determine the quality of the fires.

So you have the main indication by which you can distinguish the manifestations of the ignition of the centers from the lower psychic manifestations. "An Agni Yogi is the carrier of the Synthesis of the Chalice—by this indication you can judge." Therefore, fill your chalices with the realization of beauty, with the true knowledge of the wisdom of the Teaching of Life, and with the assimilation of it in your heart, and remember that the heart is a great magnet which attracts all knowledge, all possibilities, and all achievements. You should remember also that there is nothing forced in the manifestations of an Agni Yogi, as the Agni Yogi is his own laboratory. He, himself, by the force of his spirit, transforms his fires. The Teacher gives the Indications of the Teaching for broadening the consciousness, but the pupil himself must apply it. The Teacher watches over the process of igniting by covering the centers with layers of soma when the ignition threatens to become a conflagration. But without the participation of the spirit of the pupil no transmutation is possible.

Of course, you should be careful in your answers, and particularly in the definitions given to the questioners because it is always necessary to remember the principle given by the Teacher: "The answer must be as the ray of a physician, not as the nail of a coffin." It is necessary "not to interfere," taking into consideration the level of people's consciousness. By carefully broadening it, it is possible to achieve the true understanding; but often this is a very long process, and then it is necessary to show the same kind of patience as the Great Teacher shows toward us. In the beginning, everyone needs encouragement and recognition of his abilities. It is easy to scare away and much more difficult to hold, but the Great Teacher instructs us to retain the newcomers. Moreover, sometimes a spirit with great accumulations may receive a mediumistic structure of the organism for some definite purpose, and then, through the development of a strong will, with the assistance of the Great Teacher, he can conquer the unconscious manifestations and subject them to his will. But it is not easy.

* * *

We are experiencing a difficult time, but we shall recall it with joy, as only in difficult action can strength be developed. The technique of a musician also develops only through constant exercises after which all the fingers ache.

8

15 January 1930

Sometimes I feel so much like being with you physically, so that I might share the joy of your creative tension. You know already that the attraction of possibilities is inevitable when all the forces are strained. The law is one in the whole Cosmos. And we have already learned to love the obstacles, and we know that "the obstacles which produce weakness of spirit will produce failure, while the obstacles which call forth all the fire of spirit to battle act like a creative element." The ancient wisdom says: "Welcome the day of battle; do not turn away from obstacles." When there is deviation there is only detention, not salvation. The one who is not afraid to become a participant of eternal and infinite motion, truly, can accept the part of a fighter. The readiness, the undeferred rhythm will rush him into the radiance of Cosmos. Notice: "Fear and hesitation are as dams to the spirit."

We must become accustomed to the constant battle and try to love it. Each atom of Cosmos is fighting! After one victory is achieved, we must be ready for the next still greater one, for in proportion to the growth of our consciousness our actions also grow, and the battle grows wider and becomes more responsible. In the whole of Cosmos the endless battle is taking place, and all of us, visibly and invisibly, are involved in it. It is time to realize this because by realizing, by strengthening our spirit, we shall become the real victors. Directed by the High Wisdom, which indicates to us the right direction, we shall cross over all abysses! And without being dazzled by the vision, joyously and luminously we may look into the future. Where are other similarly fortunate ones who can say this? Think of the advantage this knowledge gives us! What an assurance it gives to all our actions and decisions! Is it not the greatest happiness to be able to move ahead to the indicated goal, fully realizing the events and knowing that our destiny is to achieve a maximum broadening of our consciousness for the best service to the Common Good? The threatening time is very near. Do not the heat-lightnings already flash out, and are not the ominous messengers of the awakened subterranean fire breaking through? And we who know about it must urgently transmute our inner fires in order to assimilate the approaching fiery storm, as only this will give us stability in the battle, will bring us near the Hierarchy of Light, and will help to fill the chalice. Thus, let us transmute all our energies. We should start from the most stubborn energy, which is egoism (that furious dragon of selfishness with its long tail); self-conceit; love of power; self-love; touchiness; irritability; fear; doubt and other similar decorations. And we should replace them with the wings of affirmed unity; complete solidarity with all the co-workers; acknowledgment of Hierarchy; joyous strengthening of the given tasks; tolerance and gratitude for the right directions. We should conclude with—trust to the very end. All this transmutation is so simplified when hearts burn with devotion and love to the One who calls to construction and who points out the way to the Tower.

Let everyone crucify himself. Let him severely judge himself and be most considerate to all co-workers. It is necessary to crucify only oneself! We shall grow immeasurably by practising this severity upon ourselves. If someone has not finished something that was entrusted to him, do not blame him, but if possible finish it yourself. And I do beg of you, do not criticize each other. From continuous repetitions of condemnations, calluses will appear on the brain, and then how can one achieve the broadening of consciousness? Every spare moment must be utilized for progressive action, for the enrichment of the treasury, for the assimilation of the Teaching, which is still so little understood and applied. Every line evokes so many questions, comparisons, and requires immediate application in everyday life. And what is applied? The Teacher wants to see us united, wants to look at us as one heart, one spirit, one organism. If one part of the organism is ill, do not the healthy parts fulfil their work, giving the sick organs an opportunity to recover? You must act similarly.

It is said, "We offer the best armor; therefore, if they do not wish to substitute the old habits for shining armor the approach to the Tower is closed! Yes, yes, yes! It is necessary to realize the threatening time and not to continue with old habits." It hurts me to write this, but I feel that it is timely, otherwise something irremediable may happen. Superficially, things may appear as they were, but what is not seen and cannot be replaced will depart. The sorrow of the Teacher is so evident, and my spirit knows and sees the sculpture of the spirit of the co-workers.

Who will be the first to emerge from this very painful battle? But remember—there is no other way. If the spirit be too slow in awakening, will it not be terrible to wake up in front of closed doors? In the spiritual world as in the subtle one, the laws are still more immutable; the limits of relationship are immeasurably finer than on the physical plane because the great selection takes place there. Take all the above-said courageously; courageously crucify yourself, remembering the pressing time.

In addition, I shall quote a page from *Infinity*:

"In the cosmic creation the energies are combined in the greatest tension. The combinations of united energies grow with the force of tension. The synthesis of tension is confirmed by the power of higher fires. In all cosmic creation the law of tension can create a new combination. With the growth of tension new and different energies are attracted. When the energies joined to the combination of the magnet attract similar currents, then it is possible to establish harmonization of the energies. But when the energies move in different directions, a wasting of the energy of the magnet takes place. It is similar with human actions.

"Why is the spirit of humanity attracted toward the disharmonious currents? Of course, the currents which are diverted to the spatial fire may give a better formula, but this formula must be created independently. Initiative should be understood as the basis for synthesized activity. When the spirit can find its seed and can cognize the coverings which surround it, then the beauty of the Cosmos can be realized. The husk which accumulates upon the human spirit has closed the way to affirmation. Therefore, Our co-workers must understand that these husks do not belong among Our requirements. It is necessary to understand that it is unfitting to manifest the garment of spirit like a husk when We honor so much the radiance of the garment of the Mother of the World. Thus, remember and strive after the Teacher! Only in this way will you succeed. Self-activity of the centers is being built like an ascending spiral."

Let us discard all husks, let us show initiative, let us strive toward the refining of the quality of thought, and we shall succeed! The care for quality in all things is the most necessary care. The high and the low differ only in quality, showing similarity in everything else.

9
24 February 1930

Truly, only the small consciousness can be annoyed by the authority of the Guru. For what is the authority of the Guru but the authority of the Hierarch? The authority of the Hierarch does not mean domination over the aspirations of everything inferior. The authority of the Hierarch and Guru is not a tyranny. This authority is the highest knowledge. It is said: "The Hierarch uses the power for cosmic progress. We Brothers of Humanity possess this power of acting in unison with the Cosmic Magnet." The Hierarch and the Guru are those experienced Pilots who, during the violent storm, are guiding through the destructive waves, through all the rocks, the boat entrusted to Them, the boat in which we, as the "precious" cargo, all have our place. Therefore, let us not forget this; let us not leave the Hand which is out-stretched in salutary Leadership! Power and domination are two different things. Domination is the lowest form of consciousness because it is caused by fearful, all-excluding egoism; while power, blessed by the highest knowledge and strained by the heart, is the highest sacrifice. Let us remember the book about "Sacrifice." Heart was always considered to be the symbol of the Leader.

Try to feel with your heart the power of joy in devotion and love to the Leading Hand. I affirm by the knowledge of spirit and heart that you have not a greater Friend and Guardian.

We should realize how small are all our offerings, if there are any such, compared to the salutary power and pricelessness of this dispensation. The broadened consciousness will understand it. Nobody is demeaned, all are honored, the way to the highest achievements is opened to all, if only we ourselves do not throw away the possibilities. There are moments in difficult mountain-climbing when the only possibility is to move ahead; every hesitation threatens disaster. A loose stone cannot support the one who delays for long. At the moment we must ascend, and the only open way is the path ahead, without doubts, without regrets and recounting of the small knots of offerings. Each thought of this kind will mean extra weight for the legs and will complicate the dangerous ascent. We need the wings of love and trust in the Leading Hand, the wings of joy in the Great Service. Every application of the words of the Teaching to life will relieve our burden immensely.

I beg you from my heart, do discard all self-conceit, every thought of exclusiveness in your offerings, every thought of doubt and suspicion, as the time is too ominous and heavy with responsibility. And is the duration of the struggle so long? Almost half is already done, and, really, nobody has lost anything. The future is so beautiful and so broad. Let your names be written down among the names of the great co-workers of evolution. What can be higher and more beautiful than cooperation for the General Good of the culture of nations!

Pages from *Infinity*:

"Great unity in Cosmos holds sway like a powerful law. Only those who accept this law may truly participate in the cosmic cooperation. The unity of essence in everything directs humanity toward creation. When the consciousness draws from the treasury of space, then the Cosmic Magnet exerts its influence. The manifested treasury contains the affirmation of energy saturated with unity. Therefore, each seed of spirit must feel similar unity. Each seed of spirit belongs to the cosmic Unity, in which all cosmic creation is contained. Man deprives himself of this truth by adopting the way of isolation. The law of Unity is immutable in all its variety. Only by this law is it possible to construct because when the attraction creates, then in the power of action lies unity. All affirmed Be-ness is founded on unity. The administering law is so powerful that cosmic construction is upheld by this principle. In all its manifestations this law gathers its particles, unifying all which belong together. This great law is the Crown of Cosmos!

"In the eternal creation of life, the law of Unity acts. The cosmic creation moves onward like a fiery, manifested edict—an edict which destines unification; an edict which destines a designation; an edict which destines the replacing of one by the other; and edict which destines a crowning; an edict which destines immortality; an edict which destines life to each atom; an edict which destines the approach of new energy; an edict which destines the New Era. The creativeness of Cosmos is expressed in this way by the magnet of life. How is it possible to disunite the cosmic creation? How to disconnect parts which belong together? How to disunite what, verily, issues one from the other? The Cosmos in its saturation impels toward fiery unification. Only the Cosmic Mind can give humanity the Image of Unity. This Mind gives to humanity the highest Image of the most fiery Heart! This Mind collects in sacredness. Therefore, in Cosmos this law is created by life. Where is the end, if all the cosmic manifestations issue from the dual Origin? When the spirit comes into contact with the highest spheres, then the cosmic creation is revealed in the law of infinite unification.

"The spirit is terrified by the thought about death. But when the consciousness penetrates into the essence of Life, then the concept of Unity is affirmed. When the spirit realizes how endlessly all the manifestations of life are flowing, then it will be possible to point to the continuousness of all the chains: the chain of thought, the chain of action, the chain of results, the chain of strivings, the chain of lives. One chain predetermines another. The creativeness of the magnet of life consists of these chains. And the spirit must be terrified not by death and dissolution but by the very thought of breaking the chain. If one could investigate the records of these broken chains existing in space, verily, the spirit would be terrified! When the great shifting has been confirmed, only those can succeed who accept the unity of evolution."

Let us not break the chain which connects us with the Leading Hand. How else can we approach?

Let us draw more from the same book:

"The cosmic dates are determined by the assertion of the subterranean and supermundane fires. This correlation is connected with the spheres of human actions. When the date is approaching and comes into action, it is always possible to watch how, together with the cosmic perturbations, the human consciousness is shifted. Of course, the immutability of the law unites all the spheres, and the communion of all the cosmic forces becomes the assertion of rational action. Thus, the date is filled by all the events and is not limited to only one sphere.

"Now, truly, the fires of all the spheres are very much strained, and the cosmic decision turns the events. The magnetic currents attract intensively the subterranean fire.

"Just as the conductor of electricity depends on various conditions, the human aura forms up receptively for the cosmic messages. When the spheres of men need certain shocks, then the cosmic sendings are in accordance. Only those elements which can penetrate into the confirmed auras join those spheres. When the sphere requires strong shocks, then it is impossible for the sphere to accept the flowing messages of Cosmos. Therefore, the darkness, which surrounds the planet, will not admit the assertion without the manifestation of explosions. These purifying forces will enlighten humanity. The cosmic fires attract the confirmed dates.

"The purifying fires of the Universe are penetrating into all regions of the planet. The sparks of fire spread over all the channels of the actions of karma. Like volcanoes the affirmed fires flash out. The force of karma shifts and moves the power from hand to hand. The cosmic flow rushes toward the purifying fires; and hence the comet, hastening through the Infinite. The tension of the currents is very marked, and the effect corresponds to the fires of the planet. The centers of the Agni Yogi record all cosmic currents."

* * *

How many warnings and signs are sent regarding the approaching threatening time! But great is the ignorance. I remember reading in a scientific magazine that a northern scientist had investigated the activity of volcanoes and found that the present volcanic belt revealed a period of unusual tension, and all the so-called extinct volcanoes were awakening once more to fiery life. Unexpected eruptions are being seen in new places. The most dangerous disturbances are at the bottom of the oceans. The scientist concludes his deductions by admitting the possibility of a gigantic, planetary cataclysm, and even in the very near future.

The following paragraph from *Infinity* partly explains it:

"If humanity would but understand the meaning of existence, it would join the cosmic creativeness. How is it possible to advance without realizing the eternal cosmic shiftings? Only when strivings beyond the boundary drawn by our life are manifested, only then will it be possible to perceive the cosmic creativeness. The wall of stupidity has blocked the way, as has also the fog of contentment. When it becomes possible to enter the spheres of true cosmic creativeness, then the cosmic consciousness will come.

"Those are right who speak about human ignorance. When we approach the threatening time it is necessary to exert all strength for such a powerful step. The epoch of Maitreya is already predicted, and the signs are already scattered like fiery seeds. Therefore, for those who follow the Cosmic Magnet, the threatening time will be full of Light. And for those also who struggle for the significance of the New Epoch, the threatening time will prove to bear the Light of the future."

But people still do not want to understand how uneasy life is on our planet now, and where and into what one must look for the cause of the imminent danger.

10
24 June 1930

In your last letters you emphasize how happy you are to have responsibility, with which every co-worker is charged in his management of the department entrusted to him. The realization of personal responsibility is quite correct, but I would also like to hear something from you about cooperation. I am afraid that my understanding of responsibility will be somewhat different from yours. Personal responsibility is not only connected with the broadest cooperation, but, truly speaking, this cooperation or collaboration is the basis of personal responsibility. The Cosmos is built upon cooperation; and man, being part of and a reflection of the Cosmos, cannot exclude himself from this law if he does not wish to destroy himself. Each institution, with one of the co-workers at the head of it, must cooperate as much as possible with all other departments or institutions. All the sections work according to the same plan, and we must see that they work together like the fingers of the same hand, not disturbing, but helping and complementing each other. The withdrawal of one of the sections from cooperation is similar to a gangrenous process, and will cause general disintegration unless a salutary operation is performed in time.

If you think that responsibility means withdrawal and independence of action, you reveal a well-concealed sense of ambition and possessiveness. And we know how all such feelings are disapproved by all Teachers. If we do not destroy within ourselves the sense of ownership in all aspects, we cannot easily reach the next step. It may be that we consider possessively not only our own section but even our pupils and acquaintances, and we would become hurt if some of our collaborators also evinced an interest in them.

The slave-holding attitudes arises from the sense of ownership, and you know how difficult it is to eradicate such feelings. But are such atavisms permissible in the epoch of the Mother of the World, the epoch of utmost cooperation?

The societies and institutions do not exist for our personal aggrandizement. We must, therefore, work according to the general plan for the development of all of them. By elevating their significance we elevate ourselves, but if we think primarily of enhancing our own personality we shall weaken the societies and institutions and ruin ourselves.

I fear that my directions may be disliked by some, and I have reasons for thinking this. But, as it is said, "The Teaching is not soothing syrup, neither is it silver jackstraws. It is a severe crucifying of self and a tense transformation of one's lower nature through the finest fires. Soothing syrup perhaps may be appropriate on the first step, but the Teaching requires the severe and beautiful flowers of self-denial. Those who prefer soothing syrup had better not touch the fiery food prepared for those who choose self-denial."

Yes, all the dark corners should be lighted up, and the dust of yesterday should be cleaned out. Otherwise it will be impossible to build the next step.

Please forgive my severe remarks. I write with all my heart. I want to help you and to give you a new understanding. Sweet speeches put our consciousness to sleep and deepen our ignorance, but ignorance is stagnation and retrogression. Give joy to the Teacher. Let Him see your ardent desire to comprehend the joyous ascent. Tread this new path with severe self-control. The foundation of the higher joy is full of suffering. "Suffering precedes joy"—let us remember this.

The souls united by the same striving comprise one whole chain. United by the same Teaching, this chain is unbreakable.

11

17 August 1930

With all my heart I agree with the Teacher's Edict about the pressing necessity to commence a new step. What does this new step mean? Not just exclamations and enthusiasm about the wisdom and beauty of the Teaching, not just assurances of devotion and a new understanding, but action according to the new comprehension of the Teaching. Thus, let us apply the Teaching in life, let us honor the Hierarchy and let us begin a friendly and sensible cooperation.

Let us attentively and carefully carry out the given tasks; let us strive to understand all the majesty of the plan of the general Good and our own responsibility. Let us put into the foundation all the given confirmations of the last ten years. Gather together and read them with all your heart. Everybody's place was clearly indicated because only in such a way could there be achieved the greatest and the most beneficial results.

Also, beginning with the very first days, some of the co-workers showed certain characteristics in their natures which should have been immediately eradicated. But what was done regarding the fulfillment of these useful and salutary indications? Was not the most unpardonable light-mindedness shown toward this most urgent problem? Verily, it is most urgent, and only honest effort to eradicate our faults can advance us on the path of Service. Let each one look into the depth of his own consciousness; let him awaken his heart; let him give to himself a severe accounting of all the motives which direct his actions; and let him start immediately the eradication of all bad accumulations, as time is short!

The Teaching points out vices, namely, ambition, self-conceit and selfishness, suspiciousness and light-mindedness, which should not be allowed to grow up among the co-workers if they wish to build the foundation of a new step. Let us become firmly aware in our hearts that the Teacher disapproves of the tendency toward bossiness. As I have already written once before—domineeringness and true leadership are antipodes. While the former is the offspring of darkness, the latter is of the light of knowledge in the eternal striving toward perfection. First of all, bossiness is vulgar; that is why it is so easy to fall into this attitude. "Domineeringness is the main obstacle in the path of discipleship." Self-conceit and bossiness are inseparable and lead to spiritual impoverishment and destruction.

The Teacher does not use force. He acts according to the intelligence of the co-workers. Often, the leader sees a short and simple plan of achievement, the very simplicity of which is above the consciousness of the co-workers. Then the wise leader will not insist upon his own way, but, after considering the abilities of the co-workers, he will select a line of action which is of easy access for the majority.

Not tyranny but true cooperation is necessary. Broadest cooperation is inscribed upon the Banner of the New Era. The main quality of a leader is to be able to assemble co-workers of the most diverse natures and unify them in the same striving. Is not our unification achieved by our devotion to the Teacher? Thus, let us remember that the Teacher directs our advancement by magnanimous cooperation, not by force. Wise concessions in small details to the consciousness not fully grown may not give completely satisfactory results, but at least it will not breed a ruinous atmosphere of irritability and disagreement.

For the sake of benevolent cooperation in the creation of a new step it is most necessary to assimilate the significance of thought. It is necessary to create a better atmosphere in our daily life by the purifying of thought. In such a way we shall attract better possibilities. In all the books of the Teaching so many discourses are devoted to this question, but until now we have not been able to realize the foundation not only of our welfare but even of our very existence. Cosmos is built upon thought. Both happiness and destruction are based upon thought. Thought brings life, but it can also bring death. When will this be understood by people? There is no stronger lever in the Cosmos than thought saturated with psychic energy!

Thought is a magnet, and each dark thought creates a stratum of heavy fluids which is attracted and gathered by similar consciousnesses. "Joy may, by a magnetic current, attract joy from space." Remember that thought acts as a boomerang; therefore thought, upon being sent consciously to a person whose vibrations are not identical, will return to the one who sent it, reinforced with identical vibrations which are oscillating in space and are seeking reunion. It is easy to imagine what destructive results a thought may bring to one who sent it evil-mindedly. Also, during the temporary weakness of the defensive auric net in the case of illness, the malicious sendings will complicate the struggle of the organism and in such a way cause irreparable harm. Will we not be foolish in breeding such dark thoughts? Chase away every impure thought; replace it with a thought of benevolence. Hasten to purify the spirit by broad creative thoughts about the wonderful future.

Also, it is necessary to remember constantly the ruinous effects of irritability. "Irritability makes our vessel fragile." The poison of irritability, with all its consequences, is pointed out in Agni Yoga. This poison corrodes the precious precipitations of psychic energy. And what can be achieved without the accumulation of psychic energy? Stupidity and destruction will be the results. Of course, everyone has the free will to destroy himself, but it is criminal to spread this dreadful infection. Thus, bearing in mind the significance of thought and of irritability, we shall commence the creating of a benevolent atmosphere.

* * *

While building up the relations between the co-workers, you must not forget all the small workers. The real leader will be very careful not to offend by word or action the least of the workers. Only treachery must be severely condemned. Our atmosphere and all our possibilities will be considerably improved if we are surrounded by friends. It has been mentioned many times how you should appreciate each devoted heart and how important are the small helpers connected with our daily life. Even the kindly treatment of animals improves the atmosphere around us.

The Teaching provides the most vital and practical advices. We must make an effort to absorb the Treasury of the Teaching entrusted to us. Let us remember the donkey under the load of grain—mentioned in the Teaching—and let us not be like unto it.

So many disappointments, so many failures would have been avoided had the Teaching and all the indications been applied in a literal sense in everyday life. By giving us understanding of life, understanding of the foundations of existence, the Teaching brings us, if there is application in full consciousness of all that is given, to fiery purification or transmutation of our centers into the higher fires, and thus gives us the chalice of Amrita.

Only this fiery purification opens the way to the Tower. But this transmutation may come only when the spirit has conquered selfishness. It is said:

"Selfishness is the breeder of all grey accumulations; therefore, when selfishness obscures the spirit it can be positively said that the transmuting fire cannot reach us. ... When the spirit surrounds the manifested power of its essence with burdensome accumulations, it departs from striving. The burdens are so heavy that the spirit loses its approach to the Tower. That is why those who know this affirmation move ahead by transmuting their ego. When the spirit does not strive to outlive its burdens, it attracts the affirmed obstacle. Thus, there is a balance between striving and consequences. The wings of spirit bring the power of soaring to the higher spheres, but the heaviness of selfishness draws one to the lower spheres. ... Only those surrounded by the wall of selfishness may affirm self-conceit. Therefore, an obstructive wall remains on the way, and only the destruction of this wall will bring us to the first step of transmutation. If the center of ego exists separately, it will be destined to solitude. Only cooperation of heart and spirit leads to the keys of the Teaching."

Self-conceit is bred by ignorance. Self-conceit closes all the ways to knowledge. Self-conceit deprives man of the wonderful striving. What remarkable definitions of striving—this key to all the Gates—are given in the books of the Teaching!

* * *

It is necessary for each one to give account to himself as to how and in what way he passed the probations of the last seven years. Let us recall all the probations which were given to those who came into contact with the Teaching in the first days of the Call of the Great Teachers. Everyone had a chance to show his nature completely. Read attentively the letter about "Probation and Chelaship" in the book, *The Mahatma Letters to A.P. Sinnett.*

They are very edifying. I have mentioned it already, but a useful exercise of memory is always good. The Teacher follows a system of continuous probation. Otherwise, how can the deeply concealed accumulations be revealed? How can they be burned over the fire of devotion and striving? Many psychological ways are used by the Teachers for probation and guidance of the pupils. The ardent pupil, who appreciates every hint of the Teacher, who is severe to himself but benevolent to other workers, will successfully pass all the probations. But woe to him who confirms himself in his own importance and considers himself a pillar of the Teaching; frightful will be his downfall!

I may as well warn you against low, vulgar suspiciousness. He who suspects others proves that he himself possesses similar accumulations. By suspecting, we show that we are inclined to do the things of which we suspect others. Let us be ashamed to unveil our nature so openly. Let us ardently destroy even a hint of this vulgarity. A slave to suspicion will suspect everybody. The king of spirit sees all as beautiful and thus calls to life the best there is. The law of the magnet is everywhere.

All words and hints which come from the Guru have deep significance. There is no effect without a cause. Every indication of the Guru, if precisely fulfilled, brings good results, not only to the work but also to the one who did the work. By rejection or careless fulfillment we often deprive ourselves of irreplaceable possibilities. And later, when our intellect has grown, we shall realize how irremediable is the situation, and we shall moan with acute distress, "The happiness was so near, so possible!" Inscrutable are the ways of karma, and we never know which link, which string may bring us the expected happiness. Therefore, let us not lose a single knot, wisely woven by the hand of the Guru.

Let us drive away all the dark shadows. They stand behind our back and whisper, and so much happiness may fly away!

* * *

Most human faults and vices are developed from light-mindedness; therefore, by getting rid of this greatest evil we shall approach perfection with the steps of a giant.

* * *

One more request. Write your letters to me with a copy, and before writing your next letter reread your previous one. In this way you will understand the design of your own spirit better. There will be fewer contradictions and moods in your letters. And if you write about the new comprehension, point out what actions confirmed and strengthened this comprehension. I would also like to see more questions about the true understanding of events but not the selection of favorable circumstances. Show more sincerity, more concentration, show a broad consciousness. From not a bad (but a wrong) desire to cause me joy by good news, your letters often do not reflect reality.

"Too little time is left for burning oil in your lamps." Please realize how serious is this Indication. Those who do not approach the Hierarchy of Light during this life may forever lose this connection. You know how I dislike to frighten, how all my being is striving to bring only joy, but you also know about the limited time.

Do not break the wonderful connecting thread. After the break, the fall would carry you far away. Be of good cheer and courage, and find joy in the salutary Indications of the Hierarchy of Light. Let us firmly remember that the most powerful force, which transmutes various energies, is the magnet of the heart. "All currents are transmuted by this magnet. The human being is attracted to this magnet; that is why the transmuting power is in the heart."

Let us try to develop this power in ourselves. This will give us the highest joy of existence.

12

7 October 1930

The idea of creating the unity of women the world over is more than timely.

In the difficult days of world upheavals, of human disunity, of the neglecting of all the higher principles of Being, which are the only true givers of life and which lead to the evolution of the world, there must be heard a voice calling for the resurrection of the spirit and for the bringing of the fire of achievement into all the actions of life. And, of course, this voice must be the voice of woman, who during millenniums has drunk the chalice of suffering and humiliation and has forged her spirit in the greatest patience.

Now, let woman—the Mother of the World—say, "Let there be Light," and let her affirm her fiery achievements. What will this Light be like, and which of her achievements will be the great fiery ones? The banner of spirit will be raised, and upon it will be inscribed "Love, Knowledge and Beauty." Yes, only the heart of the woman, the mother, may gather under this Banner the children of the whole world, without distinctions of sex, race, nationality and religion.

Woman—mother and wife—witness of the development of man's genius, can appreciate the great significance of the culture of thought and knowledge.

Woman—inspirer of beauty—knows all the strength, all the synthesizing power of beauty.

Woman—bearer of the sacred power and knowledge of spirit—can indeed become "The Leading One."

Let us, therefore, without delay raise the great Banner of the New Era—the Era of the Mother of the World. Let every woman enlarge the boundaries of her hearth to encompass the hearths of the whole world. These countless fires will strengthen and embellish her own hearth.

Knowing that limitation leads to destruction, and that expansion gives creation, let us strive with all our forces toward the expansion of our consciousness, toward the refinement of thought and feeling, so that with the resultant creative fire we can kindle our own hearth.

Let us lay into the foundation of Woman's Unity the striving toward true knowledge, that which knows no human demarcations and limitations. But we may be asked how the true knowledge is to be reached. We shall reply, "This knowledge exists in your spirit, in your heart. Be able to awaken it!"

Striving toward beauty will be the key to it. This knowledge is in each striving toward the General Good. It is indicated in all the Great Teachings which have been given to the world. It is in every manifestation of nature. In forgetting to observe the cosmic manifestations, humanity lost the key to many of the mysteries of Being, and it is just these mysteries that could provide understanding of all the reasons for the present upheavals and miseries. Therefore, while gathering the warriors of spirit, let us direct them toward an awakening of this sacred knowledge.

Humanity should realize the majestic cosmic law of equivalency, the law of the dual Origin, as the foundation of existence. The predominance of one Origin over the other has created a lack of balance and destruction, which may now be observed in all of life. But let not the woman who has realized this law, and who strives toward equilibrium, let her not lose the beauty of the feminine image; let her not lose tenderness of heart, subtlety of feelings, the self-sacrifice and the courage of patience.

Woman, the bearer of sacred knowledge, can become a calling power, kindling with fiery words the souls that are ready. It is necessary to give to every woman according to her consciousness and without impeding her natural and individual growth. It is necessary, with careful touches, to broaden the mind on the foundation of the Teaching of Life. Let every soul develop in a natural way, bringing out the best she can according to the level of her consciousness. Beauty is in variety, but all should have one general foundation—the foundation of striving toward the General Good. The broadest cooperation is inscribed on the Banner of the Mother of the World. Therefore, let us display the utmost tolerance.

Sisters of the Golden Mountain, a dangerous but beautiful time is ahead of us—a time of great achievements. I send you the call of my heart. Let us arm ourselves with flaming striving and with courage, and over all obstacles we shall carry the Banner of the Mother of the World—the Banner of Love, Self-Sacrifice and Beauty—so that in the hour of victory we shall plant it on the Summits of the World.

13

13 October 1930

I have received a series of letters which give me an idea of the course of your work and also of your attempts to apply some of the laws of the Teaching to life. I was happy to see your penetration into the Teaching. The thoughts you quoted from the book *Agni Yoga* are very timely. It is indeed necessary to affirm the great usefulness of creative activity, together with courageous striving and firm faith in final success. We must face the enemy with complete presence of mind. The enemy is often nothing more than a repulsive but harmless beetle on a sunlit wall, and only neurotic individuals will be frightened by it. Some enemies assume the guise of yaks, but we use yaks for crossing the most dangerous mountain summits. A wolf, too, will sometimes assume sheep's clothing, but we have already been warned against excessive confidence; and we know that we must suit our weapons to each individual case. We would not, for example, oppose a tiger with an arrow designed for a sparrow.

Fearlessness and striving are two of the foundations of the Teaching. It is almost impossible to stop something that is in striving motion. Similarly does striving thought surmount all obstacles. You will have received by now the new book of the Teaching. You will find many wonderful formulae in it. Assimilate them and apply them to life. Note all that is said about the qualities of action. Only knowledge of the Teaching will bring you the presence of mind for your answers because the Teaching foresees every situation of life.

Also, it is useful to remember what was said about daring, and how reproved were all standardized concepts—these destroyers of ascent in small things as well as in large ones. You can speak about the necessity of new ways, but do it tactfully and carefully because immobility and dullness resent being disturbed. "Better to move to the cemetery than to be limited by dead laws." All the laws are in the depths of our consciousness. Thus, by deepening our consciousness we comprehend the laws. From this comes great mobility. But what do we see in reality? Criminal stagnation of mind! Countries maintaining dead laws decay because they oppose the laws of evolution. Look around "with the eyes of a hawk." Study the present situation and approaching events on our planet! Verily, one may say that coming events already cast their shadow upon the Earth. It is impossible to arrest the awakened force of the new consciousness or understanding among the masses. All delays will only cause greater destruction. But we are not destroyers. We are creators. Therefore, let us ardently build the bastions of culture, knowledge of the Living Ethics, and Beauty. Knowledge and Beauty are the foundation and crown of cosmic evolution.

How I wish to strengthen you in courageous patience, fearlessness and resourcefulness!

Only thought and a great consciousness will conquer everything. Therefore, use all means to broaden your consciousness by absorbing with all your essence every line of the Teaching. A profound and many-sided consciousness and the application of the Covenants of the Teaching into life will give you the key to everything because you will possess a synthesis.

* * *

By comparing all the given indications with the current events, we shall see how wisely and timely every one of them was given. How considerately, how carefully was our consciousness prepared for the next step. Blessed is the Hand which lightened the burden!

Years of stubborn but beautiful struggle are ahead of us, but the result of this battle is predestined. Therefore, we should examine our armor and temper the steel of our swords. It is necessary to have the given shields always ready because we must raise the right shield for the right occasion. Write down and recall in your memory as often as possible each encounter, each defense, and the protection given to you by each shield. The number of the shields exceeds that of the institutions. Your entire activity is covered and protected by them. Exercise together! Every co-worker can show resourcefulness and can display the strength of the shield from a new, unexpected point of view. It is extremely useful to conclude discussion by such exercises. You may even imagine the hostile questioners and then prepare and practise your answers to them.

When defending the work of our societies and communities, let us not forget our scientific expeditions and the great idea of the Banner of Peace, our international contacts, and, finally, our struggle against the cruel and ignorant attitude toward cultural creativeness! Often, it is difficult for us to comprehend the whole significance of our constructive work, and in urgent moments the most significant data and proofs are not evident to us. It is not always that our memory can muster the necessary thought. That is why it is so important to practise the reviewing of our tasks, together with the inspection of our shields and general accumulations. To begin with, let us firmly realize that we are constructing a great work of world importance and that we are invulnerable beneath our shields.

Perhaps the concept of a City of Knowledge is less clear in the consciousness of the co-workers than the other ideas. Therefore, I shall give you—rather, will repeat to you—a few ideas for your outer protection. As to the inner one, you already have it. The center should be developed into a city of knowledge.

In this city we wish to create a synthesis of scientific achievements. Therefore, all branches of science should eventually be established there. And, since the source of knowledge lies in the Cosmos, the co-workers of the scientific center should belong to the whole world—that is, should include all nationalities. And, as the Cosmos is indivisible in all its functions, the scientists of the world should be indivisible in their achievements. In other words, they should be united in closest cooperation. The location of the center, in the Himalayas, is selected quite deliberately and purposefully, as innumerable possibilities are open there, and the attention of the scientific world is being directed toward these heights. The discovery of new cosmic rays, which bring to humanity new precious energies, is possible only on the mountain summits because all the finest and most valuable energies are found only in the pure layers of mountain atmosphere.

Are not mountains the greatest of magnetic stations? Would it not be appropriate to explore their magnetism and electricity? Would not the study of magnetic currents bring safety into aerostatics? In the sphere of magnetic currents science is still in its infancy, and modern instruments are nothing but toys, while "great discoveries could take place with proper study and research." The reason we wish so much to begin this research at our center is because the conditions of this locality are particularly favorable. Would it not be timely to pay attention to all meteoric precipitations which fall on the snowy summits and which, by the force of the mountain streams, are carried down to the valleys? For astronomical observations the conditions here are exceptionally good, and in nearby Little Tibet it is possible to establish a section of the main station.

Geologically, the Himalayas are also very interesting, and their caves hold many mysteries for archaeologists, zoologists and anthropologists. There are a great number of hot springs. Also, other unexplored springs and salt lakes, which have various properties according to the statements of local inhabitants. As for botany, zoology, and ornithology—you have already learned from the letters of our botanist-zoologist how pleased he was with the results of his work. On these mountains the rarest medicinal plants and grasses are centered, and the variety of botanic species is unexcelled.

In archaeological respects our valley, of course, is one of the richest and most ancient. There are traces of ancient Buddhist culture. Quite remarkable is the number of local dialects among the mountain tribes. Two neighboring villages frequently do not understand each other. Fiery atmospheric manifestations also could be observed here, and the so-called "Himalayan lights" may often be seen. It is most desirable to establish here a meteorological station to start studying and observing the magnetic currents, with the idea of broadening it eventually, bearing in mind the favorable local conditions. In connection with this, let me quote certain indications: "Further movement of magnetic currents over the surface of the earth manifests the lines of the atmospheric changes. Observation stations should be established in various places, and collaboration between them should be as close and precise as possible. It is true that the trouble lies in the absence of synthesis and that much energy and valuable studies are lost. Therefore, an organization of true cooperators is necessary on Earth."

Let us think of broad possibilities. "Breadth of thought and consciousness will be your test." Have you noticed that all pessimists usually possess small consciousnesses and poor imaginations?

The establishment of a city of synthesized knowledge is a problem of world significance, and that is why we must not ask for help but should demand it. We work not for ourselves but for humanity. Everyone of us is ready to apply his best efforts for the General Good. Let other people also understand this pure striving, and they may become aflame with the desire to advance humanity further toward synthesized knowledge.

Thus, insist that your co-workers examine and cleanse their shields. Search for those shields in every indication, every thought given in the books of Living Ethics. We must have the beautiful, constructive formulae ready. With all our imagination we are unable to embrace the significance of present events which gather around the cultural activities. Therefore, let us absorb the idea that a great world task is being performed and, striving ceaselessly, let us continue to carry the stones for building the Temple of Knowledge.

Once more, I ask all participants to think what great cooperation means. I quote an example given by the Teacher: "Forces which act against each other are mutually destroyed. Forces which act along parallel lines in the same direction manifest the sum of these energies, and forces which act separately are weakened, according to the angle of their divergency. People cannot realize that this fundamental law of physics is also a fundamental law of cooperation." Therefore, straighten out your divergencies so that your forces move in the same direction. Consider the consequences of divergencies. In true cooperation, no one is belittled, and he can help the better who knows and sees more. The more ignorant a person or a nation is, the less cooperation is in evidence. But who would wish to assign to himself the label of stupidity and ignorance? The saying, "I know nothing of it, I meddle not," is very characteristic. But he who knows nothing may never know anything.

14
3 December 1930

We are so happy about the development of your cultural activities. Each cultural thought applied in life is a precious treasure! And we have an immense fund of such thoughts ready for practical application. Those who approach this fund may draw upon it and use it in accordance with their striving. Therefore, our main problem is to awaken striving in the newcomers. Each one, becoming aflame, will discover his own potentiality, will develop it in his own way, and thus will enrich the communal treasury. But in order to inspire one another, we must carry this inextinguishable fire in ourselves. We should keep it in complete purity and should struggle with the welter of petty thoughts born of selfishness. You may be assured that thought created selfishly can never be harmonious with the great plan of cosmic evolution. Therefore, in all your failures, look for this worm which gnaws all the foundations. Look just for this. Verily, selfishness is narrowness, but narrowness leads to stagnation and death, while the Cosmos exists by the principle of Infinity.

How to destroy this worm? Only by tolerance, broad-mindedness and understanding of the great law of co-measurement. In other words, by the broadening of our consciousness. Therefore, let us ardently strive to broaden our consciousness. All the contributory steps toward this liberating aim are given in the books of the Teaching. Let us enrich our life with these treasures, remembering that the striving of spirit and will can transform life.

The spirit which seeks to kindle its energy by striving is a fuser of matter. After fusing matter, he will refine it, and then the finest perceptions will be reached. These are the only possibilities for true life and immortality! The spirit of striving must be the foundation of one's life.

Thus, strive toward the greatest because those who draw a small circle are doomed, and their possibilities will be limited according to the radius of their circle. A limited consciousness attracts imperfect energies or small possibilities. And even if by reason of karma the orbit of spirit catches broader possibilities, a small consciousness will try to build a chicken coop out of them! Only the consciousness that apprehends the world in its greatest actions may cooperate with the Cosmos and with the Great Brothers of Humanity.

Realization and concrete understanding of the existence of the magnet that connects our spirit with the higher energies, which carry the broadening of consciousness, can bring us closer to the consciousness of the Cosmic Magnet and will actually draw us into the current of Cosmic Evolution. This will lead us to the great Sacrament—the consummation of Being, which is called the Crown of Crowns.

Hasten to light the guiding fires of your spiritual magnet by the awakening of the heart. Only in joining the fires of the heart with the fires of the spirit can we attain creativeness and great results.

* * *

All your motives should be checked by your heart. Your heart is the only judge, accumulator and guardian of the acquired precious energies. The structure of these acquired and accumulated energies is our individuality and destiny. The law of correspondence is a basic cosmic law. Therefore, each acquired energy will attract an identical energy from space and also will evoke a corresponding reaction from the people one contacts. Here is an explanation of sympathies and antipathies, and also the reason why one person can find contact with many people while another, in spite of all his efforts, creates only antagonism. But, as all possibilities come from people, the significance of the quality of energies we accumulate is quite clear.

The accumulation of the precipitation of energies does not take place in just a single life. Thousands of years are necessary for filling the Chalice. So essential are the continuous, never-interrupted, benevolent strivings, which deposit the priceless treasures in our treasury. People possessing great accumulations of the Chalice are the treasures of nations. Sometimes very little is needed in order to complete the filling of the Chalice, and this little could be completed in one self-denying life. But by carelessness people postpone the achievement, and by this they throw themselves back. Nobody and nothing can stop eternal movement and the transmutation of energies. There exist only two possibilities: either to strive ahead or to fall back. But who would want to vow himself to retrogression—in other words, to unite himself with cosmic waste? Striving is the great moving power for all beings!

Now as regards Agni Yoga. How can we interpret Agni Yoga if we do not broaden our consciousness? All the words about it and about its achievements will be void of conviction if we ourselves do not light the fires of our own hearts. Someone writes about the necessity of tolerance toward every interpretation. This idea is correct. It is, however, necessary to learn how to make each individual interpretation correctly understood. Otherwise, such bushes may be planted that the instructor himself will be lost! Often a false interpretation is more harmful than none at all. Each instructor must realize completely his responsibility for making a correct interpretation of the first principles. He should exercise the maximum caution not to give thoughtless explanations of some statements of the Teaching which are not clear even to himself but which, nevertheless, he might wish to interpret in order not to lose his authority. In perplexing cases it is better to admit honestly, "I shall forbear any interpretation, as I would like to consider the subject carefully." As for myself, I shall always be glad to explain with the help of the Great Teacher everything that is not clear to you.

You write beautifully about your striving for harmony. Apply it in life, as everything is of worth *only in life and for life*. Show the finest discrimination; avoid hypocrisy. Patches are better than holes, but everyone would rather have strong fabric; so let us try not to make holes! Let us practise severe discipline of speech. Let us consider every word and remember that "the consequences of a word cannot be destroyed even by an Arhat." Let us broadly apply the indication that "each word should be like a ray of light and not a nail in the coffin." Know in your spirit when it is goal-fitting to tell the truth, even if it is bitter, and when it is better to be silent. But flattery and exaggeration, as well as belittling, are inadmissible.

Each one of you has his particular qualities; nobody has been set aside. Therefore, you must not envy each other. But of course it depends on each of you to develop your capabilities. And the only lawful competition between members of the group may be a competition in the best direction of striving and understanding of the thought for the General Good. Each one should understand that this capacity in each individual consciousness is the only indicator of progress and that the spirit stands on a corresponding step-not higher and not lower. I would like to quote the Teacher's words: "When it is mentioned about selfishness, it may not be interpreted individually. Everything *in* life, everything *for* life. The Teacher sees. The Teacher knows. The Teacher will not affirm anything without life. The one who repeats his own formulae does not know the formulae of the Teacher. The old formulae will not lead toward new ways. It is necessary to say: 'The channel of selfishness builds its dams everywhere.'" Also, it is indicated to explain that the channel of selfishness cuts the conduit of communication. Let us remember that the quality of a motive will either move us toward the Teacher or thrust us far from Him. There is no place where one can hide from the all-seeing Eye, which penetrates into the most secret recesses of our heart. It is necessary to manifest the power of spirit and to strive tirelessly to eradicate the persistent, heavy accumulations, as otherwise no refinement will be possible. Only refinement of all feelings brings the best possibilities.

My heart is longing to see growth of understanding of the Teaching; growth of sincere striving, free from any expectation of reward; growth of self-denial; the offering of practically everything for the benefit of the General Good; growth of a correct approach to entrusted work; and, above all, growth of the sense of co-measurement. It must be understood that one may exhaust oneself in action and tension; but, without commensurability, action and tension will result in an accomplishment similar to that of a squirrel which runs continuously in the same circle. Action not balanced by commensurability, action without the creative fire of the heart, will never create a worthy step.

* * *

I welcome very much the method which is being used for developing attentiveness among children. It is very good to use art gallery pictures for this purpose. So much can be seen in these treasures of art. Attentiveness is a foundation for accumulating knowledge. Attentiveness is a first step in the refinement of receptivity, and we know that only refinement gives broadening of consciousness and that creative power is affirmed by the centers of fine receptivity. The finer, the higher; the higher, the more powerful! Nothing holds back evolution so much as coarseness of receptivity!

If we want to approach the High Consciousness, we must first of all refine our own receptivity. Only where there is equilibrium, as is found in a balance, is true cooperation manifested. That is why the structure based on the principles of harmony is so greatly valued. The subtle perception of thoughts will lay a foundation for an alert action. The creation of the beautiful is based on this principle. The reason there is so little beauty in people's creations is that even the best ideas are executed only partly, and therefore the beauty of the original intention is distorted.

Remember that you are surrounded by possibilities, but they will materialize only if your consciousness will realize them. Every thought is born from contact with the reservoir of space. Just imagine how many unapplied thoughts are flying in the higher layers of space! Try to seize them by refining your receptivity. That is what we call cosmic cooperation, but first you must kindle your inner fires.

There is no greater joy than the joy of a growing consciousness! In the waves of consciousness lies all the joy of Being!

Once more I call to you. Please have an open heart for all the qualities of your co-workers. Learn to be tolerant without showing too much indulgence. By the fire of your heart inspire your co-workers to display in life their best qualities. Try to unite them in the highest feelings of devotion and gratitude to the Teacher who has given them so much.

Make haste to learn how to love and appreciate each other. But nothing requires such delicate and attentive care as love!

Oh, if you could manifest at least a small amount of that

tolerance and care which is manifested by the Great Heart who called us to build unitedly the Temple!

Hearken to the call of the heart!

15
17 December 1930

In the days of victory I wish to greet you and prepare you for new and more strenuous battles! In the days of victory I wish to remind you of the words of the Great Teacher: "Know the thrill of the battle." In the days of victory let us thoroughly examine our weapons and prepare our shields, for our enemy is ready, and with vigilant eye he watches our weak spots, so that he can strike through them. He knows how victory lulls the mind and lessens striving and watchfulness. Therefore, after each victory we must strive with redoubled force toward the next, still greater battle and victory. A slackening of striving results in defeat. Truly, only a broad consciousness will be aware of the danger of the lessened watchfulness that results from the first victories.

Thus, let us acquire the joy of constant watchfulness and striving. They are among the foundations of the Teaching and of life. Only striving carries us toward the next steps. Only vigilance enables us to overcome successfully all obstacles. The Teacher calls us to pressing labor for the sake of victory. All victory depends upon the strength of our striving. Therefore, if striving decreases either because of the short-sightedness of a limited consciousness or because of internal discord and disunion in the actions of the warriors, defeat will be unavoidable. Therefore, I ask you not to weaken yourselves by internal discord when approaching a dangerous passage. It is also fatal to push each other because the one who pushes may very easily share the fate of the one pushed.

It is also necessary to manifest maximum discrimination when you give responsible positions to new warriors. Give them tests and do not hurry to promote them to the first ranks. Imagine what complications may be caused if a worker falls short of meeting an occasion!

Do not allow outsiders to criticize and condemn any of your co-workers in your presence. Always try to find worthy words with which to stop evil-speaking and condemnation—for this you will receive respect. Remember that as long as you are united you will be able to pass through all obstacles, but the least disunity in your actions will create a rift to the very foundation. And what structure can be built upon a cleft foundation? The first storm would ruin such an edifice. Come closer together and strive to fulfill the smallest Indications of the Teacher. This is the only way to victory.

You must remember that the Guru has not a single personal thought; absolutely everything is directed and given to the service of the General Good. Therefore, the one who alters the indication, or allows himself to doubt, should lay the blame on himself. All that is done in a halfway manner will bring halfway results. We know that a full dose of a salutary medicine brings life, while but one-half gives only temporary relief which may end in death. Hence, let us accept completely the precious indications, in order not to lose a single bit of life-giving energy. Complete obedience to the indications and the precise execution of them gives health and leads to great victory, to great Light. In ancient times obedience was a step toward the next ordainment. The one who was unable to realize entirely the discipline of obedience could never reach the higher degrees. Only the one who knew how to obey and to execute could take great responsibility and understand all the immutableness of the order.

With all this, one must firmly understand that all the given orders can never enslave the spirit of a disciple because there is always left the freedom of individual expression, and we know how endlessly we may refine the quality of the fulfillment of every task. Only a slave of yesterday may revolt against an order. Only a petty consciousness is afraid to lose its individuality by fulfilling the plans of his Guru. To rely only upon our own accumulations, rejecting all that which we can assimilate from the high consciousness of the Teacher, means to reject any new accumulations. Individuality is formed from these new assimilations combined with previous accumulations.

Extremely happy is the one who can draw upon the Treasury of the Great Consciousness. I wish to quote from the book, *Infinity*:

"The idea of obedience to the Teacher seems to be alien to people. But how can the spirit lose when the Teacher is the Leading Light? How can the disciple lose his fire when the Teacher lights all fires? How can the Shield of the Teacher hold back the pupil if he is already inspired by his Teacher? How little does humanity desire to strive toward mutually beneficial work! But humanity must learn to act interdependently and to materialize all the thoughts affirmed by the Teacher. Thus, the Cosmic Mind fulfils evolution. Thus, humanity must learn to construct by higher measures. Verily, by following the Teacher you assimilate his Image.

"How can we achieve comprehension of the magnet if we doubt the Indications of the Lord? How can we conquer an enemy if we doubt the power granted to us? How can we expect to build anything strong if we do not admit the ineradicable Indications of Hierarchy? It may seem that I repeat myself, but because of your hesitant pace in action there is need for an attentive study of the Indications. Remember how the Teaching promotes the progress of work."

I also advise you to give a positive tone to your speeches, remembering that only positiveness leads people. And only the unusual approach to action attracts attention. Many people may see even "lack of tact" in such unusualness, but by this they would only show their denseness. Only unusualness attracts and holds strong and courageous people. All great events were created not by the masses but by individual strong personalities, and time will mark them out. Many are called, but few are chosen. Thus, work out an unusual language, a language of power and affirmation, a language of builders, as only such a language is appropriate for the entrusted task. All gushing, sugary words are the words of incompetent sentimentality and of ruinous mediocrity. Do you remember how all of you used to admire the lectures of a certain person? At the same time, however, you correctly noticed that he only criticized and attacked. But we must be creative, and we shall confirm and indicate the right direction. You must remember that all the Teachings condemn lukewarmness. Therefore, let us be fiery. Let us become aflame, manifesting the most careful discrimination in order not to create a conflagration when it is but necessary to kindle. A broadening of the consciousness will lead to the right way. A broadening of consciousness will change the quality of thinking. A broadening of the consciousness will bring the power of Victory.

But drive away petty thoughts. Avoid belittling because the belittling of the entrusted work is equal to the belittling of your Teacher, which would be traitorous and would injure the foundations on which your own welfare as well as the General Good is based. Drive away all doubts, for where there is doubt there is an arresting of the development of consciousness. The one who doubts, who does not trust, cannot hope for the confidence of the Teacher. Therefore, it is impossible for him to move ahead.

I would like so much to teach you to treasure every Indication, every hint of the Teacher and Guru, as they are so precious! Find within yourself the fiery impulse of striving toward the great task, carrying the light of culture. Imagine that you live in a house of glass and must be careful in all your words and actions. Imbue all your work with the beauty of Service. Remain joyous in battle because of your knowledge of the victory that is predestined provided you are full of self-sacrificing tension.

16
7 January 1931

The one who belittles or distorts the Will of the Teacher ruins himself. The one who belittles his Guru resembles a man who tries to cut off the branch of a tree on which he is sitting. The greater our Guru the greater are we, but this simple axiom is not comprehended. The whole history of humanity proves that the great historical figures, the true leaders and philosophers, had reverence for their Gurus, whose leadership helped them to become giants of spirit and doers of great deeds.

Hierarchy is soon to be published. Verily, the immutable cosmic law of Hierarchy is so much ignored at the present time. But humanity must once more recognize this law. The principle of Hierarchy is a leading law, verily the giver of Life. Therefore, we must imbue our consciousness with understanding of this law if we wish to grow and to contribute our share to the General Good.

The law of the chain of Hierarchy is most firm and is strictly maintained by the White Brotherhood. Nobody can avoid the nearest link because this link has been created by long approach and by the accumulations of thousands of years. Therefore, let us firmly hold the nearest link, so that we do not lose union with the whole chain.

There is so much beauty in devotion and gratitude toward the Guru! In the Teaching it is said that the flame of devotion and gratitude is above all other fiery offerings. But alas, these two qualities are particularly rare among the inhabitants of this planet. But precisely possession of these qualities helps greatly toward the creation of the giants of spirit and will. The spirit gifted with brilliant talents but not possessing these two qualities will never be allowed to approach beyond a certain limit.

It is useful to point out everything that is said in the books of the Teaching about the relationship between the Teacher and the disciple. It is said that each reverence shown to the Teacher indicates a right understanding of the Teaching. But for the one for whom guidance is burdensome there can never be any approach to the Teacher. The Teaching is not abstract but gives most practical suggestions for application in life. Therefore, let us hold in our hearts all that is said about Hierarchy, and let us watch the purity of our thoughts, for the maintenance of the purity of thought is similar to ozone.

I quote from the book, *Hierarchy*:

"Mean thoughts have been compared to crawling reptiles. Nothing is more analogous to this scum of the consciousness. Can one sit calmly in an armchair, knowing that beneath him crawl poisonous snakes and scorpions? One must free oneself from reptiles, and first of all along the path to Hierarchy. Condemnation and blasphemy against the Lord are irreparable. Thus, each one who condemns the Hierarch must remember that his levity and crime will infect his karma for many ages. Verily, if there is only one way—through the Lord—to the one Light, then only extreme ignorance will allow destruction of this single path. One must assert striving to the Highest as the essence of life and assume a reverent attitude toward this striving for salvation. By diminishing the Hierarchy one may condemn oneself and inflict perilous harm to many near ones. It is time to remember this! Verily, it is necessary to hold the connecting thread, which brings both well-being and blessing.

"One cannot expect success when the very foundations are rotting! Of course, We shall do what is needed, but it is important to arrest light-mindedness and treachery. Treachery takes many forms, but are they not all similar? It is essential to ponder who has the right to complicate the already-predestined path. So much of the beautiful is destined and the dates are already approaching. Let the connecting thread radiate!

"When space is being clouded by the mist of non-understanding, then it is certainly difficult for the creative rays to penetrate. Each layer is permeated in conformity with the complex of its striving. Therefore, the earthly layers are so impenetrable. Hence all manifestations of the quest of spirit must proceed in a tense tempo. The quests of the spirit must attract it to the Magnet of Hierarchy, since each power has its correspondence upon Earth. Thus vitally must the law of Hierarchy be applied."

"It is also necessary to know that the dark forces are trying to penetrate into the foundations. Therefore, it is necessary to be attentive, to watch with the greatest care. The dark forces may even use a Shield of the Teacher. They will outwardly praise the name of the Guru while insidiously undermining it. Therefore, it is necessary to stand on guard and to manifest resistance. If a victory is to take place, it is necessary to realize all the importance of the Stronghold. Therefore, let us strengthen all positions. Thus, it is necessary to learn how to treasure the Name of the Teacher. The power of victory comes only when the foundations are strong. Thus let us guard the foundations. It is necessary to affirm victory; that is why caution is so necessary."

All the indications are full of concern about the broadening of consciousness. Be watchful; exert all your caution, for the enemy may enter the house under a mask of friendship! Close ranks more tightly and watch carefully the attempts to disunite you! The ways of flattery and the fanning of ambition are the surest ones, as who does not love to hear good reports about himself? This is common to everyone, and all weak points will be taken advantage of by the dark ones. Puffing up our pride, they may imperceptibly belittle the highest we have and that by which we live. Be on guard!

17

15 January 1931

I shall answer the questions about service. Service to the Hierarchy of Light is service to the General Good. Of course, striving to the General Good opens the gates of higher knowledge and Service. But I would like you to realize clearly what qualities you must first of all develop in yourself for advancement on the path of Service. Many people are dreaming about the General Good and even are ready to work for it as long as it does not interfere with their habits and prosperity. But true service to the General Good, which leads to the gates of the Stronghold of Light, requires sacrifice and complete disdain for everything personal, in other words, the complete abandonment of selfhood. When the consciousness is broadened, when all feelings and comprehension are refined, the law of sacrifice will be accepted as the highest achievement. There will be no room for self-pity, fear for the future, offenses and envy because with every breath will sublimity, beauty, and the highest joy of service be realized.

The mature spirit who consciously chooses the path of Service knows the joy of a broadened consciousness and the fiery striving to the Highest Consciousness; he knows the joy of fulfillment of the Higher Will; he knows the joy of discovery and the destination of life; and in the appointed hour he will learn the sublimity and beauty of the final sacrament.

And so, after understanding and accepting with our heart the significance of the great liberating and crowning sacrifice, let us strive to develop in ourselves love, devotion, gratitude and obedience to Hierarchy. Let us be ready to take any burden, remembering that the heavier the burden the shorter will be our path. Truly speaking, from love and devotion issue all the other qualities which help our advancement. Thus, let us cultivate them as the most precious flowers; and, since these flowers of spirit grow and nurture each other, the greatest love will bring the greatest answer. Therefore, let us surround the Great Teacher with the fire of love. Let us guard our respect for Him. Let us evince the most careful, the highest understanding of the Teaching and the Indications, and sacredly, reverently, with the tremor of the heart, face the beauty and the majesty of his creativeness. Remember, those whose understanding is higher will ascend higher.

And now to quote from the book *Hierarchy*:

"Some people pour a daily gruel over the Image of the Teacher and imagine themselves to be in the Great Service. The Teaching and Service first of all presuppose the expansion of consciousness on the basis of adherence to the Teaching and reverence to the Teacher. In studying Infinity one should first of all realize the limitlessness of love and devotion. It is not wise to say that love has overflowed and devotion has withered because the consequence will be disintegration of one's self. One should understand the limitlessness of love and devotion as the first steps toward Service and Yoga. One should set oneself this task at least as a means of self-progress. One should advance only in the direction of the Teacher. Then only does relief come. But making a daily onion-gruel out of the Teacher will not lead to success. Sacredly, limitlessly, let us sustain our love and reverence to the Teacher, as a healing remedy toward regeneration."

So, my dear friends, the vulgar conception, the scoffing at the sacred ideas by small consciousnesses because of their lack of co-measurement, and the belittling of the highest and fundamental must all be banished from our life if we wish to enter the path of Service.

Some are searching for the happiness of life, but bliss can come only through the fulfillment of the Will of the Teacher. There is no other way. And one must keenly grasp these wonderful, profound words of the Teacher and constantly remember them: "In fulfilling My Will, thou givest Me the possibility to fulfil thy will." For who else, if not the Teacher, knows our sacred wishes and strivings? And by purifying and crystallizing them by the given Teaching, that is, by the broadening of our consciousness, who but He gives us the possibility of realizing them? Would one want to be so foolish as to ruin one's own happiness?

Let us ardently strive to fulfil the saving Will, which leads us toward the envisioned service of the General Good!

"When thought comprises striving toward the fulfillment of the Higher Will a direct connection with the Shield of the Higher Will is established." How can this Shield protect us if we only partially fulfil the indications? Therefore, those disciples who strive to guard sacredly the testaments and to practise and apply the smallest indications will develop their creativeness and will broaden their consciousness.

From the book *Hierarchy*:

"Can one reach the understanding of Cosmos without striving to penetrate into the higher spheres? Only succession gives foundation to all strivings. The all-existing proceeds by the law of sequence. Hence, each insulation results only in the loss of the predestined. Thus, thought is generated as the carrier of the law of sequence. Thus, the law of the Higher Will creates limitlessly.

"The law of the Higher Will is the creator of all goal-fitting deeds! This law saturates space and only the fulfillment of the Higher Will crowns our deeds. How is it possible to turn away from the Indication of the Higher Will without losing victory? How is it possible to find better ways when the Shield of the Teacher is affirmed by the guarantee of Hierarchy? The executors of the Will of Hierarchy are leading to victory. Therefore, the disciples must apply the most precise strivings to fulfil the Higher Will. Only thus shall we succeed. Only in such a way shall we affirm victory.

"Devotion to an idea, devotion to a leader, works miracles. In all times people realized the significance of devotion, and according to their consciousness used various means, from the demanding of an oath up to the church's anathema and Inquisition. And now also, only the small-minded betrayers, full of envy and doubt, driven by fear before the extraordinary Light, rise up against the invincible power of Hierarchy. Let us tell them, 'Pitiful fools, you are afraid of everything powerful and beautiful; you are afraid of spatial thoughts and creativeness; you are not our companions. We cannot find room in your burrows, and you would not be comfortable in our spacious chambers, as our rooms have not that musty sultriness that you enjoy so much.'"

I affirm by the Name of the Teacher, I affirm by my spirit, I affirm by my heart that the most devoted will be the greatest. Is it not said that Ananda, the most devoted disciple of Buddha, was a thousand times greater than the other Buddhist Arhats?

Let us pay attention to certain formulae of our enemies; how much stronger and sounder they are than many timid formulae of sympathizing friends. The enemies may teach us how to defend and to exalt, but friends often do not admit our greatest success. The wise Romans used to say, "Tell me thine enemies and I will tell thee who thou art."

Accept with your heart all the aforesaid, and ardently apply it in everyday life. Let unquenchable striving carry you toward the great Magnet, in the same way as a needle is attracted by a magnet. All the sense, all the joy and beauty, of our existence is in this Magnet. Perhaps it is not quite clear to you at the moment, but when the Teacher indicates I will explain it more completely.

Do not forget about the constant three-year tests. It is much more difficult to go over again the same probation because the surroundings have changed and it is difficult to make up for lost time and to find the lost rhythm, which moves up and does not wait for the delaying ones. Therefore, let us work with unremitting tension. Let us heighten our vibrations in order to receive the Rays that are sent to us which otherwise may pass us by.

Time is short and so much experience should be gathered; the work is growing. It will be difficult if the amount of work outgrows the consciousness of the co-workers. Broaden, broaden your consciousness by purging yourselves of destructive petty thoughts, of commonplaceness, of mediocrity. One petty thought may ruin a world, just as a leaf of grass on the mountain path can cause the fall of a giant into the abyss. Petty thoughts belong to slaves. Be the kings of spirit and broaden the boundary of your thinking up to the planetary scale! Remember that refined organisms cannot stand the atmosphere of petty thoughts; they feel suffocated. Therefore, leave all condemnations and in every one look for the best. Be kings of spirit!

18

21 January 1931

In this difficult time we are now experiencing let us give an account to ourselves of the causes of these difficulties. With complete honesty let us analyze the fundamental reason for these difficulties. We shall see that the root of the evil lies not so much in outward circumstances as in the misunderstanding of the indications, in the neglecting and rejecting of them, and especially in disagreements among the co-workers. Unity is the foundation of every constructive work, but was it manifested?

Can the disciple create, can he be successful, if he fails to work harmoniously in fulfilling the Covenants of the Teaching? No, a thousand times no! Let everyone think and recollect how many indications were not absorbed, how many were fulfilled only partially, and how many precious advices and hints were not applied at all. Let us manifest honesty, as there is no path without honesty.

Please try to understand, my friends, that every cell of our being should rejoice when we fulfil the Higher Will, as only in this way can we learn and broaden our consciousness. The one who fulfils more precisely will approach closer. Imagine an ordinary teacher and an ordinary pupil. What would happen if the pupil protested against all the experience and the indications of the teacher and followed his own methods? How much energy would the fool waste in order to obtain the synthesis of the teacher! By giving to a pupil the synthesis of his accumulated experience, a teacher helps him to save precious time for quicker and farther advancement and for individual creativeness. Without the continuous handing down of accumulations, what would happen to evolution?

If everybody had to learn by using only his personal experience, rejecting the Leading Hand, we should not move far from our ancestors of the Stone Age! Let us realize that the fulfillment of the Teacher's Will does not mean the subordination of our individuality to an alien will, as some superficial people think, but it means the greatest development of our sensitiveness and creativeness because there are so many reasons and so many possibilities of fulfillment in the Teacher's Indications. But usually a disciple does not see and does not fulfil even a tenth part of them. Can we say which one of the indications that we did not fulfil in time relates to the present difficulties we are experiencing? Everyone knows that if we strike an object in a room its echo may resound in an entirely different place and on the most unexpected object. Let us remember that nothing can slip away from the all-seeing Eye, and that all of us are under perpetual test, and that the one who is more gifted is expected to contribute more. Only when a better understanding of Hierarchy becomes part of our life will something higher be given to us. Do not thrust back the prepared possibilities and do not destroy what is given you. Will you not have to use much energy afterwards for a dubious repair? Here I shall quote from the Teaching:

"How vividly, then, must the disciple realize the power of perception and of the comprehension that there exists only one law which governs the entire Cosmos—the Higher Will; along this line the evolution of the spirit is created. This law unites all pertaining and manifested units. The striving toward the fulfillment of the Higher Will leads to the sensitiveness of perception. Only this path offers a corresponding decision of the realization and fulfillment of the Higher Will.

"Thus the Higher Reason creates upon Earth through the power of Hierarchy. Our creativeness requires the affirmation of Hierarchy in its entire scope, in its entire understanding, in its entire beauty. The manifestation of understanding of Hierarchy reveals all possibilities. It is correct to view the law of Hierarchy as the summit of cosmic creativeness. Light pours from it. Thoughts strive to it. Thus one should direct the best strivings to the summit of Hierarchy. Only when the highest affirmation enters consciously into life can the highest be given to the highest.

"Therefore each striving leading to the union of the disciple with the Teacher leads to cognizance of the highest laws. The disciple rejecting the Teacher acknowledges by this his own ignorance because he thus arrests his development. Each force attracting the spirit upwards is a force of development.

"Already you know how tense is the time; and to those who are seized with fear, say that when the Lord lives within the heart no hair will fall from one's head and to each one a place for body and spirit is allotted. But preserve pure your heart in order that I may enter there and surround you with armor. Remember that if you have given in spirit to the Lord what has been taken, He will reward you a hundredfold. Thus, direct your thought to the Lord and let the Lord enter into your heart. Without the Lord it will be narrow in the empty heart; and as peas in a dried sheepskin, wrath will jar within the empty heart. Fill your heart with the Lord so greatly that no enemy can force his way through. Peace unto you."

Our way is not the way of conclusions accessible to everyone. You may vouch that until now the events were developed not according to ordinary logic. Observe the current of events. By such experience you approach the predestined. You may notice that the Hand of the Teacher acts at the last moment; remember this formula. We should learn to act independently but should remember that success comes only if the heart is filled with the Lord. Verily, such a heart sparkles like a Sword of Light; it flames, succors and sustains. Thus, I advise to strive with all the forces of spirit in order to surround the heart with armor. There have been plenty of doubts and condemnations. You must consider the Indication received as a result, the immutable answer.

Much was rejected, but we should not look back. Therefore, I want you to test your hearts by filling them with the Image of the Lord. More complicated tasks than the present difficulties have been solved by the Teacher. You must remember how you were led by the Teacher when your hearts belonged to Him.

In the same way will He lead all those who do not break his Indications. Do you remember a Persian tale about a long-nosed man who broke his nose against the smallest stone?

"Hence, when the highest striving toward the Lord is offered, the manifested orbit and focus should be guarded. Therefore, all our abutments should be protected because clouds are about. Victory is predestined but all foundations should be protected, and the highest striving can bring all possibilities. The time is severe but wondrous. It is a time of consummation and of constructiveness. It is a time of highest tension and of earthly battle. It is a time which inscribes a great page and which builds a great future. The enemies thus rage because the highest law enters into life.

"Let everyone be as a rock—carrying responsibility in the name of the Guru. Verily, his name is a shield of Light! Let everyone listen attentively to the opinions of approaching people, but even the least belittling of the Guru should be considered as the best identification of the enemy. Only in this way shall we learn how to distinguish Light from darkness."

The aura of the Guru is the surest surveyor, the best touchstone for the newcomers, and as for those who might wish to belittle the Guru, they also belittle the Hierarchy of Light. Therefore, let us manifest double vigilance and caution when we meet those who disparage and slander.

Day and night, remember about the great time. All incautiousness, all light-mindedness, all inattentiveness may create the most difficult results. Put on your complete armor and manifest the most unremitting, the greatest devotion to the Foundations, as only in them is your salvation during this menacing but beautiful battle. Remember the words of N.K. [Prof. Nicholas K. Roerich.] "We must build upon the true facts; all our words and actions must be clear as crystal, as we are watched by the whole world."

19

13 May 1931

I continue to write about Hierarchy, as this concept, which embraces the complete foundation of life, the evolution of spirit and all constructiveness, is not yet correctly understood.

We must hasten to comprehend it, as we have little time because the severest Armageddon is raging. Only by accepting with all our heart the great principle of Hierarchy can we broaden our consciousness, which is so necessary for success. By manifesting every day the highest caution toward everything entrusted to us, we shall complete our work victoriously.

First of all, let us be honest and let us admit that all difficulties and failures are the results of manifested neglect toward the given indications, of forgetfulness, light-mindedness, doubts and selfish envy. It is impossible to conceal the worm of doubt; even an inexperienced observer can notice it. Let us apply against this parasite the most effective remedy, and this remedy is gratitude to the Great Teacher. Sometimes it is helpful to compare oneself with the millions of souls tossing around—those who have no idea of tomorrow. It is helpful to look back and to give oneself, if possible, an impartial account as to what one used to be and what one has become. It is helpful to exercise our imagination and to picture to ourselves what our destiny would be without the wise and benevolent Guidance. And indeed it will be most helpful to remember constantly about the indicated constructive work for the culture of the future.

If after such an honest and many-sided review our hearts do not overflow with gratitude, devotion and love toward the Giver and the Leader, then verily they have dried up and our consciousness has become small. If for one moment our intellect could grasp all the power, all the beauty and all the immutability of the great law of Hierarchy, our petty and low feelings and thoughts would melt away in one infinite striving to fulfil the purpose of the leading and creative principle. We should firmly remember that by fulfillment of the given indications, we first of all help ourselves. Never is an indication given unless it can be applied and fulfilled. The apparent non-applicability only means that our small consciousness is not ready, that we do not exercise presence of mind, and that we have a habit of giving up with the first obstacles; also, that we respect the opinions of shallow-minded, vulgar, conceited people and are afraid, whispering, "What will they think of us?" But *who* will think? It is time to realize your own power and dignity. As a great thinker said: "The one who is interested in the opinion of the masses will never rise above the crowd."

The Teaching severely opposes self-conceit, but to have confidence in one's power does not mean to be self-conceited, and, if combined with heartfelt reverence to the Hierarchy, it will surely affirm the best results. Self-conceit is not compatible with reverence of Hierarchy, as one excludes the other. The self-conceited one will never fulfil the indication exactly but will always distort it according to the level of his own consciousness, which is limited by selfishness. It is very easy to imagine the results of distorted indications! Will they not often bring just the opposite results? It is said that "a distorted indication is similar to a train that has run off the rails." Similarly, "a half-fulfilled indication is like a house without a roof or a half-dose of a salutary medicine—either may bring harm or death."

If we wish to remain unharmed during this trying time (which is trying for the whole world), we must affirm ourselves in the foundations of the Teaching of Light, and, with all our attention, watchfulness and straight-knowledge, we must apply the Teaching to life without delay, as success depends primarily on timely fulfillment. All the indications of the Guru are given and were given with the idea of their timely fulfillment. The untimely fulfillment of an indication may be destructive, or at least fruitless. The knowledge of dates is a great knowledge, for in all branches of life success depends on the maintenance of the right time and on the knowledge of the right direction. Thus, you to whom both are given—take care of these Treasures!

Now you may see how all the persistence of N.K., all his affirmations about the necessity of maintaining the public character of our cultural institutions (not just personal interest), all his struggle against vulgar titles—all this had profound significance. And the incomplete realization of this brought and will still bring its difficulties.

* * *

The time is not far off when the representatives of the countries will publicly support the cultural projects on a large scale. Let all women and all the younger generation rise in defense of culture against all oppression and persecution; let them guard this life-giving flame with all their power. Nations cannot live without this creative fire. Destruction is inevitable where the Cult-Ur dies away. I want to believe that the powerful "Woman's Unity" will make itself heard and will give a new healthy direction to the mind of youth, will show them the true values and will help them to find the joy of existence by enriching it with a new understanding of each life and each labor. Women—it is your turn to say something new!

* * *

Quoting from *Hierarchy:*

"How many unnecessary manifestations people create for themselves! How many superfluous karmic impediments they create for themselves! And all this only because of unwillingness to admit the Hierarchy in their hearts. Thus, all affirmations can only then enter into life, when consciousness can accept the Hierarchy. Each evil in the world is generated because of resistance to the great principle of Hierarchy. Each victory is carried out only by the principle of Hierarchy. Therefore one must be so strongly affirmed upon the manifested Hierarchy."

I would also quote further paragraphs about love, as these two ideas, Hierarchy and Love, are inseparable.

"Let us turn back to the concept of love. In each book a considerable place must be allotted particularly to that fundamental concept. For under the concept of love much of the opposite is understood. It is correctly pointed out that love is a leading and creative principle. It means that love must be conscious, striving, self-denying. Creativeness requires these conditions. And if love is marked by self-enfeeblement, disintegration and service to self, it will not be the highest concept of humanity, which extols the concept of achievement. The heart filled to the brim with love will be active, valiant, and will expand to its capacity. Such a heart may pray without words and may bathe in Bliss. How greatly in need is humanity of the realization of the fire of love! To such a fire will correspond a purple star of the highest tension.

"It is necessary to realize very accurately the fundamental conceptions of Be-ness. The love of achievement is not austere for those aflame in heart, but it frightens those who love their weaknesses and who hesitate while embracing their own illusive 'I'. Love which can move worlds does not resemble the love upon the marshes where the bones of outworn remains are decaying. Above the marshes are the will-o'-the-wisps of decay, but the eternal creative fire of the heart does not wander; it impetuously ascends by the steps of Hierarchy to the Highest Light. Love is the leading creative principle. Unbearable is the Almighty

Light, but Hierarchy is the link to that dazzling Summit. To that point where one might even be blinded, the Hierarchy leads an illumined spirit. Love is the Crown of Light."

* * *

With these beautiful lines, I shall end my letter. Friends, fill your hearts with love! Does not the Great Adamant stand at the head of our temple? Remember this, and welcome the obstacles. Only these obstacles will show the wonderful design of our luminous battle. Does not the great victorious conclusion come at the last moment? Many times we have been witnessing this wonderful law. Stand firm! Great right is with you, and there has never been a case where the predestined was not fulfilled if the nearest co-workers were firm and devoted. Battle with all your might and with a joyous spirit. Draw into the treasury of your experience every page of difficulties, for only these pages and nothing else will bring you a crown of victory and will affirm your name in the history of culture. The joy of battle is a fundamental note of Being. Through struggle comes the great power of spirit and the great gift of immortality. Do not exaggerate the significance of the temporary failures. Try to learn your lesson from everything, and please be ready—ready for further surmounting and advancing. There is nothing stronger than the human will when it is directed with concentrated power and is sharpened with love toward the Hierarchy of Light. Rejoice in the great task entrusted to you! All will come, all is ready—only help with your firmness and devotion to the Hierarchy.

20

29 May 1931

It is said: "It is necessary to acquire the regal mind." Therefore, be kings of thought and spirit. Be the most devoted, the most ardent executors of the Will of Hierarchy; accept every indication with all your heart. Devotion and loyalty are the highest qualities; therefore, they are so condemned right now. Only loyalty creates; but the world is moving toward destruction, and that is why the subverters immediately banish this fundamental and constructive quality. Loyalty is the quality which adorns everything great, or rather, without loyalty there is no true greatness. Therefore, let us manifest this creative power in all our thoughts and actions.

If one cherishes devotion in his heart, it is not difficult to follow the right direction. While cherishing our striving, we must also develop our watchfulness, which is so necessary for success. Let us be like a vigilant mother, whose spirit feels and foresees all the dangers which threaten her child. Who knows how many fateful flows are avoided by such vigilance of spirit!

In time of danger and great battle, let us be firm in all foundations, and let us manifest invincibility of spirit. Now is the time for courageous actions, the time for broad actions and the most resplendent affirmations. Therefore, let us look over our arsenal and we shall see that it is inexhaustible. It is only necessary in each case to choose the most suitable weapon. With all attention let us examine the treasures we possess. Let us not profane the pearls which are sent to us, but where it is necessary to manifest our wealth let us know how to do so wisely. We shall not allow our best treasures to be neglected just because there are some who do not realize their true value, but we shall appreciate even the smallest among them, as their value is not necessarily in proportion to their size. To put it plainly in general worldly terms—it is necessary to take advantage of everything and to know how to call forth the best, for such ability is true economy of strength, and every wise builder should possess it. True economy does not mean dispensing with foundations; it means wise application in co-measurement.

Yes, everything will change for the better when we begin to apply the Teaching in our life without alterations; when we practice true cooperation; when we stop constructing with one hand and destroying with the other; when we understand that the work we have started is not personal but for the General Good; when we understand that inadvertence, negligence, mistakes, and the breaking of the principles by even a single co-worker should be considered as the negligence of all the members—only then will true responsibility be understood. The idea of responsibility has nothing to do with alienation, lack of will, and so-called "bossing." First of all, responsibility lies in looking for great balance, goal-fitness, co-measurement, which can be achieved only by ardent cooperation. Every co-worker must have in mind a synthesis of all activities of all the sections. It is not so simple, but it is necessary to exercise it because without such synthesis it is impossible to use correct discrimination, and therefore impossible to make a true prognosis for each section. All the societies or sections are together like a single organism, and it is the duty of all of us to watch its general growth and development. But, of course, a healthy spirit and heart can easily correct the temporary deficiencies of the other organs. Therefore, let us pay double attention to these foundations!

We are sorry that in the reports there was not a single proposal, not a single specific opinion regarding the discussed problems. It is difficult to imagine that at such a stage of consciousness all the decisions could be in unison. Therefore, it would be advisable to insert special opinions and proposals into the journal of the session's work and consider them when a more unified consciousness is achieved. This would be very valuable for the history of the Institutions, and many slanders and troubles might be avoided. When opinions are in print one cannot deny them, pleading a slip of memory. For instance, at the moment, it is very important to know how and what kind of remarks and proposals were expressed as regards publishing the pamphlet about the Banner of Peace. If the opinions expressed were not written down, perhaps the most valuable ones will be forgotten. People forget so easily, especially those things which are disagreeable to them. But the knowledge that our opinion is to appear in print will force us all to brace ourselves and to use our strength in creative work, as everybody would wish to have only his best in print. The fact that not a single thought, not a single impulse, transient as it may be, is lost—since it is recorded in our aura and in space—this fact does not trouble us because our imagination is so poor and our intellect cannot comprehend it. Therefore, let us help ourselves in this important realization, and let us put everything on record. We shall enlarge our comprehension immensely if we check our decision and compare them with the consequences.

* * *

I also wish to send you my thoughts about lack of prejudices and lack of principle. Frightful as it is, there are people who confuse the lack of prejudice of an open consciousness with lack of any principles whatsoever; whereas, these two ideas are opposites. The unprejudiced mind seeks everywhere for fundamental truth, and therefore is always exercising its ability to discriminate. As for discrimination, it is the first step to true knowledge. And true knowledge is always based on firm principles, or else it is not true knowledge. A principle may have many backgrounds in its applications to life, but its foundation will always be the same: the foundation of validity or truth. In other words, principle or law is always goal-fitting, and we already know that cosmic goal-fitness is the principle which leads to beauty. Therefore, all the actions of an unprejudiced person must be marked with truth and beauty.

An unprejudiced person is firm in his fundamental convictions because they are based on the *leading* truth. A person who has no principles has no convictions in general, as he has deprived himself of discrimination, *consciously* and *voluntarily*, and his destiny is like that of a ball that is driven by the accidental strokes of circumstances. Is it not said in the Teaching regarding such a person: "Oh ball of destiny! Where wilt thou fall and whither wilt thou rebound? The light has been given to thee—succeed, thou ball, in reaching it in time! Restrain thy evil, cunning whirl." May the Forces of Light guard us against the evil whirl! Let each one of us build firmly upon the established foundations and principles, so as not to violate them even in trifles. How can we always discriminate where are those trifles which may cause downfall?

Therefore, let us quote from the book *Hierarchy*:

"Sometimes one can demonstrate the most complex laws by means of the simplest apparatus. The law of Karma is complex, but take the Ruhmkorff coil or any other electric coil and you will get an evident image of karma. The current runs along the spiral uninterruptedly but the protective winding is subject to all outside reactions. In addition, each thread contacts the thread of the preceding round, carrying upon itself the consequences of the past. Thus, each hour changes one's karma, for each hour evokes the corresponding past. Thus, one may contact the entire line of past manifestations.

"But the same obvious example shows how the seed of the spirit is unharmed; and striving into the heights it sustains its shell without fearing the past. Verily, karma is threatening only to those who are plunged into inaction. But a striving thought is liberated from the burden of the past and, like a heavenly body, strives forward without retreading its path. Thus, even with a difficult karma, one may evince a useful liberation.

"Let us see how people understand service to the Lord and Hierarchy. He who thinks of ascending only by prayer is far from service. He who in his labor hopes to bring the best effort for the welfare of humanity must adopt the Lord in his heart. He who does not yield his own comfort does not know how to serve Hierarchy. He who does not accept the Indications of the Hierarchy does not understand service. Only when the heart is ready to accept consciously the affirmation sent by the Highest Will may it be said that the manifestation of service is adopted. Thus, We are no lovers of funereal rites and of empty invocations of the Lord. Thus, We venerate the striving of disciples to the service of the Hierarchy. Thus, it is so easy to observe how the one who does not accept the service in spirit venerates the Lord and Hierarchy so long as the way is convenient to him. Thus, We take into account each effort to remove the burden from the Hierarchy; so in the great as in the small. Thus, in Our creativeness, We affirm reverence not in words but by deeds. Thus, We deplore it when We see reverence in words but not in actions. ... So, when the wise Guru carries the entire burden of the earthly battle, we must know how to alleviate his burdens. ...

"The striving of people is always measured by their service either to Light or darkness. By this may be judged their destination in life. Thus, the worst is halfway thinking and striving. The destroyers always build only upon halfway striving. There is nothing worse than a halfway servitor, for he screens himself by the manifestation of halfwayness. Therefore, a direct enemy of Light is preferred by Us. We do not admit the small worms which creep in the mist into great battles. Thus, halfwayness must be cast aside. One should always and in all ways avoid any intercourse with halfway people. Thus, halfwayness manifested by the disciples throws them back a millennium, and therefore one should know when to affirm one's own consciousness. Thus, the servitor of Light will not admit halfwayness.

"Most pernicious is it when this halfwayness insinuates itself into one who is affirming himself upon the Path because then there results duality of thought and action. Hence, halfwayness is the enemy of the Teaching, and when We see halfwayness in relation to Hierarchy, this destructive circumstance must be eradicated. For without integrity there can be no structure. Hence, the disciples must understand how important it is to have an integral striving. For this, one should renounce personal comfort, conceit, self-pity, self-deception, and always remember that Hierarchy must not be burdened. This should be remembered by those who misunderstand service as relying upon the Lord and the Hierarchy."

* * *

Thus, we are facing a majestic and threatening time, and only by the extreme tension of our entire strength can we conquer. Think in the broadest way, discuss together how you can best understand and apply what is sent to you!. Learn how to oppose with dignity all the ignoramuses and destroyers of culture. Today, it is necessary to manifest the broadest understanding of the Banner of Peace. It is essential to understand the Banner of Peace and Culture as the greatest symbol. Yes, I can see that in the very near future the League of Culture will be established, in which will gather all the best representatives of thought, knowledge and creativeness, and where woman will have her full say; and this League of Culture will replace the extinct League of Nations. The events in Spain, once more, should manifestly prove to the world how timely is the idea of the Banner of Peace! The new events are coming, and they will force the adversaries of culture to beware... but will it not be too late? It is necessary to know how to answer all ignoramuses and all those who try to suppress culture... You have all the formulae ready. Besides, each day brings affirmation of their timeliness.

Today, every country must think about the best ways of preserving its cultural treasures, and must, by no means, try to stop the activities which beautify the image of the nation and the country. These activities attract the attention of the whole world toward the possibilities of the cultural significance of America. Let us not conceal from ourselves that until now America has not been among the so-called leading cultural countries. America has been considered only from the standpoint of the dollar and mechanical civilization. And the formulae pronounced by an American official, whose words you have quoted, only prove the aforesaid. If we were to talk to such an official about the Banner of Peace and about the cultural activities of our organizations, he would sincerely wonder, "What is the use of bothering about such annoying and unnecessary things? But since they are so eager to concern themselves about culture, why do they not use their apparently not meager imagination and their knowledge of art for organizing something like a gambling club, and let us say, a movie theater with modern shows slightly risqué? It would be acceptable and pleasant and very profitable." Such people will never be able to grasp the meaning of culture. How can they comprehend the historical significance of the union of the true representatives of culture, united under the Banner of Peace?

In his essay, N.K. has given a remarkable definition of culture. He says: "An ignorant person must become civilized first of all; then educated; then after education is acquired, a person becomes intelligent; then comes refinement and realization of synthesis, which is crowned by the acceptance of the idea of culture."

Not a single narrow specialist, regardless of how high his professional skill, can be considered a cultural leader. Culture is synthesis; culture understands and knows the foundations of life and creativeness because it is the cult, or worship, or reverence of creative fire, which is life. But who has realized the foundations of life?

But the new events are coming, and a revaluation of values is predicted. Consciousness is growing and there is nothing that can stop this growth; this gigantic wave will overthrow everything in its way. There is safety only in finding oneself in the launch directed by the powerful Hand of a Pilot not of this world. All those who sit in the launch are advised not to push one another, not to change seats, not to lean overboard, and not to look back; instead, they should make every effort to ride with the rhythm of the speeding launch, which can no longer stop, even if someone falls overboard, for the salvation of the rest of the people depends just on this speed. Therefore, let us gather all the fire of our spirit and, with the understanding of all the danger of this time, let us increase the tempo of our work; let us rise in our thoughts, so that we can realize the majesty of events and of everything that is timely. Avoid an indifferent attitude toward details which may not seem important to you. Now, at this time, the least little detail should be considered, the least action should be cautiously started. Verily, light-mindedness in these days of extreme tension approaches treachery. It is especially difficult if the right moment is missed.

Observe how many wonderful things are taking place! The pieces of shattered mosaic are being reassembled by a powerful Hand into a majestic picture. The details spring out unexpectedly, but an attentive mind will notice how, in this complicated design, there are marked out the degrees of a wonderful new step in evolution.

Therefore, friends, tense your consciousness and forge the future! Affirm yourselves in the beautiful and lawful foundations, and learn how to protect them! Remember that only thought can win, so you should always have a ready answer which will render your adversary helpless. How can we win? Only by the power of thought and by the strength of convincing arguments.

21

3 June 1931

I would like to quote further discourses from the book *Hierarchy* which I consider very timely:

"Let us observe how the dark ones labor. It is necessary to observe their peculiar habits. They are not indignant against a nonentity. They consider that the first steps of service are particularly useful for them. A nonentity is negligible even in treason. Treason is precisely the main basis of undermining by the dark forces. For treason, one must know something. This relative knowledge, not strengthened by devotion, may be found on the first steps. One must know that condemnation reacts like fire upon a wavering devotion. It is sad to observe with what unnoticeable deviations the disciple begins to steep himself with indifference, finding eloquent justifications. Like the blade of a knife, the heart loses its protective net. Without its sheath, the blade injures itself. But such spurs do not lead to achievement, they lead only to irritation. If one day has passed successfully in humiliation of the Teacher, why may not tomorrow be also blazing with blasphemy against the Highest? And if the silvery thread be broken, the blade of fossilization is already irrevocably sharpened.

"It is necessary to observe the wavering ones, for the contagion from them is great. Often they themselves are already about to sink into the black mass, yet the blasphemy disseminated by them wounds many innocent ones. You arm yourself rightly against indifference; it corrodes all beginnings, and what fires are possible from the frigidity of indifference? The manifestation of the affirmation of the Teacher is also like the watering of flowers. The watered garden will not wither. We are concerned in moving the works forward. We affirm new dimensions. Indifference to Our affirmations is not permissible!

"When the spirit is filled with striving, there is no place for indifference. When the spirit is aflame there is not place for in difference. This quality is an immunity against indifference. Only when the spirit tends to egotism the death of spirit may occur. Therefore, one should flamingly protect the spirit against indifference where the evil generated by neglected striving will nestle, where the evil will inflict a blow that will bring its effects. It is difficult to detect the root of evil generated by indifference. Only in endless vigilant striving may one find protection for construction. Hence, while constructing great works one must understand that egotism and indifference are inadmissible. Therefore, We demand that the first thought be dedicated to the Teacher. Is it possible to succeed when the disciple puts himself on the first place? Did We not put Beauty at the foundation? We have given the great foundations for the world. Therefore, each thought must be appreciated as the foundation of a great structure. Verily, the future is great.

"Amidst the concepts of courage, the most invincible is the courage of the flaming heart, when in full decisiveness, in full realization of achievement, the manifest warrior knows only the path of advance. To this achievement of courage, only the extreme degree of the courage of desperation is comparable. With the same speed that the courage of the flaming heart overcomes the future, desperation flees from the past. Thus, where the courage of the flaming heart is lacking, let there be the courage of desperation. Only thus can the warriors conquer, when the offensive is great. All other aspects of courage are of no significance because in them will be halfwayness. This quality, next to cowardice and treason, must be avoided."

So, let each one equip himself with valor, which should be close to his spirit. Happy is the one who possesses the valor of a flaming heart! Everything is easy to such a one, and joyous is the battle under the leadership of the Hierarchy of Light. He will sacredly treasure the weapons entrusted to him, and he will remember all the biddings and indications because all will be contained in the flaming heart and not in dead writings. There will be no necessity to remind him again about the same suggestions and to point out the forgotten shields hanging upon the wall. His heart will be an inexhaustible source of strength. His consciousness will not be divided because the purpose of achievement will be sparkling brightly ahead of him, and all his thoughts and all his aspirations will fly like steel arrows, obedient to the commands of the Hierarchy of Light.

Yes, it is time to purify the consciousness, to rid oneself of old habits, as time does not wait. It will be terrible if events get beyond us. I beg you to forget the old misunderstandings and to think only of helping the united work. Everyone must make his best contribution toward the whole work. Let us learn to ignore the petty stings of injured self-love. Let us discern why we must not be offended by the little complications caused by some co-workers. Verily, the one who is able to meet pettiness with a smile will be a conqueror. And how contemptible is the one who casts stones under the feet of his co-worker! He will not escape the glance of the Lord! As it is said, "These stones will grow into a mountain for him."

* * *

You ask how to lead the ones who show a desire to study the books of the Teaching. First of all, it is necessary to become acquainted (at least in some measure) with the personalities of such people, with the conditions of their lives, their occupations and abilities, etc. In every case, advice and guidance can be only individual. It is advisable to ask them to what extent the ideas of the Teaching influence their everyday routine, to what extent their lives are changed. But the best thing is to observe personally their lives. If the Teaching for them is no more than a pleasant stimulant which distracts them in their daily life, it is better not to bother with such people. They may read the Teaching—and perhaps even with more benefit—in solitude. As to their interest in the higher worlds, it is necessary to remember that it is most inadvisable to give certain details of life in the higher worlds to such souls, who do not quite realize even their responsibility on Earth—it is more than light-mindedness. In the books of the Teaching, of course, it is mentioned often enough that people must be conscious of their life in the higher worlds and of their bond with the Cosmos. Therefore, let everyone aspire to such consciousness in his own way. But a desire to know more than the books of the Teaching give, and the inability to show the right to such privilege, proves much light-mindedness and harmful curiosity. It is necessary to note particularly the people who, at the very beginning, demand some *special* knowledge, *inaccessible to the rest*. Usually, such people are the ones who do not apply the Teaching in life.

It is also characteristic of some people who have read one book of the Teaching to ask, "Is it possible to find out what the seven ingredients are in the above-mentioned emulsion?" or, "Does not the above-mentioned preparation of L. mean salts of lemon?" or, "Could not the rhythms of Mahavan and Chotavan and the formulae of psychic energy—could not all these be sent to me?" And not a word of the true foundations of the Teaching. It is amazing that such questions are asked by so-called intelligent people! These people are reading the books without any comprehension of their contents. Often such people remind one of young sparrows. They grasp the first grain they see, but as soon as they notice a second they give up the first. Then they fly for the third, and so endlessly. As a result, they lose instead of gain.

Therefore, the people who wish to approach the Teaching should thoroughly analyze to what extent their habits have changed after their acceptance of the Teaching. What happened to their prejudices? Have they changed their lives, or just their words? Let them confess their thoughts to themselves or to the chosen Guru. There are too many parrots; what is the use of multiplying them? Often, parrots place their owners in awkward positions; they utter blasphemy instead of praise, and vice versa.

It is also useful to note our worst habits and immediately start to eradicate them. Every day the disciples should enter into their diaries what has been done in this respect. Let them first struggle with one habit, as it is not so simple to alter oneself. It is very useful to watch the quality of thought and not allow any malicious, petty, and, in general, mean-spirited thoughts. The purifying of consciousness is the first step. After that, we advise the discipline of thought: to learn how to think in one direction, without being distracted even for a moment. It is wonderful if one can concentrate on the Image of the Teacher.

I send to you all my best wishes. May your consciousness grow and broaden! What joy there is in the unity of such consciousnesses! There is no obstacle which cannot be removed by such power.

I want to finish this letter, but I thought it would be useful to quote some further paragraphs from the Teaching, as they are very appropriate.

"The reorganization of the world intensifies all forces of the Cosmos. If humanity would understand that reorganization requires the striving of spirit, it would be easy to establish balance in the world. But the nations do not ponder about what to place upon the scales and where the balance is; hence the chaos of thinking is so destructive to humanity, and thus the shifted nations sink to the depths without taking measure for spiritual transfiguration. Therefore, it is time to consider the affirmation of spiritual quests. When the cosmic perturbations require a powerful tension, humanity must know where to look for the center of salvation. Therefore, the quest of a spiritual center will lead unavoidably to Hierarchy. Humanity has lost the urgent formula of salvation. Hence, the anchor of salvation is the focus of Hierarchy. Only a conscious quest and the affirmation of Hierarchy will afford salvation. Yes, yes, yes! Therefore, We gave the foundation of actions and works which are founded on Beauty. It is necessary to manifest complete comprehension of all thoughts and treasures of beauty. It is also necessary to understand the fires of the centers. Only thus can we attain victory. Of course, the dark forces seek to injure. It is necessary to watch them; their fear is great. Thus, let us guard the foundations.

"The disciples on the path of Service must apply all the best strivings of their spirit and consciousness. While creating, one should understand that only the application of the best manifestations affords corresponding results. Let us not expect beautiful results where the spirit has not applied its best strivings. Often people wonder why their undertakings are unsuccessful. Let us say then—did you apply all your best strivings? Did not superficiality, the dullness of inflexibility, negligence, and lack of ardor to the Hierarchy intrude themselves? Thus, one may expect correspondence between the cause and effect. One must understand that each inconsiderate action, each non-goalfitting deed, may bring so many unnecessary and harmful consequences. Thus, the disciples on the path must display their best strivings and ardor to the Hierarchy."

Hence, one must chiefly develop vigilance in oneself and watch untiringly the creativeness surrounding the Sacred

Hierarchy. Only when disciples will attain this quality may one hope that the predestined success will come. Therefore, one should manifest an extreme conscientiousness and vigilance toward all that occurs around the Focus. Each unnoticed mistake will yield its own blossom.

"It is asked why We so often delay in destroying the enemies. There are many reasons. Let us name two: the first—karmic conditions. It is easy to harm the near ones by touching an enemy bound to them by karma. This may be likened to most delicate surgery, when a surgeon does not amputate a sick limb because of the danger attendant upon severing a major artery. With the karmic bonds the interacting relationship is unusually complex. We consider it more useful to insulate the dangerous fellow traveler than to obstruct the entire caravan. The second reason is that enemies are the source of tension of energy. Nothing can so greatly increase the energy as counterattack. Therefore, why invent artificial obstacles when the dark ones attempt with all their strength to increase our energy?

"It is necessary to understand the entire significance of the world's struggle when, instead of poisonous gases, the projectiles of psychic energy are flying around. It is necessary to observe the unusual events. ... The idea of culture will survive, and you are right in thinking of the world rulership of culture."

My friends, please realize upon what firm ground you are standing when you are defending all the achievements of culture. Therefore, keep high your spirits, and find the necessary fiery words! Do not forget that only enthusiasm, faith, and ardent striving can inflame and inspire the spirit of people whom you contact. Kindle the creative fire in your hearts. I am sending you a command: "Attack as if pursued by fire."

Do you remember how Tamerlane the Great achieved one of his mightiest victories? He set afire the steppe behind his armies. Being pursued by fire, the armies rushed forward and destroyed the enemy, which was much stronger than they. You must also understand the majesty of this formidable time. You must realize that everything is in conflagration behind you and that the only salvation is ahead of you. So, strive forward, and hold fast to the entrusted Banner!

We want to feel in your letters the note of revolt in your spirit, and also your ardor. Look for fiery co-workers, those who comprehend the significance of culture! Notice and reject all that is dead and ignorant, and always welcome a battle. Verily, you can increase your possibilities only by fighting. You should be able to speak with strength about your international cultural activities! The Pact for the Defense of Cultural Treasures and the interest which it aroused in the cultured strata of the world—you received many letters which prove this interest—this alone gives you the right to demand attention and to facilitate your efforts to uplift the level of your country's cultural standards. Point out how history remembers the names of those who help to develop humanitarian and cultural ideas. Mention the fact that the widespread response of the countries to the call of the Pact for the Defense of Cultural Treasures proves how the consciousness of all people is awakening, how it demands the defense of the treasures of human creativeness. Therefore, every government which progresses in rhythm with evolution should listen to these cosmic demands and should guard the achievements of culture. Space is filled with these demands. It is urgently necessary to struggle against the approaching events caused by the convulsions of the dark forces. Several more years will pass—and how much that is irretrievable will occur!

Thus, collect all the facts, look through all the material you have, and then affirm yourselves in invincibility. You are representatives of the New Epoch, the epoch of broad cooperation and the proclamation of the supremacy of culture.

There are many more dangerous signs than people suspect. Subterranean fires are piercing through, and many things will blaze up like straw. Only the blind do not realize on what kind of volcano they are dwelling!

22

11 June 1931

You have already received the call to battle and the command to attack as if the fire were raging behind you. We ask you not to delay in applying this command as, verily, there is fire behind you, and every wrong step or delay may burn you. Go forward—forward without looking back—because it is necessary to rescue from destruction all that can be saved. "Let them understand in America that the crisis in the country itself is nothing less than a battlefield." There is no better possibility! The Teaching says that while the human spirit is in happy and comfortable harbors it will never awaken. Therefore, only in the days of shocks is it possible to expect spiritual ascent and the realization of true values. The threatening time will compel many to look for a way out and salvation. Try to be at your best, and connect yourselves with the great Focus without delay! Let nobody be deceived by apparent calmness, as it is very deceptive—such calmness may be more dangerous than a storm.

Battle with all your might. Insist on your rights in the name of the General Good, in the name of culture! Halfwayness is always pernicious. Look for complete victory, complete liberation so that all your forces are concentrated on the broadening of the culture of your country. Action is necessary today, the broadest action. Therefore, do not fear the increased number of your committees and the intensified work; your work is beautiful and your actions lawful, as indeed are all your intentions. You should sow broader than the broadest, as you never can tell from where the greatest harvest will come. "The bells of all countries are necessary, and their ringing makes a symphony." In the time of approaching downfall and destruction, we shall build and create; we shall guard all cultural achievements and affirm the foundations of Being.

23

17 June 1931

We are extremely happy to see your boldness and daring, your forward striving, and your plans for the future. Yes, it is only the one who has spiritual aspiration who can be carried over the abyss. Verily, over the abyss, for indeed are we not witnessing so many destroying themselves? The "requiem" of the American banks alone is extremely significant. The unhealthy, inflated, unbalanced prosperity of the country cannot continue for long. The hidden abscess must be opened, and woe to those who fail to protest in time against the evils by improving the spiritual health of the whole population!

How blind are those who think that by withdrawing themselves, by abusing the "Chalice of the World," they can exist and flourish! Chastisement is approaching and will inevitably fall upon them. Fearful will be this chastisement in its cosmic correspondence and righteousness, for it is impossible to plunder from the organism of the planet its most essential part without self-destruction. Therefore, sharp-sighted as a hawk, look far ahead; observe events and foresee the future.

The future League of Culture will manifest its authority and will confirm the balance in this world; but as yet it is too early to talk about it. Even though this League already exists invisibly, first of all the Banner of Peace should be affirmed. People must be imbued with the significance of the value of spiritual creativeness and must learn to respect every manifestation of it. The carriers of spiritual fire will become the true treasures of their countries. First, let women realize all the significance of the raising of the Banner of Peace and Culture, and in powerful union, not only theoretically but practically, let them carry the stones for the building of the New World. Mountains are built from stones. Let us not neglect the smallest stone!

* * *

Again I must write and ask you to pay double attention to everything that was said regarding responsibility. We are looking forward to a time when the correct comprehension of this idea will be assimilated by the human consciousness, and only then will commence true, successful, creative work. I have already written many times that responsibility is correctly understood only by those who manifest in their daily lives the greatest cooperation. Each one who is in charge of a certain department has a personal responsibility for its creative fulfillment. However, every director must understand that he is but one member of a whole organization and that he must collaborate with the other members harmoniously, in order not to interfere with the normal growth of the organization and thus harm his own vital capacity. Each one, with all his attention, must guard the general development. Of course, "it is ridiculous for seven people to carry one chair," as N.K. has said, but it is necessary to discuss together where this chair should be placed, as only by general agreement will it be placed in such a way that none of the co-workers will break his nose against it.

* * *

Time, time, time! Unless we properly realize the significance of time, many possibilities may fly away. How can we build a successful future if we are neglectful and always too slow? We must follow the cosmic rhythm, which is indicating "presto prestissimo." Let us leave all moderato, diminuendo and morendo to our enemies. We are experiencing extremely significant events. Verily, there is no greater time in the history of our epoch!

* * *

Why are the societies of South America silent? I hope I shall not be a prophet in this case as I was in the case of the President of Peru! One can be a very eloquent and successful lecturer, but only the magnet of the spirit can uphold the results of success. But the spiritual magnet can be developed only when there is sincere aspiration and complete self-renunciation. The fruitfulness of every action is sustained by the magnet of the heart.

It is also very necessary to manifest the most careful, thoughtful and cultured attitude toward the press. Many articles written by our enemies which still frighten you bring joy to us because they arouse interest in readers and at the same time they cannot really belittle us. Most to be dreaded is the colorless and "precise" (according to their consciousness) interpretation of facts of so-called "friendly" people. But perversion of facts by enemies is always striking and helps us greatly. Now is the time of the "hot" and "cold"—all "lukewarm" ones will be forced out. Revolt with all your spirit; be courageous; be conscious of the great time and of what you possess!

Realize your personal significance without self-conceit, self-sufficiency, and arrogance. The pride of self-sufficiency diverts from the blessed seeking and, therefore, from further advancement. Without seeking, one cannot find, meet, and accept the Ray of Hierarchy.

* * *

I hope very much that you do not spoil the growing warrior! Teach him to be studious, attentive, and assiduous. Develop his sense of cooperation, sense of help, and compassion toward animals and the needy. Let him learn to help from the earliest age. Children are so happy when grown-ups ask them to help. You can create the occasions for such help. You must teach him to be obliging and respectful toward adults. Let him learn to think about other people and to be happy if he can bring some cheer to others. The most terrible thing is to develop in a child selfishness and stinginess, as these vices will limit the growth of a child's mind. There is nothing more fearful than an egotistic or mean person. No wonder that the literature of all peoples perpetuates this terrible plague of humanity in immortal images. These vices have brought about the present degeneration of humanity and will bring a terrible catastrophe. A complete sterility of creative powers is the result of egotism. Let us see what the Teaching of Living Ethics says:

"Individuality and egotism are as birth and death. The building of individuality evinces the conception of a New World, while egotism can mirror itself in the dead volcanoes of the moon. But not only does egotism deaden itself, but it strikes with sterility the surroundings, whereas individuality kindles fires in all adjacent camps. Cooperation is the crown of individuality, but the scourge of egotism is like the sting of a scorpion. Can one rely upon egotism? No more than upon a viper! But true individuality contains in itself the foundation of universal justice. We must gather individualities because a new diamond is in need of cutting, but egotism must pass through many incarnations. Certainly, this law may also be changed by the fire of the heart. Therefore, one can advise egotism to be kindled by the proximity of a fiery heart.

"Not without purpose do We kindle the beacons of the fiery heart, as a refuge for travelers. It is not easy for the flaming heart, but it sacrifices itself for its neighbors, which is precisely the Commandment of Bliss. But joy is a special wisdom." [Hierarchy]

Let us strive above all difficulties, guilt, and even treacheries. The broadened consciousness will help in everything; therefore, let it be directed to where the great Light will very soon be kindled. The scale is in the hands of the Higher Will, and what do we care for the discordance which, in blindness, is directed against us? It is impossible to deceive spatial justice. The whole history of humanity proves this. What remains of those who considered themselves above those great workers who labored for the good of humanity? Complete oblivion of their names and silent contempt.

And now I would like to quote a few remarkable lines:

"In extreme suffering and privation, in starvation, in blood and sweat, Russia took upon herself the burden of seeking the truth for all. Russia searches and struggles, is looking for the

Realm of Light. ... The pathos of history does not notice those who are content with their limited knowledge of truth and who are conceited and satisfied. The fiery inspiration does not come to *Beati posedentes*, but to those whose spirit is in tension. The wings of the Angels disturb the water of the font.

"It seems there are no changes in the world... except that in the comfortable civilized world there is no more Russia... and in this absence there is a change, as in this particular 'non-existence,' Russia, in a certain way, becomes an ideological center of the world.

"If translated into the language of reality, this would mean that on the stage of the world's history appeared a new 'culturally-geographical world,' which until now did not have the significance of a leading power. We look into the future. Does not the goddess of culture move toward the East from the European West, where she was settled for such a long time?... Does she not go to the starved, to the poor, to those who have suffered so much?

"We are under the power of presentiment. ... There is a danger of conceit through presentiment—a certain type of self-conceit, conceit of suffering. *To allow conceit means to be defeated.* One should not conceal what one considers to be the truth. But it is impossible to be satisfied with mere presentiments. *History is not made by quietism, but by the heroic achievements of those who seek perfection. Those who are self-conceited lose the bliss of searching. And the self-conceited are condemned to sterility..* ... There is no inevitability; there is possibility.

"Only by way of intensive creative work, not fearing to admit one's mistakes and weaknesses, only by the price of continuous efforts, which are materialized in the frames of 'Plastic World' (which is opened to our wills), will possibilities become Reality."

It was written in 1921.

24

30 June 1931

You write that even some good people do not understand the book, *Hierarchy*. This only shows us once more how careful one must be in order not to frighten those whose consciousness is not yet sufficiently developed. The process of the growth of consciousness and assimilation of new ideas is very, very slow. Therefore, forcing is dangerous. Only a developed consciousness can completely realize and ardently accept the great law of Hierarchy. Let us recall that our own consciousness also was gradually prepared for accepting this great foundation of cosmic creation and evolution. Please try to practice the maximum tolerance toward newcomers, and do not demand too much. We may expect extreme tension only from the nearest co-workers, whose consciousness is growing together with their work. They know the significance of the cosmic battle that is going on. They know that the more direct their path is, the more difficult and responsible is their achievement. They know that the difficulty itself is a sign of the quickest achievement. They are used to overcoming difficulties by the striving of spirit, and they know and have witnessed many victories.

Neither should you think there will be a swift improvement of the conditions of life in the world. No, the predicted threatening time is here, in all its full strength, and everything is even more complicated now. Therefore, possessing certain knowledge, be sure to treasure sacredly all warnings, hints, and indications. Only by the most intensive cooperation, by the urgent and precise fulfillment of the suggestions, will you be able to succeed during this trying time.

Beware of co-workers with small consciousnesses, as the small consciousness will try to belittle everything. But we know that destruction results just from *belittling* and *non-appreciation*. Co-measurement is a quality which is most difficult and necessary to achieve; without it, it is impossible either to advance or to construct. The Teaching states that without the quality of co-measurement a person cannot be considered spiritual.

Please realize the significance of the work that you started! How can you expect understanding from other people if you yourselves do not possess this affirmation? How can we impart strength to our co-workers if we lack it ourselves? The Banner of Peace and the Unity of Women in the name of the New Era of Culture are two of the gigantic historical tasks. Please try to realize how serious is the world situation, and apply all your abilities in order to introduce these salutary ideas. Every step of yours should be thoroughly weighed, and should be in conformity with your great tasks. But never listen to the advice of grey conventionality! All delays will bring even worse wreckage.

Uphold the Banner of Culture and the pure affirmations you have received. "Sow widely; it is not right to spill the precious seeds only in your own garden." The most important is not to be afraid of any hostile condemnations because all our offerings for the General Good have not in them a trace of destruction or selfishness! Insist on your rights in the name of the offerings you bring to your own country!

* * *

I fear that many wonderful advices and declarations of N.K. are not applied and are not quoted in defense of your rights. Do not be lazy, and reread them; remember, not everything can be immediately assimilated. But if you will assimilate or even memorize certain formulae, you will simplify a number of things; also, you will develop an alertness and vivacity of thinking that is most essential. Never forget that *we conquer by thought.*

Furthermore, do not be impressed by the superficial amiability which leads to nothing. Discriminate between real, true friendliness and hypocritical amiability. A good battle may sooner bring victory than a fleeting amiability! Attack courageously; have your weapons and shields ready—demand! Some of our co-workers did not experience a hard struggle for each of their achievements. They reached the heights too quickly. Therefore, they are not able to appreciate completely the achievements of the others who had to struggle very hard. Grow—grow in your consciousness; remember the significance of our time, which brings great possibilities. Be inspired by thought and every little boat will bring its valuable cargo! Please remember that today we have to deal with large masses because people are already able to assimilate the living fire of creative and constructive work. Among the common people there are many searching souls who are capable of sacrifice in the name of the General Good.

I enclose herewith some very essential counsels:

"Do not be perturbed by the necessity of seeming repetitions. In the first place, nothing is repeated. Even the same words at different times appear completely different. Secondly, one should reiterate day and night about Hierarchy. You are right that the hierarchy of thraldom is ended, but the emergence of a realized Hierarchy is followed by human sufferings. There is too much slavery in the world, and each flame of consciousness is too oppressed. Slavery and a consciously realized Hierarchy are as day and night. Hence, do not be dissuaded from repeating—a consciousness of Hierarchy—Hierarchy of freedom, Hierarchy of knowledge, Hierarchy of Light. Let those who do not know the inception of the New World scoff, for each concept of a New World frightens them. Is not Infinity terrifying for them? Is not Hierarchy burdensome to them? Being ignorant despots themselves, they do not understand the constructiveness of Hierarchy. Being cowards themselves, they are horrified before an achievement. Thus, let us place on the balance the most urgent concepts of the great approaching age—Infinity and Hierarchy.

"Hierarchy must be adopted as an evolutionary system. To those spirits who have not yet outlived slavery it should be repeated that Hierarchy differs completely from despotism. But even a chimney sweep must climb to the roof in order to clean the chimneys. This cannot be done from below. One cannot compose a symphony without a single key for all instruments. Many analogies may be quoted, beginning with a jest and finishing with the touching examples of bees, ants, and swans. But the best example for contemporary humanity is the comparison with chemistry. It is easy to understand that a reaction can take place only under precise conditions. Hierarchy likewise corresponds completely to the astro-chemical principles, which even a neophyte of science will not deny. We already justly agreed upon the importance of the discovery of psychic energy; for the coordination of its realization, Hierarchy is as indispensable as a helpful chemical process.

"Many salt pillars are spread upon the face of the Earth. Not only did Lot's wife turn back to the past, but numberless are those who looked backwards. What did they expect to see in the conflagrant city? Perhaps they wished to bid farewell to the old temple? Perhaps they looked for their cosy hearth or looked in anticipation of seeing the house of their hated neighbor collapse. Certainly, the past chained them for a long time. Thus, one must strive onward for enlightenment and health and for the strength of the future. Thus it should be always; but there come cosmic knots when an impetuous onward motion is urgent. One should not be disconcerted and mourn over the past. Mistakes are even obvious but the caravan does not wait, and the very events press onward. We hurry and We summon to hasten. The future is crowded but there is no darkness ahead.

"Some people cannot tolerate Our frequent reminders about battle. For them, let it be not a battle, but the opening of the Gates. The process of opening also requires energy; but for you, without need of hypocritical palliation, it may be said that the battle of Light against darkness proceeds incessantly. Many warriors help in this battle, otherwise we again would be engulfed in chaos. Often, the participants of the battle ask why they do not remember the achievements of their subtle bodies in their physical shells. But it would be criminal on Our part to permit this. The heart could not withstand the realization of so gigantic a battle. Only a specially flaming heart retains in its consciousness the black projectiles. The heart is stopped either through realization of consciousness or through sclerosis. But the cosmic battle can destroy the strongest heart.

"Thus, let us recall the battle. When the clash assumes such colossal scope, the subterranean fire is equilibrated with difficulty and the layers of magnetic currents are intercrossed. But let us not deny that this perturbation brings renewed possibilities." [Hierarchy]

25

20 July 1931

I was so sorry to see that our train again ran off the rails. Can it be possible that so clearly explained a structure was not understood? For two years, it has been repeated daily about the necessity to treasure every pearl of knowledge that was given to you. I heard recently, "One more pearl is lost." When shall we learn not to throw away these pearls but carefully weigh each grain in order not to cheapen their value? Can you expect success when the true values are thrown away and are replaced by cheap surrogates?... In our affairs, cheap actions should be out of the question. Thousands of eyes, from all over the world, are watching our Institutions. This obliges us to use the maximum of ability and determination for fulfilling the given programs. Have we so little individual creativeness and alertness that any dull outsider can cut off our possibilities by his vulgarity and obsolete standards? Surely not. We need co-workers with a broad outlook, courageous and cultured. It seems to me that with your defenders you will not go far. Of what good are the advisers who give up everything at the first opposition!

We and our co-workers must know how to defend our rights immediately. We must find ten new points and attacks to each opposition. First of all, we must demand a complete understanding of our cultural activities. We must be able to unify the consciousnesses of our co-workers with our own. Indeed, it is impossible to expect at once similar thoughts, but we must watch their ideas and when necessary we must tactfully correct them. We have already experienced a successful example of such leadership. Therefore, you must also be watchful and straighten out the thoughts of your advisers and co-workers. We must not only listen to the Teaching and agree with it, but we must become active and creative in our fulfillment of the tasks.

It seems that the "requiem" of the banks, as well as all present and coming events, sufficiently prove how just, how wise, and how timely were all the indications. Let us remember how many of these indications were not applied in time, or else they were distorted! How I would like to see you fearless! How I would like to hear from you a lion's roar! The power of spirit can conquer everything. Everything small and mean is afraid of power, while everything great has respect for it. Therefore, proceed like lions!

And then, please do not discuss with unreliable co-workers those ideas which you yourself have not yet completely assimilated. Every great idea can be easily ruined by tactless actions. Do not forget that we expect to be supported by the members of women's organizations and other cultural societies. So many good connections are already made, and it is possible to suggest the spreading of the series of postcard reproductions, "The Realm of Culture." Three millions of purchasers means three million dollars! How many women would purchase a one-dollar share in the name of their own womanly dignity!

Friends, I would like to tell you that what was promised will come about, and is really not so far from you! Only open wider your eyes and make an effort to broaden and refine your consciousness! And what can be better for the growth of your consciousness than the alert and creative utilization of the rules of the Teaching? Indeed, develop your creativeness! Penetrate more deeply into every idea that has been given to you! The ideas are growing, together with the opening of possibilities, but these possibilities should not be missed. The time will come when the Banner of Peace and the Banner of Culture will cover the whole world. Do you sense the beauty and the power of this Symbol?

26
21 August 1931

Please reread often my letter of July 29th. In this letter you will find an urgent Advice of the Teacher which should not be deferred. Assimilate this advice with all your heart and follow it, both in large and in small things. Who knows wherein lies the great and the small? Who knows where is the little blade of grass or grain of sand that threw the giant into the abyss?

Therefore, let us be watchful, and let us not belittle. Let us realize completely the danger of our time and the significance of that on which everything is based. Let us clearly remember that each disparagement and omission will bring the belittling and destruction of the work and of all co-workers, and tenfold so, as such revolts are against the affirmations of the Hierarchy. It was said long ago that "all your trunks will remain empty and your writing pens dry, if you will not understand the affirmations of foundations. If the time when the school was established was difficult, it is a thousand times more difficult now. If the time was considered serious when you were on your way, it is a thousand times more serious now. If then the time was great—now it is a thousand times greater." So it was said.

Let us remember this and not permit ourselves to be lulled to sleep or made quiescent, and let us not rejoice in the flattery and pleasant words of the numerous dugpas. The circumstances will become more and more complicated. Therefore, follow the Teacher. If you cease belittling, your Guru will carry you over all dangers and will bring you to safety. There are certain times when belittling and concealing are even worse than the most ferocious vexations and slander. No wonder that belittling and concealing are considered by the Great Teachers as subtle betraying. Is it really possible that we could be so guilty? We may well remember that the desire for self-glory at the cost of belittling the leader will not result in anything. By glorifying him, we glorify ourselves. By belittling him, we destroy ourselves. The cosmic law of correspondence is inevitable. The best pages of history were written when at the head of a movement was a leader who was followed by devoted and conscious co-workers, ready at every moment to sacrifice everything for the glory of the work. And do we not also revere their names alongside the name of the leader? Even in schools we learn the names of the co-workers of the great leaders, teachers and thinkers. And does not history point out the backsliders? And are they certainly not regarded with contempt?

Let us always remember that all possibilities come only with the Ray of the Teacher, through the way illumined by this Ray. But if we are full of doubt, if we deviate in lack of confidence and in fear, then of course we fall out of the path illumined by the Ray, and, falling into darkness, we at best risk breaking our nose!

* * *

We received a book, a beloved book, unfittingly and cheaply published. N.K. was so unhappy about it that he immediately sat down and wrote an article about love for a book. Unless we understand that there must be refinement in quality, we shall never move farther in cultural growth. And how can we speak of refinement of consciousness and culture if we fail to realize what that means? Of course, perfection never comes at once, but deterioration of quality is unworthy of disciples. Also, it is most vexing to see cheap postcard reproductions of some paintings. The admittance of such deplorable quality discredits the artist. And do we not know the old truth that the purchasing of things cheaply is dear in the long run? Do you not remember how, after certain expenditure, we were compelled once more to spend again for reprinting? All our beginnings should be introduced worthily. We must search and demand the highest quality. Only in this way may we serve culture.

* * *

We are also concerned about the popularization of our books and publications. There must be a certain system, a certain organization, regarding this most essential matter. We must find a person who is fond of this work and who knows it well, and he should give an account regarding the exact destination of the books and the amount of money received; also, in what catalogues our books are included and where to find the best sale. Really, there are so many bookstores all over the world! We must also carefully watch that our publications come out without delay! So many possibilities have gone because of procrastination. The publishing must become a source of income.

I know that you will accept all this advice with the right spirit because I have proof that you will, but could I say the same about certain other co-workers? Some may be offended, but by being so touchy they will only cast a slur upon themselves, for they will show that they are far from self-perfection and that regality of spirit is unattainable for them. The king of spirit is happy whenever he has an opportunity to perfect himself. He will never repeat his mistakes, and an eradicated, expiated mistake is a step forward, an approach toward the predestined. Therefore, let us completely realize how severe and pressing is the present time. Let us follow the Hierarchy and let us fulfil all suggestions.

* * *

No weakness can be excused today, even if it is dictated by good motives. The stake is great and we shall pass only through affirmation. You must affirm, you must spread the benevolent thoughts. Use all your knowledge and all the strength of the messages you receive from the high source of Knowledge and Creativeness for wide dissemination. Try to realize in the name of culture the great task of creating the new step, the epoch of refined consciousness, of unprecedented discoveries in science, and of world-wide cooperation.

The saturating of space must take place in all directions. Not a single possibility should be missed. You must be able to utilize a small hint for creating a great deed. The power of saturating space is very great. Let the image of your Guru be manifested on the world scale. Do not allow it to be depreciated in the smallest degree. Do not be afraid to look ridiculous, as you can always tell a scoffer, "You are laughing at yourself. Try to know more." Scoffing is a sure sign of ignorance, and nobody who really knows would ever ridicule anything.

We were very happy to hear about the approach of a new co-worker. We welcome him most heartily in this service for human welfare. His name will live in our hearts because we appreciate one who at the beginning offers a willing hand and helps the growth of sprouts. The best tree will rightly be his.

When the tree grows there will be plenty of those willing to find protection under its shade. But very few can note the significance and power of the seed. Therefore, let us particularly appreciate the new-comers. Joy and greetings of the heart to the new co-worker.

* * *

We have received letters from America from which we learn that even prominent business leaders cannot maintain their influence and cannot balance events. The same is true all over the world. The old formulae are outlived, while the new, constructive ones are not yet assimilated. The consciousness of the masses outgrows their leaders. The dams erected to hold back the growth of consciousness always are dangerous; inevitably, however, they are destroyed by terrible upheavals. And since the law of correspondence is immutable, the more tenacious is the resistance, the stronger is the final overthrow. The true leader is always in the forefront of events. But, verily, he should hold fast to the Hierarchy of Light.

The salvation of the world is in new formulae, in a new spiritual and cultural approach toward all questions of life, be it in government or private life.

The Banner of Peace and Culture, when completely realized, will become a foundation for new creativeness. Beginning from school days, the future generations should learn about the vital significance of constructive and creative work in all its aspects. In the New World there can be no room for the luxury of destruction; ignorant, wild violence cannot exist there. Such achievements will not come at once and everywhere, but it is already possible to see where the dawn breaks.

Even now, the idea of peace and culture is so differently understood! The majority associate culture with superficial civilization, with all the frivolous luxury which goes with such civilization, while by peace they mean "a peaceful invasion" of markets and discussions about disarming. By this, they mean the replacing of old, obsolete weapons by new and more powerful ones. It is burdensome to ponder upon the condition of the world! The situation is terrible, and of course it will get even worse, as it is impossible to stop those who, in their blindness, are ready to tumble down into the abyss. Gathering momentum, they will roll faster the nearer they get to the bottom. But we know there is a Stronghold of Knowledge and Spirit and that those who are searching for Light will always be helped. Therefore, let us most ardently call to our still-unknown spiritual brothers to join us under the Banner of Culture. The fire of spirit and the enlightened consciousness will stop all the terrors of destruction. Thus, let us sow the benevolent seeds, and in due time they will bring forth fruit. The answer you received in regard to the Banner of Peace and Culture is very characteristic. In such an answer is contained all the impotence, all the inability to understand the offered possibilities, and reveals complete irresponsibility. What a handsome gesture could be made, and recorded in history, by participating in the conference of the Pact and the Banner of Peace! But small and ordinary minds are satisfied to be in the rear. What do they care for history, since their consciousness does not embrace the idea of responsibility, to say nothing of responsibility on a world scale. Their whole idea of responsibility does not stretch beyond their desire to keep for themselves a warm, comfortable place. And for this purpose, ordinariness, dullness, and ignorance are considered the most suitable. But they forget one thing: conditions change, and sometimes only extraordinariness and fiery readiness of mind can save them and preserve for them their beloved comfort and felicity. Yes, the world is full of automatons, of shadows, and of the active assistants of evil. The automatons who thoughtlessly repeat the outlived formulae, and the shadows who do not protest against evil—should they not be put alongside the assistants of evil?

Thus, let us struggle against every bit of dullness and ignorance, in ourselves and in our nearest co-workers, and let us not be depressed by the accidental newcomers. But, with a smile, let us write into our records one more page about ignorance and stagnation, which together are building the karma of a whole country.

* * *

It is true, we should not accept flattery. Great is the contempt of a flatterer when he sees how easily we fall for his sometimes rather crude stratagems. Let us not be as bribed slaves, but let us develop the pride and independence of lords of spirit, for whom flattery does not exist. Nothing lowers and destroys a person so much as his acceptance of flattery. Certainly, the one who loves flattery is a slave of yesterday. A person who is guilty of flattery, or one who accepts it, can never become a close co-worker. Great is the mercenariness of such people—let us remember this.

* * *

I was glad to hear about the attempts toward a closer cooperation and sense of justice among the co-workers. A strong spirit will know how to rid itself of certain atavisms, while common sense and realization of the great Image of the Teacher will remind that a conscious cooperation is noble and joyful. A heart warmed by love will emanate the most beautiful power of attraction. Aspiration of spirit brings courage and justice.

All of you are dear to us; and are we not united by the same Teaching, by the same Teacher? If we are able to drive away the whispering shadows, irritation, touchiness, and a careless attitude toward work, we shall move ahead with gigantic steps. Really, is it not distressing to remain static, in the same place? The worst obstacle is touchiness, which holds us back, which destroys all sense of striving. Wonderful possibilities flee from us when we are busy analyzing outrages against us which, in many cases, are imaginary and self-suggested. Let us discard these destructive habits and let us give all our hearts to the fulfillment of the entrusted work. Let us put all our interest, our whole lives into our work, and a miracle will occur. This very self-denial will bring us the most unexpected, most lofty joys.

A selfish person condemns himself to dreadful loneliness and complete oblivion. Happiness is in giving love; and happier is the one who loves rather than the one who is loved. When this truth is realized, all happiness will materialize. Therefore, learn how to love, become accustomed to love everything beautiful, and develop active compassion toward everything that is not yet perfect. Be kind and polite to your subordinates, as such is the privilege and beauty of a lord of spirit!

I love the legend about Akbar, describing how, in the days of solemn feasts, when all the dependent rajahs and peoples brought their gifts, Akbar, amid loads of costly gifts, would pick up the humblest and, holding this simple gift near his heart, would appear in front of his people. In this manner he expressed solicitude toward the humblest of his subjects, emphasizing that he appreciated not luxurious gifts but those given by a devoted heart. Let us do the same, and judge not by outward appearance and position but by the inner thought and the inner quality.

And, of course, the best thoughts and the most devoted hearts are more often hidden under poor cloth and modest position. Appreciate your humble co-workers! Punctuality, as well as politeness, in the ancient days was considered a privilege of kings.

27

7 October 1931

We are glad that you understand the importance of dates, and we are grateful for each hastening. It becomes more and more pressing to hasten the development of our work, in view of the accumulation of events. Only a developed spirit can fully realize this necessity to proceed with the rhythm of the Cosmic Magnet. All who are retarding or hindering belong to the lower grades of consciousness, and we can only be sorry for such state of thought. We should try to transpose part of their burden to those who are looking ahead and striving toward evolution.

Prepare co-workers for yourself; do not forget what is said about the replacing of faded roses by wild flowers! Every day try to learn something, and be grateful to every co-worker who can help you develop the right attitude toward petty personal affronts and thereby liberate yourself from them. Only when we try to understand the main point can we learn to ignore the attacks of an uncultured heart. N.K. always recollects with gratitude his most hostile associates because those were the ones who helped him develop his vigilant eye, his readiness of wit, and the essential firmness and discipline of spirit. Thus, you too must learn to regard the conduct of captious people as based on whims that cannot insult you but can only make you feel sorry for those who return to the nonsensical habits of childhood.

We know how complicated life is today, how difficult it is, and we feel distressed about each lack of understanding, about each delay, about everything that complicates the progress. The neglect of one's duties can never be expiated. Your task is not an easy one, but with easy things one will not perfect oneself. Pure striving is always supported by the Great Teacher. Therefore, be victorious! The Great Teacher is always ready to give a helping hand to the striving disciple, but such help usually comes after all possibilities have been exhausted by the disciple himself. And herein lies the greatest wisdom and a great cosmic law of evolution. Only at the very limit of tension are our forces transmuted into the finest energies. Our thoughts are with you, and we know that all will come about safely unless we ourselves sever the silver cord by our selfishness, sluggardliness, and superficial attitude toward the Advices.

* * *

In order to be able to judge about the height of a mountain, one must move away to a certain distance. The same with work. Sometimes, it is advisable to get away from it in order to realize its cultural significance. It is necessary to realize the cultural movement in its world scale, and this is the most important thing; because if we do not realize it our actions will be lacking in co-measurement and, without the latter, success will be quite impossible. Why do all Teachings insist so much upon the necessity of faith, or on complete understanding of a given task? Just because the intuitive knowledge or faith makes a giant out of a man. By destroying doubt, such faith creates an invincible persistency which inevitably leads to the goal. We, being limited by our physical bodies, cannot see through the accumulating events. Therefore, we cannot by ourselves fulfil the preordination. And thus, if we are lacking in faith, we withdraw from the direction indicated by the Teacher, or by misunderstanding the terms we break the outlined combinations in which we are a needed ingredient and eventually were supposed to act. Faith is great knowledge and wisdom. A person who lacks faith or knowledge is like a weathercock. He depends on conditions which are constantly changing and which, in his blindness, he cannot foresee and cannot avoid.

* * *

"It is correct to affirm the principles of the Banner of Peace wherever it is possible. Please remember that possibilities issue suddenly. Resisting evil by itself brings the new possibilities." The articles written against the Banner of Peace are so petty that one can only be surprised that people can produce such thoughts. I am a little puzzled as regards the League of Nations. Why should one be so interested in the opinion and support of such an organization? It seems that a movement of cultural unification and the development of a true understanding of spiritual achievement in art among the younger generations is so extremely essential that there is absolutely no necessity to wait on the approval of such stillborn organizations. Each far-seeing government should notice in the Pact and Banner of Peace just the very movement toward protection, order and constructiveness. Therefore, whether or not the League approves the Banner, this should by no means influence the establishment of the great Banner of Culture.

Could it be possible that the women's organizations in America will remain indifferent and will not support the Banner of Culture? I do hope that we are not over-estimating their spiritual receptivity. Long before the first conference, in Bruges, I learned about the real value of many modern organizations, and I understood how much one must work in order to awaken the consciousness of the masses to make them understand the true values and cultural creativeness. This can be achieved only by the *persistent and systematic spreading of ideas,* but not by convulsive bursts. Therefore, let us not be discouraged by the attitude of indifference shown by governments and certain groups of civilized society, but let us use all our efforts for destroying superficial thinking among the nearest co-workers, as well as for deepening their understanding of the pressing necessity to fulfil this idea.

"Thus, My Advice is once again to transform the Teaching into the daily necessity. My Advice is to observe the extent to which one's surroundings will become successful. In small groups one should especially watch mutual thoughts in order not to burden and interrupt the current. Many teachings advise this simple discipline, but each book should give a reminder of it because that which is most vital, most needed, is not applied to life. And it is a great happiness for Us when We have as complete confidence in someone as in Ourselves. Thus, powerful is the citadel of the open heart.

"Unceasingly, and during all times, the Teaching of Life is poured upon Earth. One cannot imagine earthly existence without this link with the invisible world. As the anchor of salvation, as the guiding light, the Teaching strengthens our advance in the darkness. But amidst the shower of benevolence, as with sea waves, one may notice a rhythm with special definite expansions; it is then the Teachings appear. Thus, one may explain the rhythm of this entire world by noting the growth and submergence, all together inscribing the evolution of existence.

"Interruption of rhythm is due to many conditions, but the

best means for avoiding this perturbation lies in unity. Direct yourself to Us, where there is the decision for all. In comparison—as a grain of dust may arrest a tremendous wheel, so the breaking of rhythm interrupts the current. Whereas, just now is the date of the great tension. Thus, the possibilities are so near, the events already gather as a rolling ball, and the terrifying will be revealed as salvation."

Let us not break the salutary current!

28
21 October 1931

The last mail brought us the description of a most characteristic conversation. What an illustration of feeble-mindedness and decay! What can one do if the official representatives of various organizations fail to comprehend the significance of education? For them the word "culture" is synonymous with everything they despise—what they call "abstract ideas," or else they associate it with something that may interfere with their beloved habits!

Yes, it would be out of place to mention to such people the names of Pavlov, Bechterev, Pupin, Abel, Millikan, Rutherford, Einstein, Jagadis Bose or Tagore.

The words of Lord Buddha that "ignorance is the greatest crime because it brings all miseries to humanity" should be, by now, assimilated by the consciousness of people. Until the leaders of the countries possess brilliant intellects and especially a spiritual synthesis, which helps to embrace all the planes of existence, there will be no real progress. But as there is no such thing as immobility in nature, all ignorant humans must retrogress, followed by the usual degeneration and decomposition. Are we not already witnessing such things? Some outstanding scientists have already pointed out the threatening signs of such degeneration, which is demonstrated in increased numbers of psychic diseases and feeble-mindedness among the younger generation. And many people begin to wonder whether such sad abnormalities are not due to wrong education and upbringing. Generally speaking, modern education is lacking a cultural basis, which should include, primarily, a development of synthesis in the abilities of man. One-sided specialization always leads to a loss of balance and results in the psychic diseases which we observe today.

Let us disregard fear and mockery and let us boldly march to victory under the Banner of Culture! But always keep in mind that you are taking part in a most responsible preparatory stage, which requires the manifestation of a refined intuition and close attentiveness, so that not a single detail, useful or harmful, may escape the vigilant eye. It is also necessary to show a maximum of tact in dealing with people. Remember that open enemies are far less dangerous than masses of small worms. The firmest tread can slip in this mire.

Let us apply patience as well, for without patience nothing can be achieved. Verily, very often people give up a brilliant beginning only because of lack of patience. They forget that all great tasks are accompanied by difficulties, but by shunning those difficulties they condemn themselves to a fatiguing and endlessly reiterative course. One cannot skip over the following steps without mastering the first ones. Certainly, we can run swiftly through all the steps by great striving. Even so, however, our feet should touch each step. The degree of striving will determine the amount of time spent on each step. Therefore, with all our strength, let us prepare ourselves for a new and higher step, remembering that our time is limited. You must know that our patience is supported by our knowledge; we know that there is a crowning step. We also know that our wait will not be too long. But preparatory stages require the maximum sharp-sightedness, caution and tact. Make all possible speed, and fly on the wings of the great epoch of the equilibrium of the dual Origin and of the broadest cooperation and culture based on spiritual knowledge.

The eyes of the heart will not miss anything, but will sense and will direct. Blaze like a torch; kindle everything with purifying flames; illumine the right direction! Unify your hearts in this wonderful action, in this spiritual aspiration. Try to resound to all calls, all strengthening of thoughts, and to feel all the fluids of the heart's energy, all that strives toward you in a fiery motion and is ready to bring you help!

By unified efforts, let us raise the very heavy burden. The raising of this burden is difficult only at the beginning. Once it is raised off the earth, it will become lighter than a feather.

Let us not forget that the main success of the dark ones

is in their methods of creating disunity. They succeed when the co-workers fail to realize the seriousness of the moment, and when they neglect and put aside urgent matters. We must remember that irritability and touchiness are the easiest channels through which everything dark can approach.

"You understand quite correctly that the attack in its final form will result in nothing but benefit. However, you must learn to wait till the flower of Satan has blossomed. The battle is intense; you must apply all your carefulness. Watch your health; do not weaken it by irritability. Hold tightly to the silver cord and purify your thoughts!"

N.K. is finishing his "Introduction" to Spinoza and Goethe. It is wonderfully written, and it should be translated in such a manner that the beauty of the original is not lost. When we read the description of Spinoza's life, we can see once more how necessary were all the attacks and slanders against him, and how they strengthened and made clear his image in the consciousness of the following generations. Yes, in this stage of our evolution, all sorts of Judases and all the dark forces of ignorant resistance are absolutely necessary. But do not these very forces of darkness give us the possibility of tensing all our strength and our alertness, and do they not broaden our opportunities for action? Are they not the ones who spread information about us, and in such a manner that they attract the attention of valuable people? At first, such people may approach merely from curiosity, or even indignation, but later their breadth of mind will enable them to realize the true value of things, and they will become our friends. There are many friends who are temporarily masked as enemies. Such metamorphoses are not so rare in life.

* * *

Let straight-knowledge be especially developed in these days. Let nothing valuable be neglected. One must remember that often the most insignificant trifle may turn out to be a strong weapon against the enemy. How many beautiful and ready-to-hand formulae are in your arsenal! Learn how to use them so that you can disarm your adversaries! Talk effectively; consider the mentality of your interlocutor, and always base your speech on positive facts, of which you have a considerable supply! The trouble is that we do not always appraise events in the right proportion, and often a certain detail or fact not very striking but of great significance we do not take into consideration at all. It is necessary to remember that everything that is being formed alongside the constructive work for the Hierarchy has the profoundest significance, and if today it is as yet not evident, tomorrow everyone may exclaim about it. Who knows the ways of evolution? Who can predict how the present chaos may end? Who knows what forces will be raised? Therefore, act boldly but with discernment and complete confidence in the Hierarchy of Light! Let all the co-workers endure the battle until its end. Difficult will be the battle, but there will be continuous help if, for your part, you show constant determination—then you will go through everything triumphantly. Only one condition is absolutely essential: complete confidence, to the very end, to the very bottom of despair. The invincible "Tactica Adversa" will lead the enemies into absurdity, and as a result all hostile aggressions will be scattered by the very reason of their evident absurdity. So, remember this when the evil and the ugliness accumulates and reaches its maximum; then you can pierce through its center with "just one arrow." Remember also that only by the contrasting of Light with darkness comes the possibility of creation. All cosmic laws are reflected and reproduced in human life. Thus, courageously and carefully bear a little longer the burden of these times, and help will come to you in due course!

Furthermore, please make sure that publicity regarding us is not presented in a flowery and artificial manner but is based on facts. And when talking about the personality of N.K., it is very important to point out how N.K. gives to everyone who comes into contact with him a creative stimulus, and how he demands the highest quality of work. Point out his wonderful ability to get the best out of everyone, and what powerful results are achieved by such guidance! How he teaches to draw benefit from every circumstance by concentration on the positive aspects! N.K. is not only a benevolent prophet who calls for pure thinking, abstinence and all-forgiveness, as people do see him, but he is also a true leader and builder, for he knows the battle of life and he arms his co-workers for participation in this battle. He strikes at everything dark and ignorant. Sometimes it seems that his wisdom and foresight are endless, and his near ones can confirm how he has predicted events which later came to pass and were witnessed by many. Has he not also, so often, pointed out the right direction humanity should choose in order to avoid misery?

The main condition for salvation is in his call for the unity of the whole cultural world and for educating the young people in a new understanding of creative thought and broad cooperation, based on the concept of great culture, the Cult-Ur, or the Cult of Light. Much could be utilized for the better understanding of N.K.'s personality by reading his "Introduction" to Spinoza and Goethe. N.K. is the same "Sun-carrier" as Goethe is in the interpretation of him by N.K. Can you sense all the power, the invisible power of this man, who builds life full of sunlight? The sun of his life burns up all that is dark, malicious, and destructive. So, one can collect many strong and beautiful facts. But it is better to avoid comparisons. Let every great spirit stand in his own power and in the beauty of his own achievements. We really are not the ones who should compare. Every great spirit fulfils his own task and every individual manifestation is beautiful in its *inimitability*. Long ago, it was said: "How can we compare the light of distant stars?" This formula is applicable in many cases.

29

8 November 1931

I received your kind and sincere letter, and I want to tell you that I was especially touched by the feeling of joy which you experienced in your approach to the Teaching. The degree of this joy is, in fact, the true measurement of our readiness to assimilate the foundations of the Teachings of Light. Preserve this joy and gratitude throughout all the grey days of life because this is the quickest way to broaden your consciousness. And is this not the aim of the Teaching?

Judging by what I know about you from the letters of close co-workers, I feel that you will not remain on the first steps after the Call, but that you will find enough courage to follow the very difficult path which may be before you. When reading the books of the Teaching, please apply first of all to yourself everything that is said there. Many are reading the Teaching, but mostly people think that what is written there is meant for someone else but not for them. They do not notice, or they reject, that which mainly concerns them. Thus they retard their advancement. But a true disciple will apply everything to himself. And really, who can be sure that he or she has not certain good or bad qualities still in their embryo state? But if we apply everything first of all to ourselves, we shall be able to penetrate into the depths of our nature, and we shall find such things as may be very surprising to us. These unexpected discoveries, provided we are firmly prepared to follow the path of self-perfection revealed by the Teaching, will be most helpful in our further advancement.

It is absolutely necessary to realize that the disciple must demonstrate complete confidence, even if something is not clear to him. With the further broadening of his consciousness, much of what seemed even contradictory will find its place. My favorite formula is: complete trust to the very end. Accept it—this is the shortest way! If you follow this path, joy will come to you!

I can also tell you that if one seriously devotes oneself to the service of Light, one is never alone spiritually. In all moments of your life, learn to remember that you are watched continuously by the Eagle Eye and the Flaming Heart of the One who called you! Our gross body and the insufficient refinement of our senses are the only obstacles that prevent us from realizing His Presence. But if you have already had the beautiful experience about which you wrote to me, it is a good sign; it means that such experiences may increase. But be patient, as really "you know neither the day nor the hour"—a profound truth is in these words. The aim of the Teacher is not to weaken our organism but to forge it for the highest receptivity, which requires extreme care. Joy, gratitude and confidence are the best aids.

Love and help others to love!

And thus, I greet you on the path of Light and send all the joy of my heart to the dear new co-worker.

30

12 December 1931

In this difficult moment of your life, my heart sends you all the firmness and striving of my spirit. You know that the hour of the Great Battle has struck. Many prophecies and revelations have been given at various times in all Teachings. The Great Armageddon started at the end of the year 1931, opening with the Great Battle for which the Teacher was preparing us. We must understand the proportions of this Battle, which takes place on all planes or worlds. We must understand the rigor of our time and that the heavenly battle is followed by the earthly one. Therefore, let us not be surprised by the accumulation of events. "So much has been said about the Heavenly Host, about Michael, the Archistrategist, about the manifestation of an affirmed Leader, and all calamities. Therefore I say—caution!"

We already are not on the outer fringe of the battle but marching in the vanguard. Therefore, while carrying the Banner entrusted to us, let us hold close to the leading Hierarch. Remember this, for the enemy's projectiles are bursting only in the midst of the last ranks, as was shown to me in the wonderful vision of the victorious army led by the Leader. Let not your hearts tremble under the heavy aggression of the dark ones, as the nearness of the Great Heart will give you the necessary strength of resistance. Let us manifest intrepid kingliness of spirit. Let us inscribe a page of valiance, of a great deed, into the history of our lives! Let it not be said of us, "Verily, the Great Battle is hardly yet mentioned and someone already expresses weariness. What will such a one say when he sees the numerous host of the enemy?"

In this connection, I shall mention several prophecies regarding this Great Battle: "Every Yuga has its significant time, as a preparatory period, but there can be accelerations which must intensify unusually all forces. One must not understand the great decisive Battle as just a war. The manifestation of that Battle is far deeper. It will proceed along the entire Subtle and Earthly Worlds. It will express itself not only in battles, but also in unusual clashes of peoples. The boundaries between the belligerent ones will be as anfractuous as those between good and evil. Many decisive battles will be inaccessible to the earthly eye. The threatening clashes of the Subtle World will be manifested as catastrophes on the earthly path. Likewise will the earthly courage be reflected upon the Subtle and Fiery Worlds. The Great Battle will be the first link of connection of the worlds. Thus, one can expect swift actions along all directions. Cooperation has a tremendous significance in this Battle. The star of the Flaming Heart already brings great help. This help may not always be visible, but one can cite the example of a writer who exerts tremendous influence yet nevertheless does not know his readers. The same is true in the cooperation of the two worlds. One must be highly strained in the days of battle. Of course this does not exclude all other daily labor, and during each labor one must remember to dispatch it by thought for the benefit of Light. So with each hostile arrow, one must realize that this blow is accepted in the name of the Great Battle." [Heart]

"I would like the present time to be the turning point in your life. What was possible yesterday may not be possible tomorrow. Truly, courage unthinkable yesterday may be attained tomorrow. The battle on the Earth will be as terrible as it is in the Subtle Worlds. The world is broken into numerous factions. Only complete striving toward Us will save you. Of course, the least little sign of disorder and hostility among you will be painful for Me. Remember this! Thus, I confirm the development of Our actions in spite of the unprecedented attacks! But in this battle there is no reconciliation. We shall note disturbances in Europe, we shall witness many treacheries, but the Great Battle will solve the problems of the world. We also should realize that Light is invincible. The manifestation of darkness is a sign of ignorance. I repeat that tomorrow we shall awaken entirely different. In the Subtle World collisions are taking place along the line of the dead hearts. You will shortly see the results of these actions on Earth: everywhere there will be incoherence. The fall of countries, epidemics and poor harvests also will be manifested, and the world will split into new divisions."

Thus, all forces are at variance with each other. The situation of the world is terrible, and it is important to be firm until the new circumstances contribute their help. Everyone should be firm.

"Besides the fact that the dark forces are active in all countries and are influencing their allies in various classes, some of ours are weak because of their narrowness. It is absolutely necessary to maintain the position until we prepare the new circumstances. This present period is unavoidable, but one must accept it as a path toward the future. However, great care must be taken. ..."

31

5 May 1932

You are experiencing a terrible time and you should make a great effort to maintain internal unity. Verily, only unity of heart can overthrow the enemy; he can never penetrate this armor! And all hostile attacks will be warded off by the bountiful energy which emanates from hearts that are unified. This is not an abstraction but a great scientific truth. Let us not be light-minded and ignorant. You know already from the books of the Teaching what a terrible destructive whirl results in the megaphone of space from human irritation and disharmony, and how the most negative forces, including disease, are attracted by this whirlpool.

Is it possible that one of us, out of shameful weakness of will, would allow the success of the work to be overthrown? This would involve him in misfortune, and he would realize it only after the opening of the eyes of his heart. *Unity* now is the order of the battle, and there cannot be complete victory without the precise fulfillment of this essential order. It is most beneficial to reread the indications, as they are given not just for a particular day; and it is good to have them always in mind. Last year, for example, the significance of the Banner for the defense of the treasures of art in times of war was constantly emphasized, so that the idea could finally be assimilated. Let us remind the doubting ones how the Red Cross was started, what difficulties this movement had to go through in dealing with ignorant officials, through whose hands this highly humanitarian project had to pass. Really, sometimes one would think that the human conscience is going backward instead of forward.

I beg you with all my heart: remember about *unity*. My heart is concerned about every one of you. I would like so much to relieve the hardship of the present time, but such periods are absolutely necessary. Let us apply our most vigorous efforts in helping each other as much as possible. Let the very difficulties beautify and uplift our deeds which are meant for the General Good,

My courageous fighters, remember about *unification*!
I sign this letter: "Woodpecker."

32

28 June 1932

Just as we must be able to give to everyone who comes to us everything that can be assimilated by him, even so we must be able to receive from everyone what he can offer for the General Work. Do not drive away the newcomers!

Do not be afraid of extreme tension; only tensed strings can sound. And we know that by cosmic law energies can be transmuted and forms can be refined only in *extreme tension*. This law sets two fundamental rules in all the Teachings. First, for spiritual perfection the disciple must use all his strength. This is held within certain limits, as the Teacher watches that this tension does not injure the health. Secondly, every particle of conscious psychic energy is most precious, and therefore the Great Teacher can give it out only in cases where all earthly possibilities and means are exhausted. These two rules explain why the help comes at the last moment, in time of despair. But what a large number of feeble souls are unable to endure to this limit, thus condemning themselves to descent and then to a perpetually repeated burdensome ascent! There are many such Sisyphuses, rolling their stones of cowardice and doubt.

All perplexities and seeming contradictions are caused by the difficulty for the undeveloped consciousness to embrace antitheses. But unless one realizes this, one cannot advance in spiritual life. The encompassment of antitheses, for the majority of people, is the most difficult thing. But every spiritual Teaching considers this most essential; for instance, a complete indifference to fame but at the same time self-affirmation; renunciation of possessions but at the same time life in the midst of possessions; complete freedom from worldly desires but at the same time profound interest in the earthly work. All these antitheses should be harmonized in the consciousness of a disciple. The main thing to comprehend is that all renunciation primarily is achieved *in spirit*. Remember how Buddha admonished for possessiveness one of his disciples who had sacrificed all his possessions, while at the same time He permitted another to retain all his property. Why? Because one of them, in spite of actual surrender, was in thought constantly preoccupied with them, while the other, although still remaining in possession, was unattached to them. There are so many people who appear indifferent to their possessions and yet, in their thoughts, are constantly coveting more. And so many self-styled "unassuming" people, who "would not even think of any publicity," in their inner selves are hoping that they will be noticed.

And what about those who fast and who are yet longing for the renounced food? And also those who are hoping to be doubly compensated for their labor and sacrifices! Poor, self-deluded prisoners! Who can explain to them that their efforts are useless and will never bring them joyous liberation but will rather harden their hearts? Spiritual liberation is achieved not by force but by the realization of the heart. A person who is free from all worldly attachments will not talk about them because his renunciation will be natural, simple, and taken for granted. This "taken for granted" attitude is the most important achievement because if there is left even the slightest regret, or condemnation of others, all the efforts will be fruitless. The disciples should not struggle against their lower nature by torturing themselves; rather, by the development of their hearts and by the breadth of wisdom which they should acquire from the Teaching of the New Life.

For the most part, condemnations come from people who themselves suffer from these attachments. These are the Pharisees, who expect great regard for their smoking candles! And if the reward were sent to them they would fail to appreciate it. Would they not treat it like the cock who found a pearl?

* * *

Truly, those who do not accept the Hierarchy should be reminded that according to all laws, physical and spiritual, there is no action or work that can be developed without a focus. Each country has its focus in a government, each political party has its representative, and every firm, every establishment, has its manager. Every energy must be focused in order to be manifested. Evolution in Cosmos is built wholly on these focuses, bonds, links, ties—call them what you will! Point out to those of limited understanding the chapter about Sacrifice in *Leaves of Morya's Garden I*. Renunciation is so joyous! But the reverse concept is verily dreadful. The Burden of the World, the Chalice of Redemption, the Drinking of the Poison of the World, thus do we name the various missions on the path of great responsibility and Light. And these extreme burdens are placed only upon those who understand spiritually the idea of liberation. It seems to me that further explanations are unnecessary.

* * *

Do not forget your cultural and international contacts! If we ourselves do not cultivate them, who will do it for us? The time will come when things will be regulated, but now we have continuously to struggle and work. The scope of the cultural tasks should be always in your minds. And please do not ignore even the small indications! They might seem little to you, but you can never tell how significant they may be. All of them have in view the very great, although they may sometimes appear to have no direct connection with the daily work. Remember that even the smallest flies can spread deadly infection! Always have in mind the scope of everything. Only great thought can encompass all the contrivances of our enemies.

33

7 July 1932

Let the disciple firmly realize what harmful results are brought about by neglect of the wise Advice of the Teacher. Neither should they doubt or be disappointed if the fulfillment of the Advice does not bring good results immediately. We should always remember that sometimes we have no idea what result the Teacher has in mind. Often it is something entirely opposite to our expectations! Sometimes the Teacher wants to throw a bridge across an abyss, and we can never tell where is the person, thing, thought, or word which can be used as a bridge! A careful fulfillment of the command—that is all that is expected of us. The significance and the result of the applied indication will be revealed in time.

Here are some paragraphs from the Teaching:

"Often the Teacher finds himself in a very difficult relation with his pupil. The pupil promises to follow all the Commands of the Teacher, but no sooner is one received than immediately reasons are found to alter it. The Teacher experiences a similar difficulty when He is blamed for inaction. Imagine to yourself the position of an archer when he is tensed for his shot and behind him someone cries, 'Why does he not shoot?'

"Small children, even without perceiving the reason, obey the guiding hand. But adults attempt to add to the prepared reaction something fit to their mood. One may compare them to people who, when the house catches fire, neglect irreplaceable manuscripts but save their cherished bedding.

"Whence comes this disrespect of the Command? Also from mistrust. It is incomprehensible how readily the gifts of the Teacher are accepted and how neglected are his best Commands. How many premeditated transmissions were rejected, how many effectual actions disrupted, because of light-mindedness! With one hand reverence is rendered, and the other scatters the pearls over the precipice. The fact is forgotten that permeating space with personal sendings is an infection of space, and that the chosen Guide, with his experience, will not humiliate the pupil. Hence, how greatly must one value cooperation, firm in trust!

"When you yourselves will become teachers, insist on the immediate execution of a command. Do not give commands often. They may become commonplace. but if the work demands it, give a concise command. Let it be known that a command is irrevocable. One must follow more simply, combining independent labor with cooperation. The distorted command is like a train that has been derailed." [Agni Yoga]

34

6 October 1932

I am sending you the first pages of the new book called *Fiery World*, with the hope that this inexhaustible source of wisdom will continually nourish your hearts. Take from this book all the power, all the protection, all the possibilities; all this and much more is in this Treasury, which comes from the Eternal Source.

When reading about the great creative fire—the life giver—let us try to awaken in ourselves the fire which warms our hearts. Let us be like the ancient priests who, once the fire was kindled, had to guard it even under the threat of death. In this guarding of the fire was a great symbol, as the extinguishing of the flame of the spirit results in the death of the soul. The fire of the heart will protect us from delaying or distorting things, as well as from being frightened by anybody or anything, for it will enlighten our consciousness by awakening the fiery straight-knowledge.

As it is said, "Let us be like those who await the Great Advent, hearkening for the tread and knowing that our hearts are dedicated to the service of humanity. We shall not allow weakness or negativeness to enter our hearts, as these failings will turn the tongues of the flame against us. Let us, therefore, not be frightened by the battle for the culture of spirit and for the rights of existence, as it is only through spiritual values that the world is sustained. Let this call to the battle not confuse you. Those who remain static are a thousand times more in danger than those who strive. Of course, striving should be in your thoughts and in your hearts, rather than in your feet! And remember that on the great Path it is better to be slandered than to go against the decision of the Forces of Light. Indeed, we should become accustomed to being slandered, for no fiery path exists without these flower carpets of evil.

"This concerns all the friends who are doubtful and uncertain and who do not understand whence come so many attacks. But let us remind the bigots and hypocrites about the Teaching as well as the destiny of the Great Teacher, whom they ceaselessly continue to crucify."

The excessive burden is accepted voluntarily only by the fiery heart. Let us be these fiery hearts; let us accept the greater burden, which will bring us sooner to liberation. And while those who did not accept the whole burden will have to return for the part left behind, we shall, with all the joy of our hearts, fulfill the next coming task. Let nobody be so low as to allow himself to count his contributions or so-called sacrifices. This would be equal to the blocking of the path. All real contributions and sacrifices are weighed on the innermost scales of conscience which exist in everyone.

If we are calculating our contributions (even if it be in the depths of our secretive minds) we deprive ourselves of the privilege of giving something for the benefit of the world. The fire of such sacrifice will spread over the Earth like the fire of sacrifice brought by the Biblical Cain. So vital are all the ancient symbols. The Forces of Light value sacrifices made with joy, as only such are productive and victorious. The Book of Sacrifice should be carried in our hearts.

Do not forget that the qualities of sacrifice are manifold. Of this we should remind those who, from the very beginning of their approach to the Teaching, expect an immediate reward for their supposed sacrifices. Let them read:

"The Teaching about sacrifice was already given to you. Sacrifice is power. Power is possibility. Consequently, every sacrifice is first of all a possibility.

"It is time to cast aside the hypocrisy that sacrifice is deprivation. We do not accept deprivations, but We give possibilities.

"Let us see what possibilities are born from the so-called sacrifice. Where is a true sacrifice which can demean? In Our Treasury there is a large collection of sacrifices, and each one was useful to the one who made it. We dislike to speak about sacrifices because a sacrifice is the most profitable undertaking.

"Small tradesmen love to cry about the expenditures and to feign a loss. But a real provider in life considers each expenditure as only a business guarantee. You have lost not through sacrifice but pillage.

"Christ advised to distribute spiritual wealth. But, as the keys to it are far away, people have applied this advice toward the distribution of pillaged money. First to steal and then to giveaway with a tear and become enraptured by one's own goodness. As if in speaking of distribution the Teacher could have had in mind chairs and old coats! The Teacher meant imponderable wealth. Only the spiritual gift can move the cup of the scales.

"Let us examine the row of co-workers. Was anyone deprived of anything? No, all have been enriched. Is it not enrichment to become a ruler of a new kingdom? So rich is that kingdom that without too much harm we can break a few dishes. Positively the hands are growing, and the book of gratitude can be examined.

"I advise the providers in life to have substitutes for all positions.

"In large enterprises the business stands upon the business, and not upon personality.

"Who can justly assert that he has been the giving one? We will open Our account books and show how much every one received. For it is not at all easy to sacrifice when a sacrifice is a possibility, and the possibility is a benefit, and the benefit is a sound cooperation, and the cooperation is the Alatir-Stone, which either resurrects or consumes.

"But self-abnegation can open the Gates of Understanding, and the decrepit sacrifice of unneeded things will swing upon one branch with self-love." [Leaves of Morya's Garden II]

35

12 October 1932

I was so happy to learn of that unity which you wrote about in your last letter. But it seems that even broader and more complete unification is needed, as I was told to write to you as follows: "Great unity is required. If the road is broad you need not push each other. It must not be forgotten that even a tiny stone can hit very hard. The battle against the darkest forces must evoke the most noble thinking. Let us be pure and cautious."

Indeed, the broadened mentality obliges us to be twice as careful of our thoughts and actions, and first of all toward each other and the people who come into closest contact with us. Remember that thousands of eyes are watching us with great attention, and—let us not deceive ourselves—this attention arises chiefly out of the desire to find our weak spot for their destructive purposes. It is most important that all the co-workers respect each other and do not belittle each other in front of employees and strangers. Little things, trifles like sharp words and cutting jokes, crooked smiles, etc., destroy the respect of other people. By no means should you allow strangers to lose their respect through hearing unkind insinuations. Respect once destroyed cannot be re-established; and it can be destroyed so easily by the most ordinary things, such as unfitting remarks. More than once has it been said, "Even in jest you should not belittle or criticize each other. It is time to realize the harm that small flies can do. The sting of a small fly can poison the whole organism. You must remember that the enemy tries to enter not through the door but through the smallest crack." Quarreling with each other is not just a crack but a wide open door!

In dangerous attacks of the dark forces, even the slightest hint of condemnation is fatal. Imagine how many useful people may be driven away. it is said, "Useful people may be sent to you, but you should know how to keep them." Imagine the position of people who have heard about your cultural activities and, after meeting you, have found out that you do not differ at all from other people! How will such a discovery affect their attitude toward you and your work? Think, too, about those who approach you through the books of the Teaching—what disappointment they will feel when they find that you do not practise the fundamentals of the Teaching! Think of your great responsibility! I shall not enlarge on the diversity of this responsibility, as it should be clear to all who have the seven books of the Teaching. But you must think about it more often, as well as about all the results of spiritual deafness and neglect.

Your life will become such a joyful fairy tale if only you are able to realize the daily High Guidance, and your own responsibility. So much joy if you accept the responsibility with all your heart and if your fairy tale is not covered with the dust of the commonplace! You must be able to remove the dust and look objectively at everything that is happening around you and your work.

Let us perfect ourselves; let us watch ourselves especially; let us illumine with the fire of our hearts all the Indications of the Teaching; let us be closely united in the hour of danger. Only to a superficial mind does this demand remain an abstract ethical idea inapplicable to practical life. But a serious co-worker, and particularly a disciple, will concentrate on this idea with all the fire of his heart because he knows that unity is the basis and strength of the whole work. Therefore, the request for unification should be your first consideration in all your decisions. More than ever, all the institutions should complement each other. Our first duty is to guard and advance the plan of all our cultural activities. Therefore, everyone should learn not to limit himself within his particular work and section. Most impersonally and wisely, he must see what is especially urgent, and therefore requires help, and which work may be temporarily put aside. One-sidedness is not permissible among the builders. We know the great Plan of our work, and such broad creativeness cannot be limited to two societies or to one country.

36

10 November 1932

Lately, I have been greatly depressed, as I feel that the foundation is decaying. Could it be possible that the hearts of some co-workers have hardened so much, and their consciousness darkened so, that they do not see the abyss into which they are about to fall? Will they not realize the terrible danger of our time and stop serving the dark forces? Was it not said that "every bad word, every disagreement, is already an encouragement to the darkness"? And remember: "The dreadful knife is not in your pocket but, verily, on the tip of your tongue. Some time you will have to realize that a word and a thought cannot be erased. Everyone who thinks of the General Good may rejoice, and vice versa. Morals and customs of the dark ones are not to Our liking."

For your own sake, consider what has been said and endlessly repeated. Only by our united efforts can we reach the goal. It is hard to think how many wonderful possibilities have vanished because of hidden discordance! What can be built on the aura of irritability, offense and unfriendliness? The principle of the magnet has been thoroughly discussed. We cannot make ignorance our excuse! From the very first day, the necessity of harmony was emphasized, but, it seems, all in vain. The most terrible thing is that the sense of honesty has been lost, and someone is ready to blame the others, forgetting that his inner soul is an open book to the Guru. It is time to be ashamed of our childishness and to understand that when we do not follow the Advice we behave no better than traitors. Forgive the use of this word, but my heart bleeds when I see what kind of difficulties you so obstinately continue to create on your path. Try to imagine what will become of you if the Teaching ceases to lead you. Where will you go? Which way will you turn? Who will hear you and help you in your misery? Who will point the way out of the difficult situation? The threatening time, the dreadful time is coming for all. And just think that you were the ones who were permitted to work for the salvation of so much and so many! Is this the way to do it? Is this the way to justify the confidence of the One who called you?

I want you to feel all my pain, all my longing to see you working in complete harmony, in realization of the tremendous responsibility of your work. What is the best way to make you understand it? How to strengthen in you this understanding? I hate to threaten, but how can I help warning you, when I see someone falling into the abyss and pulling the others down. How to hold him back?

Some time ago I thought that the endless calls for unification would be properly understood. I was hoping you would understand that friendliness is important, not when your authority is accepted and when your vanity is satisfied, but rather when you have to give in, in many things, for the sake of successful cooperation.

Heartfelt words are being written, but you should show friendliness and attentiveness in action—words are like running water. In my dreams I saw one of you as a faithful standard-bearer of the name of our Guru. I dreamt that the words of the chosen one would be full of magnetic power and beauty. From the time when it was indicated that the New Society should be established, seven years have passed,—a long time and a significant one in every respect. During this time a complete spiritual regeneration could have taken place if real aspiration had been applied. It was precisely told in what circles these words should be spoken, what connections should be made. But if we look back, we must admit that the inner condition prevented this development. If in the first few years there were various obstacles which were not easy to remove, in 1926 there were many new possibilities; but the old, not-outlived habits asserted themselves. I still do not lose hope that your hearts will kindle again and that you will express yourselves in fiery, beautiful deeds. The achievements can be so great!

It is so sad to write accusing letters instead of sharing the joyful news of the successful work of other groups of co-workers.

It is heartbreaking to know that the most precious energy is spent on negative, corrective work, that all the warnings were useless, and that all this is happening at a terrible time when the dark forces are making their strongest and most aggressive assault! At such a time, when you should have developed maximum energy and inner stability for preserving all your achievements! In great distress, I beg you to help me—find the courage for patience and peacemaking... "blessed are the peacemakers..."

Try at least to relieve my worry and grief a little. It might have been my own fault. Who knows—perhaps I could not unite you sufficiently, could not impress upon you a love to the Great Heart and a striving to selfless action. Perhaps I failed to show you by personal example how to apply the Teaching in your everyday life, and, above all, failed to kindle your hearts with the fire of self-perfection and tremendous responsibility. You cannot approach the Teaching and the Service without being responsible for all your actions.

Please do help me in my own responsibility for you! My heart sends a call to each of you. Help!

37

17 November 1932

It is hard to express my grief. Again I see that the inner decay continues its dreadful course. I see that the consciousness of some co-workers does not grow, and the treasures of the Teaching are accepted as empty words. Verily, it is the inner unsoundness which is so fatal. "You can win all litigations, you can meet new friends, but this inner decay may drive away your best friend. When there is a lot of pepper in the air, people start sneezing. In the same way imperil can spread. Many times you have seen how new circumstances arose, but one has to understand how to meet them. Therefore, you should understand at last how infectious is imperil. You cannot treat decay carelessly. This process is as contagious as leprosy. There is either strengthening or decay—no third condition is possible."

Who would choose decay for himself? At present all events are happening with such fantastic speed that it is impossible to remain on the first steps. It is said, "We cannot suggest strengthening by force. Neither can we save from leprosy by force, nor can we hold back from imperil. Friendliness cannot be achieved by force. You cannot rudely compel the heart to grow, but the beautiful garden will grow only through beautiful deeds. Slandering of the Hierarchy is irreparable." Knowing this law, I feel desperate that I cannot help in anything, as what can I do if even the words of the Guru are not accepted? How can I expect that the desire of my heart, intense and passionate as it is, will reach your hardened souls, your clouded consciousnesses? It is dreadful to think that the ranks may thin out and someone will remain utterly alone, that the greatest privilege of the approach to Light can be given up for the sake of disgusting selfishness, this eternal enemy of Light! And to think that this may come after twelve years of discipleship! Apart from personal destruction, inner disharmony may result in the destruction of the whole work! The terrible danger is that instead of concentrating on the most essential—on our cultural construction which holds us all together—we shall become accustomed to concentrating on trivial matters, disagreements, offenses, envy. How can we guard all our positions? How can we expect to be successful? Will not friends run away from us if they sense the polluted atmosphere?

I regret that I have to quote another sad page:

"It is necessary to learn not to waste labor. Obstructed minds neglect the principal matters. Observe how the two letters which you received are lacking in essential contents. I do not blame the writers so much as those who caused the obstruction. Such neglect of the most important things is fatal. A person who confuses his brother is sinful. He will not make his own life happy either; dark will be his life, as his consciousness is distracted by the non-essential. To discern what is essential and to concentrate on it means to be on the path of victory. But to lose the path means to become a burden to those near you. The distinction between the most important and the least essential should be the test which everybody must clearly hold in his consciousness. Nobody has a right to pierce someone's heart, or even to cause a headache, while irreplaceable treasures are passing by! People do not consider irreplaceable what they do not notice."

To those who are full of doubt and are lacking in steadfastness, I suggest writing down from the books of the Teaching everything that is said about doubt, instability and suspicion. Nowadays there is an especially large number of these real servants of darkness. It is very useful to have at hand the definitions of all these hateful vices and to reread about them often.

Although a merely formal unity is not very high, it is better than nothing. The animal nature of man is a combination of habits. Therefore, by watching oneself, it is possible to create certain good habits. Finally, you will kindle a little flame in your hearts and then this long-torturing process of practising good habits may, in one moment of illumination, become a joyous part of your enlightened consciousnesses. And once more, I ask you to be honest with your own selves. Lying to oneself is the most terrible sin. It injures the consciousness and leads to so-called death of the spirit.

38

10 December 1932

What must I write about? About the same old thing, about the great unification as the only salvation. In the meantime, everything has already been said, all reasons already stated, but the consequences of disunity are still present. Now to one of you is given the order to repeat all the time the Indications of the

Teacher. ... I do not lose hope that from now on all the advices and Indications will be written down and will be reread with much love, much care, so that they will not be forgotten or distorted.

Turn a new page in the books of your lives and begin to fill it up with beautiful deeds of tolerance, understanding, generosity! It is said, "There is no sense in stirring dust." All this digging in the dust of yesterday will not lead to anything, and it will infect your eyes and nose. Will you please abandon it, as it is beneath your dignity. So much time will be saved for productive work, which is now more necessary than ever. So little time is left for the strengthening of our foundations and the magnet of our works. Strengthening of the foundation is our first duty if we care for the promised success! Realize what a firm foundation is needed in order to accept the promised success! Let no trivial thoughts and suspicions stop your victorious movement! With your hearts you should feel that there is nothing personal in my requests, but only my care for the beautiful Plan! The Indications should be accepted with your hearts. You must concentrate on them with all your determination; only then will come complete understanding which will simplify many things.

It is not right to overburden the Forces which carry on everything. It is hard to believe that the Eastern concept of and reverence for the Teacher is dead in the West. Try to understand what it means to overburden the Forces of Light and what price you yourselves pay for it.

"Those will come who extinguish, who slander and violate, they who, verily, are the darkest souls. *Decay once started cannot be stopped.* But the wise will not look back, as they know that the fire is undying when it is kindled."

No wonder that I insist on repeating the Indications of the Teacher. Even the mere repetition could strengthen the foundation. "It is not right to dig in dust when clouds are gathering. It is not right to turn back when crossing the path on the edge of an abyss. I remind you that the main foundation is one anchor for all.

"So, unite simply in the name of salvation. If we were able to count all the stars, if we were able to measure all the unseen depths, we would still not be able to improve the present time. With all the courage of our hearts, we must realize the terror of darkness which approaches when the fires are dying down.

Many think that unity is an old, unnecessary concept. They consider that individuality is better preserved by separatism—such is the logic of darkness. But during dangerous epidemics, one sometimes thinks of simple remedies and finds salvation through them. Unification is this simple remedy; manifestly it defeats the darkness. Thus, let the sword over the dragon be not asleep.

"I can only advise you to remember the Indications. The times are complicated, and the thread should not be lost. Therefore, I ask you to remind them about the exact fulfillment of the Indications."

I trust that the clouds which darken your sight will vanish and that you will understand with your heart and your mind what the result of disunion will be. Let us not condemn anybody or anything, but with all honesty let us examine ourselves and eradicate all that retards our progress.

39
29 December 1932

The Battle of Armageddon cannot be a straight victorious march because Great Forces are involved in it on both sides. The victory of the Forces of Light, however, is evident, as they are allied with the Cosmic Magnet. The latter attracts the greatest powers, against which the dark ones cannot hold out. The element of pure Fire burns them. But we must have patience. The battle is started by the dark ones because in their fury they are trying to destroy as much as they can before their days are over. From them, and from their best collaborators—the tepid and neutral ones—come all the terrors of revolutions, all the violence. They try through general spiritual impoverishment to create confusion and complete disorder. The heavy currents of Saturn and of other unfavorable combinations of the planets are especially helpful to them. At the moment, all the Forces of Light are focused on the bridling of the elements disturbed by the dark forces. Nobody can imagine how much divine energy is now being spent on just controlling the underground fire! The dark ones try in every possible way to kill what is light and pure. That is why unification is so necessary. As it is said, "Notice the inexplicable attacks, which depress the whole planet. It is not accidental that the constant Rays are sent for defense. Serious dangers already have been avoided."

During the last week, there were prophecies in our valley about a great earthquake which was supposed to start on the 22nd of December, continue three days, and ruin our whole valley. But on the 21st a great snowfall suddenly took place, and the temperature dropped. This continued until the 27th of December. We were told, "Pay attention to the people's prophecies, which very often correctly forecast the cosmic events. But of course, you cannot rely on them completely." It was further told, "We can confirm that the deadly danger was avoided. You know how many currents were used. Besides, the meteoric snow formed ice vapors. It is quite understandable that you are feeling tension and indisposition. So the dark ones did not succeed, but you helped by not disturbing Our currents, being harmoniously united. It is essential to understand how even indirect resistance to the Rays is dangerous, to say nothing of real arguments and quarrelling, which may paralyze the valuable currents. Many other horrible things are planned by the satanists. Tightly hold Our Hand. I speak to whom it may concern.

"Observe how alike in action are paralysis and disunion. Paralysis does not come immediately after wrong actions. Paralysis requires a long cure, and often is incurable. Therefore, I demand unification. Be above all kinds of moods and recollections. I demand unification, otherwise I refuse to heal. The unity must be firm. Do not permit mere hypocrisy—the times are much too dangerous. *Who among the co-workers can say when and by whom the paralysis was caused? Where is that spot, that aura, i.e., that combination which caused the paralysis through which the power of the salutary Rays was paralyzed?* Who knows how much time will be required to cure the aura which cut the contact with the Hierarchy by its irritability? Meanwhile, the enemy does not lose time and uses the black fire which, of course, is so easily ignited and fanned whenever the magnet of irritability is evident. The black fire is nothing else but irritability, so beloved by the dark ones. At the moment, conditions for them are favorable. Therefore, tremendous caution is required. Remember that where the Ray is accepted it is stronger than any armor. Therefore, the satanists are looking for the weak spots, so that they can pierce through these cracks. They do not care where or through whom or in what part of the world they must look for these holes. They will use all opportunities, thinking that My Rays cannot fill up the whole world. They use the most fantastic masks in order to deceive our watchfulness. You are right, the satanists are spread all over the world. We know the traitors and We also know that only unity can defend and lead to victory. True, the right circumstances will come, but we must live up to them.

"I would like to concentrate all the energy on many outer events. Therefore, your unification is essential, so that the chalice may be sound. Unity is always good, but in certain cosmic circumstances it is particularly necessary. Imagine somebody pushing the hand that has raised the brimful chalice! What fire may start from the spilled fiery drops! When I was warning about the time when the finest fulfillment of the Indications would be required, I meant this particular time. You can well imagine that I am accumulating the energy, so do not let one scorpion escape!"

I hope that this loving and austere warning will create the right impression and someone will be sorry, if not for others and for the work, then at least for himself.

I beseech you to find the courage to defeat the main inner enemy—disunion. Everybody patronizes it, but the overcoming of this enemy would secure victory. Let us tell ourselves that hypocrisy is impossible among co-workers, and let us practise tolerance and friendliness, which is really not so difficult if the heart burns with striving toward our Teacher. But everybody, *without exception*, should do it. Let each co-worker apply all that has just been said to himself first of all; let him not discard it as something which concerns his neighbor and not himself. Frequently, the one who really should pay attention selfishly blames everything on his neighbor. But the wise and true disciple will apply everything first to himself, not to others, as otherwise how can he perfect himself?

Also, once and for all, let us drive away all offenses and consider them as real poison. Touchiness must not reach the disciple, as otherwise he is far from progress. Long ago it was said, "There is not much honor in planting a garden of offenses." And also, "A person who feels himself offended attaches himself to the offense and loses mobility of thinking, and if we lose mobility we inevitably become dull. In everything, we should have a sense of proportion, knowing the great scale of our work! Where will be the place for offenses? The four bases which were given in the beginning of the Teaching should always be in your memory." I shall remind you of them: (1) Reverence for the Hierarchy; (2) Unity; (3) Co-measurement; (4) Great Tolerance. Therefore, let us not look back into a dark corner where all the bad habits are stored. They only deprive us of joy. With all our hearts let us strive to the Teacher of Light who so tirelessly sends us his Rays of joy and loving care. Let us open our hearts to accept this bliss.

Do not confuse by your disunion the newcomers and those who have already joined you. It is so harmful to you, to the work, and to them. We can foresee the harm in this and are deeply grieved. The newcomers should be inspired and not confused by absurdities. I suffer when I see that we who proclaim the principles of unity are practising disunion. How can we construct and unify this way? Only personal examples inspires and advances one.

I believe that you will apply all your diligence to sympathetic, tolerant cooperation. I know that it is difficult, but so much more wonderful will be your achievements.

Part II

LETTERS TO EUROPE

1931-1934

1

24 April 1931

I wish to send you a few words from my heart. The Ancient Wisdom says that sincere words can never be flowery. Therefore, in all simplicity, I tell you that we are profoundly touched by your steady striving toward the Teaching and by your creative work, which is so full of beautiful feeling.

Sincerity and simplicity are two powerful magnets. The great art of human relationship is based on them. Very few realize the importance of this art, which is the foundation of all constructiveness and evolution! This forgotten art, which requires so much sensitiveness, alertness, and synthesis of the spirit, must be introduced into life without delay. It is the most essential accomplishment; and how can we build the New World of beauty and powerful cooperation without it?

It seems to me that your steadiness and heartfelt approach will be an example, a lighthouse, which will guide others in the right direction. You will call them joyously, you will teach them to love obstacles and struggle—for how otherwise will their inner fires be kindled? You will direct their attention to the joyous service of the General Good; and to the most courageous ones you will whisper about the joy of self-denial, about the constant readiness to give oneself completely to the service of the Great Hierarchy of Light!

We are forwarding to you (and shall continue to do so) pages from the books of the Teaching. They will come as great support to you in strengthening the young souls, including such lovable ones as our little friend Serioja.

Accept these words, which come from a heart that is open to you. We often think of you and you have a place in all our labors.

Give our heartiest greetings to all those near to you; for whoever is near to you—is near to us.

2

28 August 1931

You are right that "to understand Agni Yoga completely and to apply it in life is not a task for everybody." But without application in life, knowledge is worthless and will not give the expected results. The first formulae which a disciple should assimilate are the following: "All for life—nothing should be abstract; all should be done by human hands and human feet; without the tension of all forces, no transmutation (or perfection) is possible." We all know that in physical and chemical experiments new formulae are born only at the edge of greatest tension. Therefore, using the great analogy which exists in Cosmos we must continually strive and intensify all our abilities.

First of all, the Teaching requires independence of action from the disciple. The Teaching gives direction, generously giving the precious hints, but the disciple must himself "with his own hands and feet" build his path. Therefore, do not expect ready-made formulae. From small hints build the great structure.

Now I shall answer your questions.

1. The various branches of Yoga have been partly translated into European languages. The best works are those of Patanjali, Vivekananda and Avalon. In addition to these, it would be advisable for physicians to get acquainted with the recently published little book of an Indian doctor of medicine. We shall try to get it for you. But Agni Yoga is the synthesis of all Yogas.

2. Musk is the deposit of the substance of an unconscious psychic energy, about which so much is said in the books of Agni Yoga. Musk has nothing to do with narcotics, which kill the intellect. It is not a regular stimulant in the full sense of the word. It balances the nervous system; it regulates the sympathetic nervous system which so strongly vibrates in advanced Yogis. It is also true that while using musk the demand for food lessens because psychic energy, by strengthening the nervous system, also nourishes the physical body. Dose: medium-sized or small-sized pellet once a day, but some take two such pellets at once, which is considered a strong dose. It is difficult to find a substitute for musk. Perhaps the nearest to it is castoreum and the spermin of Dr. Pell. "Precipitation of the unconscious fire" is also a definition of the same substance, psychic energy; therefore, musk can also be considered as such a fire. The "phosphorus of spirit" is another name for that same psychic energy. And you know already that psychic energy is the most powerful, most penetrating, most transmuting energy, which protects from all diseases and from many other things. Of course, it acts in this miraculous way only when it is consciously mastered, or

at least realized. But even the unconscious precipitation of this substance is most precious.

3. Valerian remains in the category of "life-givers" and its significance is equivalent to the significance of the blood in the body. Occultly, valerian is considered as the blood of the vegetable kingdom. It should be taken continuously as daily food. It can be taken in the form of a tincture, made with alcohol, but definitely without mixing with such additions as ether. Dose: ten to forty-five drops. But best of all is the valerian tea made from infusing the valerian roots in water—once or twice daily.

In general, bear in mind that narcotics are not advisable for the followers of Agni Yoga. Also, smoking is harmful, as well as the immoderate use of alcohol. Even meat is harmful, as it fills the organism with decayed particles. Of course, as a physician, you realize how carefully one should change one's habits so that there will not be any harmful reactions. But are there many people who could do it gradually? However, Agni Yoga is inaccessible for smokers and drinkers.

4. Cedar tar and other tars or resins, such as eucalyptus, are the products of the psychic energy of the trees, and therefore they are extremely beneficial for strengthening, purifying, healing, etc. Knowing these qualities, everyone should try to apply them in the best possible way. The best tar is from Siberian cedars.

If purified, tars or their oil may be taken internally. Dose: five drops or more. Everything is very individual. Perhaps your intuition will help you to find the successful combinations.

The emanations of pine trees are, of course, irreplaceable. Pine trees, like electric machines, accumulate vital forces, a condensed supply of prana, or naturovaloris. The Druids considered a chalice of pine essence as a chalice of life.

It is always beneficial to have in rooms small pine trees or to spray the pine essences. In this way, the atmosphere is purified, and the undesirable entities, which are so numerous around the human emanations, are driven away.

Essence of peppermint is also very good for this purpose—either sprayed in the air or put in hot water for evaporation. A cup of such water should be placed near the bedside. In all the cases you mentioned this would be useful.

5. Peppermint or menthol preparations are first of all irreplaceable in local anaesthetics, as well as for the relief of

inflammatory processes which are so common among the beginner-yogis. Most of the pains of the yogis are connected with the inflamed condition of the nerve centers and glands because the channels of the nerves are closely connected with the glands. Therefore, the common "migrenstift" (migraine stick) is very useful, as well as applications of Baume Bengué, which contains a large amount of menthol. This has been proved by personal experience.

6. It is advisable to protect the crown of the head from the direct action of the sun's rays. Therefore, yogis put up their hair in a knot on the crown of their heads. Besides the heat, the sun's rays contain certain "chemism" which, during the periods of increase of sunspots, may be harmful. In general, during the opening of the centers one should avoid direct contact with the sun's rays. Excessive physical exercises, such as sports, are also quite harmful.

7. "The third eye" certainly has its physical substratum in the center of the nervous system. Pay most serious attention to the two glands of the brain—pituitary and pineal. The molecular movements of the pituitary gland develop psychic sight, but for the spiritual, highest sight, there should also be movements of the pineal gland. The radiations or emanations of these two glands, when unified, bring the highest results.

I should also give you advice to pay most serious attention to the nerve centers, which sometimes are not consciously realized and, being partly opened, often show the symptoms of tuberculosis, asthma, rheumatism and other diseases. One of the most important centers in the process of Yoga is the center of the solar plexus, but it is not given any attention. And it creates many painful sensations in the development of the yogic process.

I am afraid you will not be satisfied with my brief explanations, but it is necessary to display an individual intuition and initiative, as without these qualities there cannot be any true progress. As you ought to notice, the Agni Yoga requires first of all a spiritual development. Without it, all these indications and secondary measures are useless. Therefore, from the bottom of my heart I wish you to be successful not only on the physical plane but also in the spiritual one. You will always receive help in the latter, although you may not realize it at once.

Avoid all magic and pseudo-occultism! Without the proper development and broadening of consciousness, all the widespread suggestions for the sliding out of the astrosom, and other externalizations, conjurations and other manifestations, might be harmful.

First of all, start firmly your spiritual development and unprejudiced, real scientific researches. The rest will come naturally.

By the way, what do you think about the cure with colored rays?

In conclusion, I want to remind you about the absolute inevitability of the New Era. The fiery energies are in their greatest tension attracted toward Earth, and if not accepted, realized and assimilated they will cause terrific earthquakes and other cosmic perturbations, and also revolutions, wars and new epidemics. We are now at the very entrance of a New Era, a New Race, and therefore our time may be compared with the times of Atlantis, the existence of which becomes more and more evident to our science.

Watch out for all unusual and destructive signs in all spheres of life, and many things will be clearer to you. You will see where are the sparks of the New Era, the era of spiritual knowledge and great cooperation of peoples under the sign of culture. Realization of the coming of this great time should multiply the strength of every sensitive person and should direct him toward joyous, constructive work for the General Good under the Banner, which we shall call the *Banner of Peace and Culture*.

3

26 December 1931

Your program of educational activities is really beautiful. Everything you point out is most essential, and, if it is applied in the refined conception of the heart, it will give wonderful results. Of course, we presume that the proposed curators (not only men, but women as well) will not be just formal officials, but will be really spiritually advanced and experienced advisers in questions of education.

Moreover, the idea of pacifism should not be considered as something passive and therefore negative, but as pure, active peace creation. Therefore, in general, it is advisable to replace the rather specific expression "pacifism" by the beautiful word "peace-building."

Certain information about the legends you may gather from the essay of N.K., "The Soul of the People." Naturally, in every country, in epos, the people have their own heroes who are particularly dear to them. Therefore, you should never limit the imagination of the young generation, and should let young people show interest in whatever inspires them most for heroism, for good. But in what costumes or in which century certain heroic deeds were performed really does not matter! When you study the books of Living Ethics, you will find many precious ideas on all these problems, as they are discussed very broadly.

Verily, your country should be welcomed, now that such an idea as "The Sisters of the Golden Mountain" is already materializing. Are not the nurses you mention representatives of General Good and of a New Era? It is excellent that you have your little community which trains itself in spiritual discipline and where all help one another to practise good deeds and to realize the ideal of joy as "special wisdom." You know how essential it is to develop the initiative and to encourage every good possibility, as nothing is impossible for those who are facing the Infinite, regardless of how difficult everyday life may be. It is correct that you are cultivating your thoughts for the coming generations, as it is only for the future that we preserve the Covenants of the past. And in the name of these luminous Covenants, which will open every heart and will materialize our hopes, we send you our greetings. Only culture, the most lofty, most refined, will conquer all the unnecessary, disturbing distinctions, and will create that beautiful army of Spirit which, in active peace-building, will create the luminous future of humanity.

4

15 January 1932

Once more I wish to tell you how happy I was to learn about your program. When I recall that among your members there are country and city teachers who spend a third of their salary in order to be able to travel to your meetings, I feel touched. Once more it is proved that the best thoughts and deeds are not born amidst abundance and luxury.

It is perfectly right that you pay so much attention to children's and youth's literature. This is a most essential problem, as not only in childhood but later on a person's mentality depends very much on the first, and therefore strongest, impressions. So often a good book could correct the results of imperfect surroundings of the family! Certainly there are many valuable books in the literature of the past. It is only necessary to choose correctly, and particularly to discard what is harmful.

Almost everybody knows that the material and spiritual welfare of whole countries depend on foundations built into the consciousness of children. Nevertheless, almost nothing is done in this direction. I agree with you that books which deal with heroic deeds are most essential. Such books can influence a child's mentality and will guard against the terrible evil of today: the *superficial* attitude toward sacred concepts and the inferior quality of thought. Due to this, the whole structure of life is being built on sand, and it will crumble and disintegrate with the first shock.

Teach children to understand the significance of each thought and each action, as well as of each manifestation of nature, which has its unfailing laws. Tell them that the violation of these laws is strictly punished. Point out that the vitality and creativeness of people, as well as of other creatures of the kingdom of nature, depend on the invisible world and the invisible vibrations of the great spiritual Sages of the past and present. Children are ready to accept the invisible as reality because their minds are not yet demoralized by destructive doubt. Moreover, today there are so many experiments with rays which prove the subtle influence of the invisible. Even such an example as photographic negatives will be most convincing to the child's mind. The most complicated scenes may be on a negative, but unless it is chemically developed, they will not be visible! Likewise, a sensitive film records the most distant stars which cannot be perceived through the strongest telescope. The same is true about scientific records of other manifestations invisible to the physical eye. It is necessary to impress upon the child's mind most emphatically the existence of the subtle spheres that surround us; and to eradicate the terror of death and of contact with the Subtle World. The Subtle World is as unavoidable as our earthly life, and when realized, being the sublimation of the earthly world, it will open to us unutterable beauty. Therefore, you must teach children not to be frightened by death, which is an illusion, and not to be afraid of so-called "ghosts." Usually children who have an open psychic sight are not afraid of what they see until the grown-ups influence them either by their mocking attitude or by their stories about ghosts and "that deadly cold of the grave." This "deadly cold" is nothing but a simple chemical reaction of the contact of the subtle with the gross.

I am glad that you have certain perceptions of the Subtle World. It seems that your explanations are right, as the seer, judging by his own spirit, knows better. The symbols are very individual, and they correspond with the consciousness of a person. Very often the same symbol has an entirely different meaning for each of two people. Listen to your heart and you will not be mistaken!

5

24 November 1932

Thank you for your confidence. The account of your life touched me very much, as all your aspirations are extremely dear to me. What work can be higher than the healing of physical and mental disorders? And especially during this fearful time of disunion and the threatening signs of new, still-unknown epidemics. I am sure that you will find a spiritual approach in treating the diseases of the body. May I wish you all success in your tasks.

I welcome the idea of our dear Felix Denissovitch to give you such responsible and important work as to bring together many scattered little cultural societies and unite them under the one League of the Banner of Light. Of course, I agree with all my heart regarding your ideas concerning the League of Culture. The dome of culture is all-embracing; the League of Culture is like a great temple in which everyone who wishes to practise self-perfection and serve humanity will find his place. Everyone with the right desire for self-perfection—let it be in science, in art or in other fields—is already contributing a stone toward the building of the great future League of Culture. May all such masons gather, and let there be no boundaries, no narrow limits in your work! Whoever wishes to give his best, whoever thinks of his fellow men has a place in this temple. It is quite desirable to include various groups of cultural workers, and it would be excellent if different nationalities could be included. All the societies ought to maintain their original names and should only add the title "League of Culture." If for some reason this is not desirable, they may simply make known their affiliation with the League.

In this manner all the individuals of the various organizations will become members of the World League of Culture.

Now I shall mention the various societies which may be considered eligible for affiliation with the League of Culture.

First—peace societies; second—societies for spiritual development, which includes the study of religion and philosophy; third—representatives of the sciences; fourth—arts; fifth—motherhood and education; sixth—crafts and labor; seventh—cooperation and industry; eighth—security; ninth—agriculture and architecture; tenth—health and safety. It is easier to cut than to add; therefore such wide scope is given you. Take advantage of a big program and do not be discouraged by small disagreements. The ability to yield is absolutely necessary, especially in the beginning. Therefore, practise patience and tolerance. With tolerance, with kindness and patience, it is possible to change the most stubborn opponents. I quite approve of your "cup of tea"—moderate, clean food never will be an obstacle, and, as you say, it might create certain intimacy.

Of course, you realize that every start should have its focus of unification, and blessed are those who will understand and accept it, as this would strengthen their own position. It is so important to strengthen the achievements. So, good luck to you! Start to unify, applying broadly the principle of tolerance, the canon "By thy God." But beware of betrayers, for great is the infection from them. It is our duty to protect all who have joined us in trust under the dome of the Temple of Culture! Weakness and non-resistance to evil is not for us. When necessary, we raise the sword of the indignant spirit and defend that which is entrusted to us.

A great task is given to you. Let us sincerely collaborate in this difficult but joyous task! Bright is the future! Joyous is labor in the name of Beauty!

6

1933

I hasten to answer your questions about obsession. All your questions are correct. One should know that there are a great number of these cases. There are many kinds and degrees of obsession. And the obsessors themselves can be of the most varied order.

We knew, for instance, one pious old lady who was possessed by her great-grandfather—a bishop. There was nothing bad in the old lady. She was a charity worker and was preaching the ideas of her great-grandfather, the bishop, who apparently did not fulfill his mission during his life. Nevertheless, such cases are very sad, as an obsessed person *always* gradually loses his own will and becomes a victim of the obsessor. The whole life of such a victim is spent without any true achievements and accumulations. People are so afraid to lose their individuality and freedom of will. At the same time, most of those who are so "conscious of individuality" do not possess it (in the real sense of the word), and—even more often than ordinary people—are possessed. Most people think that individuality is just strongly expressed selfhood. It would be quite interesting to ask a number of people how they understand individuality. The answers would be most curious!

Regarding the League of Culture and the Woman's Unity, do not be disappointed by the slow development. Nothing should be forced. First of all, only a very small group is necessary. Very carefully test the newcomers. It is a great art to know how to talk to people according to their consciousness, to give them no more and no less than they can assimilate at the moment.

As to calumny and slander, knowing that it comes almost always from envy, you should react very quietly; but you should try to ascertain its source. To know the enemy is already half the victory. You must always remember that a true individualist will never listen to aspersions, rather he will never judge a person by them, neither will he himself cast a slur upon others.

It would be very desirable if the members of the Woman's Society could start their work with the tasks of self-perfection and self-education, and would try, with united efforts, to apply them in life. In the coming era of the Mother of the World, great numbers of cultured women are needed—women educated in various branches of knowledge, arts, crafts, etc. Every woman should be also a trained nurse, or at least should know elementary hygiene and medicine. In addition, would it not be wonderful if they could learn also spiritual healing?

Why gather into groups and societies if there is no desire for self-perfecting and for giving willing help to one's fellows?

Certainly they are not gathering for frivolous gossip and conventional parties! All newcomers should realize the threatening time and meet it fully prepared. It is necessary to broaden the consciousness, to observe events, and to realize how unusual is the time. Therefore, I think that firstly such groups should consist of those who are already acquainted with the principles of the Living Ethics. And above all, do not solicit. People thus drawn in will be of no use. As always and in everything, quality is important, not quantity.

It would be possible to suggest many activities, but unless they are realizable by the consciousness of the members, nothing can come of it. It is important that members should develop independence of thought, in order to be fruitful. We see it every day. We see how long it takes even the advanced disciples to realize the given Teaching. It strengthens our thoughts, which, of course, for quite some time were already directed by the Loving Hand, without any forcing of the process of assimilation.

So please do not be disappointed by the slow progress. The time will come when your ark will not be big enough to shelter all those who seek salvation. And the impure will be in greater numbers than the pure. And you, the Noah of today, will be in a rather difficult position! Your work is most valuable, and we greatly appreciate it. It would be desirable to have more such workers!

7

27 January 1933

Heartiest thanks for your letter, in which you express such lovely aspirations. I shall try to answer all your points.

1. Your opinion that the League of Culture may be opposed by "strong individualists" certainly could concern only the very ignorant who do not realize what the idea of the League of Culture really is. However, if you explain that the League of Culture has in mind the refinement of consciousness by means of real spiritual enlightenment and therefore cannot disturb true individuality, hardly anybody could insist upon opposite, ignorant concepts. No refinement of thought, in fact, is possible without a distinct individuality. The trouble is that people

always mix individuality with selfishness. The latter excludes cooperation, and is therefore unsocial.

It is most essential to learn to discriminate between these entirely opposite conceptions: selfishness and individuality. Selfishness is the most terrible scourge of humanity, the source of destruction, and, first of all, self-destruction. Selfishness is a dead separatism. The old truth about the unity of Cosmos and its humanity being an integral whole is very poorly realized, but it should finally reach the consciousness of the people. What would happen if someone tried to separate or isolate one organ of the body from the whole organism? Individuality is a life-holding receptacle. Individuality is beauty, is the crown of man, the synthesis of all his accumulations. But how can he accumulate if he separates himself from all other life-holders? Individuality is as honey, gathered by the man-bee from the best flowers, and of different meadows. But what kind of honey can a person gather who locks himself in the darkness of selfishness?

The thought about the League of Culture is more than timely. There are stupendous, lifeless manifestations of selfishness on one side, while on the other is the terrible, grossest materialism, which denies the creative fire of spirit, which depersonalizes and equalizes by reducing man to nihility. The League of Culture should introduce educational problems in the light of this new spirituality. Thus, it would give the growing generation a new comprehension of education and a real appreciation of the true values of the human spirit, which in most cases are entirely forgotten. And so, let the League of Culture consist of very small groups. In time they will develop, but let these groups realize the tremendous significance of their task. Threatening and merciless is our time, and the conscious elements of every country should use all possible spiritual means in order to be able to stand against subversion. No doubt everyone is looking for some outlet from this bewilderment, but the majority run after mechanical solutions, forgetting that the true change can come only by means of the expansion of consciousness and by the acceptance of spiritual leadership. As it is said: "Only by broadening the consciousness is it possible to solve the problems of life. One can see how mechanical hypotheses ensnare the hopes of people. This is what was known by the ancients as *Maya*, which could be destroyed by the slightest blow."

2. You write that the members of your groups greatly differ.

But you should not worry about this; neither should you criticize it. Each one has his own approach. Again, I may quote the words of the Teaching: "Some choose the easiest, others prefer the most difficult. Some cannot speak but are most sharp-sighted. Others have the gift of words and fly after them. Some realize the most significant, but there are others who prefer to remain on the fringe. Endlessly We can enumerate these differences, but only the fire of the heart will justify the person. Thus, We shall never tire to repeat about variety. The gardener knows how to mix his plants; otherwise he would not be the master of the garden."

Pay attention to the words: "only the fire of the heart will justify the person." Therefore, particular care should be taken where the fires of devotion are kindled. Never mind if in the beginning they are somewhat fanatical. When the disciples will better comprehend the Teaching of Life their consciousness will broaden and they will be kindled by *real* devotion, which actually is a sublimation of fanaticism. Precious are the kindled fires! The disciples are quite right in their desire to give up all reading and concentrate only upon the books of the Teaching in order not to divide their thinking. For the serious student who wishes to become a disciple of the High Hierarch (and not to remain just among the listeners), such complete immersion in the first steps of devotion is most essential, and it should be continued until the complete realization is reached. Otherwise, how can a disciple create unity of consciousness with his Teacher? How else can he create the silver cord which unites him with his Teacher? As you already know, this union with the Teacher opens up all the possibilities. And this union is created by stubborn efforts and by the unfailing striving toward the One Focus. Similarly, a tender plant is fenced about so that nothing can harm its growth.

Those who memorize the words of the Teaching are not so wrong. In school, the pupils learn things by heart in order to strengthen their memory. Even so, when the Teaching is burning in one's consciousness, it can be affirmed by short, firm formulae. For some, it is easier to grasp the sense by memorizing the original. Do not prevent anyone from following the path of his karma! "Better not to compel when a person's own fires are burning"—so speaks the Teaching.

Therefore, you are right in not stifling these fires of devotion;

let them burn. Their very burning is already a purification of the surrounding atmosphere. And who knows how many other little fires they may kindle without even knowing it! Strong is the power of the fires of the heart, even though invisible.

In the East, people assure one that the presence of a Bhakti Yogi in a given locality purifies and sanctifies for a distance of many miles, and all neighboring villages are spiritually uplifted. Thus, let us appreciate every manifestation of selfless love.

3. Now your question about how to acquire the right information on the events. I shall answer by the words from the Teaching:

"The Guru may ask his disciple, 'What are you doing... what do you desire... what torments you... what gives you joy?' These questions will not indicate that the Guru is unaware of his disciple's condition. On the contrary, with complete knowledge, the Guru wishes to see what the pupil himself regards as most important. Through lack of experience, the pupil may indicate the most insignificant of all circumstances. Hence, the Teacher does not inquire merely out of politeness, but as a test of the consciousness of his disciple. Therefore one should carefully weigh one's replies to the Teacher. Not the so-called amenities but a constant broadening of consciousness is the Teacher's concern.

"The pupil must also remember about divisibility of the spirit. One must strive in consciousness so as to realize in spirit the presence of the Teacher." [Fiery World II]

You should read in the Teaching about the divisibility of spirit. Like everything else it has its various degrees; but sometimes in its crowning development it becomes of cosmic scale, and then its applications are really of many kinds. Not always is it possible to impress upon the physical brain everything in detail, as in the polluted earthly atmosphere the heart could not stand it. Nevertheless, the essence of events is felt acutely. For instance, practically always N.K. and I know the acute moments in the lives of our co-workers. Sometimes it is a concrete knowledge; at other times it is certain painful impressions precisely corresponding in dates with certain events. Often we know the results quite far in advance. Just as often, we feel as if our psychic energy is departing. Sometimes it is so strong that we even feel dizziness and a transient absence. Then we know for sure that our energy was needed elsewhere. Manifold are the manifestations of divisibility of spirit!

Many mysteries are in the life of the disciple. The real discipleship refines all the reactions of a disciple. Verily, he becomes a golden harp under the Hand of the Teacher. So much joy there is in the unified consciousness. We have many cases—rather, they are constant—when we see the proof of such unity with our old co-workers. Often, we hear their voices and know about their troubles. We also see the sculpture of their spirits. Our letters always answer their needs, although you know what distance separates us.

Many miracles are around us; we must only notice them. Verily, wonderful is the life of a disciple. But it is not so easy, for he carries a tremendous responsibility and there are so many difficulties, especially in the days of Armageddon when all the dark forces try to attack him. But with the development of consciousness these very difficulties become joyous because the heart is so full of devotion to the Teacher and wants to prove in reality this devotion by overcoming all the difficulties. Self-sacrifice becomes so natural, so full of joy. The whole spirit is already separated from earthly things and realizes where its true home is. The only thing left is an ardent desire to fulfill the mission as well as possible, to justify the confidence of the Teacher, without any care for the results. They say in the East, "We must work without thinking of results." I understand it this way: we must learn to do our work as well as we can because of love and not for the reward. Only then will our work be beautiful. The key to all achievements is in such selfless love for every work we undertake.

4. Now about your remark that "the Teaching covers the whole of life and is not just enclosed within a number of books." I must agree, life is the best teacher, and without life nothing can be learned. But someone has to open our eyes, and without the leading Principle all evolution would be retarded for endless centuries. Therefore, the books of the Teaching are so essential. In concise formulae here is collected the profound knowledge and the manifold experience of ages. In the books of the Teaching a studious disciple will find answers to the most complicated problems of life, which are explained from various points of view, as well as many concrete affirmations in all branches of science. And the correct approach to science comes only after the firm

many-sided comprehension of the Teaching. Only then can we concentrate on the most essential, without spending long years on the wrong path.

The books of the Teaching, which, of course, include all the pearls of the East as well as *The Secret Doctrine* and *The Mahatma Letters*, give real food to the spirit and mind; and it is doubtful *whether one life is enough to study them all well*. Thus, knowing *The Secret Doctrine*, even if not perfectly, we rejoice when we see the new discoveries in science more and more confirming what was given to us in these volumes. Therefore, I personally prefer to inform myself thoroughly with the Teaching. This will save one from backwardness, or from something still worse—being incorrect in one's own calculations. We are ready to welcome all branches of science, especially if free from orthodox scientific limitations. Prejudices and superstitions in science can be even stronger than in religion! But to be liberated from such prejudices and superstitions is possible by following the way of the Teaching, which points out clearly and firmly the ascension to the synthesis of true knowledge.

So, try carefully to discriminate in questions of superstition and prejudices! And please do not conclude that I am in general against other books. But I must admit that there are not many good books, and even the best often contain together with beautiful pages a lot of harmful nonsense. Therefore, it is most important to cultivate an open, unprejudiced consciousness and to be able to discriminate.

It seems to me that I have answered all your questions. Please remember that I am always glad to answer as much as I can. If you do not agree—object. Exchange of opinions is always useful, as it sharpens the thoughts.

And so, let us desist from all forcing and manifest a maximum of tolerance, care and benevolence. Let everyone develop according to his abilities. Only careful touches are permissible; otherwise, we may frighten a nightingale who visits our garden!

8

10 May 1933

Do not avoid sleep. Sleep is beneficial and absolutely necessary for the nourishment of our subtle body. Only during sleep can we easily exude it and nourish it intensively with the finest energies, to say nothing about the great lessons we receive while in this state. Not only do we learn to merge into different spheres, but we also fulfil the commissions of our Teachers, and often we participate in battles with the dark forces. Why should we deprive ourselves of such a great privilege, which first of all is given to the disciples of the Great White Brotherhood? Everything artificial is against the Teaching of Light. If it is necessary to decrease our food, our organism will indicate it. The same is true about sleep. Often the work in the Subtle World is more significant than the work in the physical world.

The Teaching says that on the border of sleep we enter the worlds above the Earth. And this should come about quite naturally. We only have to train ourselves to be on guard, to be attentive, and the Subtle Worlds will open to us and, at the right moment, we will hear and see as is necessary. When I wanted to hasten my own experiment, which was practised under the supervision of the Teacher, I used to ask, "What am I to do? Which regime is best for the purpose?" etc. I always received the same reply: "Just be serene." In this serenity and balance lies the whole secret of achievement. And now, in the days of the terrific battle between the Forces of Light and the dark ones, we always hear the same thing: "Be careful, guard your health; this is the most important."

You should also remember that the currents are very heavy now, and all sensitive organisms react by experiencing periodic anguish, dizziness and depression. But, knowing the reason for such depression, you should patiently await the change of currents, or rather their new alternation. And so, my dear, do not consider these times of periodic anguish and depression as plungings of your spirit, that is, of failure and instability. Much more often, this is just the result of these interchanging currents. It is indicated: "These currents are like the clanging of swords." Let us always remember about the great happiness of being co-workers of the Forces of Light. The name of the Great Teacher, pronounced with love, will always protect us.

The Teaching has never mentioned the desirability or possibility of doing without sleep. The only thing that was just mentioned was that on heights of twenty-one thousand feet it is almost possible to do without it. But where are there people who live, and who can live on such heights? Passing across such altitudes during our traveling in Central Asia we experienced the truth of what was said, but living in the valleys requires sleep. For instance, when we stayed in cities we were told to sleep not less than seven or eight hours. The same is true about food. On heights, the quantity of food should be reduced; and this is done quite naturally because the organism does not require much. But in the polluted cities food is necessary.

Also, on a height of seven thousand feet, during a great experiment with fiery energies, it was indicated to put on weight, so that the nerves should not be too much exposed. In ancient Teachings the "Golden Mean," or *Equilibrium*, was indicated. And those who wanted to approach the great knowledge were expected not to go to any extremes. Nothing is so much distorted as this concept of *Equilibrium*. It seems to me that this has happened, and still happens, mainly because of the difficulty for people to practise discipline. It is much easier to go to extremes and to start exhaustive fasting, to encumber oneself with fetters—in general, to practise austerities—than to achieve vigilance and self-control together with complete preservation of strength. But without self-control nothing is possible.

And again I must add that, while food and sleep are absolutely necessary, there are different norms for different organisms. It is advisable to take as a warning sign a decrease of strength; and this decrease may not become evident until after some time, then appearing all of a sudden. Therefore, avoid declines and with all your might try to preserve the precious substance of the fiery energy.

9

19 June 1933

I received your "Address to Women" and must say that I greatly approve of it. This is just what is necessary and, as you say, it will appeal to the consciousness of people. Of course, it is necessary to spread this address as widely as possible so that the ideas will be assimilated by many. Time is so short, and sometimes I am afraid we shall not be able to fulfill everything. The New World is coming and we must prepare groups of people who will be able to introduce the new concepts. The awakening of woman is taking place all over the world. Already, from 1920, the women of the Far East have begun the struggle for their rights, and the same is true of the women of India. Indian women, in spite of difficulties, are achieving wonderful results.

* * *

In the sentence you bring to my notice, I would rather that you replace the word "militant" by the word "aggressive"—if you have nothing against it. First, because in this particular case the word "aggressive" will have a greater sweep, and, secondly, because I personally am too fond of the concept of the warrior and cannot use it in a negative sense. In all religious Teachings the people who start upon the spiritual path are called warriors. All Bodhisattvas, and even the most sacred images of Buddha have in their hands, or by them, a sword—as an imprescriptible attribute.

Let us recall our own saints—Michael, the Archistrategist, and St. George, the Victorious. Also the great Educator and Protector of the Russian Land, Saint Sergius of Radonega—did he not bless Prince Dmitry at the commencement of the great historical struggle against the Tartars, and did he not send his own monks to help? Verily, are not all the *Heroic Sages* warriors for the General Good? And do we not often hear about the luminous arrows sent against darkness and the satanic hordes? The struggle against chaos is the very foundation of the life of the Cosmos. And this struggle, in *proportion with ascent*, is increasing in tension and is changed only in *quality* and *motives*. Nothing can be compared with the rigor of the struggle against the invisible chaos!

I shall quote a page from the Teaching:

"Some people may think—how easy it is for the Lords, when They have passed beyond the boundaries of earthly burdens! But whoever says this does not know the scope of reality. Precisely as it is upon Earth, so also in Heaven. The earthly burdens pass away, but incomparable cosmic cares take their place. Truly, if it is difficult on Earth, then so much more difficult is it in Heaven. Let us not count the moments of Devachan, when illusion may conceal tomorrow's labor. But in action amidst chaos, it cannot be easy. You suffer from darkness and chaos. In all abodes it is as difficult from many aspects of darkness and the same chaos. But, fortunately for you, you only feel the attacks of chaos and do not see its murky movements. Truly, it is difficult for people because of their ignorance and their servility to darkness. But it is more difficult when one sees the movements of the masses of matter being turned into chaos. When the destructive subterranean fire tries prematurely to pierce the earthly crust, or when layers of gasses poison the space, the difficulty surpasses all earthly imagination. Not burdens, but only comparisons help now to speak about the difficulties. For ignoramuses think that hymns and harps are the lot of Heavenly Dwellers. Such error must be dispersed. Nowhere are there indications that it is difficult only upon Earth; in comparison it must be said—if here one is annoyed by devils, the Archangel is threatened by Satan himself. Thus one must understand action and the everlasting battle with chaos. One must realize it as the only path and grow to love it as the sign of the Creator's trust." [Fiery World II]

That is why I am so fond of the word "warrior" and admire every heroic and courageous deed. By nature, I myself am quite courageous and militant. Nowhere is it said that we should practise non-resistance to evil. And did not Christ Himself drive away those who scoffed at and violated the sacredness of the Temple?

Therefore, every mother must bring up her children in the spirit of great deeds, heroism and self-denial for the General Good. This is not approval of war in its usual sense; but we cannot deceive ourselves—we do live in the midst of the most dreadful and ruinous wars of all kinds. But the spiritual war is far more exacting than any other war. That is why it is so important to cultivate courage and fearlessness, the qualities which the disciple of the Masters of Light should first of all develop. However, if there is a strong bond with the Hierarchy, courage and fearlessness come absolutely naturally, as the Hand of the Hierarch will always hold back the final danger and will point out the way to victory. But I repeat, this is only so when the Image of the Master is constantly kept in mind. More than once have we had the opportunity of experiencing this wonderful influence. In a moment of danger we would become suddenly and amazingly serene and we knew that everything would be concluded perfectly.

I, personally, prefer a courageous self-sacrifice in the performance of one's patriotic duty to such an attitude as that of the contemporary youth of a certain country which was expressed recently in a resolution not to fight for their country in time of war. You may ask, "What about the Banner of Peace?" And you might even think that I am a secret supporter of war! No, for me war is unspeakably dreadful. I cannot imagine a manifestation of worse ignorance! But since we live in a world where physical power is still highly respected, we have to instill into the young generations the idea of the *illegality of killing and violence.* At the same time we must teach not to be afraid to perform one's duty for one's country, as this is beautiful and courageous. Who would wish to be a defenseless sheep in front of a wolf or a tiger? But tigers and wolves are lurking in every unprotected corner. Until there is real cooperation among the peoples we shall be under the threat of constant wars and invasions. Only the World League of Culture, correctly understood, could solve for the future the many problems which seem insoluble today.

* * *

Let women remember about courage, so necessary for them in the fight for their lawful rights. But let them not understand courage as violence, as in the case of the suffragettes who used to break windows and burn mail boxes! Such measures are very ugly, but there are other ways of showing real courage. First of all, it will be in firm striving toward knowledge and beauty directed toward the General Good.

* * *

Now let us talk about straight-knowledge. Someone has said, "Often a simple woman has a better sense of straight-knowledge than a woman-graduate of a university." Here I must remark, "Such a woman is 'simple' perhaps in the sense of not possessing social position or education, but not simple in the sense of lacking spiritual serenity." People often confuse great straight-knowledge, which is a result of many experiences (of many incarnations), with a certain psychism. The latter manifests itself in more or less correct presentiments, dreams and certain perceptions of the astral plane, according to the consciousness. On the other hand, straight-knowledge knows unfailingly, knows just the essence of things, the direction of evolution, as well as the future. Straight-knowledge is the synthesis of spirituality and, of course, only a developed spirit with an accumulated Chalice possesses it, regardless of how modest his or her position is in life. Often the modest position is purposely chosen for a certain mission. The one who listens to the voice of his heart will the more easily awaken his straight-knowledge. The heart is the best instructor in all the problems of life.

* * *

And now let us turn to the subject of abortion. To deal with this problem now is quite timely. There appear currently the most disgusting articles about it and some of them are written with the approval of the clergy. On this subject I shall quote some paragraphs from the Teaching:

"The spirit is connected with the embryo at the moment of conception. It begins to enter in the beginning of the fourth month when the first nerve and brain channels are being formed. The formation of the vertebral column brings in the next degree of possession of the body. Wonderful is the moment of birth, when the consciousness of the spirit flashes up brightly and then blends with matter. There are even cases when words are pronounced at birth. The final possession of the body takes place at the seventh year of a child's life." It is also said, "Even as hunger directs toward food, so the spirit is directed toward incarnation, as only matter can give the new impulses."

Therefore, it is not hard to imagine how much suffering the spirit that is ready to incarnate endures from the forced interruption of life already begun, or from the averting of an incarnation even planned by karma. What a difficult karma the ignorant and criminal parents prepare for themselves!

* * *

I will venture to add several words about the art of N.K. His art is valued for purity, translucency and an endless diversity of color combinations which go together with an unusual power and depth of tone. Each painting is a beautiful symphony of color consonances. We know that the colors, the shades and their harmony create an occult impression upon the viewer. It is known that beautiful paintings have the power of healing, and we have had many opportunities to witness this. But, of course, for such reactions one must have "an open heart and an open eye." As it is said, "It is possible to remain in full darkness even while facing the most beautiful art creations, if darkness is in us."

But no less attention should be paid to the quite exceptional gift of N.K. in composition, which, by the way, is very rare. All strange—to put it mildly—deviations in the life of art, which we notice periodically, come mainly because of this lack of the gift of composition. But each creation of N.K. is striking by its harmony in the combination of all its parts, and this harmony carries real conviction. Nothing can be added, nothing can be taken away. Everything is just right. This harmony of form and color, this mastery, is that gift which is characteristic of a great creator. The creations of N.K. are also dear to me because of the beauty of their thought, expressed in majestic but simple and sometimes profoundly touching images.

For me, a constant witness of his art, it is a source of endless amazement—this inexhaustible thought combined with daring and unexpected color combinations! Just as remarkable is the ease and certainty with which he calls forth his images. They truly speak, live on his canvases, and very seldom has he had to change something or to abandon the first sketch. Verily, in watching the process of his work one does not know which is more amazing—the beauty of the painting or the virtuosity of its execution.

* * *

I do not agree that the Greek art is lacking in spirituality. I think that the spirituality of ancient Greece was higher than ours, which is proved by their high philosophy and by the contributions of their greatest workers, creators and thinkers. Their philosophy put great ideas into lovely forms. It seems to me that we are the ones who have lost spirituality and therefore the ability and sense to appreciate beauty. Because of the fact that art expresses the character of its people and the conditions of nature in which it originated and developed, very often it is not understood by other peoples who live and create in different environments. For instance, the marble statue of the Greeks may be out of place in our northern clime, but it was lovely under the bright sun, on the purple sands, and with a background of turquoise waters and the dark cypresses of Greece.

Art, in all its manifestations and in all its conventional forms, remains basically spiritual. It awakens our longing for beauty, for the Highest; and here is its chief and great significance. As you correctly write, "The true problem of art is to move man toward the comprehension of beauty." Verily, the true striving toward the beautiful will lead us to the understanding of the higher beauty of the laws which rule the Universe and are expressed in the Perfect Mind and the Perfect Heart.

* * *

And so, fulfil your great mission to restore physical health and to sow the seeds of spiritual knowledge wherever it is possible. The main thing is—*do it according to the consciousness of your patients!* To give too much is still more dangerous than to give too little. Consult your heart!

Do write about yourself and remember that our thoughts are often with you. Tell friends to drive away all doubts, as these are our most dangerous enemies! And what doubts can we have when the pure Teaching gives us such clear and most beautiful solutions, where nothing and nobody is belittled but everything is elevated and broadened infinitely. May the Blessing of the Forces of Light be with you!

10

8 February 1934

Your excellent work brought great joy to us. It is just what is particularly necessary today. We must awaken the consciousness of people, which stagnates in musty prejudices and is depressed by the threatening events. The dawn of the New Era already shimmers in the distance, and it is essential to be able to face it with the new, awakened spirit. I am looking forward to the continuation of your work, which should be printed and widely distributed.

"It may be proposed to co-workers that they accustom themselves to such work. They can select portions of the Teaching near to them, and compare them with other Covenants. In this way there can be observed the imprint of the times upon the very same truths. The task of investigating this evolution will in itself be a much-needed labor. We are opposed to condemnation, but the comparison will be, as it were, the polishing of the stone. Through love for the subject one can find new comparisons and beautiful points of contact. Such meditations are as flowers in a meadow." [Fiery World II] Keep this program in mind!

You write, "No wonder Christ did not find it possible to reveal this truth (the law of Reincarnation) directly and openly to the undeveloped human minds." But I think it would be more correct to say that although the law of Reincarnation was a cornerstone of every ancient religion of the East, and of course the religion of the Jews was no exception, already in the days of Jesus this law was badly distorted by the priesthood and maintained its purity only among individual sects. In the New Testament we have plenty of proof regarding this knowledge of the Jews; Christ Himself confirms it. For instance, in the Gospel of St. Matthew (17:10-13), "And his disciples asked him, saying, why then say the scribes that Elias must come first? And Jesus answered and said unto them, Elias truly shall first come, and restore all things. But I say unto you, That Elias is come already, and they knew him not, but have done unto him whatsoever they listed. Likewise shall also the Son of man suffer of them. Then the disciples understood that he spake unto them of John the Baptist." And, in the Gospel of St. John (9:1-3), "And as Jesus passed by, he saw a man which was blind from his birth. And his disciples asked him, saying, Master, who did sin, this man, or his parents, that he was born blind? Jesus answered, Neither hath this man sinned, nor his parents: but that the works of God should be made manifest in him." Indeed, how could a person blind from birth be responsible for his sins without the law of Reincarnation! There are other very clear hints, but you should find them for yourself.

You write that "the Eastern man became so passive because of his knowledge of reincarnation, and this finally resulted in a slowing of the tempo of life, stagnation and lifelessness." This is not quite so. Many other reasons are responsible for this stagnation. Of course, all that hardens and develops the strength of man—severity of nature, severity of climatic conditions and the struggle for existence in connection with this—is almost entirely absent in the East. On the other hand, climate and other conditions were favorable to the meditative life. But the real evil of India, which resulted in stagnation and degeneration, is not "in their knowledge of reincarnation" but in the dead system of castes. This system, with the loss of a real knowledge of the past and with the corruption of the governing class, became like an iron vise upon a most capable nation of teeming millions. Who has not lived in India is unable to imagine completely the terror of this slavery! At the moment, there are, apart from the four main castes, a vast number of all sorts of subdivisions—as many as there are occupations and professions. Each caste is limited by all sorts of absurd prohibitions, and the higher the caste, the more prohibitions; hence, the well-known degeneration of the higher castes.

Even if we take into consideration the unsurpassed heights of their main spiritual Teachings and, on the other hand, the covetousness and ignorance of most of their present priesthood, even then it is hard to understand how could such absurdity, such crying cruelty, such criminal monstrosity of forms take place! But such is the sad reality. Apart from the caste system, child marriages are bringing degeneration. It is not unusual to see a nine-year-old girl married to a sixty-year-old man and already a crippled mother of a stillborn child. Yes, there are many wonders in India, but also many terrible things! It is as if this would prove the law: "the brighter the Light, the deeper the darkness." That explains why nowhere else do you meet such spirituality and refinement as here. If this beautiful country could succeed in curing the dreadful scourge which is destroying it, the development of this country would amaze the whole world. There are some signs of revival. The woman of India is awakening and her heart reacts to the suffering of the degraded; therefore, she is destined to revive her country.

Always I shall be glad to help you in case of some questions and misunderstandings. Your work, in which you so clearly discuss the foundations of Being, is most precious, and we hope that you will continue to write along these same lines. The Teaching of Life indicates so many new, untouched themes!

We are happy to see you so able to apply the Teaching. Apply it freely and broadly; these seeds are given for great sowing. Moreover, much is given only in hints and is only slightly revealed but the broad masses need to be prepared and more detailed explanations are necessary in order to reach their receptivity.

The studying of the works of H.P. Blavatsky would help you very much to understand many things.

11

17 February 1934

Everything you say about the so-called occult groups does not surprise us but confirms what we expected, as we know of the sad situation within many organizations and we know that human nature is everywhere similar. The evil is always the same: lack of tolerance and a terrible exclusiveness which destroys all foundations. The presidents of numerous societies and lodges pretend to have an exclusive monopoly and authority over everything concerning the Teaching given by the Great White Brotherhood. In addition, some wish to be the sole channel through which the High Teaching may be introduced. But in the poverty of their imagination they fail to see that the Great Brotherhood, which leads the evolution of the whole of humanity, cannot limit itself to one or even ten currents or recipients who are, in any case, just temporary!

The Great Brotherhood is constantly working for the General Good of the whole world and, therefore, uses widely every possibility to reach through with their salutary Teaching. The vessel of humanity is sinking, and only the blind or stupid do not notice all the danger in the life of today.

Of course, the Great Hierarchy of Light has on the earthly plane co-workers of various degrees, conscious and unconscious, as well as the particularly trusted and dear ones. There are also quite a number of persons who receive beautiful messages often without even knowing the true image of their Messenger, but they all bring their seeds for the great sowing. It would be most ignorant to associate the Great Hierarchy of Light with any limitations or conventional forms! The Hierarchy lives and acts using the *law of great commensurability*, the only law which guarantees true evolution.

There is also no doubt that at the due time the Great Brotherhood selects one or two person for the renewal of the human consciousness and for introducing a new degree of the Teaching. This was the case with Blavatsky and, after her death, with Francia la Due, through whom the Master Hilarion gave his Teaching. Unfortunately, Francia la Due died in 1923. She was the founder of the society in California and the editor of the magazine *Temple Artisan*, in which the Messages were published. But I repeat that, apart from such main recipients who receive the "Ocean of the Teaching," as one of the Great Masters said, there are many others through whom are given individual small messages, and we know quite a number of fine little books, mostly written automatically or, which is rather rare, by dictation. And the beauty of the moral value of such books is not any the less because they are written without the approval of certain authorities! As far as I know, not one of these "authorities" during the whole of his lifetime was illumined by a single book given to them from the Great Source. On the contrary, such books were systematically criticized by them and were condemned and banned. Would it not be quite appropriate to inquire about this? Why do they not give the continuation of "The Book Dzyan"? And the continuation exists. It would also be interesting to know what such blasphemers of the Living Ethics (which they even did not study) think about the society founded by Francia la Due and William Dower and about the books which appeared through them. This society was founded in the nineties of the last century, and has its branches in other countries as well. The great Teaching which was given by them does not contradict the statements of the Living Ethics, and we are on friendly terms—we do not exclude each other! There is the Arcane School in the United States, which has special classes for studying the books of Agni Yoga. The books of Living Ethics are spread throughout many countries and are attracting many new groups. Today, there are many searching souls, but certainly intolerance will not attract anyone.

Some authorities after reading one book of Agni Yoga found great danger in it and forbade their followers to study it. Of course, we shall not try to find out in what they discovered this danger, as we never force the given Teaching. but those who were confused by this verbal statement may find out for themselves. What would these self-created authorities say (and one of them pretends that he belongs to the Great Hierarchy of the Sun) if we told them about the remarkable meetings and events we experienced and showed them the sacred things which were entrusted to us? Probably they would consider us to be impostors. And in their "righteous indignation" they would unite with the fanatics and bigots of the church, and together would fulminate and anathematize us now and forever!

It is a great pity that such valuable books as *The Mahatma Letters* and the *Letters of H.P. Blavatsky* are still not translated into Russian. They explain much about the environment of H.P. Blavatsky.

But all these aggressions are not important. What really is terrible is the intolerance of some churches. Verily, "most difficult of all is to reveal the true Image of Christ," as one of the

Great Teachers expressed it. The main cause of intolerance is ignorance. But things cannot continue this way, and the new generation already demands a new explanation of the problems of Being. If the spiritual authorities do not want to be entirely ignored, they should consider this demand and should be able to satisfy it. The consciousness of the masses grows and expands, and it is impossible to keep it locked within mediaeval torture chambers! The Western Church is also alarmed, but in order not to lose entirely its authority, it begins to watch the movement of science and even some of the Eastern Teachings. Some of the clergy even admit the existence of the Great Brotherhood. And truly speaking, what is the Hierarchy of Light if not "Jacob's Ladder"? Others pay attention to the law of Reincarnation. The New Testament, the words of Christ Himself, confirm this law, which was a cornerstone of all the most ancient religions. From these sources Christianity later borrowed all its symbols and ceremonies. A recent Conference of Bishops in the United States proposed to study the works of the great Origen. This is a great step forward, as the studying of Origen may broaden the ecclesiastical framework and its dogmas. We should not forget that the law of Reincarnation was rejected only in the sixth century by the Council of Constantinople. And we are supposed to accept as revelation and dogma the authority of the Fathers of the Church who, with great seriousness, discussed such problems as "How many spirits may be placed on the end of a needle?" or such similar pearls as "Has woman a soul?" And these reverend Fathers, the educators of our consciousness, did not hesitate to slap each other and tear each other's hair and beards! Even now, there are some people, quite educated in some respects, who sincerely believe that they will be raised from the dead in the last day of judgement—in their physical bodies! That is the main reason why they are so against cremation. How to understand this self-delusion, by hypnotism or by atavism?

It is time to understand that the world needs vivid souls, able to perceive quickly, intensely and profoundly that the essence of the events of today is evident proof of the uselessness of outlived ideas and structures, and that amid unprecedented destruction the new ideas of great tolerance and cultural leadership are engendered, like heat lightning against a black sky.

However, among the Russian Orthodox priests, we know of some thinking and broad-minded people. They were our real friends. I am sure that we shall find souls full of light in the New Country. Now, as regards the lodges of Freemasons. It is quite certain that among them are many that are purely political and very harmful. In some countries, with the rarest exceptions, Masonry has degenerated into buffoonery. Such a degeneration of originally highly moral and beautiful inceptions is very tragic, and the Great Teachers feel inexpressible grief because of it. Bear in mind also that today there is an unprecedented amount of the most terrible black magic and sorcery, and this is almost everywhere. Often, not bad but ignorant people are caught in this black trap. Therefore, the Great Teachers are against any kind of magic. The black lodges are very active just now; that is why the forces of Light should immediately unite and, with conscious activity, work against the dark forces of evil. But alas, at the moment there is much less unity among them than among the black ones. The latter are unified by fear, and thus they act, driven by it.

* * *

Certainly, blasphemy against the Teaching of Light is not a trifle, as this is blasphemy against the Holy Ghost. And dreadful is the destiny of such a blasphemer in all the worlds. But in order to paralyze the blasphemers it is necessary to educate the listeners. Great is the ignorance! This is proved on every step. However, sometimes complete ignorance is better than a little education, as small knowledge creates self-conceit and thus arrests all possibilities. People are accustomed to all sorts of prohibitions and limitations. And most of all, they are afraid of broad thinking because they sense that broad-mindedness will bring greater responsibility. And who wishes responsibility? Everybody tries to avoid it and to lean on somebody else. In general, if in due time there were fewer prohibitions and negations, and if the necessity of responsibility were strongly emphasized, many would avoid the cup of bitterness that they now have to drink. Therefore, the one advice could be given to all abnegators: Do not negate, but know more.

* * *

Great ignorance and an amazing poverty of imagination also is shown by those who can believe that all the volumes of the given Teaching are written by only one person, which would be impossible, regardless of how ingenious this person might be.

Verily, ages of experience of life and a tireless study of human nature, with all the cosmic influences upon it, are necessary in order to think of all the questions and problems introduced by the Teaching and to throw light upon them so completely and all-embracingly.

* * *

Verily, life is full of miracles if we approach everything with an open heart and with striving to beauty and self-perfection. And not by way of all sorts of artificial meditations and concentrations and other mechanical means, but in the great deed of everyday life. This great deed of life in all its severe beauty is practised by N.K. His life is the life of complete renunciation; he lives for the great service to humanity. Nothing belongs to him and he himself belongs not to himself. The greatest tolerance is his nature, and, like a magnet, he attracts the most diverse people and groups them around his name. The wisdom of the Master is his wisdom. Had it been otherwise, how could he be such a prophet? How could he succeed in the entrusted mission in spite of the dreadful obstacles which are raised by the dark ones at the end of Kali Yuga, during the dreadful Armageddon?

* * *

And now I must tell you how wise you are in being so careful with what is entrusted to you. But you ought not to be afraid of the enemies because they are the ones who attribute to us the most fantastic powers and possibilities, and in their furious anger they fail to belittle you; rather, in this way, they direct the attention of people to you. In our life we have met many enemies, but they have only increased our success. Let us remember what is said about slander in the books of the Teaching: "Let slanderers look over the list of everything slandered by them. Will it not contain the names of those who have contributed most to human evolutionary discoveries?... Therefore, let us define slander as the torches of savages. But during the night crossings each fire is of use!"

So we have learned by experience the usefulness of enemies. Therefore I shall finish by praising the enemies.

* * *

As regards the spreading of the Teaching, also do not be too disappointed. You should never force anyone. Only great harm comes from such pressure. Remember how the Teaching warns against anything forced: "The Teaching conscious of its knowledge, will not expose itself in the bazaar. ... There is but a fine line between affirmation and obtrusion. It is easy to degrade oneself to no avail. Every drop falling aside turns into burning acid. But a forced swelling means only dropsy, and you know that its cure is impossible. Therefore—only *quality*, not *quantity*.

"He who knocks takes the responsibility upon himself, but the forced one will be as a millstone on the neck of the bell-ringer. Therefore, ring the bell only at the right time. Thus you will avoid coercion." [New Era Community] And so, do not worry about the popularization of the Teaching of Light. The Teaching is spread in unexpected ways. Just keep your heart on guard; do not ignore the knocking of the sufferer and of the comer!

12

17 April 1934

Your letter came almost simultaneously with the grievous news about the passing of our dear, unforgettable Felix Denissovitch. We have lost a real friend and a devoted, self-denying co-worker. We had plenty of signs regarding the impending loss, and the brain tried not to accept it, but the heart was contracting in anguish. This loss is a great shock to all our friends and co-workers. As you say, he really could unify and warm with his heart... The best respect to the memory of F.D. will, of course, be the unification of all his co-workers and the strengthening and development of the great work begun by him. Therefore, I much appreciate that you feel such responsibility for all the works that have been started, and I hasten to answer all your questions in their order.

1. Of course, the Society for Unity of Women needs the hand of a woman. However, man's collaboration is not undesirable and can be most beneficial. Often, man is a better co-worker, apologist and defender of women's rights than many women.

2. The statutes about the Unity of Women which you worked out are beautiful, and may God help them materialize, even if only partially. I particularly approve the point regarding equal education for both sexes, or, as you call it, "equal rights." This is a very important matter. Equal education will eradicate the

harmful superiority toward women and will give a necessary balance in many other respects. Equality of rights for both sexes, as well as for all nations, should be one of the first foundations of each government. Everything concerning the upbringing and schooling of children is very dear to me, and I shall willingly share my thoughts about it with you.

3. You mentioned a most painful problem of today's life—the question of the legality of abortion. Of course, there are no two opinions on this subject: abortion is most definitely murder. Therefore, only in cases where the mother's life is in danger should it take place. But it is wrong to think that a woman who is guilty of abortion always attracts low spirits. The karma of the whole family should be taken into consideration. Often we can notice that in a family where one of the children is worthless the other children are not bad. Karma ties groups of people for long, long thousands of years. And often, even a high spirit has not unimpeachable, irreproachable parents. And it is significant that the dark forces are especially against the reincarnation of highly developed spirits, and they try their best to prevent the reincarnations that are dangerous for them. And, once more, it is not the purgatory of the Subtle World that prevents spirits from reincarnating, but only the crime of the parents. There is not a more powerful purgatory than the earthly life, if all the potentialities of the individuality are intensified. It is said in the Teaching, "As the one who hungers longs for food, even so, the spirit that is ready to incarnate longs for the new incarnation." Therefore, one can imagine what suffering the spirit undergoes by reason of artificial prevention. The spirit is connected with the embryo at the moment of conception, and gradually enters the body in the fourth month when the nerve and brain channels are being formed. Therefore, abortion is permissible only in exceptional cases.

4. Of course, woman should not only be a giver of physical life; she has her other high duties. And for that purpose there is the most natural abstinence, which can easily be practised and the increase of the family thus regulated. This is quite possible when high interests occupy the head and the heart. Of course, I expect plenty of opposition; still, I insist on it. No doubt, in the present state of the family it is quite difficult, but already there are such families and they will increase in the future. In remote antiquity, people knew how to regulate their families

by the phases of the moon. Later on this was considered black magic, but nowadays even such measures would be better than the dreadful abortions that cripple women and therefore the coming generations.

Now I shall discuss the two cases you mention in connection with this difficult problem. Your first case concerns a woman who "out of love for children" chose the profession of schoolteacher. The case is rather illogical. Since she considered it a prejudice to be afraid to have a child illegally, she should have abided by that opinion. And once she had decided to have an illegitimate child, she could not possibly expect it to be legitimatized. Moreover, she should have known the rules of the school; I cannot imagine that she did not know them. Thus, very much light-mindedness is manifested in this particular case, and I should say a very dangerous light-mindedness, as it ended in crime. But what seems most contradictory to me is her "deep love for children," as this very love should have stopped her from taking such a foolish step.

In wise India, the exclusive love for one's own child is considered as one of the types of animal egotism. When there are so many unfortunate orphans around us, can we be so indifferent as not to find great motherly feeling toward them? With "her deep love for children" could not this woman then adopt one of these unfortunate homeless orphans and thus satisfy her love for children? There would be so much nobility in such an act, and (who knows?) perhaps she would bring up her true son or daughter. Karma amazingly directs us toward souls that have bonds from the past with us.

You write that she had read *Sister Beatrice*. But Sister Beatrice was motivated by a powerful love, while this woman speaks only of a desire to have a child. It is inconsistent. I shall never throw a stone at a woman who neglected all conventionalities for the sake of her passionate love, provided that she does not build her happiness on the unhappiness of others. Obligations toward one's family and children I consider sacred.

In the second case which you describe, the woman deserves more sympathy. But in her case also, so long as the desire to have her own child was dominating, we can apply the wise saying about the egotism of such love. In order to be able to judge correctly, it is necessary to know first of all the real motives and circumstances. But always and in everything, it is most essential to have complete harmony between the heart and the intellect, this great balance which is the basis of perfecting and which is confirmed by all the great Teachings. A strong mother feeling cannot be limited by love for her own children only; such limitation should be outlived. And very often strangers by blood are more harmonious with us than our own children. Spiritual affinity is much stronger than the bonds of blood.

5. You ask, "Has every woman the right to have her own child?" If we discuss this question from the standpoint of Cosmic Right, then of course—yes. But as the cosmic laws have nothing to do with their man-made distortions, I shall have to say that not every woman has the right to have her own child. The conception of family is a sacred conception. But as things are now, there is nothing sacred in it, or almost nothing. Many families are sinful. And I repeat that I shall never condemn a woman who is sincerely absorbed in her love, as we know how many conventionalities and all kinds of circumstances interfere with the legalization of such unions; so much more sinful is it to punish a child born from such a union. But today, there are many men and women who do not deserve to have children because of their profound spiritual corruption.

6. The lines you quoted from the book of Ernst Bergman definitely reflect the ideas of the future, and correspond with the nearest problems. Is it not mentioned in the Teaching about the high significance of woman in all the activities of life? Is it not indicated that the cause of so many miseries of our planet and of humanity is because of the loss of balance between the two sexes? Cosmos is based on these Origins, and on the Cosmic Scale both Origins are equally great and necessary, for one cannot exist without the other. But what do we see in life and in its customs made by people? Woman in some countries is degraded to the level of slavery, and even in more civilized countries all privileges belong to man.

No doubt, in many respects, it is woman's own fault, especially now when she tries to imitate all the vices of man, instead of expressing her own character and originality. The result is an indecent caricature. Of course, there are no limitations in spiritual creativeness of either of the sexes. The creativeness of thought, art and construction of life are from the spirit and belong to both sexes. Both sexes have their characteristic features and this makes life more beautiful. And these features should be manifested most powerfully in order to revive the salutary beauty of romanticism and heroism. After the refinement of consciousness and sentiments, the beautiful destiny of both sexes will be vividly expressed.

In conclusion, I may tell you that many families have no right to such a term because they are united unlawfully. Verily, many unions which are legalized by all human laws should be considered illegal. True lawful union is a great science of the future. This science will be based on the immutable cosmic laws. Much was said and is said about the affinity of souls. But who knows and understands this truth in all the grandeur of Cosmic Law? You remember that in the books of the Living Ethics it is said that people should be united according to the elements. Only parents who belong to the same element can give life to healthy and well-balanced children. "And in life we often see that fire is united with water, or air with earth. The degeneration of entire nations is the outcome of such mixtures." The time will come when this truth will be understood in all its glory and people will apply it in life as the most essential. The forms of life and all functions of humanity must be rebuilt according to the laws of Cosmos—that is, if humanity cares to continue its existence and evolution on this planet—otherwise, the destiny of Lemuria awaits us, i.e. destruction by fire.

7. Certainly, I approve of the fight against abortion, but how will you fight this evil? There are no laws which can either preserve or forbid anything. That is why I, personally, think that first of all you must battle by uplifting the level of consciousness of the growing generations, directing it toward the right comprehension of the human cosmic mission in general and that of motherhood in particular. Thoughts should be directed toward creative work and broad problems of the General Good on a cosmic scale. It is important to establish the *world's scale*. Again, we return to the same fundamental question: *upbringing and education*. As the Great Mind expressed it, "The source of all suffering is ignorance," which is so true; and the history of humanity, with all its dark pages of persecution of the best representatives of knowledge, proves it.

8. Without doubt, every mother and every child have the right to security, and here also there is no place for dividing into legitimate and illegitimate. But we may go further and say that

every citizen has a right to security of work. So much has to be altered. And here the voice of the heart—woman—should help.

9. You ask, "Is it in the plan of the White Brotherhood to preserve the old family forms and to revive them spiritually?" Of course, the forms themselves are almost meaningless. The main thing is the spiritual consciousness which animates these forms. I already answered this question when I discussed the great science of the future, which is based on immutable cosmic laws. Therefore, we should not worry about the new forms, but should animate the old ones with the new understanding. I shall add these lines of the Teaching: "If, instead of so-called innovations and statutes, humanity would pay attention to cosmic laws, it would have been possible to establish the balance which is being more and more violated, beginning with the law of begetting and ending with cosmic crowning. The confirmed laws are unitary. Unity could be confirmed on all planes. The way of evolution is like a thread which goes through all the physical and spiritual degrees; therefore, governments and social systems can apply the cosmic laws for their improvement."

10. And now, as regards the groups. It is desirable to form the groups according to the level of consciousness. But the ideal way would be to group the people according to the composition or color of their auras because the ray which unifies harmonious auras acquires the power of increased attraction, whereas inharmonious combinations repulse. Two harmonized auras may guarantee success because the reaction of unified rays advances every undertaking. But as we are far from determining even the colors of auras, although there is some progress in this direction, the only thing we can do is to combine the people who are sympathetic to one another. The instructor should attentively watch the characteristics of his pupils.

In the Teachings of Life, there is an indications about this as well:

"The instructions should be goal-fitting. For the one who shows more progress, there should be created possibilities for further advancement. If the swiftest boat would lower its sails for the sake of straightening the front line, would this not involve a diminishing of its own possibilities? The teacher with a vigilant eye should discern those who are able to progress. They should not be praised but their path should be cleared. It is advisable to arrange intermediate courses; the pupils will then the more quickly ascend, using these steps. Do not conceal the difficulties from them! For a certain type of consciousness, every heroic movement is already a source of light and joy. It depends also upon the teacher to determine quickly the direction of the thoughts of the pupil, as a wrong viaticum is very sinful; it can drive away the best workers. Every static program is like a corpse, which is unbearable under the sun of knowledge."

You are quoting some paragraphs from the book *Agni Yoga*, correctly thinking that in arranging the groups it is necessary to follow these indications. It is necessary to remember that these indications have in mind three different groups. While in paragraph 137 the indications concern a very close group of the nearest co-workers, in paragraph 310 they concern people in general and not very close co-workers in particular, with whom tolerance should be practised, as it is taken for granted that the nearest co-workers do not "look in different directions" lest they illustrate the fable about the pike, crayfish and swan. Paragraph 311 is about a group which is still being formed and preparing to become united by the Teaching.

The unification of consciousness does not come at once. It is achieved by great effort. Much mutual patience, tact, sincerity and generosity should be practised. But when it is achieved, really everything becomes possible, as then comes the constant High Guidance.

But if it is difficult to collect harmonious groups, it is still more difficult to find a suitable instructor. It is particularly important to have already experienced teachers for the beginners. Of course, the abilities of the teacher are developed during the conjoint work. By the way, teachers often learn more from people whose consciousness is not very well developed than from those who are approximately on their own level. It is because the simple ones, in putting their questions, make us intensify our resourcefulness so that we can succeed in explaining according to their receptivity. As a result, we have a wonderful exercise in clear thinking. Verily, we learn while teaching.

Yes, in all questions, we should rely upon our straight-knowledge, or heart; there is no other measurement. Every case is entirely different and quite original, especially if there is an extraordinary concurrence of circumstances. And the heart must find the right decision for everything.

Now you are at the threshold of new, responsible work.

As you beautifully expressed it—the "Burning Heart," which knew how to give joy, has left us. But every one should learn to find this joy inwardly, as Light is within us. The "Burning Heart" kindled the fire. It is your duty, and that of the nearest co-workers, to preserve this fire and to fan it into an inextinguishable flame. The work that has been started is so great, so beautiful, so all-embracing and essential, that one should rejoice in the very fact that one is participating in it. What can be greater than work for the General Good and for the Hierarchy of Light?

Great events are about to come and many new workers will be necessary. Those who have assimilated the foundations of the Living Ethics should help to maintain the balance of life and confirm the coming epoch based on the true comprehension of the spirit of beauty and cooperation.

And so—good luck in your new task; be brave and joyous, as the Leading Hand will not leave those whose aspiration is sincere.

13

11 April 1934

You ask for advice on how to be most successful in work and in personal development. But, meanwhile, you have the books of the Living Ethics, in which are given the most precise indications and advice, and if at least one tenth of this is applied, good results will not be long in coming. I can only add that for the quickest self-perfecting and development of spirituality the most essential is a constant thought about the Highest Hierarch; this is the sacred concentration about which so much is written and which so often is misunderstood. Remembering the Luminous Image every moment of the day and night and doing all our work in His Name, we are gradually establishing the sacred union, which will finally give us the great power of Hiero-inspiration.

Knowing your literary talent, I would advise that you use it for the fiery invocations, for the awakening and reviving of spirit. Verily, the future lies in the resurrection of the spirit! After reading the books of the Teaching, you have realized, no doubt, what a crucial time we are experiencing, and, knowing how slow is the process of the broadening of consciousness, you must understand that not a moment should be wasted. The very existence of our planet is being weighed on Cosmic Scales, and only humanity itself can place the deciding weight on either one or the other cup. The rebuilding of the world is taking place, and we must firmly decide whether we wish to proceed with the Cosmic Magnet or to share the fate of cosmic waste.

The trouble with most people who approach the Teaching is that while admiring its all-embracing wisdom and beauty they nevertheless consider it as nothing more than a beautiful poetic creation, and they do not understand all the *essentiality* of it and do not even attempt to apply it in life; they do not surrender a single habit, a single comfort. Meanwhile, the threatening signs of the fiery storm, about which so much is said in the Teaching, are already appearing, and those who are not spiritually awakened and strengthened will be destroyed in thousands by the dreadful, unprecedented epidemics.

It is time to think of hygiene of spirit. Hygiene of body is not so important as hygiene of spirit. No vitamins, no injections, no inoculations will save the one whose psychic energy is exhausted or benumbed. How essential is the understanding of the profound significance of the word "service," great service, great deeds for the sake of humanity! The word *podvig** is so beautiful! It has in itself the idea of self-perfecting and self-denial, the result of which is the advance of consciousness, not only personal but of the whole country. Verily, now is the time to call for *podvig*. All countries, the whole world, is involved in a dreadful struggle, and only the spiritually strong will conquer. We should not deceive ourselves that everything somehow will be settled. No, each country must realize that it can survive only if its best representatives understand that the struggle with ignorance and the forces of destruction is not to be deferred. All countries are being tested. Will many pass? The map of the future is already formed in the Subtle Worlds, but much can yet be eased.

And so, be inspired! Write fiery articles in defense of the culture of spirit; praise heroism and *podvig*. As it is said in the Teaching, "Where the idea of heroism is considered ridiculous, or even indecent, there is real decay. By this sign, one can judge the decrepitude of nations. The last words of the Greatest Spirit

---

* The word *"podvig"* is untranslatable from the Russian. It means a great or heroic deed plus spiritual achievement

to his Brothers when He was leaving the Earth was: 'Create heroes!'" The time has come when *we all must be heroic and must create heroes.*

14

26 April 1934

I was so happy to receive the letters from my distant co-workers. We are all united by the same Teaching and we should feel like one big family. While it is not yet possible to be together physically, it is good to know that such a time will come. So let us prepare ourselves for that great time. Let us look forward to the holiday of spirit and heart. We shall keep strict spiritual fast in order that we may, in complete purity of body and spirit, welcome the Eve of Easter—the Resurrection of the Spirit. Let us aspire in all our thoughts toward this near future, and many of the dull and difficult things of daily life will be eased because in our hearts we will accept the unavoidable blows and difficulties as a part of a great probationership and will live in the joy of the coming future.

Please tell the dear co-workers to preserve the flame of their hearts and to apply all their creative efforts toward bringing the happy message of the Teaching to the yearning hearts. All those who are striving for knowledge are very dear to us. A person cannot come to realization without difficult probations, and lucky is the one to whom these probations come in youth. In the work which we all shall share we should appreciate all the difficult moments which tempered our spirit and acquainted us with the life and soul of a nation. It is quite right to think that humanity will be saved by a great miracle of illumination. "The miracle comes at the predicted time."

I am so glad to hear that you decided firmly to dedicate yourself to the work planned by the Great Teachers for the General Good. Without such a decision it is impossible to advance along the Path. We were given a prayer: "Thee, O Lord, I will serve in everything, always and everywhere. Let my path be marked by the attainment of selflessness!" May this prayer be yours also and that of everyone who wholeheartedly enters the path of Service to humanity. In connection with this, I shall quote from the Teaching:

"When the disciple realizes in his heart the joy of the path, a path which knows no friction because all is transformed in the joy of Service, then it is possible to open before him the Great Gates. Amidst higher concepts the disciple must remember in his heart the records of Light. Amidst the frightening manifestations the disciple must remember about the records of darkness. There is inscribed upon the Shield of Light: 'Lord, I come alone, I come in a manifested achievement. I will reach the goal, I will reach it!' And upon the Shield of Light is inscribed: honesty, devotion and self-abnegation. But fearful are the records of darkness. Let the hand of the disciple refrain from inscribing upon these permanent scrolls: lie, hypocrisy, betrayal, self-hood. ...

"Among the manifestations which are particularly harmful for ascent may be noted halfway service. It is impossible to advance without casting away this dreadful halfwayness. It must be remembered that, having once chosen the Teacher, the disciple must always act with an understanding of all the harmful effects of halfwayness. Not only is an obvious betrayal dangerous (against such one can openly fight with a sword), but these pernicious burrowings of halfwayness are so harmful.

"One must direct the consciousness of people along the path of honesty. People must understand that the most important thing is the honesty of Service. How can one affirm the growth of the spirit, how can one prove devotion to Hierarchy, how can one purify the consciousness? Only by this single law—honesty of Service. Thus, let us always keep in mind the harmfulness of halfwayness. The records of darkness contain all halfway decisions and actions; therefore, on the fiery path one should remember the consequences of halfwayness. If it were possible to make manifest all the records of the Subtle World, humanity would be terrified at the grey shadows around destruction, halfwayness, betrayal, incitement to strife, blasphemy, intolerance and selfhood. Thus, on the fiery path let us remember about the dangerous undermining effect of halfwayness." [Fiery World III]

Therefore, all newcomers should not expect immediate relief and special results if in their heart and spirit they are not entirely prepared to serve the Light. As it is said, "One should treasure the Teaching as the last fire, the last piece of bread, the last water. One must manifest love and care as toward the last possibility and the last drop of water." If there were such striving our possibilities would increase. A true disciple moves forward, being impelled by irresistible love for the Teacher of Light.

Now I shall answer your questions.

1. Of course you are right: first of all one must personally apply the Teaching in life and must perfect oneself. Otherwise how can we attract sincerely striving souls? Each one who has approached the Teaching is obliged to spread the seeds he received. But will such sowing be successful if we ourselves are not able to appreciate and to test the seeds entrusted to us? Will there be many who will value our seeds? Most of them will want to see the sprouts of these seeds. Therefore, the concrete personal example of those who possess these seeds is most important. It is important to show the reality of the Teaching, to prove to what an extent it can alter the character and life of a person. Long ago it was said, "Faith without deeds is dead." Thus, the Teaching without application to life will bring no benefit.

2. You ask whether you should continue your meditations. Everything that develops the concentration of thought is most useful. Clearness and the crystallization of thought should be greatly encouraged. Just now there is so much chaotic thinking that one should be particularly on guard and try hard to harness one's thoughts and not permit their capricious jumping. Sequence in thought and action is so essential for the broadening of consciousness.

I have read your meditations. The theme concerning thought is so broad; verily, thought is the Universe! Therefore, it is advisable to take this subject all-comprehensively and to make it as concrete as possible. It is also most useful to meditate upon thought as the creator of karma. The theme "And we open the Gates" should be expanded. Try to picture the whole path of ascent divided into seven Gates, and point out in sequence the qualities which should be developed for the unlocking of these Gates. If not for all the seven, then at least for four of them. And another theme, "Smile at the difficulties of your path," also should be broadened. You should emphasize even more what actually gives us the strength to withstand all the difficulties and to "smile at them," and in what we find an inexhaustible source of joy; then enlarge the idea of "joy as the highest wisdom." These are only brief remarks; such meditations on subjects from the Teachings are most valuable. It would be very good to take such ideas as "Simplicity" and "Podvig." These two ideas are especially emphasized in the books of the Teaching.

Now I shall discuss your fourth meditation, "The quality of Air and the serenity of Spirit." In this meditation I cannot agree with the phrase "first we must prepare the temple and then educate the soul." The spirit builds its temple, it is not vice versa. Of course, the psychic and the physical are closely linked, and to be perfect it should be completely balanced; however, without the body we can exist but without the spirit we are absolutely dead. I quote from the Teaching: "Rightly has it been said that the spirit can live without a body because a deformed body can contain a luminous soul, but a body cannot, in spite of all external perfections, contain a spirit which does not conform to the accumulations of the past. It is correct that since for the most part the human spirit is suppressed many illnesses are a blessing, for they unite the spirit with the Subtle World. Each manifestation is based on two principles which correspond to the measurements of the subtle and physical worlds. Indeed, these measurements often are inversely proportional." There is a page in the books of the Teaching about the danger of giving healthy bodies to undeveloped, wicked souls; verily, evil would be yet more triumphant! It follows from what is said that we should concentrate more on the development of the spirit, and should cultivate the physical body only as much as our common sense demands. And the famous saying, "a healthy spirit exists only in a healthy body," I would use vice versa—"a healthy body belongs to a healthy spirit." If we start only with strengthening of the body, we may never advance., I encourage all co-workers to learn how to meditate.

If one has literary talent, and has assimilated the essence of the Teaching, it would be very useful to write little popular booklets, in which the ideas of the Teaching would be annotated for the broad masses. These short popular commentaries are so essential! For instance, it would be valuable to write about the significance of the Teacher, about the power and importance of thought and of psychic energy, etc., and to collect the separate references to the concepts given in the Teaching and add simplifying comments. In general, there are endless possibilities to work on in the Teaching, and I always welcome literary abilities that can be utilized. So much work should be done in the near future, so many hands will be necessary in all fields! One should always try to learn as much as possible along the lines which are within one's capacity, bearing in mind the necessity to utilize and eventually apply the knowledge.

3. You ask whether you should study the medicinal nature of herbs. Every knowledge is beneficial, and this field indeed is very noble and extremely interesting.

4. You want to know how to apply the Teaching in life. with all simplicity, with all the heart, just as it is indicated in the books of the Teaching. Of course, you may have misunderstandings and queries in regard to certain statements of the Teaching. Please do not hesitate to inquire. I shall always be happy to help you. The Teaching was given for daily life, and it often contains answers to definite questions and explanations of events and, therefore, these places may not always be clear to those who are not familiar with our life. I have often met interpretations of the sense which were entirely opposite to what was meant by some pages of the Teaching. This is unavoidable, and I am always glad to answer your questions concerning the Teaching. This will give us the necessary spiritual contact. *Unless there are questions, there can be no Teacher.* And particularly when we are in different parts of the world, direct contact helps a great deal, as it is very important to have constant and long communication between auras. Meanwhile, let us exchange the thoughts and aspirations of the heart, and let us send our psychic energy, stratified on the paper.

My heart is full of the desire to give joy and relief to everyone. Please remember about the seriousness and solemnity of the moment, and tense all your forces for self-perfection. The future is great and beautiful.

15

5 May 1934

It is incorrect to call the subtle body formless, as its shapelessness is relative. The Teaching speaks of incorporeality but not of shapelessness. Moreover, there are statements in esoteric Teachings that those primordial subtle immaterial bodies had beautiful, perfect form. It is impossible to declare that they had nothing in common with our present physical forms. We should bear in mind that the subtle body is the prototype of the physical body. Of course, the primitive physical high-animal type was, in its appearance, very far from the subtle body or the spiritual essence which was clothed in it.

It would also be more correct and more understandable to say that in the very beginning of its earthly evolution the human being did not possess an intellect, but that in its spiritual development it was ahead of us. Spirituality, first of all, is consciousness, and consciousness is the foundation of the Universe. Each atom has its consciousness, as wherever there is life there is consciousness; but, of course, its gradations are infinite. It is true that in the Subtle World there are half-conscious, or even unconscious, posthumous conditions, but only in those cases where spirituality is either dormant or absent, or when a person in his earthly life failed to develop his higher abilities and thus severed communication with his spiritual centers, which alone can give us the true immortality of the Man-God who possesses clear knowledge. Verily, only in the case of the Man-God, or Arhat, when union of the mind with spiritual consciousness is achieved, is it possible to use the terms "straight-knowledge," "clairaudience," and "clairvoyance." Therefore, speaking of the spirituality of primordial man, it is better to apply such expressions as "spiritual consciousness," "spiritual hearing," "spiritual sight."

I shall now quote some extracts from my book which I shall soon begin to put together; it might be very helpful to you:

"The sacred Teaching says that the hermaphrodite never existed in reality. There were some individual, unsuccessful cases, which soon ceased to exist. But the theory of twin souls has a real basis, and in a way completes the symbol of the Androgyne. All symbols of the Androgyne have as their aim the showing of the necessity of the twin Elements in the Cosmos in all their manifestations, for the maintenance of life and equilibrium. All legends about the affinity of souls are based on a great truth because, in primary law, the union of the two Elements is basically meant. ... Fire is dual in its nature; hence, all the chalices in the ancient mysteries had a dual flame above them. All the gods of antiquity had with them their consorts, who personified the cosmic energy. All scriptures and sacred images point out this fundamental cosmic law. Differentiation results in separation of the Elements and the separated Elements are driven into distant spheres. The magnet which has existed in the Elements during aeons of time will, after the complete transmutation and purification of the elements, collect and unite them again. This is called the Great Crowning, or the Crown of Cosmos."

Until now, this knowledge has been purposely obscured, for humanity was not ready to accept it in all its purity and beauty. But at the moment, humanity has reached its turning point when spirituality will have to dominate, or else the planet may be destroyed. Therefore, this most sacred cosmic law must be gradually introduced and assimilated, so as to check and purify our dreadful sexual licentiousness.

There is a great beauty in the spiritual union of the dual Element, but things on the physical plane are far from being spiritual. A change of forms may be in conformity with the broadening of the consciousness. Beautiful vessels should be used only in beautiful surroundings. But in everything there must be the command of Spirit. Therefore, the ugly hermaphrodite, or people with two spines or with similarly fantastic peculiarities imagined by some ignorant and ugly-thinking writers, have no place in the future evolution. Evolution proceeds by way of beauty, and the future races will be improved and refined according to their spiritual progress. Toward the end of the sixth and the beginning of the seventh race, there will occur the materialization of the astral bodies. This improvement of forms and the growth of spirituality could be hastened by correct union or marriage. The Great Brotherhood is ready to help humanity apply this sacred knowledge.

Now, to continue, separation of sexes means that after immersion into gross matter the magnet of the elements became weak and people began to mix and to unite incorrectly. The great martyr Origen expressed it wonderfully: "Widows are those souls who have left the husbands to whom whey were wedded illicitly but remain widows because they are not yet perfect enough to be united with their Heavenly Bridegroom." Of course, we must take into consideration that, according to Ruffin, the biographer of Origen, the writings of Origen suffered many "corrections"; otherwise they would never have been published, and might even have been destroyed. It is obvious that here also a "correction" took place and the word "bridegroom" was written with a capital "B," to imply that Christ was meant. But in another place in the same work, *On the Elements* (where it is also spoken of women who no longer live with their illegitimate husbands, but are left alone and regarded as widows because they do not yet deserve their bridegrooms), the word "bridegroom" is written with a small letter. Certainly, there are also opposite cases, when the bridegroom does not yet deserve his bride. But could such things be written in those days! It is not scoffing at sacred things when the church of today declares Oecumenical Marriage (although symbolical), having in mind Christ? I always have felt indignant about it.

And now as to your question about karma. In each life a person can neutralize a certain part of his old karma, which reaches him in this incarnation, and certainly he then starts a new karma. But if his consciousness is broadened he can outlive more quickly the accumulated karma, and the new karma he then creates will be already of higher quality. Moreover, the old karma will not be as fearful because of the purified thinking; therefore the purified aura will react entirely differently on the return blows. And in this way man can emerge from the spellbound circle of karma. But this concerns only the earthly karma, which attracts him to Earth, for karma cannot be entirely eliminated so long as there is consciousness and thought. Karma which corresponds with the cosmic laws will infinitely improve its quality, entering new cycles and coming out of them, and so into Infinity.

Individual karma is always the basic one. And firstly, it is formed by the inclinations, thoughts and motives of man—actions are secondary factors. The Buddhists say, "Karma is thought." If it were otherwise, man could not rid himself of his karma. Verily, the individual karma, being fundamental and determinative, can influence the creation as well as the liquidation of all other types of karma. By injuring himself a person injures others. Everything is linked in the Cosmos; everything is intertwined, and nothing can be dismembered from all the rest of karma. Therefore, individual karma also cannot be dismembered from other types of karma, such as group karma, race karma, etc. It is said in the Teaching, "With difficulty do the sparks of creativeness seep through on the path of karma; and even less understood is the truth of karmic action. Not from without comes the proper estimation of karma. Every cell contains within itself its karma. The spirit carries its achievement and weapon within."

* * *

If in the past the system of castes and classes had its purpose, today it is most foolish and stagnant. Classes and castes are responsible for the great misunderstanding between the so-called "educated" class and the common folk. This terrible gulf, this difference of consciousness, is very tragic, and now it threatens our whole culture. There is great progress in the consciousness of the broad masses; people instinctively sense the fundamental equality of spirit. But in their ignorance they cannot perceive the great principle of true *lawful* Hierarchy, which is based on the law of evolution, and so their furious protests are endless over the entire planet. Therefore, the main problem of governments should be care for the education of the masses; otherwise, the hydra of darkness will swallow everything. Only knowledge should bring privilege, not class distinction. The followers of the class system, deprived of true knowledge, kindle the passions of dark consciousness. Fearful, terrible is the hydra of darkness and ignorance!

It is wrong to think that the mixing of classes can affect the karma of people in a negative way. At the present time, quite often, the healthy, spiritually sound peasant family offers the best environment for a highly developed spirit. One's having been born in a palace or in a corner of a cobbler's shack should not be deemed the result of a mixing of classes, but, rather, to have been for the purpose of fulfilling a personal karma or else a certain mission. Thus, Boehme was a cobbler, but this was for the very reason that in those days this was the way in which he could best fulfil his great mission, in comparative peace. The dreadful karma of humanity is the result of the violation of cosmic laws, beginning with birth, but it is not the result of the mixing of social classes. Thus, marriage will be scientifically treated in the future. It is even said that people should conjoin according to their affinity with certain elements.

By neglecting these fundamental cosmic laws, humanity has created the grievous karma of degeneration. Therefore, the contrast between the accumulations of a highly developed spirit and the modest environment in which he may be born is not so important as is disharmony between the basic elements of parents; the latter is the cause of all manner of spiritual degradation. Poverty and hardships will but develop the power of a strong spirit. The efforts he makes to overcome difficulties are more valuable and beneficial than success.

Now regarding the Lords of Karma. Much confusion surrounds this concept. Can it be imagined that the Lords of Karma are distributing portions of karma to all the billions of incarnated souls! But we hear even such absurdities. In the books of the Teaching we read:

"Forces manifested for the Service of Light do not invade karma, as some who are not initiated into the power of karma think. The Forces of Light observe human actions, giving the direction but not invading life. Many are the examples of this. Messengers appear, warnings are sent, the direction is given and the paths pointed out; but the choice of designated affirmations is determined by the human will. In this way appears the manifestation of cooperation between the two worlds.

"Precisely, self-activity of the spirit can bring near a better karma. Thus it can be explained why the Forces of Light do not stop the spirit from certain actions which often violate that which has been ordained. Often people are perplexed as to why other paths are not indicated. Likewise, they wonder why the Sendings are affirmed through diverse channels. They wonder why the Forces of Light do not ward off various currents. Let us reply, 'The Forces of Light never invade human karma.' This law must be remembered on the path to the Fiery World.

"The law of free will often prohibits Us from clarifying a manifestation which appears to be obscure. The very same law indicates Our crossing of paths when the free will directs a heart toward a heart." [Fiery World III]

The spreading of karma in the Subtle World during the intermediate state of the soul could be emphasized more strongly. I quote a paragraph from the Teaching:

"Karma is diffused in all actions, in all worlds. Just as karma can be hastened, it can be prolonged as well. A deepening of karma is reflected not only upon the succeeding life. All intermediate states are also affected in an aggravation of karma. The Subtle World is held in close bond with the earthly, and it is necessary to intensify thinking in this direction. He who understands the meaning of the connection of the two worlds will be careful of his earthly actions. Care toward all energies is of assistance to the striving spirit. A chief impediment is non-understanding of the truth of spatial life—that all is transmuted, all is atoned for. Correctly has it been pointed out about the law of Karma—indeed, about the law of Karma unto Infinity. Precisely, aspiration reaches into Infinity; and so also do possibilities. On the path to the Fiery World let us affirm a conscious relationship to the law of Karma. ...

"Transmutation of the centers intensifies the creative energies which are necessary for crossing into the Subtle World. Each spiritual striving produces its sediments, which assume the aspect of subtle energies during the passing into the Subtle World. Thus, it is important to aspire into the higher spheres. Ecstasy of spirit and joy of the heart yield those energies which nourish the subtle body. Indeed, only a feeling imbued with higher impulses provides the needed energies. It must be understood that imperil and gross earthly desires produce their ugly ulcers, which the spirit must heal in the subtle body. Ulcers of the spirit are carried over into the Subtle World if they are not gotten rid of on Earth. Liberation from the physical vehicle does not mean deliverance from spiritual ulcers. When the spirit, faced with breaking away from Earth, realizes how it has used its energies, then the consciousness can atone for a great deal. But the consciousness must be impelled toward the thought about the higher worlds. Even the most hardened criminal can be directed toward the understanding of the burden of karma, but for this it is necessary to change the social conditions. Thus on the path to the Fiery World one should become accustomed to the thought about transmutation of the centers because liberation from the body is not deliverance from spiritual ulcers."[Fiery World III]

* * *

Please use occult literature most discriminately. And do not become too abstract; things must be introduced as concretely as possible.

16

6 May 1934

You declare that you are monogamic. This, no doubt is a very important quality for every serious disciple. But for true success the devotional love should be focused on a single Teacher. There are several Teachers of the Great Brotherhood who accept disciples and direct them. Each one who enters the path of discipleship (and this is not just studying occult literature) must firmly decide in the depth of the heart which of the Great Teachers of the Brotherhood is the nearest for him; then, one must completely surrender oneself to this High Guidance, without any limitations, any conditions. But quite often the called and aspiring one, in the desire for immediate progress, squanders his forces and looks for other Great Teachers and Teachings. By this dividing of himself, twice, sometimes thrice, he loses his place in the scale of ascent. Think of everything that is said in the Teaching about choosing the Teacher!

I shall quote a paragraph from the Teaching:

"To be affirmed in the heart upon the Lord is the first condition on the path to the Fiery World. It is impossible to arrive at the ordained Gates without this fiery requirement. Of course, Guidance must be recognized in spirit and heart, for the acceptance of the Hand of the Lord is alone insufficient without devoting the heart to the Lord. One must understand that law which unites the Teacher with the disciple because without the manifestation of complete attachment to the Lord there can be no bond. A full acceptance of Guidance means a conscious relationship, for one must understand and feel in the heart the warmth which arises from the depths of the spirit. It is especially necessary to feel and to learn to discern that by which the nature of the Lord is linked with that of the disciple. Thus, one must remember that vibrations and karma are as connecting links on the path to the Fiery World." [Fiery World III]

Yes, it is most dangerous to scatter one's forces on the first steps. Do not forget about the years of probation and of the adjustment of the organism; all the various disciples who enter the path of Service must go through this process. Even the very high spirits are not exceptions in this. Of course, all the aforesaid is not applicable to the theoretical occultists. But, as I understand you, you wish to be accepted in the group of real disciples and, as you say, your sole desire is to meet the Teacher and to work under his Guidance. I certainly have not yet met anybody who, after becoming acquainted even if only superficially with the Teaching, would not like to give up the earthly burdens and join the Teacher in his Community. It is mostly those who have only superficially learned something of the Teaching who are the ones to demand entry into the Community of the Great Brotherhood! But they have not the slightest idea whether their physical bodies could stand the extremely tense atmosphere which surrounds this Stronghold. One must remember that the transmutation of the organism and the nerve centers must take place here, on Earth, amidst the spiritual struggles, amidst all the burdens and difficulties of life, amidst all the testing trifles of every day. Only this struggle evokes the necessary energies for the transfiguration and the outliving of all the gross habits and attachments. The earthly life is indeed a purgatory, and without going through it it is impossible to enter Paradise, or to come to the Brotherhood. The fires of the higher energies would burn the overloaded aura. The Community of the Brotherhood is too far removed from the ordinary earthly environment, and therefore it could not provide the necessary test conditions.

Moreover, the Lords never invade the karma of man, and do not make exceptions. Only karma can bring a person into their Community. So, if such karma is ready, nothing can stop its realization, unless the man himself wills it. Let this law inspire you. Apply all your aspirations to practising in life what you have learned from the books of the Teaching, and leave the rest to your karma and to the great knowledge of the Lords!

Not always have the Great Souls, who had to fulfil certain missions, entered the Community of the Brotherhood during their earthly life. For instance, Apollonius of Tyana was called to visit the Brotherhood, but He, in his incarnation as Origen, accepted the most difficult task of guarding the purity of the Teaching of Christ, and for this He suffered imprisonment instead of dwelling in the Abode of the Brotherhood and participating in the joyous work there.

Tell the friends that they must not expect the end of the world in 1936, as predicted. Nothing so final is likely to happen; however, there will be important events. In any case, be assured there is no danger of being destroyed by cosmic cataclysms and catastrophes for those who with all their hearts are attached to the Great Teacher. In due time, all the scattered wayfarers will be gathered together—but not necessarily in the Himalayas, as there are other places just as important. One should not overburden space by fixing definite times; however, it is very advisable to be always spiritually alert and ready to leave. Thought of the future is the best exercise for achieving readiness to leave at any time, but for this so much more quality and care should be demonstrated in our daily routine.

* * *

One should not overestimate the achievements of Hatha Yoga and think that "the adepts of Hatha Yoga are equal to those of Raja Yoga in ability to awaken the kundalini and to acquire various siddhis," and that "they reach bliss and liberation from matter." It is not so! The degree of bliss reached by such adepts is very relative, and they never reach liberation from matter (in the sense which is meant by the Great Teachers) by means of Hatha Yoga. As it is said in the Teaching, "We know of no one who reached the goal by way of Hatha Yoga."

Even the development of the lower siddhis, to which the Hatha Yogis come by stubborn and terribly difficult mechanical exercises (Western literature has no idea about even half of these horrors) is not lasting, and in their next incarnations they may lose all these siddhis. Only those achievements are valuable and permanent that come naturally, for then they are the result of inner spiritual development and can never be lost. Only in such way can the all-powerful manifestations be reached. Exercises in Hatha Yoga should not go beyond a slight and very careful pranayama, which strengthens health, as otherwise they might be dangerous and could lead to mediumism, obsession and insanity. Quite correctly, the Hindu people of high spiritual development consider Hatha Yoga most undesirable, and they say that at best it is useful "for fat and ill people." Even Vivekananda, who is so often mentioned now, though he cited examples of fearful demoniac persons whom he knew who were able to perform the most amazing miracles and cure the hopelessly sick by a glance, was very much against the so-called siddhis and these miracles.

Therefore, the main test for all spiritual Teachers is the magnet of their own hearts, their occult ability to change spiritually the surroundings and to transform the consciousness and the very nature of their disciples. It is by no means their ability in so-called miracles. This requires the fiery ray of synthesis, which is inherent in the opened centers but not in the lower siddhis. No pranayama can give the necessary purification and high results if the consciousness does not correlate with the High Ideal. The higher forms of Yoga do not need pranayama. Every coolie in India knows about pranayama; the average Hindu performs it every day, but nevertheless they are far from spiritual achievement. Therefore, do not rely just upon pranayama!

The highest achievement of a Yogi is the opening of the eye of Dangma, and it is not what we call clairvoyance. It is the awakening of perceptions which never can be developed by any mechanical means but which comes as the result of accumulations of uninterrupted spiritual aspirations and self-sacrifices over thousands of years; and these results are manifested in the most subtle energies, which are stored and preserved within the Chalice. A true Yogi should try his very best to awaken these old accumulations and to preserve and protect the new ones; otherwise, he is a mere book-taught occultist.

It is also quite wrong to think that "the occult sciences would never have obtained the correct idea of the astral plane, had it not been for the selfless work of the Hatha Yogis." Such an assertion is equivalent to a statement that the foundations of physics and chemistry would have been unknown to Ruhmkorff and Crookes without the work of present-day college freshmen! Or that an agriculturist knows less about the chemistry of the soil than an ordinary ploughman.

Moreover, the difference between Hatha Yoga and Raja Yoga is precisely qualitative, and not quantitative, as you think. Hatha Yoga can never rise above the lower psychic phenomena. And there has never been a case when a Hatha Yoga became a Raja Yogi—their paths are entirely different. The true "efficacious pearls" include Raja, Jnana, Bhakti and Agni Yoga, but not Hatha Yoga, as some ignorant people think; just as artificial pearls cannot be compared to real ones. Furthermore, I cannot quite understand the following thought: "But nevertheless, Hatha Yoga gives to its adepts efficacious pearls of high achievement, and in the same manner every occultist must look upon the achievements of Agni Yoga as a similar tremendous victory of spirit over the flesh." Here again, Agni Yoga is put on the same level with Hatha Yoga, whereas these two Yogas are *diametrically opposite*. As it is said, "Verily, Agni Yoga *has nothing in common with* Hatha Yoga: this must be thoroughly realized." Agni Yoga deals with the highest fiery transmutation of all the centers, which cannot be achieved by any mechanical methods but requires the direct controlling influence of the Great Teacher. The high attainment of Agni Yoga can be reached only by a spirit which possesses agelong spiritual accumulations, collected in the center of the Chalice, while the latter is not absolutely essential for the Hatha Yogi. Another thing that is characteristic of Agni Yoga is that its achievements must be attained during everyday life, while all the other Yogas (except Karma Yoga) demand isolation from ordinary life, and thus are not sufficient for the present and future evolution.

It is also a mistake to call every beginner of any of the Yogas a "Yogi." Yoga, or *communion,* is achieved by hard and *constant* spiritual practice, and can be hastened, as it was said above, only by karmic accumulations. Therefore, it is wrong to say that "A Raja Yogi sometimes becomes a fanatic; a Jnana Yogi an intellectual speculator; and a Bhakti Yogi a religious zealot who rejoices at the 'righteous' punishment of heretics." Rather, it would be more correct to say that "those who have certain inclinations which may lead them to become in their later incarnations Raja Yogis may first manifest themselves as fanatics; those with tendencies toward Jnana as intellectual pedants; and those with Bhakti tendencies as religious hypocrites." Once, however, a high degree of true Yoga is achieved (either Raja, Bhakti or Jnana), there can be no real perversion of the guiding principles in such an intense way. A king of spirit cannot become a fanatic, and a Jnana-Philosopher possessing the eye of Dangma cannot become an idle intellectual pedant; neither can a Bhakti—a lord of the cosmic magnet of the all-embracing heart—rejoice at "righteous punishment." When the Teaching mentions there are "signs of the Hatha Yogi in the unbearable athlete, signs of the Bhakti Yogi in the hypocrite, and signs of the Raja Yogi in the Fanatic," it is pointing out characteristic inclinations which, if transmuted by spiritual fire, would lead into one or another of the different types of Yoga. But not vice versa!

One should also take into consideration that Hatha Yoga is dangerous because, in a peculiar way, it strengthens the astral body and holds it for a very long time in the lower astral spheres, which prevents the evolution of spirit. In the temples of India there was, and still is, a custom of keeping Hatha Yogis for certain lower phenomena of the astral type. They are supposed to lead a very pure life, but even then are never initiated into the higher spiritual powers. And if such a Hatha Yogi leaves the temple, he is not accepted back again, for, by becoming free from the higher control while having an easy access to the lower strata of the Subtle World, such a yogi becomes a victim and sometimes even an instrument of the darkest forces. Here is also the reason why the Hierophants of Egypt never accepted mediumistically inclined disciples, and even avoided lymphatic servants. Not a single medium, not one lymphatic, can become a true Agni Yogi.

The Great Teachers are grieved because of the predomination of lower psychism at the expense of true spirituality. Without the understanding and application of the Living Ethics, without spirituality, the lower psychism can lead to the most grievous results. Therefore, in order to be accepted as disciples it is necessary, first of all, to practise self-perfection, to improve morally and spiritually, and to apply the Teaching in life. This will broaden the consciousness and bring the necessary balance. The Teaching is beautiful and true when it is realized, but no tricks of pseudo-occultism and magic will lead to true discipleship. In order to fill one's vessel from the High Source, one has to establish the corresponding high vibrations. The application in life of the Living Ethics is the quickest way to reach the goal.

Great is the mission to kindle the consciousness of people by *podvig* (great deeds), which can change the whole essence of people. Perhaps never was the idea of podvig so necessary in life as now. What a beautiful word—*podvig*! How expressive! And note how remarkable it is that it has no equivalent in any other Western language. So please remember that communion with the Teacher is achieved through the heart, through purified thinking, and by way of the long, tireless work of self-perfection.

And now one more warning: theoretical occultism is most dangerous. Many most harmful books flood the market. Perhaps (and fortunately) not all of them are translated into the Russian language. As it is said, "Many of them are the creation of hands that are lacking in beauty, knowledge and honesty."

It is said by the Great Teacher, "Only Blavatsky knew," and it is our duty to rehabilitate the memory of this great woman martyr. If you only knew all the slanderous literature about Mme Blavatsky, all the betrayals and the perfidy around her, you would be horrified. So much ingratitude, viciousness and ignorance. Of course, all hideousness results from the latter.

* * *

You asked whether you wrote something superfluous in your article about the Banner of Peace. My answer is this: By too many prohibitions it is possible to frighten and to stop aspiration. Sometimes so-called carelessness, if committed when the intentions are good, may bring happy results *However, do not make a rule of this. Care and cautiousness are among the first qualities of every disciple*, for he must know with what energies he is dealing.

I beg of you not to be annoyed by my remarks. I know that you are courageous and are able to become a serious disciple and co-worker; that is why I write to you without sentimentality and compliments. You remember how the Teaching says, "The Teaching is not soothing syrup... only the spiritually strong can reach the goal and become accepted disciples. The Teaching of Living Ethics is beautiful in its *vitality* and *austerity* and in the *brevity of its clear formulae*."

17

25 May 1934

You are writing about the inability of people today to perceive spiritual ideas. But when were there better times? It seems to me that today there is much more seeking after truth than ever before. Serious calamities compel many to think about certain things and to look deeper for the reason for present events. We are fortunate in having met many beautiful souls; and some of them have gone through great distress without losing firmness, still selflessly continuing to work for the General Good.

You are right: in our days we need synthesis. But the majority cannot accept and realize it because synthesis, or illumination of the spirit is the rarest achievement. This synthesis is an accumulation of many energies which have been crystallized during innumerable selfless lives. But are there many selfless workers for Light? Therefore, the kind of synthesis which is publicly lectured upon and preached cannot bring the right results. As you say yourself, the lectures are visited by people who are not ready for them, and often they come from mere curiosity. Sincere seekers are welcome, and it is up to them to accept as much as they can. Of course, the spiritual leaders should possess spiritual synthesis and should give wisely, studying individually each case and imparting according to receptivity just as much as is necessary. The leader should find the right language for each one. In his all-embracing heart there should be a place for everyone who sincerely seeks his help. Nobody should depart from his presence feeling depressed by the breadth of his views. He should know exactly what a person can assimilate, for then he can give joy.

You write that perhaps "in your country it will be easier to build the synthesis." Let us hope that the chosen leader will possess such synthesis, as verily one can build firmly only through synthesis. *And the failure of the present time comes from a lack of synthesis in the spirit of the leaders.*

I quote from the Teaching:

"The leader stands on the crest from which there can be no departure. Only a born leader can find the boundary between opposite conceptions. From the hidden boundaries, victory is built. Every day, every hour, the leader conquers riddles. Here he finds condescension, and here is want of firmness; of course, one may result from the other, but between the two is a sword of justice. For condescension is of Light, but lack of character is of darkness. On the crest between them lies the sword of the leader. Narrow is the place wherein the sword can be laid. Just as narrow is the boundary between courage and cruelty. Only the leader's heart can sense the boundary.

"The riddle of justice is not only in great things; the whole life is full of these riddles. Therefore, the leader never divides things into 'big' and 'small.' The attention of the leader is always equally alert regarding all his decisions. The leader does not ask for advice; however, he is quite ready to accept advice. He is never late, but will not overburden anyone by staying too long. He knows the advantage of appearing unexpectedly; and he can, in advance, calculate how much time is needed for everything. He is not depressed by slander, and he knows how to utilize every word. He cannot be bribed, as earthly wealth does not tempt him. He understands the significance of color and sound, for he is a healer of human hearts. He rejoices at Truth, but he rejects illusion. Thus, the path of the leader is the path of Truth."

So many suggestions are given to leaders in the pages of the Living Ethics. Every book speaks of tolerance, of ability to embrace and comprehend—are these not actually the foundations of synthesis?

18

26 May 1934

Enclosed are the answers to your questions.

1. The idea of the Unity of Cosmos was introduced to humanity from the earliest times in the "First Revelation," the memory of which is preserved in many sacred traditions, in the images and writings of all the peoples of antiquity.

2. In ancient times, among all nations, there were, and are even now, always two types of religion—one for the initiates, and one for the masses. In other words, one esoteric and the other exoteric. And it is quite understandable, considering the stage of development of the masses in those days.

3. For the initiates, all the gods were only the personifications of certain cosmic forces. This sometimes explains the strange aspects of these gods, and also the animal symbols.

4. Moses truly was a great leader, and you say correctly that he was the creator of Israel. However, Moses was not responsible for the idea of monotheism; *this idea had existed from the most ancient times.* Therefore, the belief that the Jewish people brought this idea into the world is not exactly correct.

Moses, being a disciple of the Egyptian priests, was initiated into their secret knowledge: Unity of Cosmos, unity in all its multiformity. And this idea of unity he affirmed as monotheism—*precisely to the masses,* giving them Jehovah as one aspect of the Divinity. There were also other reasons why the image of Jehovah was chosen as the Ruling Element or God for the Jewish people. Let us remember how highly advanced was the science of astrology in ancient Egypt. *Jehovah was connected with Saturn,* and Israel, as an individual nation, was born under this planet.

In spite of the fact that the idea of monotheism is very pronounced in the exoteric religion of the Jews, their sacred pantheon is as numerous as those of other people, including Christian: the Hierarchy of Forces, the Ladder of Jacob, and all the Planetary Spirits worshipped by the Catholic Church.

5. Moses was a Jew, and all the stories about his Egyptian origin are most erroneous. Even from a purely psychological point of view, such an opinion is beneath criticism; the whole movement, the whole development of the epic of Moses, strongly contradicts it.

6. Moses was a leader and ruler in the fullest sense of these words, and he had to undertake the hard task of creating a nation out of a nomadic tribe, which for a very long period had been enslaved and therefore had developed many negative qualities. From such a tribe he had to build a nation and give it the foundations of constructiveness and the concepts of organized government. All hints about the cruelty and revengefulness of his laws are not quite sound; when one studies his laws objectively one is amazed how wise and merciful they are. In may ways they are more generous than our present laws. And if we speak as realists we should not even attempt to criticize the cruelty of Moses when we consider our own times, full of the most cruel crimes and terror.

Moreover, would you consider the destruction of savage, beast-like men cruel? For among the Israelites who were taken out of Egypt, many were such uncivilized, beast-like creatures—the Bible also states this. The leader had to save the best element, from which he hoped to build the future nation. Hence, severity was necessary for the sake of justice and mercy. Severity and mercy are based upon the same concept.

7. Also, regarding the oft-quoted proverb "Eye for eye, tooth for tooth" (Exodus 21:24), which is always considered as an example of revengefulness, do you not think that it deals with the inevitable law of Karma? And consider the following words of Christ: "Ye have heard that it was said by them of old time, Thou shalt not kill; and whosoever shall kill shall be in danger of the judgment: But I say to you, That whosoever is angry with his brother without a cause shall be in danger of the judgment: and whosoever shall say to his brother, Raca, shall be in danger of the council: but whosoever shall say, Thou fool, shall be in danger of hell fire." (St. Matthew 5:21-22.) These words expressed by Christ we shall find still more severe than the words of Moses, unless we take into consideration the very same law of Karma. Therefore, let us be just.

And in the same chapter (17-18) Christ says: "Think not that I am come to destroy the law, or the prophets: I am not come to destroy, but to fulfil. For verily I say unto you, Till Heaven and earth pass, one joy or one title shall in no wise pass from the law, till all be fulfilled." And the Jews, as we know, lived by the law of Moses. The following verses (38-39) in the same chapter may seem somewhat inconsistent: "Ye have heard that it hath been said, An eye for an eye, and a tooth for a tooth: But I say unto you, That ye resist not evil: but whosoever shall smite thee on they right cheek, turn to him the other also." But this statement of Christ, we must also again associate with the law of Karma. I shall try to explain it still further.

Now let us imagine the situation of Moses if he had not resisted evil and had allowed the worst and crudest elements to destroy the best—the one which was able to assimilate the ideas of morality and order. What would have happened to his task? His duty as a leader and an earthly lawgiver was to protect his people and to maintain order. Therefore, the resistance to evil was basically necessary. All teachings of antiquity declare active resistance to evil. Thus, the well-known sage and lawgiver of China, Confucius, used to say, "God for good, but for evil—justice."

In the Cosmos there is a perpetual struggle between manifested chaos and the unmanifested. It is the struggle of the Forces of Light with the dark forces. Christ Himself actively resisted evil, if we decide to believe the Gospel. Let us recall how he drove the merchants from the Temple, and all his severe accusations against the scribes and Pharisees. Would we accuse Him of contradictions? And again, if we try to read objectively the words which are attributed to Christ, we shall see a Teaching which is severe in its mercy. Therefore, the words "resist not evil, but whosoever shall smite thee on thy right cheek turn to him the other also:" I accept from the point of view of karma. If this law of Karma, "an eye for an eye, and a tooth for a tooth," is inevitable and exact justice, it by no means follows that we ourselves, personally, should attempt to fulfil it in this way. If we do so, we shall never emerge from the magic circle of karma. Indeed, we must forgive our personal enemies, as who knows but that the blow one receives is a return blow, well-deserved under the law of Karma? By returning such a blow with another and with a feeling of revenge in our heart, we do not outlive this karma, but we continue and even intensify it in the worst way for ourselves. Moreover, by forgiving our enemies we decrease the amount of evil in space and become immune against many blows. Similarly, let us understand the words "Love thine enemies." However, with all this, *we must resist evil*, if we do not want to be entirely overwhelmed by it.

There are many ways of resisting evil. First of all, by the

power of spirit—certainly, resistance performed without hatred, occultly speaking, is a hundredfold stronger. All these assertions of Christ prove that He was an Initiate, and that He knew the strength of the reversed blow. Similarly, one should understand the words from Deuteronomy (the book of Moses): "To me belongetha vengeance, and recompense." The Apostle Paul uses this very apophthegm in his Epistle to the Romans. Again, we see that Christ came not to destroy the law but to fulfil it.

Besides, we do not know exactly and completely the laws of Moses. Let us not forget that the whole Bible is reconstructed, to say nothing about the many inaccuracies and omissions in the numerous translations. Perhaps it is not necessary to mention the Old Testament, as even in the New Testament there are so many contradictions; for instance the differences between the English and Russian versions.

8. The Cabbala, as any other religious and philosophical system, is an echo of the Sacred Teachings of the East—through the Vedas, Upanishads; the Teachings of Egypt, Chaldea, Assyria; of Orpheus, Pythagoras, etc. In any case, the substratum of the Cabbala is very similar to other systems. The foundations of the Cabbala originated in very remote antiquity. In *The Secret Doctrine* it is indicated that the Jewish people originally came from India. One of the lower Tamil tribes came out from India and, through marriage, mixed with the Semitic tribes they met during their travels.

Further, it is said in *The Secret Doctrine*, "By not accepting the Teaching of Christ, the Jews excluded themselves from further spiritual evolution." This states the case, one which must be placed side by side with other similar cases. Of course, by not accepting the purification brought by Christ of the old Teaching, by permitting Him to be killed, and by the persecution of his disciples, the Jews severely burdened their karma. In like manner, the Indian people also created their sad destiny by not accepting the Teaching of Buddha and by the persecution of his disciples. Buddha brought freedom to India by his rejection of the caste system; but by refusing Buddhism, India chose slavery. The theoretical acceptance of the Teachings of Buddha and Christ are one thing, but it is an entirely different matter to practise them and to realize them through the heart. The true follower of Christ and Buddha is the one who realizes the single fundamental and universal Doctrine which is behind Them and which nourished Them. Only such a follower enters the path of evolution.

The Teaching of Christ is also distorted beyond all measure. And now is the time for the Christian world to choose its karma.

9. In their desire to preserve their caste privileges, the Brahmins continue to inculcate amongst the ignorant communities the most dreadful superstitions. In this conglomeration of superstitions and rituals, which have lost their original meaning, it is rather difficult to seize upon the sparks of what was once upon a time great knowledge. But the Brahmins do not deny the law of Reincarnation and do not fear it, as they are convinced that every Brahmin, being " a twice-born," will never reincarnate in a lower caste. In ancient times the term "twice-born" meant spiritual birth, or initiation, but later it became a title indicating a general inherent quality of every Brahmin.

The majority of Brahmins are regularized parasites on the diseased organism of India. The degeneration of this country is a direct result of the most terrible, most cruel caste system. But today, the more educated classes of India are already protesting against the limitations of caste. In some parts of India the lower castes are already being allowed to visit the temples. The women of India are also awakening, and this may become the main factor in the regeneration of the whole country.

10. Now, regarding "guardian angels." It is true that every human being has his or her own Guardian Angel. And we must understand them not only as concrete Beings from higher spheres but, more often, as our own spirit, our higher triad, or our true individual Ego, which, unfortunately, is very rarely able to make a person listen to its voice. Sometimes this voice is known as our conscience.

It is also quite true that many people have friends and relatives who, having passed on before them, sometimes intervene in their lives, trying to direct and help them.

The real Guardian Angels are the Great Spirits, the Hierarchy of Light, the Great Sacred Fraternity, which is always guarding the human needs and evolution. Some of these Guardian Angels (but of course in the rarest cases) become the Guides of exceptional individuals. Their Ray continuously searches for newly awakened consciousnesses and those of flaming hearts, in order to support and direct them. But in our age, unfortunately, the guardian angels of the vast majority are dark obsessors from the lower spheres, whose voices are much more easily assimilated, as they never disagree with our earthly desires. But woe to those who allow such to approach!

Here is a paragraph from the Teaching:

"So many distortions, so many inaccuracies have been admitted into the Teachings. Verily, each purification is great Service. Each striving to renew the Truth, as it has been given to humanity, is fiery Service. The black threads seen represent not only the darkness of the earthly atmosphere, but also that web which covers the human mind and heart. It is difficult to imagine how many minds have been clouded by various evil interpretations. Each man is full of tension in search of new interpretations, but goes farther and farther away from the Truth. Dismemberment is so vividly affirmed in religions, in science, and in all creativeness. Each world has its correlation with another world. Each truth emanates from another truth. Truth is revealed only to the open heart. Thus, the tensed consciousness, which senses the cosmic pulse, passes on its own beat with luminous thoughts. Verily, great is the fiery pulse, revealed to the fiery heart." [Fiery World III]

19a

2 June 1934

You say that you are tired, that you are struggling against depression, and that you are not sure whether you will be able to conquer it. But of course you will! Remember that these moods do not always come from within us, but very often they are the result of the unprecedented tension of the surrounding atmosphere. As soon as the current changes, the moods too should change. Quite correctly, you write that "an overwhelmed warrior may hope to receive unexpected and miraculous help." However, you should allow this very wondrous Power to judge when the help should come. So often, we ourselves have been in the most difficult circumstances and we thought we could bear it no longer. But then we learned that even more could be suffered, and only after having entirely exhausted our own resources did we receive help, and always in the most unexpected way.

From the Teachings of Life you know already that only through obstacles do we grow, and that only thus do we learn and sharpen our abilities. And, truly speaking, how else can we temper our spirit? Please do not imagine that the disciples and the servants of Light are treading a path covered with roses. No, their way is full of thorns; and the nearer to Light, the more difficult and responsible are the orders they receive. The path of the Teaching, the Path of Service, first of all, is the path of self-denial and sacrifice. But joyous is this path when the heart is full of love toward the Hierarchy of Light—the thorns become like fragrant freesias! An example of such service is given by N. K. If only you could know his burden you would be terrified, as verily his burden is enormous! But he is so full of love, of devotion and striving, that he accepts everything with great joy and is ready to give his whole self for the General Good.

And is it not joyous to realize that we are fulfilling our duty toward humanity? What a beautiful and powerful concept is in the fulfilment of duty! All heroes fulfil their duty. And you, being a warrior, should particularly appreciate this idea of duty. Therefore I am so convinced that you will overcome depression, all the whispers of darkness, all fears and doubts. You write that you have your weapon; therefore, if your consciousness really thinks it to be a weapon, and not just a symbol, you will win! The Teaching, well understood and applied, is our best weapon.

Of course the material hardships are difficult, but they are nothing in comparison with spiritual sores. The material hardships, if the spirit is strong, sometimes can be immediately remedied, but the spiritual sores require long years of cure. I hope you do not mind these "moral lectures," but I am longing to impress upon you that you also do not lack the possibilities of improving your material affairs. Do you know what the near future may bring you? And I earnestly ask you to be courageous during these coming years. Verily, there are only a few years before the great changes should take place. Much will be altered and it is necessary to preserve our strength. The whole world is wailing and experiencing the most incredible material crisis, which is the result of complete spiritual corruption. And only those whose spirit is strong may hope to conquer this. The predicted Armageddon is not a myth but a dreadful reality. Therefore, be strong! God is with the brave!

I was very happy that you appreciate the works of Vivekananda and Ramakrishna. Their books were and are our greatest friends. Unfortunately, both these great spirits have already left us. Vivekananda died in 1901 and Ramakrishna before that. Can you read English? And what books of Vivekananda and Ramakrishna do you have? I am sorry that my library consists only of foreign books, mostly English; I have almost no Russian ones. But if you can read English, I shall be glad to send you those books of Vivekananda that I have, although I have no other works of his except his lectures. He died rather young, being only forty, but he fulfilled a tremendous mission. He instituted the real association of the East with the West. This was the first time that, clearly and with love, India's majestic concepts, her world outlook and the high principles of the Living Ethics were introduced to the West. And perhaps he influenced the consciousness of our fellow countrymen more than our own great Helena P. Blavatsky. You know that the proverb "no one is a prophet in his own country" is particularly true about our people. But the time will come when the Russians will realize all the grandeur of the Teaching brought to the world by H. P. Blavatsky and will pay due respect to the great woman who suffered for these ideas.

Have you read that pearl of Hindu Literature, the Bhagavad-Gita? In was translated into Russian by the poet Baltrushaitis. One of my Russian friends in America borrowed it and, as often happens, forgot to return it.

You are right, as far as bad results are concerned, there is no worse crime than ignorance! Pseudopatriotism and pseudoreligion are falling away, and to replace these expiring scarecrows there is coming a future era of new joyous, constructive life, based on the great cooperation of peoples. It will be a new revival and purification of the Testaments of all the great Teachers. It will be Russia's destiny to become a real mother and not just the stepmother of the people who populate her. Real patriotism and chauvinism are two opposites. One concept is based on tolerance, and therefore is growing, while the other is based on hatred, and therefore is dying away. The laws are the same everywhere.

Did you happen to hear that even the Banner of Peace, which was raised by N. K., was declared to be unpatriotic! Are you surprised? But such is the fact; we received an accusing letter concerning this matter. Someone found in this great idea a neglect of the problems of our country! N. K. was accused of being an internationalist, indifferent to the sufferings of his motherland.

It was necessary to acknowledge this letter. Some extracts from our letter I shall quote to you, as it will be my answer, in general to all similar pseudopatriots, with whom you also have to deal:

"Only broad constructive work on a world scale, inspired by the national genius, can raise the significance of a country and its position among other countries. Can you imagine that the armchair critics, who grumble, blame and scoff, can help at all? Can they do more than those whose energy is applied for development of culture? Will not this cultural uplift awaken a true esteem for a country? For every firm structure, first of all, it is necessary to have a powerful center. But a center which reflects a narrow nationalism cannot be successful in the world structure. Where is there such a country in the world of today that is built up of only one race?

"And if some people think that narrow nationalism is equal to patriotism, they are very much mistaken. And even if at first glance some short-sighted people see power in it, they will discover that with the further development of such a movement there will result self-destruction. Each power let loose is a boomerang; and therefore we must be very careful about the way we throw into space these powers, for by the law of the returned blow they sooner or later will either destroy or elevate us, depending upon how we use them.

"True patriotism is so different from chauvinism. It is selfless love of one's country together with respect toward other nations which have in various ways contributed toward the growth and development of one's own nation. The true power and beauty of a country abides in its multiformity, in a comprehensiveness that does not preclude the fundamental oneness of the motherland. And the one who knows how to manifest this unity in diversity is really a great leader. The narrow nationalism of Germany has degraded that country and, if brought to life again, may destroy it. Patriotism is a high, most noble and sacred sentiment, but narrow nationalism or chauvinism is self-destructive. It is not sufficient to read the newspapers and to listen to the political leaders in order to understand the development of events; perhaps it is even better not to pay much attention to this information, as often it creates still greater confusion. Today, the human mentality and the whole life is similar to a ship that is adrift without sail or rudder amid the chaotic stormy elements. In order to understand the created chaos, in order to see the direction which leads toward salvation and the great future, and especially in order to know the right dates, one should possess a great spiritual vision and should know the High Guidance, or the so-called Hiero-inspiration."

And now, as regards a certain priest. It is a lie, thrice a lie, that he personally knew N. K. He never met N. K., but he had a short and rather significant correspondence with him. I may have to quote some extracts from this correspondence, in order to give a picture of the personality of this priest. From Paris we received his booklet. After reading it, I asked N. K. to write him a kindly letter about this little book and to tell him we would be glad to read some of his other works. N. K., in addition to his most cordial letter, sent his book *Realm of Light* and a few reproductions of his paintings. The answer was stunning and overwhelming. It was a veritable replication of a narrow sectarian, spiritually poor and cruel to the utmost. Not knowing personally N. K., without having any idea about his selfless work in the name of Good, of Beauty—in the name of spirituality regardless of how expressed—this venerable priest, at the end of his letter permitted himself the following reproach: "Your path, N. K., is not an evangelical one. The people make of you an idol (and in America this easily becomes a source of financial income), *but you do not stop such people.* (The last words are underlined in the original.) ... Your book does not take a person away from the world of relative spiritual values and concepts, and as far as *the cult of your name is concerned, which is encouraged by you, it is more than alarming for us.*" (Again underlined.)

Who are these "us"? Those ignorant pharisees who are trafficking in the name of Christ? This priest (monk-priest of the Russian Orthodox Church] did not realize that N. K. by his very nature is a constructor of life, a leader of culture, and that the conventional measurements of a monk are out of place!

In reply to this cruel, repulsive letter, N. K. wrote a wonderful answer, full of real tolerance and kindness. In this letter N. K. also spoke of his cultural activities. Nowhere, not by a single word, did he insult the man. This letter, as could have been expected of such a "kindly and righteous priest," was acknowledged, but with all the calumny he could collect from all the envious calumniators. He did not hesitate scoffingly to tear down everything that is sacred to us and which, according to him, is a manifestation of the devil and the jest of an Antichrist!

Seeing that we revered the Eastern Teachings, he, in order to prove that these Teachings are heretical, quoted some extracts from the works of certain orientalists. These works are not only considered obsolete by the Sanscritists of today, but are entirely ignored by a well-educated orientalists, who consider them illiterate and, as far as their very distorted translations from the Sanscrit are concerned, most unreliable. And here our correspondent revealed his weakness. It is only in the last ten years that the West has begun to discern something greater in Sanscrit (this most difficult language), and now some crying, monstrous mutilations in the first translations are revealed. Thus, for instance, he quotes from Bunge's *The History of Paganism*: "The true substance of the world is not Deity, not the Original Power, but the absolute Vacuum, entire Nihility. Everything came from Nihility, through Nihility, and will once more return to Nihility, for from the very beginning it was nothingness. Everything is vanity of vanities in heaven and on earth, for heaven and earth are equally vain. Above the clouds of the disintegrating universe reigns the eternal Nonentity."

And further comes similar absurdity, extracted from *Religious Consciousness of Paganism,* an essay by Professor Vedensky. I shall quote only the end: "If for a Buddhist there is any aim at all in life, it is only a negative one—escape from this illusory and nonsensical life, full of bitterness and suffering, into a Nirvana of Nonentity."

To this obvious distortion and to similar ignorant quotations, N. K. answered with the following:

"In regard to your quotations, I may say that the author of one of these books evidently did not know foreign languages and probably consulted only very limited and distorted translations (such as Bunge, and Keppen); neither did he know the 'Summa Summarum' of the Eastern contemplation of the world, which first of all states, 'From nothingness comes nothingness,' and secondly, 'There is no vacuum.' Do not these two statements open the way to God? Let us not forget that in the East the *Greatest Concept*, because of *profound reverence*, is not pronounced. One may choose the unfortunate, distorted concepts and follow them, or from many sources one may find most beautiful pages full of the all-pervading divine Spirit, all-merciful to his creatures.

"As for 'Nirvana,' it means, according to the original Eastern concept, the transcendental, or the *highest state of existence*, which cannot be encompassed by the ordinary human mind; in other words, it is a *complete contrast to non-existence*. Such is the ignorance of our Western translators and commentators on whom we depend!"

This letter of N. K. was acknowledged just by a short note; probably the priest felt that his opponent was above his capacity. He expressed the desire to meet N. K., and then he was not ashamed to add: "Believe me, I would like to feel that you are *higher and better* than I." A real prayer of a Pharisee. "God, I thank thee, that I am not as other men... or even as this publican. I fast twice a week, I give tithes of all that I possess." (St. Luke 18:11-12) Does it not follow from these words of the "spiritual father" that he himself suffers from what he accused N. K. of in his first letter? Is it not said that he who has a beam in his own eye sees a mote in his brother's eye?

And this last note N. K. did not leave without an answer. He sent a warm, wise letter. I shall quote only the end of it (at the beginning N. K. just thanked him for his books):

"Perhaps some day we shall meet and talk amicably and heart to heart. Once more I may affirm that I am glad to find certain things in your book. To the utmost of my power I am trying to deal with the primigenial sources of the Great Testaments in order to avoid all sorts of later accumulation, which sometimes border on sacrilege and mockery of sacred things. 'In all your works, look into their foundations and deepen the good.' These were the words of Father John of Kronstadt, which he gave me. You certainly know of all the dark slander which was spread about Father John and was repeated by light-minded people. But is not slander just another sign of a true grandeur of spirit? And so, hoping to see you personally, and in the meantime sending you my best wishes."

This was the end of a significant correspondence. But it remains a most curious example of the ignorance, pharisaism and cruelty of our spiritual leaders. This priest told the truth when he admitted that the clergy are responsible for the decline of the church. You, who admire the books of Vivekananda and Ramakrishna, will be interested to know what this "enlightened priest" said:

"At the moment I am looking through one of the most pure, spiritual and noble occult books [why occult!], *The Gospel of*

Ramakrishna, with a preface by Swami Abhedananda. One reads the preface and is astonished by the absence of real spiritual values. For instance: 'Before starting to deal with people and to teach them at all, Ramakrishna, like a scientific explorer, devoted twelve years to the study of the dogmas and ceremonies of all religions, performing their divine services and rituals full of faith and profound reverence, so that he could, by experience, realize where all the religions led. ... And finally, by following all their methods, he realized the one and only presence of Deity in all of them.' This alone should be sufficient for you to understand my perplexity, how such absurdity could be compared with the Revelation of Christ."

Truly speaking, the last sentence of the priest himself should be put into the category of "absurdity." And it would have been better if, before criticizing and anathematizing other religions and Teachings, he could have followed the honest example of Ramakrishna and Vivekananda and tried to study the true foundations of each Teaching and religion by attending their divine services, only after that giving his opinion. But without being a prophet, one can predict that the "enlightened priest" has not the spirit of goodness and tolerance that Vivekananda possessed, and which Vivekananda so beautifully expressed in the following: "Had I lived in Palestine in the days of Jesus of Nazareth I would have washed his feet, not with my tears but with my heart's blood!" Vivekananda sensed the true beauty of the Image of Christ, undistorted by ecclesiastics. But, in giving Christ tribute from his heart, Vivekananda did not forget the Great Images of his own religion. Which of these two is the greater? The spirit of this priest is so far from the all-embracing utterance of the Bhagavad-Gita: "By whatever path ye come to Me, by that path will I bless ye; because all paths are mine."

In this beautiful statement it is clearly indicated that the form of religion itself does not really matter, but it is the idea that is essential. Verily, our spiritual leaders are far from such wisdom, generosity, tolerance and comprehensiveness! Everyone knows that "as in Macrocosm, so in microcosm." Therefore, should not our hearts be like the Cosmic Heart in comprehensiveness? Could one imagine such terrible injustice as that the most Wise, the most Merciful God could send his son just to one particular nation! Then afterwards, as well as before, the billions of people, "the children of our Heavenly Father" (if we believe the words of Christ Himself), remain *outcasts*, in spite of the fact that many of them were and are much higher in morality than those who were privileged to be born under the shelter of the Christian Church!

You should not fear that the words of this priest may bring harm; on the contrary, it is always good when a person reveals his true nature. We need not be afraid of accusations of heresy. The Image of the true Christ—the Teacher—abides in our hearts and minds, and we completely join Vivekananda in his words about Christ. However, we see Man-God in Christ, and not a narrow sectarian who condemns everybody to the ranks of "anti-Christ" if they do not accept the ecclesiastic limitations and distortions of his Teaching. We have plenty of adherents even among the official representatives of the various churches. It is impossible to stop all progress, and it is impossible to share the mentality of the ancient priesthood, the *creators of Christian dogmas*, who, at their synods for instance, discussed very seriously how many spirits could be placed on the end of a needle, or whether or not woman possessed a soul, and similar gems of profound spiritual revelation. In addition, at their Councils, these ancient holy men pulled each others' beards and soundly boxed one anothers' ears! Let us not forget that the law of Reincarnation was rejected by these wise men only in the sixth century, at the Council of Constantinople. No, it is time to look through all the Teachings, discard the later distorted accumulations, and return to the pure original sources.

It would be advisable for the fathers of the church to recollect the Covenant of Christ, and of his favorite disciple, "love one another." Then everything would take its right place. It is also urgently necessary to look through and study the works of the great Origen, that true Light of Christianity. His works are now studied by some of the Western clergy in America. These fathers understand that the consciousness of their spiritual flocks requires new nourishment, and that it can no longer be satisfied by the naive ideas which once upon a time perhaps were necessary for the taming of half-savage tribes, newly-converted to Christianity. In order not to lose altogether their influence, some members of the clergy of the West are hurrying to improve and increase their knowledge. If our "spiritual fathers" were to follow their example, we could expect many good results!

Just think how many clear indications about reincarnation,

about the law of Karma, are given in the New Testament, precisely in the words of Christ Himself! But our "spiritual fathers" thoroughly avoid these questions! May God be their judge!

Today, we experience a dreadful spiritual crisis, a terrible, all-corrupting atheism, which results from narrow, lifeless sectarianism and from choking dogmatism, as well as from the fall of morality among the representatives of churches. We have never spoken, nor will we speak against any religion or church, as it is better to have some religion or church than none at all. But we will always protest against lack of tolerance, morality and knowledge. Priests are necessary, but they should be real spiritual leaders and should be progressive and not continue to exist in the chains of the dark ignorance of the Middle Ages. The spirit of the Inquisition is still very strong. Do you think that if Christ came again on earth now He could avoid crucifixion? At best, would He escape lynching, or imprisonment for life, with the title of Antichrist?

Threatening events are approaching, and it is particularly tragic to observe the increasing disunion in all spheres of life. So much incommensurability, low slander, envy and hatred among those who should be doing the work of unifying! It is time to understand that the question of the salvation of the whole of humanity, and of the planet itself, is now before us. And salvation is in the hands of the people themselves; but they, fanning the fires of hatred and personal disagreement, are only increasing the danger of a dreadful time. Nobody wants to think that the predicted Armageddon is anything but a myth, but, verily, it is a terrible reality and a great danger.

Nevertheless, we should not lose courage, for those who have heard the Call and who endure suffering to the end shall be saved. Remember about the shortness of the time, and let this knowledge strengthen you. In all your deeds, in all contacts, remember the principle you were taught: "Tolerance, magnanimity and striving into the future!"

19b

7 June 1934

The time which humanity is now experiencing is one of transition from the evolution of the intellect to the evolution of spirituality. This period will be marked by the achievement of the predominance of the spirit over the intellect. This transition will be completed during the change of races. Thus, the sixth race is now taking its rightful place. As you know, each change of races is accompanied by cosmic cataclysms. Such purification is necessary for the development of the new race. These cosmic cataclysms will take place as a result of the shifting of the earth's axis. The scientists of today most emphatically point to this shifting, which has been happening for some time and may result in catastrophes.

Precisely, the sixth race must begin the New Era, and this preparatory period is very strenuous. But it would be wrong to think that the sixth race is being born in one particular country or nationality; it is spread widely. Certainly, there is always the main kernel of the sixth race, and in the time of catastrophe its members will be gathered into places of safety.

The great fiery purification is approaching. That is why it is so important to purify thoughts and heart and attempt to assimilate the fires of space.

At the time of the change of races, there always comes a Great Revelation, and, as usual, only those whose consciousness belongs to the next degree of development, i.e., to the new coming race, can assimilate it fully. The rest will benefit insofar as they are able. It is wrong, however, to think that the remaining races will be exterminated. The best will be saved, and some may even flourish. Only the refuse, those who are unable to proceed with evolution, will die out or will entirely degenerate; we can see examples of such degeneration among many primitive peoples. Thus, the aborigines of Australia are the degenerated descendants of sub-races who at one time belonged to the great third race; this race was superior to us in its achievements, for the Great Sons of Reason were incarnated in it.

* * *

And now, why do you think that there can be no destruction of our planet? Alas, precisely this danger threatens us. Verily, the Great Forces of Light, beyond all measure, are trying to save our planet. Read carefully from the book of Josephine St. Hilaire, *On Eastern Crossroads*, the two cryptograms, "Gold" and "Darkness"; these legends are received from a High Source.

"Verily, the human spirit will make its appearance as an exploder and an impetus for volcanoes."

"Verily, it is precisely this darkness which begins to leave its previous depositories. Upon its way it corrodes all elements, and the gas forces the elements of destruction into these fissures."

And this darkness was shown to me. The dreadful anguish I experienced was so intense that I almost became ill, and during the next few days I was unable to regain my balance.

You remember how the Teaching says that the very destiny of the planet is in the hands of man, and also that man makes the earthquakes. Take these statements literally. For precisely, the low thoughts and cravings of humanity (not only on the Earth, but also in the lower spheres of the Subtle World) create this fearful suffocating atmosphere around the Earth which promotes the fusion of the fire of space with the subterranean fire. Only pure, fiery souls are able to discharge this atmosphere, acting somewhat like lightning conductors. This is the reason why the epoch of Fire is so dangerous: it brings purification as well as dreadful disasters, namely the destruction of whole polluted communities and the increase of epidemics—all caused by the subterranean fire. Only those whose auras are sufficiently purified and who are able to assimilate the fire of space will be able to withstand. That is the reason why it is so urgently necessary to apply the foundations of the Living Ethics into life and, by purity of thought and deed, to transmute our energies. The waves of the fire of space will be particularly strong in the forties of our century. But the immediate coming years will also bring many explosions. The great testing of our planet is near. Threatening is this future! Let us hope that through great disasters humanity will learn its lesson and will accept spiritual leadership, and thus will alter its destiny.

Certainly, the Lords of Light are taking all measures for the saving of the planet from this dreadful destiny. And if humanity chooses destruction, its better part (and are there many such?) will be transferred to the higher planets. The average mass will go to another planet similar to our own, which will approach Earth in case the explosion occurs. (At the moment this new planet is still not visible.) As for the rest of humanity, they will follow the Prince of the World and be banished with him to Saturn. But alas! no one realizes what retardation in the evolution of the majority of our earthly humanity there will be in the event of the destruction of our planet. What aeons will have to pass before the new "Earth" will be able to provide suitable bodies!

Therefore, it is essential to awaken the consciousness of humanity and to make them realize that they themselves are creating a most critical and dangerous situation. The East knew about this dangerous period a long time ago. In ancient scriptures there are times indicated, regarding the approach of the fiery energies, corresponding to the forties of our century. It is interesting to note that the calculations of the Hierophants of ancient Egypt show that the year 1936 is most significant; and, still further, the very years during which the destiny of our planet should be decided are pointed out. This destiny will be either a beautiful epoch of Great Balance or else it will be the end, a final total explosion. Thus, the fate of our planet is in the hands of humanity. Therefore, in your writings try to emphasize the role of man in all matters of either the pollution or purification of the atmosphere. Verily, man is both igniter and extinguisher of the subterranean fire. Also mention the Hierarchy of Light, tirelessly watching and helping us!

Yes innumerable worlds are being both born and destroyed in Infinity, and who can tell all the reasons for these destructions? Is it not the neglect of cosmic laws and the perversion of all the higher principles of Life that is the main cause of cosmic cataclysms? The cosmic laws are immutable, and all that fails to move in rhythm with evolutionary transmutation is destroyed. As refuse, it goes back for remaking. People should try to understand the events on the planet. From one of the books of the Teaching I quote some paragraphs that have significance for our time:

"During the reorganization of spatial affirmations, evoked by the accumulation of earthly structures, all measures must be taken for the elimination of dark agglomerations. Each earthly reconstruction appears as a resonance of the super-earthly spheres. Our Fiery Period is saturated with particular energies which must enter into life prior to the designated dates. For the Fiery Period can create fiery manifestations, when that time approaches in which humanity can rise to meet it. Thus must one understand the Fiery Reconstruction which will give inception to the New Epoch. But one must affirm the spirit in understanding of spatial fires because only fiery assimilation can produce the required energy. The manifestation of fiery dates draws near. Let those see who can, for a Great Time is approaching!

"Before the great reorganization of the world, a manifestation of all the dark forces is displayed, for a better transmutation. What is taking place in the world cannot be called a step of evolution, but it can indeed be said that what is being manifested is the lowest, the most intense, the most saturated by the forces of darkness. But great is the work which gathers together everything helpful for the great reconstruction. Just as the condensed strata of the earthly spheres are being made ready for battle, so does a manifestation of the Forces of Light stand on guard. The stage which the planet is going through can be compared with a furnace of Cosmic Fire. All dense energies are aflame in tension, and on guard stands the Fiery Right. Fiery creativeness is assembling all fiery energies—thus the world is being reconstructed by the tension of two polarities. It is necessary clearly to discern these turbulent energies.

"A fiery epoch has begun. As at present physical manifestations are being studied, so will be studied the fiery manifestations of the centers. Agni Yoga is being manifested as a forerunner of the Great Epoch—yes, yes, yes!" [Fiery World III]

You know the principle of the Forces of Light never to invade personal karma; therefore, all warnings are given in hints. A person must discriminate independently regarding the application of these warnings and as to what he should attribute them, for otherwise how could one learn? Precisely, the dark forces are using all methods to creep into the pure undertakings in order to destroy them.

The dark forces, in their desire to disrupt the pure beginnings, will come to the temple uttering the formulae of the Teaching, and after lulling suspicion they will tempt fools by offering to quicken the development of their psychic energy. Of course, for the fulfilment of their evil design, they must break the protective auric net. This hideous aim is achieved by various prescriptions and methods which depend upon the weakening of the organism of their victim. Thus, the dark ones penetrate through the breach in the protective net, that is why so much is said in the Teaching about the protective net, and about the need of keeping the aura in purity, in order to prevent the dark ones from approaching. And the best measure is complete devotion to a single Teacher. Every deviation (even if only temporary) from the chosen path can throw us into the power of darkness.

I shall quote a page from the Teaching which I suggest that you spread widely:

"The forces of darkness press on by various means, being affirmed in strata which are found to be near to the Light. In the Subtle Spheres this proximity is naturally impossible, but in the earthly strata, where the atmosphere is so thickened with infected gases, the forces of darkness definitely try to come close to the Light. An impulse of destruction impels the forces of darkness to these Torchlights of Truth. The enemies who uplift a sword are not so dangerous as those who penetrate under the mask of Light. There are conscious and unconscious instruments of darkness. At first the unconscious ones create, as it were, in unison with the good, and these bearers of evil infect each pure beginning. But conscious servants of evil enter into the temple with your prayer, and woe to the undiscerning! Dark snares have been laid for them. It is not fitting to admit into the Holy of Holies offenders against the spirit. Djins can help on the earthly plane, and may even build a temple, but the spiritual plane is inaccessible to them. Thus, on the path to the Fiery World let us remember about the servants of darkness who strive to penetrate into the Holy of Holies.

"It is especially necessary to employ cautiousness for manifestations of cosmic energies. The misuse of energies is a danger connected with every affirmation of cosmic force. Only a conscious and careful attitude can ward off frightful consequences. Forces called up from the Subtle World require a restraint which only a strong spirit can manifest. Otherwise this unbridled force becomes an affirmation of Cosmic Chaos. When fiery dates approach it is very necessary to know this, for vast will be the manifestation of invocations." [Fiery World III]

Everywhere black lodges are springing up, with the most disgraceful black masses and evocations. Newspapers are full of these reports, but public opinion does not seem to bother about this very great crime and calamity.

* * *

Great is the error of thinking that it is possible to develop and increase the supply of psychic energy by way of excessive straining in work or by depriving oneself of sleep and food.

The correct development of a high quality of psychic energy is possible only through the broadening of the consciousness and by the help of the Great Ones. But the cord of the heart, which connects the disciple with his Teacher, should be strong! All other, forced, methods and exercises can lead only to the lowest manifestations of psychic energy, or to the development of mediumism and eventually to obsession, and can even cause death. Therefore, all the Teachings have always stressed the Golden Mean, or Balance; care should be taken of health. Sleep is absolutely necessary because during sleep our subtle body is nourished by the vital substance of the Subtle World, which has contact with the higher energies. If deprived of this nourishment the spirit droops. In the polluted atmosphere of cities it is necessary to sleep not less than seven or eight hours; also the food should contain a sufficient amount of vitamins. All extremes are harmful.

The tension mentioned in the Teaching is not a physical over-straining but a *vigilance and mobility of consciousness.* This in turn influences our vitality, as the awakened, broadened consciousness makes a person twice as strong. (However, vigilance of consciousness does not mean that one should try to do without sleep.) The centers also can be opened only in the cases where the consciousness is broadened. But the opening of the centers is not the final achievement; afterwards comes their fiery transmutation. The path of discipleship is not as simple as many think. It is made easier for those who have striven to fill their Chalice. Therefore, do not expect opened centers in every kind of psychic manifestation. Even should there be a slight opening of one of the centers, there are such endless gradations of these partially opened centers! Therefore, remember what is said in the Teaching about "the rings of keen sight and hearing."

* * *

You may call the Teaching "The Living Ethics," if you would rather avoid the Eastern terminology, which sounds strange to some people. I have already mentioned the study of the Teachings of Origen. In America the minister R. N. was our great friend, and a great admirer of N. K. He was a wonderful preacher, and in his sermons he propounded the concepts of reincarnation and karma. Many followers attended his lectures. The Gospel of Christ is full of indications about these laws. Why should we then ignore them? It is most essential to look carefully through all the resolutions of the Church Councils. What an amount of ignorance, greed, and even criminality would be discovered! If we glance through the whole history of the Church, and of the Papacy, we are terrified! And one asks oneself whether those who were supposed to be following the Great Light indicated by Christ were not guided by the dark forces! And is not Christ still being crucified today? This task (the purification of religion) is not an easy one and it may bring out many enemies, but in the long run perhaps even more friends! Therefore, one must carefully weigh whether or not one is prepared to accept this burden. But even if one would limit this task, much can be done for the shifting of the human consciousness. If anyone decides to commence this work, let him thoroughly prepare himself for it; let him collect irrefragable proofs, so that each question can be answered from the standpoint of what is most vital, understandable and benevolent. All abstractions must be omitted. It is essential that he emphasize the vital principles of all the Great Teachings. Certainly great Blessings will be with him! But I repeat that there will be much hostile opposition. In America such tasks should be much easier, as in that country there are not the many prejudices which enslave and destroy the thinking power in other lands. However, even in the United States, the life of our friend, R. N., was not an easy one; the narrow churchmen were very much against him.

And now I must tell you that you should not be alarmed by your mood of depression. Often these moods only reflect the incredible tension of the surrounding atmosphere. A changing of the currents will bring a corresponding change in your mood. Therefore be calm, and carefully wait until these heavy currents alter. In the meantime, new strength is coming to you.

20

14 June 1934

Everything you write is very good, but let us hope that the country will not remain for long on the level of narrow nationalism. Of course this transitory stage is inevitable, but the more cultured the people who represent the country are, the sooner will they deal with this question. True patriotism and chauvinism are complete opposites. The first concept is all-embracing and therefore capable of growth while the other is exclusive, compressive and therefore deathly. The laws are the same in everything. If some think that narrow nationalism is the same as patriotism, they are badly mistaken. Only the short-sighted can consider such nationalism strong. True patriotism should manifest itself not only in devoted love for one's own country and for all manifestations of its national genius, but also in solicitude and respect for each of its component peoples who have contributed toward the building of its culture. The task of the national genius is to perceive the achievements of all minorities and all nationalities resident in the country, to blend them, and to bind this conglomeration of creative expressions into a synthesized whole.

Peoples and countries must learn to preserve their character and individuality by enriching themselves with all the flowers that grow in their meadows! But every forced isolation in this age of cooperation and unification (even if in its present stage this unification takes place mostly in mechanical achievements) is ruinous. But the time is not far off, during the next step, when whole countries will aspire toward cultural, spiritual cooperation and exchange, each one offering its flowers of achievement. For this new step the Teaching of Life is preparing us. Thus, wisely, we must wait until the inevitable period of exaggerated nationalism is outlived, and in the meantime try our best to unify and never to disrupt.

Also, please follow the Advice not to argue with those whose consciousness refuses to live with the time, as it is quite hopeless. We should always follow the Advice given to us not to call or force anyone, as only the spirit that is ready can accept a broad understanding of all vital problems.

As for the alleged Eastern influence over the Teaching of Living Ethics, let us be objective and ask ourselves if there is any teaching or philosophy that did not originate in the East. Our so-called Western philosophy is a mere reflection of the thought of the East. Christianity itself came from Eastern Hands. Therefore, in order to comprehend the Teaching of Christ completely, it is necessary either to be an Easterner by birth or else to study fundamentally those doctrines upon which the Teaching of Christ is built.

It is quite certain that the Christianity of today and the

original Teaching of Christ Himself are two entirely different things. Even as the lamaism of the present time and the original Teaching of Gotama Buddha are complete opposites. One is of the spirit, the other is a creation of human ignorance and greed. All this I am writing to you, but it is not for the narrow-minded dogmatists, with whom it is useless to argue. Many souls need little fences to protect them, just as timid horses need blinkers. There is a proverb in the East which says, "It is good to be born in a temple, but very bad to die there." There are as many gradations of consciousness as there are degrees in Infinity; therefore, there are as many laws and aspects of truth as degrees of consciousness.

You write about the Pact and Banner of Peace, that his idea may not appeal to some people because they are against pacifism. But why should they take only one side of the movement? The Pact itself, first of all, mentions the significance of the Banner during war and similar destructive events. The Red Cross, for instance, is good in peace time, but its main significance is during war. Likewise, the Banner of Peace, as a protective measure, first of all, is necessary just now, when the countries are on the brink of threatening events. The most eminent military authorities of France and America were the first to approve the Banner. And official recognition of the Pact continues. Thus, the Republic of Panama has officially accepted the Pact and Banner of Peace. Likewise, the Pan-American Union (which proposed the ratification of the Pact) hopes to fulfil this pressing cultural task toward 1935.

And now, regarding the League of Culture. You write that you plan to establish the League of Culture within a certain society which approves of such work. This is excellent, and let this work also include science and art groups. And it seems to me that if you start such groups they could be excellently developed. In time it could be expanded into a very good school, something like a people's university; and, of course, it should be based on the self-supporting principle. But as usual, things should be started on a small scale, according to possibility. Nothing should be overdone; this is the fundamental rule. Hence, one should not insist upon the acceptance of the Teaching of Living Ethics. As long as the people are not bad and, mainly, as long as they do not betray, things are acceptable. Time will show us "who is who." Remember that the canon "By *thy* God" is higher than "By *my* God."

Yes, you have, so to say, mountains of work. But the members of the Society should not start too many things at once. All the tasks should have certain limits, and these boundaries will expand of themselves when the need arises.

And now, regarding those who turn aside. You know how all the ancient Teachings looked upon the breaking of one bond with the single Teacher and the replacing of Him by another. Once the connecting cord is rent, nobody can repair it. Only the one who fell away himself, after many hardships and efforts to perfect himself, completely realizing his fault, may ask the Teacher to accept him again—but no one else can do it for him. Therefore, it is necessary to warn the newcomers who are striving for spiritual advancement. They must first decide whether they are ready to give themselves completely and unconditionally to the High Guidance. Often a person, in the desire to advance immediately and to acquire great knowledge, runs after other Teachings and Teachers, and thus divides himself twice and sometimes thrice, and loses what he has already gained. But the fundamental rule of every Teaching requires the affirmation of one particular Teacher, and then reverence to all the links of the Chain of Hierarchy. The High Hierarch has his own trusted ones, and not one of the approaching disciples can leap over or omit the nearest link without danger of losing his place in the whole chain. But all this concerns only the serious seekers and those who have firmly decided to walk the path of Great Service. The rest may draw benefit from the books of the Teaching, without pretending to enter the path of discipleship or to receive special Guidance. They need not even be aware of the source of the Teaching! It was said that many will read the Teaching on retiring, taking it as a soporific. We know of such people, and never do they think about the origin of the Teaching. Thus, those who choose the quicker way of broadening their consciousness should assimilate the law of Hierarchy; otherwise no real progress is possible. The Ladder of Jacob is a great Reality and the foundation of the whole Cosmos.

And now, please point out to the newcomers that every Teaching advises the Golden Mean. All that is forced or exaggerated is condemned. Therefore, when it was mentioned regarding the decreasing of the amount of food and sleep, it was well and very clearly said that when the spirit is ready the organism itself will indicate what is required. One could lessen sleep and food to the extreme, but the final results would be very sad: a weakening of the organism, insanity and even death. A person normally sleeping seven or eight hours, eating sufficiently, but aspiring ardently to purify his thoughts, can reach excellent results. Of course, it has been pointed out that in the mountains one may sleep and eat much less, as the necessity for both appreciably decreases there; but in the polluted atmosphere of the city it is strongly advised to take a sufficient amount of food, and it is of course to be understood that it is not the quantity of food itself that is important but the quality and amount of nutritive elements and vitamins. Even so, vegetarianism is preferable, mainly because meat-eating is the cause of many serious poisonings and diseases.

There is a Buddhist saying, "If spirituality could be achieved just by eating vegetable matter, the elephant and the cow would have attained it long ago." And it is also said, "Asceticism is worthless for liberation. It is much more difficult to find a patient person than one who lives upon air and roots and dresses in bark and leaves. If a person is weakened by hunger or thirst, if he is too tired to control his emotions and thoughts, how can he possibly reach the goal which can be reached only by means of a clear mind and broadened consciousness?" And again, "In order that the strings of the vina may sound harmoniously, they should be neither too taut nor too slack. Verily, every effort that is too strenuous fails, and if not sufficiently strong it results in passivity and inertness."

Thus, exercise your sense of commensurability. Know the limit for tension, and balance your abilities!

The renunciation of earthly excesses should be performed in spirit, in one's consciousness. "The one who fasts while enjoying thoughts about food is worse than the one who actually eats meat at his meals." It is always well to remember that the spirit that is ready easily surrenders all excesses; he does not even think about it, everything comes naturally to him. So the main achievement is in the purification and broadening of consciousness, and everything else is secondary.

It is also most foolish to think that one can develop and increase the supply of psychic energy by too much work and too little sleep. The proper development of psychic energy of a high quality is possible only through the broadening of one's consciousness and by the Help from the High Sources. All other, forced methods and exercises lead only to the lower manifestations of this energy, or else they end with the development of mediumism, obsession and even death. That is why it is so important to point out to everyone the way of the Golden Mean and care for health.

The idea of eating pure vegetable food is not based upon sentiment but on purely medical reasons. Those who enter the path of Service and true discipleship should be most particular about purity in everything. Also, you should point out that sleep is absolutely essential. When the body does not interfere, the spirit can be nourished especially well by the vivifying substance of the Subtle World. Deprived of this nourishment, the spirit droops.

* * *

I was surprised to learn about the number of members. If all of them answer the first requirements of the Living Ethics, it is a great joy. However, we should remember that quality is important, not quantity. "Discrimination of people is the first test of every leader. Therefore, let us be careful with the newcomers, especially with those who merely recite the formulae of the Teaching." A large army never was a guarantee of victory; the important thing is the spirit that unifies it.

Often we see from the letters we receive that many people misinterpret some indications of the Teaching. Almost everything that is meant in a broad, all-embracing sense is taken personally, according to the domestic requirements. And a cruel, ruinous want of co-measurement is the result. I realize that some ideas are hard to comprehend, as the Teaching was given and is given according to certain experiences and events in the everyday life. That is the reason why some indications do not sound complete and may be understood only by those who have the key to them. If you have perplexities, please do not hesitate to inquire, and I shall be only too glad to explain what I can.

People who pretend to watch closely the correct interpretation of the Teachings, often are guilty in just the opposite.

Do not be surprised if the very infuriated and intolerant ones resemble the obsessed. It should be remembered that fanatics are just the obsessed. The degrees of obsession are various, and sometimes there are even cases that are not very bad. Thus, once we knew a very kindly old lady who was under the complete control (or obsession) of her uncle, an English bishop. She was constantly delivering speeches of the same type and scale as the bishop gave when alive. It was quite possible that she was even helping some people, but for the old lady herself this condition was rather harmful, as the growth of her spirit was entirely paralyzed; she was only an obedient instrument of her obsessor.

21

30 June 1934

The Teaching of Life, while revealing a new aspect of the one eternal Truth, has not the intention of replacing the great Teachings of former times; it brings a fiery purification and affirmation of them. Did not Christ say that He came not to destroy the law, nor the prophets, but to fulfil it? Verily, every new Teacher becomes a lawgiver and, at the same time, a fiery purifier of the law. If we study the historical manifestations of the Great Teachers, we shall see that They appeared when the former Teachings had lost their original purity and were completely distorted.

Verily, the Teaching of Life does not reject any preceding Teachings, but deepens them and liberates them from age-old worldly accumulations.

The paragraph from the Teaching which was sent to you offers a whole program of work. Precisely, it is advisable to compare the Teaching with other Testaments; the traces of time will be found on the same truth. However, we should neither criticize nor belittle, but try to find beautiful comparisons and connections.

It is essential to become acquainted with the foundations of all the great Teachings. This knowledge will help the assimilation of the Teaching of Life and the Teaching of Christ. We should remember that all the great Teachings issue from the One Source, and it is impossible to accept one and reject another. The East fully appreciates the significance of the succession of Teachings, and reveres only those Teachers who are links in the Chain of Hierarchy. A teacher who denies the succession of the Teachings and who affirms only his own teaching, is called in the East "a rootless tree." And no one would want to listen to such a teacher. So let us not criticize, nor diminish, but compare and find beautiful links and new extensions of Truth.

* * *

Someone declares that "in the New Era a mother must love another's child as much as her own." This statement is much too strong, and therefore not convincing. It is impossible to demand superhuman feelings from an earthly mother. Let us leave her with her natural right to love her own child more. But we may add that a true mother will find room in her heart also for another's child. All children should be dear to her all-embracing heart. The excluding love is terrible, but the containing love will have its gradations.

* * *

There are seven main centers, and they correspond to the seven principles of man. But for complete crowning, man must kindle all the forty-nine fires, which include all the fires of all the centers and their branches. There are twenty-one centers mentioned in the Teaching because their opening involves the opening of the rest of the centers and their branches. All spiritual centers depend on the heart. The heart is the great accumulator and transmuter of all the energies. It may be called the sun of the organism because of the role it plays.

* * *

The Duad, consisting of the seventh and sixth principles, does not act as a conscious entity on the physical plane of existence. Thus, in order to reach true immortality and to achieve a conscious manifestation on all planes, that is, to become an Arhat, a Buddha or a Dhyan Chohan, man must connect the three principles (the fourth, fifth and seventh) here on Earth and merge them together, precisely in the sixth principle. The seventh principle is just the eternal vital force which exists throughout the whole Cosmos. Therefore, perhaps it would be better to say: Absolute Intelligence and Perfect Heart, being one and the same Origin, correspond to the higher aspect of man, wherein his spirit, intellect, and all his feelings are fierily transmuted and are centralized in the heart—in short, when the intellect becomes a heart and the heart becomes an intellect.

With this understanding the reader will be able to avoid many perplexities.

You associate the sixth principle with the heart, and this is quite correct, as nothing can escape the heart. All energies are transmuted there. But there are many who are accustomed to connect the sixth principle, i.e., Buddhi, with the brain center, and they may oppose you. Nevertheless, precisely the sixth principle, in its highest aspect, is manifested in the heart.

* * *

Every now and then we hear the remark, "Just as the other scriptures, the book *Agni Yoga* does not offer any definite and complete directions as to what to do and how to do it." This is a great error. Precisely, *Agni Yoga*, as well as all the other scriptures, does give the most definite and clear directions how to act. But people always ignore the essential, and are looking for secondary prescriptions. As in their everyday life, they look for apothecary's doses or patent medicines. One forgets that even an ordinary honest physician cares, first of all, about the general condition of his patient, and applies his doses of medicine according to the condition of the organism. All the Teachings, including Agni Yoga, always point out the most essential; and the secondary, subsidiary measures are left for each to choose according to the peculiarities of his or her individual organism. It would be a great mistake to give the same prescription to everyone. Once the foundations are understood and applied in life, the rest will follow quite naturally.

The difficulty comes from the inability of people to realize that the foundation of achievement lies not in mechanical means but in the transmutation of the inner man, whose sphere is in the realm of thought. All the Teachings of the entire world constantly emphasize the significance of "purity of thought, word and deed." These are the three foundations for those who wish to rise above the level of ordinary humanity and join the "gods." Thus spoke Zoroaster, and thus have spoken all the Great Teachers from the first to the last.

Therefore, let us be just and ask ourselves, "Are there not mentioned in the books of the Teaching of Life the qualities necessary for the transmutation of the inner man? Are not these qualities discussed from all angles, from all points of view?" Moreover, even the auxiliary means are given there. Look through the books carefully, and you will find not a few suggestions, even the apothecary's prescriptions! It is also advisable to copy out separately all the qualities expected of a disciple. You will be surprised to find how numerous they are! Verily, it requires many lives to achieve these perfections. But then—have we not great Infinity before us?

And now I shall deal with the questions about reading other books in general. Apparently this question worries everybody. Of course there are no objections against reading books concerning various branches of knowledge, art and spirituality, for one should always extend one's knowledge. But it is quite essential to learn to discriminate as regards quality. Thus, I always warn against pseudo-occult books. And when one has the possibility of obtaining all the treasures from the books of the Teaching of Life, which deal with all the problems of life and show new ways of knowledge, and when one has the chance of becoming acquainted with *The Mahatma Letters* (now in a complete edition published in the English language) as well as with not a few works by H. P. Blavatsky, then the reading of lesser books will be a waste of time. With few exceptions, these other books are often a mere echo—frequently erroneous—of the above-mentioned ones. For instance, *Esoteric Buddhism*, by A. P. Sinnett, is based entirely on the letters from the Mahatmas received by Sinnett through H. P. Blavatsky. But all these letters are much more complete in the book, *Mahatma Letters*. I personally always advise the reading of Eastern philosophy, provided, of course, that it is not distorted in the translation.

It would be excellent if all the co-workers could become acquainted with the *Foundations of Buddhism*, the Upanishads, the Bhagavad-Gita, the Teachings of Confucius, Lao Tse, Zoroaster, Hermes, and others. Of course, one great obstacle is that so few books are translated into Russian. If correctly understood, these Teachings can strengthen the consciousness and help in the assimilation of the Teaching of Living Ethics. I always recommend the reading of the books of Vivekananda and the *Gospel of Ramakrishna*. I also love the four volumes dedicated to the lives of Ramakrishna and Vivekananda. When reading these books, one is fascinated by the refinement of feeling and thoughts of the East. Fine are the works of Sister Nivedita about India and Vivekananda, who was her teacher. Altogether, there are many beautiful Eastern books.

Of course, there are very many people who, after reading various theories which deal with the foundations of the various Yogas, will compare them with the books of the Teaching of Life, and will be disappointed because of various divergencies. That is why the reading of false books dealing with occult subjects is so dangerous for beginners who are not yet firm in their knowledge of the true Teaching. Much sorrow is brought about by spiritual errors. I shall conclude with a paragraph from the Teaching about the evaluation of books:

"The errors in books are equal to a grievous crime. Falsehood in books must be prosecuted as a grave calumny. The falsehood of an orator is prosecuted according to the number of his listeners. The falsehood of an author should be prosecuted according to the number of copies sold of his book. To fill the peoples libraries with falsehood is a grave offense. ... Indeed, one should not impede new views and structures; but incorrect data must not bring one into error because knowledge is the armor of the community and the defense of knowledge is the duty of all the members.

"No more than a year must elapse before books are verified, otherwise the number of victims will be great. It is especially necessary to stand guard over the book when its merit is shaken. The library shelves are full of abscesses of falsehood. It should not be permissible to preserve these parasites. ... It is indecent and impossible to suggest reading a false book through.

"Why turn over to a lying buffoon the best corner of the fireside?... The problem of the book must be dealt with!" [New Era Community]

There are other pages from the Teaching on the same subject, and sometime I will quote them also. Particularly one should guard children, as many spiritual as well as physical ailments of children are the result, precisely, of the reading of unfit, false books.

If the readers of the Teaching of Life, or the Living Ethics, would think more profoundly about all the problems of life, about all new domains of knowledge which are discussed therein, if they would but decide to study them thoroughly, there would be enough material not only for one life, but for several. But usually people read with their eyes, not with their hearts, and that is why the most remarkable indications, the greatest revelations, just slide over their consciousness without leaving the slightest trace. I, having the key to many statements in the books of the Teaching, sadly realize this. These books give direction to the whole mentality; they point out the new domains; they set the new signposts for all scientific research. These books are so vital, so essential, because they lead to the future. The books of the Teaching should be a perpetual source of knowledge to the scientist whose consciousness is not obscured by prejudices.

A person free from prejudices, foreseeing the future, already participates in creating that future and thus facilitates the life of the present. Technical knowledge and all sorts of comparisons are quite useful, but there comes the time when all such informative sources become useful only for certain technical inquiry. The true knowledge comes, however, only when the indications given in the Teaching are assimilated and applied; when this process does not stop for a single day; when the fiery formulae of the Teaching are leading forward, pointing toward the next steps of the broadening of the consciousness and further achievement, and opening wider the curtain into the Great Infinity.

Thus, let no one think that the reading of various books is forbidden; this would be absurd. But let people learn to discriminate regarding the quality of books. It is most useful to know about all the latest achievements of science, in order to realize once more how near these recent discoveries approach the affirmations of the Sacred Knowledge.

I have long dreamed of publishing a magazine (from our main center) which would deal with all the achievements of life. I wanted to give to broad masses of readers a full review of general current achievements in science, art and social life, and thus to indicate the trend of thought. So far, there is no possibility of fulfilling this; but later this will come about as well.

And meanwhile, once more I say, let no one think that it is forbidden to nourish one's thought from sources which are suitable to one's particular type of mind. There are no prohibitions, but only warnings against false information.

22

6 July 1934

What you write about the theater is extremely sad, but in other countries things are no better. The radio and the cinema are replacing true art, and the direct influence of the sacred fiery spirit-creativeness is departing. The same is true of photography; for, invaluable as it is in many fields, it is supplanting more and more the works of art, the paintings in the average home and building. Unfortunately, we also have to live through this stage in the slow evolution of the human spirit. But with the growth and refinement of consciousness and the correct upbringing of the young generation, and if respect is paid to the human genius, everything will eventually find its correct place. However, there is much work to be done. Precisely, it is necessary to uplift as much as possible the level of taste and the understanding of the average person, in all spheres of creativeness. And of course, for this the theater is an excellent medium. But it is vain to expect true development of cultural achievements unless there are highly cultured people at the head of governments. The direction is always set by the leaders, and in spite of so-called democracy and much-vaunted individuality, almost everyone is following, as if hypnotized, the standards established by the ruling ones. And indeed, for the most part, this standard is not very high.

Beautiful are the dramas of Kalidasa and the plays of Tagore, but I would suggest to you also not to ignore the legends and beautiful historical episodes from the life of your own country. Every country has its own treasures which should be remembered. Each nation should know its foundations, those foundations that have created its specific character. We are approaching now—or rather, we have already entered—the threatening heroic times in which many nations will be tested. Therefore, it seems to me that everything heroic, everything that uplifts the consciousness of a nation and evokes the achievements of the spirit, should be at present particularly encouraged. You know that I am very much against narrow nationalism or chauvinism, but I am always profoundly touched by the esteem with which the peoples of the nations regard that which is beautiful and heroic in their own countries. Do not mistake this for a call to militarism! No, but events are such that all of us should be ready to become warriors of the spirit and with spiritual weapons find courage to defend our spiritual achievements. It is a consolation to hear of the spiritual searchings of the young generation, and we should not miss this moment but should be ready to give them that for which their spirit longs. The Teaching of Life is exactly the right and all embracing answer to all the questions of the spirit! Not a single domain, not one problem of life is neglected in these Covenants. On the contrary, every situation is treated from many angles and many points of view, and advice is given for most practical application. So many beautiful discourses are possible with searching souls! Just do not drive away those who are knocking. At the same time, great discrimination must be practiced in order to prevent the approach of the doubting ones.

It is also a joy to hear that you sense the approach of the New Era. Yes, it is coming and nothing can stop it. The map of the whole world is changing. Many countries will go through severe hardships, but even now there are some signs of Light in the midst of darkness. I shall quote a page from the Teaching:

"The forms extant in life are the imprint of the spirit of a people. One may judge the fall or rise of a people not only from historical facts, but also from the accompanying expressions of creativeness. When coarseness and ignorance are in possession of the spirit this will be reflected in the laws and customs of the life. In this unity all the basic features of the time can be traced. Naturally, the set forms of the life give a distinct coloration to various periods of history. By what are distinguished the first three decades of the twentieth century? Wars, terrors, cruelties, coarsening and the most horrible denials! Yet it is possible to discern, amidst all this darkness, forms of Light. It matters not if they be few in number, if they be scattered over the face of the Earth. The equilibrium of Light is not established by quantity, but by potential; not by congestion, but by *prowess of the spirit.* Thus, on the path to the Fiery World let us be imbued with the significance of great forms, and let us especially esteem the light of those eyes which bring to humanity the power of beauty." [Fiery World III]

Thus, let us create the forms of Light. Let us not be troubled by their fewness, but let the potential be great.

23

21 July 1934

Your striving toward the Teacher is beautiful, and if it grows in its intensity and understanding of the Great Image much can be achieved. Do not limit yourself by any time or by your own premises and conditions, but with all your heart trust the High Wisdom and everything will be as it should be—*as is best for you*. Sometimes the most fearful, the most inadmissible, becomes the chief source of our happiness.

You write that it is clear to you that "it is not the disciple who awaits the Teacher, but the Teacher who awaits the disciple." but I must elucidate this very categorical statement. For every creative activity, for every manifestation, reciprocity and concordance are necessary. Therefore, if there is no expectation there can be no answer. Where there is no expectation there is no striving, but we are told to apply the most vigilant and intense striving.

Even so, the great Covenant "When the disciple is ready the Teacher appears" is seldom understood. There are not many who ask themselves what this readiness actually is. Should not this readiness consist of certain qualities? The trouble is that people do not want to realize that at the foundation of this readiness, and of all the achievements, there is the following of a great ideal, involving a fiery transmutation of all our feelings, of our whole character. People would rather give up various excesses and thoughtlessly, mechanically perform their pranayama, than surrender even one habit that stands in their way to spiritual achievement. But, as it is said, mechanical ways have no value. The transformation of the inner man cannot be achieved automatically, and this transformation is the chief aim of all the true Teachings. Therefore, one must always bear in mind that all the Great Teachers are concerned with the inner man, whose realm is in the sphere of motives and thoughts. Therefore, not a single high Raja or Agni Yogi needs mechanical aids, nor any physical exercises. And their only consideration is the concentration on the chosen Great Ideal, on the unwavering and constant striving to approach it. Such concentration continues unceasingly. Whatever such a yogi or disciple is doing, his thought is always occupied by his Ideal. Everything is performed in the name of this Ideal, and he always feels in his heart the love and the presence of this Image. This is the real concentration indicated by the esoteric philosophy, which deals only with the inner world, the world of Noumena.

The same is true regarding the prayer of a disciple; it is precisely this same unceasing striving of the heart, and being in the presence of the chosen Image. In connection with this, I remember a story about the great Confucius. Once he was very ill, and his friends, thinking that he was about to die prompted him to say his prayers. The sage smiled and said, "My prayer started long ago." And indeed, was not all his life an unceasing service to the Great Ideal, which is the true prayer to the Highest?

When such a constant presence of the chosen Image comes into the life of a disciple, when there is no further deviation, then there is true readiness; the Teacher appears and the disciple under observation is accepted. But of course, there can also be some communications through individuals, and sometimes wonderful little books setting forth the foundations of the Teaching are given through pure psychics, but true discipleship is something entirely different. Almost no one realizes what an extreme burden the Teacher takes on by accepting a disciple. Therefore the Great Teachers, who guard the world, who direct the universal processes toward good ends and who participate in gigantic cosmic battles, can accept only those in whom They have no longer any doubt. Only those can be accepted who have no longer any doubt. Only those can be accepted who have gone through many fiery tests and have proved their readiness and devotion, not in comfortable environment but *on the edge of the abyss;* hence, the small number of accepted disciples.

After accepting a disciple, the Teacher creates an unseen union with him and includes him in his consciousness. In other words, from that very moment the Teacher knows everything about the disciple. He can know every thought and feeling, even the most transient, and accordingly He can guide his disciple. As for the disciple, his life, from the moment of his acceptance, becomes entirely new. His dormant energies are awakened and their development and transmutation are accelerated. A veritable battery of unseen but powerful rays are directed toward him. These rays become more and more perceptible, in proportion to the striving and the growth of the disciple's consciousness and to the refinement of his organism. The object of this is to transform the inner self and to refine and separate the three bodies for independent work on their corresponding planes. Great is the tension of a disciple. The physical strength temporarily decreases, and he must follow a certain regime without abandoning his regular duties. Of course, all these rays can be assimilated only if the disciple is striving to the utmost. Everything requires a reciprocity, conformity and accordance. Therefore, without expectation there is no attainment!

It is possible that you, again insisting that "it is not the disciple who awaits the Teacher, but the Teacher who awaits the disciple," may say that I have failed to understand you. With my heart I understand you, but a certain emphasis is necessary. You yourself may have to deal and talk with undeveloped souls, and when telling about the Teacher and discipleship you must firmly emphasize that without striving and strong determination nothing can be achieved. Much has been said about the harm of halfwayness. The Teacher awaits only him who is firmly, infallibly absorbed in complete striving and going toward the goal. And when the last obstacle that separates the disciple from his Guru is conquered, the Guru stretches forth his Hand. There are many crowding at the base of the mountain and who are hoping to follow the path, but it is certain that the Teachers are not waiting for all these! For high is the summit and narrow is the path, and many will be frightened and will leave, without even traveling half the way. Only after crossing a certain point may a disciple hope to attract the attention of the Guru. As, verily, it would be a waste of time, and a great incommensurability to attend to the leapings of unstable travelers of the spirit.

Also, there are destined disciples, those who were disciples in many of their previous lives; and in this present incarnation such a disciple, from very birth, is under the high guidance of his Teacher. The conditions of his birth are determined by the Teacher, and from early childhood he knows his Teacher. Therefore, for such spirits there is no deviation, and the events of their lives, as an unrestrainable torrent, carry them toward the predestined shore.

I shall quote to you a page from the Teaching:

"Verily one should accept this symbol of the Summit as the goal in the ascent of the spirit. Each disciple should remember that avoiding of the Summit leads the traveler away from the path. Each excessive burden well hinder the traveler. The Summit is sharp-pointed, and each needless attachment to the earthly world brings the traveler to a halt. It is difficult to halt on the slope, so let us remember about the Summit when beginning the ascent. It is difficult to reach the Summit if the spirit does not grasp the fundamentals of Hierarchy."

"The slopes are steep, and one should remember also that only the foot of the mountain is broad." [Fiery World III]

To my offer to help you understand more clearly some difficult points of the Teaching, you answered that you do not want to bother me with questions of a personal character, and that it would be an unproductive waste of time for me.

I must tell you that you are wrong. You should not think that there can be something personal or profitless in the purifying of the Teaching from incorrect commentary. You cannot imagine how many perverse accumulations are gathered around the Teachings. Precisely, the Great Teachers insist on this purification. Therefore, the one who can understand, who seriously wants to enter the path of discipleship, should learn to deepen his understanding.

Many hints are scattered throughout the Teaching, and the inquiring mind of a serious reader may become interested and he may enter the path of preparatory discipleship. And then I am quite ready to answer, and it will not be a waste of time. However to answer the questions of the curious and idle I really have not the time. Moreover, why give knowledge to unprepared minds? It will not benefit them, but will puzzle their minds even more. Do you know what questions I hear most often? "What are the seven ingredients which make up the emulsion of the yogis? What is the water of L. How many carrots should be eaten daily?" etc. And all this, when the books of the Teaching are full of and deal with the most profound mysteries and fundamentals of Life! But very few are interested in this.

Now let us return to your questions. You ask, "What does Mahavan and Chotavan mean?" Literally, it means great rhythm and small rhythm.

Mahavan and Chotavan are the cosmic rhythms, rhythms of the fire of space, and at certain times these rhythms are sensed by those who follow the path of Agni Yoga. They are sensed for short periods; otherwise they would be too difficult to endure, as they follow each other with great speed and violence. All these rhythms and the rhythm of the double dodecahedron I have experienced, but it is very difficult to describe them. I can only say that every cell of the organism is vibrated by this rhythm, while the heart (which is interesting to note) continues its usual, but slightly deepened, pulse.

Do you think that this information can help on the first

steps? All these fiery experiences and rhythms come when a disciple reaches the stage of the assimilation of the fire of space. If people after hearing about these rhythms will regard them only mechanically, they will be like the army drummer mentioned in the Teaching as a "most successful rhythmist." Therefore, read carefully paragraph 401 in the book, *Agni Yoga*.

Now your next question: "How to understand the replacing of blood relationship by the spiritual?" It seems to me that this is so evident, so clear! In life, we can see that often some people, even of different nationality, by their spiritual development are closer to us than blood relatives. There are many explanations for this; sometimes it is karmic law, sometimes it is the belonging to a similar element, or there may be a similarity of potential energies existing in the embryo of the spirit.

But even if we take simple everyday examples, can we expect from a reasonable person—for instance, one who wishes to improve his business—collaboration not with able people familiar with such work but with relatives who show an obvious inability and sometimes even harmfulness?

Every one of us has direct duties toward his family, but let us not exaggerate them. Often families manifest a complete disunion and mutual antagonism and are the hearths of spiritual corruption. Would it be right and sensible to waste strength and sacrifice the high ideals for an artificial maintaining of bonds which in most cases are illicit, being against the higher law? Precisely—illicit because many unions on Earth which are justified by human laws would be considered illegal from the point of view of the cosmic law. Precisely—terrible crimes, the degeneration of whole nations and a downfall in civilization result from many such wrong marriages. The question of the cosmic lawfulness of the family is very deep; it touches Be-ness itself.

The understanding of the establishment of correct, lawful unions is a great science of the future; and this science will be based on immutable cosmic laws.

Much has been said about the affinity of souls, but who knows and understands this truth in the full grandeur of immutable cosmic law? The Teaching says that people should unite according to the elements. Only parents who belong to the same elements can have balanced descendants. Whereas, in life we see that often fire is mixed with water, or air with earth. Verily, sterility and degeneration of whole nations is the result of such mixtures. The time will come when this truth will be understood by humanity and will become most essential. The forms of life, all functions of humanity, must be built according to cosmic law, if humanity desires to continue its existence and development on this planet; otherwise, the destiny of Atlantis threatens us.

And to those hypocrites who, after reading about the replacing of blood relationship by spiritual relationship, will show their indignation and slander the Teaching "because family obligations are demeaned," we may recall the words of Christ, whose Teaching they profess to accept: "There is no man that hath left house, or brethren, or sisters, or father, or mother, or wife, or children, or lands, for my sake, and the Gospel's, But he shall receive an hundredfold now in this time, houses, and brethren, and sisters, and mothers, and children, and lands...; and in the world to come eternal life." (St. Mark 10:29-30.) By the way, what an obvious affirmation of the law of reincarnation is in these words and in the similar words in the Gospel of St. Luke (18:29-30)! Significant also is the affirmation "And ye shall be betrayed both by parents, and brethren, and kinsfolk, and friends; and some of you shall they cause to be put to death." (St. Luke 21:16.)

Let the interrogators also explain the following words of Christ: "Think not that I am come to send peace on earth: I came not to send peace, but a sword. For I am come to set a man at variance against his father, and the daughter against her mother, and the daughter in law against her mother in law. And a man's foes shall be they of his own household. He that loveth father or mother more than me is not worthy of me: and he that loveth son or daughter more than me is not worthy of me. And he that taketh not his cross, and followeth after me is not worthy of me." (St. Matthew 10:34-38.)

It seems to me that, after these words, the statement about replacing blood relationship by the spiritual sounds rather modest! There is no bigger sin than imposition upon the human spirit. And how often we see that precisely our nearest ones put such burdens upon us. The spirit will not endure imposition, and woe to the imposters!

Would you prefer to explain and discuss the Teaching with those who hate it or to converse with your supporters, following the wise proverb "Give not that which is holy unto the dogs, neither cast ye your pearls before swine, lest they trample them under their feet, and turn again and rend you"? (St. Matthew 7:6.) This also indicates the necessity of replacing blood relationship by the spiritual one.

All well and good if the family consists of spiritually united members. If not, no one has the right to condemn if one of the members looks for support outside his own family. Only the spiritual ties, the ties of the heart, are significant and can unite us over millennia; whereas the ties of blood are transitory and their obligations may be considered as a partial karmic debt. How many fathers do not even know their sons and daughters! Therefore, let us not be hypocrites.

Thus also, let us not be sentimental regarding this question, but realize what is the true duty of the family man. When we arrive at maturity of understanding regarding true, *lawful* marriages, the question of the blood and the spirit relationships will be solved by itself. But meanwhile, let us emphasize the necessity of perfecting the inner man; precisely this self-perfecting will help us to solve many problems in life.

* * *

And now, what are the seven astral qualities? They exactly correspond to the five senses which function in the earthly body plus the sixth (the straight-knowledge, or so called intuition, which is still rare), and then the seventh (synthesis, or spirituality). The astral feelings exist in the same way as the physical but as their subtle counterparts. It is impossible to separate them; unity manifests its harmony. There is a complete correspondence between the subtle and the physical bodies. Therefore, the axiom "as above, so below" must always be borne in mind.

But indeed, just as the outward feelings or energies are manifested only when there are certain conditions suitable for them, even so, the inner spiritual abilities are manifested when the astral or spiritual conditions are created on the inner plane. The outer world is only a reflection of the inner one.

And now regarding loneliness. With the broadening of the consciousness, with the broadening of the horizon of thought, a person will inevitably feel loneliness. Every educated and cultured person when rising above the general level, has more and more difficulty in adjusting himself to the thinking of other people. What, therefore, can be said regarding those who lift their mental horizons to the distant worlds? Those who learn not to judge superficially and not to accept evidence for reality; those who, seeing the consequences in which humanity is involved, can grasp the real causes of events; those who understand and know that the so-called unseen conceals all the true reasons, all the powerful factors of our existence, and who know all the beauty of the higher worlds—what thoughts, what part of their designs, of the beauty of their creativeness, can they share with people who have not risen above the earthly plane? Who will understand them? And must they not conceal their knowledge in order to avoid unfriendly feelings and not cause harm? They will have to show only the kind of personalities that can be appreciated by their companions—those who accept petty evidence for reality!

It is well said that "he who discovers a precious formula cannot cry it out of the window because the resulting harm would be greater than the benefit." Hard, very hard is it to collaborate and to converse according to the consciousness of our interlocutors; it often requires a tremendous tension. "If it is hard to sheath a small sword in a large scabbard, how much harder would it be to sheath a large sword in a small scabbard!" Thus, the spirit of such a person is full of desire to give joy to people by the light of the great Teaching, but he must be silent and adjust himself to the consciousness of those who surround him, in order that they may accept his collaboration, which has in mind only their welfare. This is the great *Loneliness*.

Verily, the Agni Yogi is both the "Lamp of the Desert" and the "Lion of the Desert."

In conclusion I will add that in spite of this loneliness we may congratulate everyone who has achieved the broadening of consciousness. Nothing else can give the sense of limitless continuation of possibilities. And only the knowledge of the spirit can give man a place in Infinity, where there is no such thing as loneliness but only a great attraction to the grandeur of the Fiery World.

We are given a certain touchstone by which we can judge the degree of our approach to the Hierarchy of Light; it is that sacred tremor of the heart in lofty reverence and love toward the Hierarchy of Light, which should be expressed in all our words and deeds that concern this greatest concept.

Bear in mind that the exact geographical location of the main

Stronghold can never be given, not even those of the individual Ashrams. Likewise, all the available portraits of the Great Teachers are only approximate likenesses or have nothing at all in common with the real Images of the Masters. Much nonsense has been spread about this greatest concept, Brotherhood.

* * *

I often receive information about the reincarnation of H. P. Blavatsky. Several English Theosophists have identified her in a little English girl born in India. Besides this, I myself often receive letters in which people address me as H. P. Blavatsky, and ask permission to come and see me! But I assure you that I *am not* the incarnation of H. P. Blavatsky. H. P. Blavatsky reincarnated about forty years ago, and in 1924 she safely arrived at the main Stronghold in her physical body.

I am very much touched by your reverence toward H. P. Blavatsky. It would be wonderful if you could write an article about this lion-hearted woman. It would be good if someone would lay a first foundation stone in reverence to her memory.

24

1 August 1934

The main power of musk is in its, so to say, "fiery laboratory", which intensifies the forces of the centers, thus nourishing the weaker organs with fire. It must be understood that the finer organism will react positively upon being saturated with fire, while those that are influenced by earthly attractions may experience the reverse. There can be signs of temporary illness, but if in such cases musk is taken regularly these strange reactions can be prevented. The fiery property of musk is its greatest power. It must also be understood that in a fiery organism the effect of musk is increased by the fiery centers. The power of the fiery centers should be treated with great care. The transmutation of centers, which tenses the psychic energy so powerfully, intensifies also every kind of reaction of the fiery substances! Therefore, speaking of musk, we must note the inner reaction, which tenses every fiery substance. Thus, *subtle comprehension will bring subtle methods;* this is the main problem for the realization of the fiery transmutation. All our aspirations must be directed toward unification of the inner with the outer, but if we rely only on the outer reactions we shall achieve merely partial results. Thus, your remark that "if the neophyte greedily uses musk and takes big doses of this precious preparation daily, he will hardly achieve any high results, as this is merely an auxiliary help" *is quite correct.*

But since this preparation because of its irreplaceability and harmlessness is given for general use, for maintaining balance, and also since it is a protective agent against many illnesses, including cancer, one should try to obtain this precious substance, which is now much cheaper. Moreover, the majority of heart remedies, with the exception of strophanthus, leave harmful sediments and if used for a long time may poison the organism.

Musk, according to all the ancient sources, is related to the Sun and not to Venus. And it is wrong to state that musk belongs definitely to the aphrodisiac category. It is true that the powerful balancing action of this preparation restores all normal functions of the organism, but it could not be considered to be a sexual stimulant. Although we know that by the odor of the secretions of musk left by the males in the bushes and on rocks, the females find them in the mating season, we must not forget that what merely increases an instinct in an animal may produce a consciously intensified action of the fine centers in a human being. And musk has precisely this property. Therefore, for mental work musk is especially beneficial.

The researches in Ayurvedic and Tibetan medicine indicate that musk is used as an ingredient in almost all Tibetan and in many Indian medicines. In India it has been used from the most ancient times. Indian medicine is older than Arabic.

* * *

And now some interesting information about the meaning of aromas. In the book, *Five Years of Theosophy*, there is an excellent article by a medical doctor, L. Salzer. It is called "Odorigen and Jiva." It discusses the role and significance of smell.

Of course, in various pharmacopoeias we often meet a statement like the following: "Its action is similar to that of ethereal oils." We must say that this statement is extremely *unfair*, as each aromatic substance has its own specific influence, but they have not yet been properly analyzed. In the future, the so-called ethereal oils—these characteristic properties of certain plants, will be considered most significant. But so far this has not been realized, and such articles as "Odorigen and Jiva" are signposts to the future.

I shall quote extracts from this article:

"That those odorous substances are by no means inactive bodies may be inferred from their great volatility, known as it is in physical science that volatility is owing to a state of atomic activity. Prevost has described two phenomena that are presented by odorous substances. First that, when placed on water, they begin to move; and second, that a thin layer of water, extended on a perfectly clean glass plate, retracts when such an odorous substance as camphor is placed upon it. Monsieur Ligeois has further shown that the particles of an odorous body, placed on water, undergo a rapid division, and that the movements of camphor, or of benzoic acid, are inhibited, or altogether arrested, if an odorous substance be brought into contact with the water in which they are moving.

"Seeing, then, that odorous substances, when coming in contact with liquid bodies, assume a peculiar motion, and impart at the same time motion to the liquid body, we may fairly conclude that the specific formative capacity of the protoplasm is owing, not to the protoplasm itself, since it is everywhere alike, but to the inherent, specific, odoriferous substances."

And still further useful information: The ancients mentioned the science of "Characteristics or Signatures." Man, knowing the characteristics (that is, form, smell, species) of a plant, could apply his knowledge for medical and other purposes "without the necessity of blind experiments and accidental discoveries." The same applies to the mineral and animal kingdoms. This is called the "Science of Correspondences." And as the whole of nature is built according to a certain plan, an open-minded explorer can detect these "correspondences" in everything. Paracelsus understood this science, and his miracles were the results of the application of these principles. Astrology is the first step in the field of this science. By the way, the article "Odorigen and Jiva" was at one time brought to the notice of Madame Blavatsky by her Guru, who wished it to be published in the magazine Lucifer, I believe. If, instead of translating the books of L., the Russians would translate the articles of H. P. Blavatsky, great would be the benefit. As for the miracle-lovers, there are plenty of these in the first volume of Olcott's *Old Diary Leaves* and in *The Occult World*, by A. P. Sinnett. Of course, much light could be thrown upon the entire movement by *The Mahatma Letters* as well as the *Letters of H. P. Blavatsky to A. P. Sinnett*.

* * *

Note that soma is not the ethereal body. Soma is a subtle secretion of the glands which can create a sort of protective net for the centers. Therefore, with such protection the transmutation of the centers may be continued, as the insulation of the centers makes this transmutation less dangerous. Even under the snow some plants live and grow. Sometimes the most wonderful plants develop under the pure snow. Thus, soma offers protection against fire.

* * *

It should not be said that the ethereal body is the precipitation of psychic energy. How can this be if the ethereal body, after the death of a man, remains within the field of earthly attraction and quickly decomposes, whereas precisely the accumulations of psychic energy, after death, carry the spirit to the level prefixed by him?

The ethereal body, or the subtle fluids (emanated by the physical body), are emanations of the physical centers. The ethereal body affirms the physical one, and strengthens the astral, being a link between these two bodies.

Do not exaggerate the significance of pranayama. The science of breathing practised by true Raja Yogis has little in common with ordinary pranayama! The Hatha Yogis are interested only in the control of the vital breathing of the lungs, whereas the ancient Raja Yogis looked upon pranayama as a mental breathing. Verily, only the mastery of this mental breathing brings the highest clairvoyance, restoring the function of the third eye and leading to the true achievements of Raja Yoga.

* * *

And now some answers to your questions:

1. For the science of the future, it is far more important to know that *musk nourishes all the nerve centers with fiery energy* than to know its occult history.

2. Everything in Cosmos is built according to one plan;

hence, the great correspondence between all the organisms of the various kingdoms of nature. Therefore, when the heart energy of nature is spoken of, one must seek in every organism of nature the magnetic, vitalizing substance which corresponds to the precipitations of the energy of the heart. In the Teaching, several particularly clear examples of the precipitations of this fiery substance are mentioned. Deodar or cedar, musk and amber—all of them belong to the life-givers.

3. If physical fire is the best purifier, how much stronger is the substance which increases the life-giving fire within us! So many times the Teaching mentions that psychic energy is a panacea against all diseases. The discovery of the crystal of psychic energy would end many diseases. All malignant diseases such as cancer are possible only in an organism completely exhausted of psychic energy. It would be interesting to test and compare the blood of a cancer-infected organism with that of a normal, healthy person. Many useful discoveries could be made in this way. However, such tests are already being carried out.

4. Everything that is directed toward purity and goodness should be encouraged and protected. But it must be understood that not a single teacher of the Brotherhood, after spending very many years in the main Stronghold, is able to live among people during the time of Armageddon. If even advanced disciples are unable to stay for long in the valleys and cannot endure certain auras, how much more difficult is it for the Teachers of the White Brotherhood! In *The Mahatma Letters*, it is mentioned how very ill the Great Teacher K. H. became after contact with the valleys and the people. The Great Teacher.

K. H. was, by command of the then Ruler of Shambhala, recalled to Tibet for a long time in order to restore his protective net. Certainly, the Mahatmas are able to protect Themselves completely from the influences of crowds, but then many, because of such defense, would suddenly find themselves in the Subtle World; that is why the Mahatmas do not use their power. Similarly, the Great Teacher M., while visiting Sikkim for the meetings with H. P. Blavatsky, almost always smoked a special preparation of ozone for protection. By the way, this started a myth that Mahatma M. was smoking tobacco. H. P. B., in her description of the meeting with M. M., mentioned an Indian pipe, but forgot to add what kind of pipe it was and with what it was filled. In this way are myths created.

5. And now, what is the Fire of Aryavarta? "Aryavarta" means the country of the Aryans. This is the ancient name of Northern India, where, after the destruction of Atlantis, the first newcomers from Central Asia settled. This name applies principally to the mountain valleys of the Himalayan ridges, but not to all the plains of India. Our Ashram is located in the most ancient and the most sacred Aryavarta. The Fire of Aryavarta signifies the great spirit and potentiality of this nation. The Indo-Aryan people also call themselves Aryavartas.

The Balsam of the Mother of the World is a wonderful medicine prepared by my son, Svetoslav, and is based on a most ancient prescription but with new ingredients added. It is first of all irreplaceable in the treatment of old, malignant wounds.

6. What does it mean "to cross Santana with your heart"? "Santana" means stream. Buddhism compares the chain of our lives, in their perpetual flowing, with a stream. Therefore "to cross Santana with your heart" means to pass through all the lives by a tireless striving of the heart.

* * *

While reading the book you mentioned, do not forget what I told you about visions and dreams in my last letter. The whole floridness and the staging of the scenes of initiation which you describe will be clear to you. The Great Teachers would not waste their precious time on such childish performances. True Initiation does not need any rituals. It comes when the inner man is ready and only the Great Teacher is present, as He directs that transmuting ray which must be assimilated by the disciple.

Remember what is said in the second book of *Leaves of Morya's Garden* (page 147) about the highest and last act of all Mysteries. Always remember—where majestic simplicity is absent, there is no beauty. Therefore, the Great Presence cannot be there. Also, do not forget that all ceremonies have been created on Earth and for Earth—precisely for the earthly consciousness; whereas the highest Mysteries were held in secret and were without ceremony.

25

8 August 1934

One should not regard life upon the Earth plane as unreal or less real than the other worlds. Only the earthly existence provides the foundation for our further perfection and conscious existence in the Subtle World. Only here, in the laboratory of this life, can we acquire new stimuli and energies and immediately transmute them into higher accumulations for the further existence in the Subtle Worlds. Verily, conscious life on Earth guarantees the reality of life in other worlds. Precisely, there is a complete correspondence in the Cosmos. Therefore, the broader, the deeper our earthly consciousness, and the finer our sensations—the brighter and more beautiful for us is the reality of all the other spheres.

The Eastern Teachings, speaking of Maya, or illusion, meant in the first place the eternal mutability of everything in the Universe. (The Buddhists say: "There is no constancy in the Cosmos, as even the simplest object in two consecutive instants is different.") Secondly, by pointing out the transitory conditions on our Earth, as well as in the worlds that follow, they seek to teach us not to be too attached to our earthly bodies and to the lower earthly attractions, but rather to aspire toward the eternal renewal (i.e., evolution) and new conquests. They wish us to strive toward beautiful spiritual accumulations, as only in this way may we continue a realistic existence in the Subtle Worlds and have a more conscious life during our next sojourn on Earth, and so on. Remember that in the Subtle World, in spite of its complete reality, *life can be very dim for the spirit possessing a small consciousness and without aspiration.* Therefore, it is correct to say that *all the worlds are real in so far as our consciousness is able to accept them.* Precisely, the Maya of the ancients is equivalent to our law of relativity. Thus, in paragraph 322, of *Fiery World I,* it is said: "The entire perceptibility of the Subtle World is relative, varying according to the development of the consciousness."

Strange is the expression of your correspondent, "not only is the consciousness of a man immortal, but also the real man." But consciousness, as you correctly state, is the real man! And, of course, being a combination of high and low energies, the consciousness must possess its own vehicle, which will correspond to its own degree and to that plane on which this ego (or consciousness) exists.

"The consciousness contains within itself all the traces of past lives, impressions of each manifestation as well as each thought and striving for revealing of a broad horizon. The consciousness is fed by the Chalice and the heart, and each compressed energy is deposited in the consciousness, unbreakably connected with the spirit. The spirit, upon becoming separated from the body, preserves a full connection with higher and lower energies. Certainly, the Teacher leads wisely in pointing out the affirmation of vital transmutation. Indeed, through the immortality of the spirit there are preserved all manifestations of vital energies. As are the sediments, so will be the future crystals. And thought, and heart, and creativeness, and all the other manifestations collect this energy. The whole fiery potential of the spirit consists of radiations of vital energies. Therefore, speaking about spirit and consciousness, one must take the spirit as the crystal of all higher manifestations. The ancients knew about the crystalline quality of the spirit, and the spirit was revealed as fire or flame in all the higher manifestations. Therefore, it is so important to understand the true significance of fiery transmutation. Verily, spirit and matter are refined in one impulse toward attainment of the higher fiery consciousness." [Fiery World III]

Further on, your correspondent writes that an evolved Ego builds the physical body according to its image. Yes, of course, a developed Ego can achieve many improvements even in the structure of the physical body; however, everything that is manifested on the physical plane is subject to the laws of that plane. Therefore, the evolved Ego, when born into a certain race, or nationality, bears all the characteristics of that race. You may tell your correspondent that in all the various incarnations of the Great Teacher he mentions there were evident the characteristics of that race and nationality in which He incarnated.

Also, it is incorrect to say that the study of astrology keeps a person back. Until now, astrology was considered first of all a science of the future. But it is true that astrology in the hands of its modern "adepts," is far from perfect. Even here in India there are few good astrologers left.

Astro-chemistry is a science of the *nearest* future. Already the chemism of the sunspots, as well as the influence of the moon, is being studied. Soon the chemism of the nearest planets will also be investigated. This will be one more step toward the official recognition of astrology because astro-chemistry is the foundation of astrology. But esoteric astrology is very little known among modern astrologers. The key to it is in the hands of the Great Teachers and They give it only to their closest disciples, and only in cases when their mission requires it. The knowledge of the secret calculations of esoteric astrology, in the hands of the evil or irresponsible, could cause the destruction of the world.

* * *

You are right that at present there is so much fantastic and, most of the time, mediocre nonsense written about the Great Teachers. Very many harmful distortions have accumulated around the Great Images, as well as around all the Teachings. Verily, the time of fiery purification has now come, as foretold by the Great Teachers. But the fantastic nonsense of some writers perhaps is not so dangerous because they at least put into their stories something of what they consider to be the maximum of power, grandeur and beauty. More dangerous are those consciously or unconsciously erroneous assertions of persons whose authority was for many years considered established. And your indignation is quite right. Of course, such incarnations as of Alexander the First or Dmitry Donskoy are not recorded in any of the Books of the Lives of the Great Teachers.

* * *

You are right in thinking that in all the attempts of the dark ones there is a certain system. Precisely, they strive to discredit every pure beginning. And the easiest way to achieve this is by bringing dark or irresponsible persons into the midst of benevolent activity. That is why the books of the Teaching insist so much upon discrimination regarding newcomers. Discrimination is the key to achievement and success. This is the first quality which a disciple should develop. Therefore, the idea of organizing groups for the study of science and art is wise and useful in all respects. Such studies harmonize with the tasks of self-perfection indicated by the Teaching more than anything else. Moreover, this should give a good opportunity to observe the characters of the students, and to accept into the Teaching of Living Ethics only well-tested persons.

Science, Art, and the Living Ethics constitute a beautiful trinity. Thus, make it a rule that the main thing is not quantity but quality, and let those who are unable to follow the path of Light leave. Let us recall that once, after Buddha had finished preaching, five thousand of his followers left Him and only a small group remained. But the Great Teacher smiled and said, "It is good that the chaff has become separated from the grain;

there remains the community which is strong in its unity." Yes, the Great Teachers appreciate a closely united body of tested co-workers, and never seek masses of people.

I shall quote from the Teaching:

"Not without reason did the ancient sages choose to occupy themselves with some art or handicraft. Each one had to acquire some manual skill. They had in mind a means of concentration. Each one, in his striving for perfectionment, thus intensified his will and attention. Even in the few objects which have come down to us, there can be seen a high quality of workmanship. Precisely at present, the time has again come to return to quality in manual work. It is impossible to place spiritual limitations within the confines of machines. It is necessary to take the time to produce a quality of workmanship that will revivify the imagination. Precisely quality and imagination are united on the steps of fiery attainment." [Fiery World II]

Do you not think this is a beautiful bidding for the establishment of new groups?

* * *

To the comment you mentioned of one of your defamers that "in the books of the Living Ethics there are too many threatening warnings and this is not the method of Christ," it could be answered that this person probably does not know, or does not understand, the Teaching of Christ, a Teaching which is severe in its attacks against hypocrisy and in its full striving toward self-denying service to humanity. Also, one might point out many stern warnings in the words of Christ. Of course, faint hearts prefer to cover their most disgusting vices with the all-forgiving smile of an Image of Christ, which they themselves have sacrilegiously created. How unjust, cruel and insignificant would be such an all-indulgent and all-forgiving love! Long ago, it was said that "all the waters of Urdar and Uruvela could not wash off the spots of contamination from the garments of Christ caused by sacrilegious hands!" Verily, the time has come for the fiery purification of the Great Images of the Teachers and of their Testaments!

Bear in mind that all the obsessed ones always speak sacrilegiously about the Teaching; this is the most characteristic thing about them.

And now your three questions. "Siddha" means a saint and a

sage, one who has reached an almost god-like degree. "Siddhi" are the attributes of perfection, or the phenomenal abilities and powers acquired by yogis through purity of life. "Saddhu" is a saintly person, a spiritual teacher, applied at the present time to almost every traveling monk and every pilgrim.

You ask about "Khatak of the Mother of the World." "Khatak" is the sacred silk scarf which Mongolians and Tibetans present to all spiritual representatives and all especially revered persons, as a sign of respect. In Buddhist shrines all sacred Images are covered by, or wrapped in, these silk scarves, the length of which varies from one to five yards, and the width from a quarter of a yard to one yard. Their colors are white and yellow in Tibet, and blue and yellow in Mongolia. Sometimes holy Images and happy signs are woven into them. The khatak is a symbol of protection and help. On the sacred paintings of Tibet and Mongolia, the so-called tankas, or banners, one can often see depicted a saint from the Subtle World lowering a khatak to a sinner in the lower spheres, and the latter climbing up the khatak.

* * *

The Great Spirit who is at the head of the New Cycle must contain within Himself all synthesis, all the greatest Images of the past Cycle. That is why the Synthesis of Maitreya includes all the Rays.

26

11 August 1934

I cannot agree with your statement: "The merit of the Inquisition was that by burning about ten million witches and sorcerers it prevented the masses from participating in black magic and nocturnal orgies dedicated to Satan," etc. Indeed not! By killing millions of its victims the Inquisition created a most dreadful evil obsession. We know from all the Sacred Teachings that the spirits forced into the Subtle World before the expiration of their natural span of life still have an unexhausted supply of the strength of magnetic attraction. This binds them to Earth, as they are unable to assimilate the currents of the higher vibrations, due to the low development of their consciousness. Yet they are longing to get in touch with this vital force through every possible means. During the Inquisition anger and revengefulness attracted these victims toward their executioners. Thus, through obsession, they compelled their executioners to commit worse crimes and even drove some to suicide, in order to absorb and enjoy the emanations of blood and to experience the illusion of life, even if for a short time.

No, the Inquisition was established not just for the persecution of pitiful witches and sorcerers (mostly mediums), but for the annihilation of all the differently minded people, and all personal enemies of the representatives of the church, the latter having decided to obtain absolute power. First of all, among the so-called enemies of the church were the most enlightened minds, those who were working for the General Welfare, and the true followers of the Testaments of Christ. Indeed, the easiest way to destroy the enemy was by accusing him of being in league with the devil. This devilish psychology the so-called "Guardians of the purity of Christian Principles" attempted to instill into the consciousness of the masses in every possible way. Small wonder that in those days the visions of the nuns and monks had the stamp of the Satanic influence, as they were full of devilish images and all sorts of ugly temptations.

The persecution of the miserable witches and sorcerers, the mediums and the obsessed, was a mere screen. The Inquisition was created to establish unrestrained rule over the poor, frightened population. The most effective means of achieving this was robbery and the annihilation of all those who aspired to bring light into the darkness of the Middle Ages—those who were too independent, who dared to talk about the General Good, who protested against this kingdom of the devil, personified in the representatives of the Inquisition. The establishment of the Inquisition was a horrible caricature of Divine Justice. It was instigated by the Prince of this World for the complete corruption and destruction forever of man's faith in the purity, goodness and justice of the church.

It is edifying to read the biographies of the saints of the Catholic Church written by its own clergy. The history of the church is one of the bloodiest chapters in human history. Another unforgettable crime was the slaughter of the Night of St. Bartholomew, which has become synonymous with mass murder! I suggest that you reread Dostoyevsky's "Grand Inquisitor." Undoubtedly, that work was dictated by his inspired spirit. Also, there was published in the West, during the last century, a remarkable book by E. D. White, *The Struggle of Religion with Science*.

You are acting correctly in warning against the interest in spiritualism. I must add that in olden times all magic rituals and acts were held in great honor and used precisely among the representatives of the Western Church, and that magic is used even now by their successors and followers. Let us recollect the grimoires of Pope Honorius and others. Many black lodges are spread over the world. And how can it be otherwise? We are now in the midst of the Great Battle predicted in all the most ancient prophecies and in the writings of all peoples. We are approaching the great decisive battle between the Armies of Light, led by the Archistrategist Michael, and the hordes of the Prince of this World. We are approaching the Great Day of Judgment, when the whole army of Gog must be exterminated. But immutable is the Law of Light, and darkness shall be defeated.

Quite correctly you call spiritualism and all magical practices "spiritual corruption." Spiritualism is a violation; it opens the doors to the disembodied entities who mostly belong to the lower strata of the Subtle World, and of course spiritualism, like magic, cannot be considered evolutionary. It may be observed that many who read occult literature rush to everything which in one way or another deals with psychism and indicates the possibility of acquiring various psychic powers. But almost nobody thinks, "What is spiritual development? How to awaken in oneself straight-knowledge, which is the only way to acquire true spiritual enlightenment?"

* * *

You ask, "Is it necessary to have an earthly teacher until one is accepted as a close disciple by the Great Master?" But let me remind you that you yourself arrange special groups and appoint the instructors! Why do you act in this way? Are you not doing this for a better assimilation of the first steps of the Teaching, and consequently for further progress? And what would you call such instructors? Are they not also earthly teachers? And were not the great Founders of religions and the great philosophers, in their time, just "earthly teachers"? And did not people scoff and revolt against them? And now they are all elevated to the status of Gods and Great Illuminati by the very same adversaries!

Have you ever thought why among the Great Community,

or Brotherhood, we meet mostly those who are Easterners by birth? Has it not something to do with the very character of the people of the East, a character which possesses special qualities? Exactly so. And the first of these qualities, which has been impressed upon the consciousness of the people for centuries, is precisely the quality of devotion to the Guru! In the East, the bond between the disciple and the Guru is considered even now to be the most sacred, and above all blood relationships. And occultly, it is quite correct because the Guru creates the consciousness of the real man, the inner man who is the carrier of his karma; and by so doing the Guru takes responsibility even for a part of the karma of his disciple. Therefore, the selecting of disciples as well as of a Teacher must be done with great thoughtfulness and care.

But those who are far from the understanding of the sacred conception of discipleship must not be forced by us. Let them go their own way. The shortest way—the way of the heart—is rarely reached, or rather rarely chosen. It requires a great degree of devotion, this rarest quality of nobility, which in our age has all sorts of substitutes, and which is being chiefly replaced by devotion to the "golden calf."

You ask, "Why do so many good undertakings not develop properly?" My answer is, "Because the chain with Hierarchy was broken." The law of Hierarchy is immutable, for it is a cosmic law. Nobody can leap over a single link set by cosmic law and the Great Teachers. Let the blind fool themselves temporarily, but bitter will be their awakening. Therefore, let us revere everyone who brings the Light of the Teaching. I shall tell you about one wonderful example of devotion. In the Great Community there is one Brother, who, in the seventeenth century, was a famous chemist. During his earthly life he had a servant who was devoted to him, body and soul, who spent most of his life working in his master's laboratory. In spite of small intellectual development, this servant, because of his profound devotion, was accepted into the Community after his death; and now, in his subtle body, he is able to help his Master as formerly. Verily, devotion performs miracles; it is the first quality that determines spirituality. In fact, spirituality is impossible without this quality.

After such definitions of devotion it may be clearer to you why the significance of the Teacher and of the Hierarchic Chain are so emphasized. With this, I shall conclude my explanations, and I shall point out once more that all who sincerely try to apply this Teaching in life are definitely under the Ray of the Great Teacher, and it is just a matter of perseverance and past karma to be eventually accepted into a closer discipleship. Therefore, let us be elated and joyously strive toward the great aim—may I say, the greatest aim—for by entering the path of real service to the Hierarchy of Light, we fulfil the object of life on a cosmic scale.

* * *

Some say that in the higher worlds there is no evil; but I would put it this way: there is no conscious, active evil in the higher worlds, but there, as everywhere, light and shadow are inevitable, for Light and Shadow is the great Balance of the Universe.

27

12 August 1934

Intellect and erudition were never the main factors in the approach to the source of Truth. Often, intellect develops at the expense of the heart and smothers the great fire of straight-knowledge. Disharmony between the intellect and the heart will distort, like a crooked mirror, the reflection of the Great Truth. People reflect every great task *in their own crooked mirrors;* hence, such distortions of the Teachings, such caricatures of the High Images. As it was said, "The purification of consciousness and of the Teachings is the greatest task of our time." There are now so many "initiates," "hierophants" and "great incarnates," etc. But it is not so difficult to recognize the impostors. First of all, they lack *simplicity.* While the true initiates or entrusted ones are entirely simple in their lives, trying not to be different in outward ways and to be silent about their achievements, all the self-deceiving ones are very fond of acting mysteriously and talking about their high initiations, as well as of using high-sounding titles and names, although they themselves do not even know what real initiation means. Real initiations have nothing to do with any kind of ritual invented for the masses; initiation can take place in diverse places and dwellings, and there is only one condition necessary—the readiness of spirit in the disciple. And this readiness is ascertained by the "thermometer" in the hands of the Great Teachers. Initiation consists of the assimilation of the higher rays of various strength and qualities. Often, those who sincerely aspire toward the good are under the influence of these higher rays, though at the beginning they do not even suspect it. The stage of preparation for the assimilation of the higher rays is sometimes very long; all depends on the accumulations of the disciple.

With devotion and love toward the Great Hierarchy of Light, everything, even the most burdensome and difficult, is solved and conquered. And so—good luck!

Heartiest thanks for your calm and cheerful attitude toward all the attempts and attacks of the dark ones. Often we have heard warnings about planned intrigues and repressions, but after investigation, in most cases, they proved to be only the inventions of the enemies, who hoped to frighten the weak and thus to sap the strength of the whole movement. But you act excellently and wisely in not ignoring a single tale or piece of gossip. By checking them and then eliminating them, you follow the best policy. We have nothing to be afraid of, as there is nothing unlawful in our activity. On the contrary, it supports all the best foundations, all that upon which life is based. The Living Ethics is so necessary now! As I wrote to one of our co-workers, "It is important to cultivate educational and cultural ideas without insisting or forcing the Teaching upon others. The more so since the principles and ideas expressed in the Teaching are not marked by any specifications or peculiarities, and since all of them can be practised beautifully under the concept of Living Ethics. Many themes for lectures could be borrowed from the Teaching. It is important now to uplift and broaden the consciousness of all who are ready to follow the Light. But it is possible to reveal this Light only according to the development of the people's consciousness, using easy methods and images accessible to them and gradually broadening these concepts from the simplest up to the world scale."

28

17 August 1934

As I have mentioned already many times, it is most important to bring into life the educational and cultural ideas without insisting upon, or forcing on people, the books of the Teaching. The more so as the principles and ideas expressed in the Teaching do not bear any specific stamp, and all of them can very well enter into a general concept of Living Ethics. Many themes for lectures and essays could be borrowed from the Teaching of Life. Thus, the fundamental rule must be not to proclaim and not to force. While it is important to raise the consciousness of those who are able to go forward in step with evolution, it should be done by simple methods and images, gradually broadening the concepts until they reach full scope. Of course, I well understand that it is difficult constantly to step down to the level of the majority, but the great joy of the possibility of perpetually receiving from the limitless source of knowledge and beauty is left to us.

You must not think that it is possible to overburden us with cares. What do we work for? Every care that concerns culture is a joy for us. Where there is no care, there is no love. Remember what is said: "Burden Me more, lay upon Me the burden of the world and I will multiply My strength. When We approach the garden of the Beautiful, We do not fear burdens." Therefore, your decision not to undertake such "negative" work (because, as you put it, "it would be wrong to bring into your life our worries") is not right. And it is not right. And it is not right because there is no such thing as negative work if it is done for constructive purposes. Moreover, nothing negative or unpleasant can frighten us; our life is full of great worries—it is difficult even to imagine them! As to your statement that "it is better to settle these things by our own strength," it is always advisable to develop a maximum degree of independent action and alertness for the conquest of obstacles, as how otherwise can we acquire experience? At the most difficult moment, when all means are exhausted, the Advice will come, but its application will also require alertness and ability.

You ask, "Is there any selfishness in initiative when it is used for the General Good and for Service?" Of course not! But human nature is so complicated that the purified straight-knowledge alone can discriminate regarding the motives. That is why all the Teachings have insisted, and still insist, upon the development of straight-knowledge, without which there can be no true spirituality. In human nature there is so much self-deception, accumulated over centuries, that it is not easy to become suddenly an impartial judge of one's motives.

Each work is appreciated by the Great Teachers according to the degree of self-denial that is put into it. Therefore, the nearest co-workers must realize the importance of self-denial in service, and everyone should do his best under all circumstances. It is not for us to judge who does more and who less. What is important is the inner fire that we put into the work entrusted to us. Time is a great molder, and with the passage of time much can become clear, molded into the most unexpected forms. The true disciple lives with the heart, thinks and judges with the heart; and because of this he develops within himself such a powerful magnet that all the newcomers are attracted to him, sometimes even to the extent of overburdening him. By this magnet one may judge a person. The magnet is built and developed by many accumulations, and it is impossible to conceal such a magnet. Even as an ordinary magnet acts through seemingly impenetrable obstructions, how much more powerful is the all-penetrating power of a spiritual magnet! Therefore, first of all, we should take care of our own individual magnet and should develop its power to such an extent as to be able to give some of its power to those who need it.

Friendliness in cooperation helps very much to emit this power, and if practised it increases its strength. People are revivified when they come in touch with a powerful magnetic aura. Of course, one must not expect an immediate rebirth; time is required in everything. But with a hearty attitude, with responsive attentiveness, miracles can be achieved. Therefore, in everything one must practise patience. This should be your great and absolutely essential discipline. As it is said, "the greatest person is the one who is greatest in patience." Let us follow this wise rule, and let us practise real patience. The time is so threatening, so great, that we should not complicate the circumstances.

Truly speaking, everyone should have only one thought—how to hasten spiritual development. For only the spirit can raise us and carry us over the abyss. Many abysses indeed are now opening under the feet of humanity. It is said: " The Teaching comes at the threatening hour in order to select and save those who can follow the Light."

"On the Cosmic Scales the destinies of countries are being weighed. Those going with the Cosmic Magnet will stand before the Light of the Future, but those going against all the illumined beginnings will realize the full weight of karma. Certainly the battle of Light and darkness saturates all space. So many manifestations are being weighed on the Cosmic Scales! Each hour brings a new cosmic wave, and on the Cosmic Scales are new fluctuations being affirmed hourly. Space resounds with the new conditions which lead to the Fiery World. In the cosmic tension new fiery conditions are being created. On the path to the Fiery World let us apprehend the law of the Cosmic Magnet in each action and each aspiration." [Fiery World III]

* * *

Life is most complicated, and only the consciousness which is united with the Higher Will can sense the right direction and steer its vessel through all storms. But the storms are inevitable and useful, for the ship as well as for the pilot and the whole crew, because only in this way are strength and firmness tested and also fearlessness and alertness developed.

Of course, one must be able to strongly resist evil-minded slanderers if they are of the kind who can cause real harm. Often, however, some kinds of slander can be like the chattering of sparrows, and then one may well decide that it would be out of proportion to use a cannon!

* * *

The group instructors should not only give lectures but should, together with the pupils, discuss the questions that arise regarding the Teaching. By all means, questions should be asked, but I know from experience how difficult it is to encourage pupils to ask the right ones. They prefer that the teacher give a subject and explain it! But the important thing is for them to ask questions, as only by the question is it possible to judge the direction of thought as well as the level of consciousness. Besides, this is the best exercise for the instructor himself. Often the pupil will approach the question from the most unexpected angle, and thus will give the teacher the possibility of checking his own understanding. The teacher is made, not born! Verily, we learn while teaching.

And now, regarding the question "In what can the majority of women cooperate?" we must proceed from the fundamental point. Therefore, I would say that they could collaborate in the task of establishing the balance of the world. Verily, the existing state of imbalance threatens humanity as well as the whole planet. How can the world endure when the foundations of life are violated! Much has been said about this in the Teaching, and one can develop the hints that are given. I shall quote several affirmations: "The Banner of the great Equilibrium of the World must be raised by woman. Thus the time has come when woman must fight for rights that were taken from her as well as those she sacrificed voluntarily."

The universal disorganization which we see today, the threatening degeneration of many countries, is the result of this continuing imbalance through the subservience and oppression of woman. By degrading woman, man degrades himself; and without the revival of true chivalry and gentleness the spirit cannot rise.

It is also said: "As the Teacher creates through his disciples, even so woman creates through the masculine principle. Therefore woman uplifts man." Hence, woman must raise herself to such a degree, spiritually, morally and intellectually, that it will enable her to carry man with her. Remember the painting by N. K., "She who Leads." Thus woman must occupy the place destined for her. She must become not only an equal cooperator in the management of the whole life, but also an inspirer. The greatest task is to spiritualize and to restore the health of humanity by filling it with aspiration toward great deeds and beauty. But woman must first of all change herself! Therefore, the call to woman must be primarily the call to self-perfection, for the realization of her dignity and her great destiny and to lay the foundation of Be-ness and for the awakening of the impulse toward creativeness and beauty. It is said: "The Equilibrium of the world cannot be established without true understanding of the First Causes. ... Therefore, let us be affirmed in consciousness upon the power of Equilibrium, as the stimulus of Existence, of the First Causes, and of Beauty. Hence it is so indispensable to affirm in the spirit the Feminine Principle." [Fiery World III]

As a motto, I would give: "Spirituality, Podvig (Heroic Deeds), Beauty." This trinity includes everything.

And now regarding the question which occupies your mind so much: "How to determine to what element a person belongs?" Certainly, the horoscope could reveal it. Even with the little knowledge that modern astrology possesses, the prevailing element in a person can be determined. But the esoteric knowledge is focused on the *fundamental origin* of the seed of the spirit.

Moreover, not only must people be combined according to the elements and to the basic luminary under the rays of which the seed of the spirit (not personality) was born, but there must be taken into consideration another fundamental cosmic law, called "The Cosmic Right." Thus, the legend about twin souls has a profound significance. And this law is indicated in the stars. The ancients knew how to read these signs. The key to this was given to the High Initiates. But today such knowledge in the hands of corrupt humanity would bring more misery and calamity than benefit and happiness. Therefore, the Great Teachers are so anxious to awaken spirituality and to broaden the consciousness, as They wish to give to humanity the knowledge of the great laws. This is why these laws can be mentioned now only as being within the reach of the science of the future. Nevertheless, it is quite appropriate to mention the existence of these laws, as it is necessary to prepare the thought to work along this line.

True, even a superficial knowledge of astrology can sometimes help to establish more or less harmonious bonds between people, or to point out favorable and unfavorable dates. But, in the hands of irresponsible or evil-minded people, this knowledge can be harmful. The key to all perplexities is in a person himself and is always at his disposal. There are people who know how to use this key, and their lives are arranged miraculously. Thus, let us apply our best efforts in order to hasten the coming of the epoch of the Resurrection of the Spirit; then the key to many mysteries will be placed into deserving hands. This epoch is approaching.

I am very sorry that I am unable to bring you that joy, but I have not received permission to reveal the mysteries which belong to the esoteric knowledge. Let us find consolation in the knowledge of the beautiful law of Cosmic Right, and let us try to purify the magnet of our heart, which can and should attract a corresponding magnet. But unfortunately, because of the immorality that has ruled for many centuries and is still at its full strength, the souls that should be harmonious have traveled so far apart that often they are especially antagonistic to each other. Karma is an inexorable law. That is why we must try our best to purify the magnet of our heart. We must emerge from the cycle of karma which binds us to the results of our own deeds and which postpones the cosmically lawful unions. Only such unions can intensify creativeness and can give beautiful progeny.

I want to emphasize that the equality of the sexes and of nationalities must be considered as among the first foundation stones of any government. The first part of this statement I have already discussed, but I may add that since the equilibrium of the world is built on the dual Origin, the equality of the sexes must be recognized as a cosmic law. Thus, only the ignorant can oppose this.

As regards the status of different races that constitute the populations of some countries, I mean to say that all the subjects of such a state, irrespective of their nationality, should be treated equally under the basic government laws, without the least exception, privilege or limitation. Of course, the question of religion is not included in these basic laws, as well as other secondary matters which should be free from law restrictions and should vary according to the local customs and conditions. One fundamental characteristic of the laws should be precisely flexibility in application. If we limit ourselves to the dead letter of the law, we may as well move to the cemetery! I was never interested in politics and in the outer forms of government because I am profoundly convinced that it is not the form that is so important but the spirit that permeates and motivates it. I have always thought that every system of government should be guided first of all by common sense, that is, by consideration for the *Common Welfare*. No other motives are valid for such a responsible, and I would say, sacred task.

I must confess that no other system makes me feel so indignant as the present way a head of a government is elected by ignorant masses! I saw enough of this most abominable and criminal comedy. Bribery, we are told, is illegal, yet, in such a responsible, sacred act as the election of a head of a country, great sums are spent and even the most obvious bribery is practised, to say nothing of other proceedings which are equally disgusting. Thus, on the day before the election one may see in some of the most important newspapers of a country the name of the possible head of the state maligned as the greatest scoundrel, and on the morrow (in the event of his being elected) the very same papers may launch into the highest praises of his unusually lofty qualities! In this way the consciousness of the people is corrupted.

Common sense should tell us that the ignorant masses, who are in addition impelled by their lower instincts, cannot be the judges of the highest. The right of electing the head of a government should belong only to a highly moral, therefore cultured and educated people, or representatives of the people of a country. But unfortunately, in an epoch when it is most necessary to have the best and most trustworthy people at the head of affairs, the power of the masses prevails. If any country should lose even one thousand of its best representatives in all the fields of knowledge and work, such a country would very soon fall to a low level.

Yes, the time has come when woman should be prepared to participate in the burdens and leadership of government. Woman, the life-giver, who lays the first foundations of education, has also the right to create better conditions for those she brings into the world. Her common sense, and especially her heart, will dictate to her many correct decisions. If we take the historical facts and true biographies of many great people, we shall see that often the source of their inspiration and their chief adviser was a woman. Thus, in ancient Egypt the head priestess often inspired the hierophants by transmitting to them the will of their goddess. Thus, they were called the inspirers of the leaders of the people.

The great epoch of Woman is coming. Verily, woman has a two-fold task: to uplift herself and to uplift her eternal companion, man. All the Forces of Light are awaiting this great deed. The Star of the Mother of the World has indicated the great date. All Scriptures are confirming that woman will sever the head of the Dragon. Let the heart of the woman become aflame with this self-sacrificing deed. Let her fearlessly raise the shining but cleaving Sword of the Spirit.

At the destined hour we will call the burning hearts and the hands ready to raise the Chalice of Salvation of the World.

Let every day of our lives be spent in self-sacrificing service to the great task.

The Great Mother is approaching!

29

23 August 1934

Christ, speaking of the end of the world and of the Day of Judgment, could not have had in mind the final completion of the evolution of our planet. For if that evolution were to follow its natural course of development, the planet would enter its seventh cycle and its humanity would enter the seventh race, with all its sub-races, so that at the crowning of such an evolution there could not be a Day of Judgment. For by that time humanity and the planet would have reached the condition of the higher worlds where there is no conscious opposition to good by any evil force.

But of course, Christ knew the difficult karma of humanity. He knew of the threatening danger, and therefore He had in mind the approaching removal of the race, which is always followed by tremendous cosmic cataclysms and is foreshadowed by the great sorting of the good seeds in advance of the final Judgment. Being an Initiate, He knew that this catastrophe could become the Last Day, owing to the terrible downfall of spirituality in the human race. Quite possibly, there may not be a sufficient amount of high counteracting, or rather, discharging energies to save the planet from the final gigantic explosion. To this explosion the Prince of the world is directing all his efforts, as he knows that in a purified atmosphere pierced by the new fiery energies the spheres of Earth will become unbearable for him, and his continued presence here made impossible. Therefore, he attempts to explode the planet in order, as it is said, "to float away on the wreck." Does not the Apostle Peter speak of the same removal of the race (Second Epistle 3:9-13)? Also, it is indicated in Revelations (21:1) and Isaiah (66:22).

In the Teaching, it is said that precisely the spirit of man can act as the exploder of the planet. It is mentioned also that the number of Those who are able to resist this is very small, and that They bear the whole burden of maintaining the planet's balance. A strong spirit can save a whole area from earthquake. Thus, in the ancient days, the Great Teachers sent their advanced disciples to places threatened by earthquakes.

* * *

It is not a decrease in food but a lack of sleep that injures the organism. A person does not need much food. Thus, for one who performs mental work it is quite sufficient to take two, and at most three meals a day. Two or three fruits or vegetables, a little cereal food, some milk and butter—this is the best diet. But it may be difficult for those who are used to eating meat in large quantities to change suddenly to a vegetable and farinaceous diet; it can even cause some undesirable reactions in the organism. Therefore, caution and gradualness should always be practised. Besides, every case is so individual! But let us remember that the majority of human diseases result from all sorts of excesses, and especially from overeating. In America, where people work very hard and eat little, they have great endurance, and longevity there is much greater than in many other countries where people habitually overeat.

* * *

Many naive people think that the dark ones act only through evil, corruption and crime. How wrong they are! Only the crude and relatively insignificant dark forces act in this way. Much more dangerous are those who masquerade under the guise of Light. And the poor seduced people who do not possess the true discrimination of the fiery heart fly, like butterflies, into the black fire, which devours them. Ignorance and lack of intuition pushes them into the arms of darkness, and deprives them for a long time of the salutary influence and support of the rays of the great Stronghold of Light. Dreadful is Armageddon; the dark forces are struggling for their very existence. Despair unites them and makes them so persistent in trying to achieve their aim. The Prince of the World has very many talented collaborators—some conscious, some unconscious—and it is foolish to think that they do not know the ways of the most cunning subtlety. They are very shrewd and inventive, and they act according to the level of their victims. But all of them lack warmth of heart. Thus intertwined is darkness with Light on our Earth. The snare of darkness is woven by skillful hands.

Many terrifying things are now practised. A great deal of the most disgusting sorcery is spread all over the Earth. Of course the biggest centers of population are usually chosen by the main dark forces and are used as their centers. Precisely, the whole brood of hell has crept out onto the surface of Earth. And their best weapon is the ignorant masses. That is why the unity of all the white and near-white forces is so essential! But the latter so easily become greyish and fill the ranks of those of whom it is said in the Bible, "because thou art lukewarm, and neither cold nor hot, I will spue thee out of my mouth." Only the power of devotion and the striving to serve the Great Hierarchy of Light can save from the widely spread snares of the Prince of the World.

Let us tense all our forces, so that by the purity of thought we may create an impenetrable armor. The attempts of the dark ones to rend our auras are inevitable, but if the protecting net is strong enough these attacks are easily repelled without bringing any harm to us. Usually, these attacks affect our weakest organs. The aura saturated with devotion to the Hierarchy is able to resist any attack of the dark forces. But not for a single moment should we allow doubt or deviation from this focus of Light. Devotion and purity of motive is our *only anchor* in the chaos of the raging elements.

30

29 August 1934

Let us talk about the accepted and destined disciples, and about discipleship in general.

In their unawareness, many imagine that so long as they are reading the books of the Teaching, and have some desire to become disciples of this or that Great Teacher of the White Brotherhood, they will be accepted and quite welcome.

But almost no one ponders what he has done in his life, or rather, lives, to deserve this greatest of privileges. Truly it is the greatest, and before we expect to receive this privilege we should realize what it means. In their naivete, the majority think that the Great Teachers are desperately seeking disciples and are ready to accept with open arms any person who is not too bad and who wishes to be accepted. There is no greater delusion! The Teachers are not looking for disciples because the fundamental rule is that the disciple must look for the Teacher, and must *find* Him. At the same time, the Teachers are indeed looking for every possibility of extending help through all suitable channels. That explains why we occasionally find beautiful little books written automatically by pure psychics. Often these psychics, after acting as a channel, never hear again from the real Author, who transmitted through them one or another precious gem. Sometimes not even the Author's name is known, as very often the Wisdom is given by the Great Teachers through a disciple who has already passed into the Subtle World. Furthermore, these psychics do not have to undergo any specific discipline, which is so completely essential for the accepted disciples. The chief, unfailing sign of nearness to the Teacher is the perpetual "Ocean of the Teaching," which such a disciple receives, together with a precise knowledge of its Source. Also, there is the broad constructive work of the disciple, the receiving of indications, knowledge of the future and of exact dates, and, of course, the very character and mode of living of such a disciple.

The great Covenant "When the disciple is ready, the Teacher will appear" is understood by only a few. Almost no one realizes that this readiness must contain in itself some definite qualities and conditions. I have already written about this, but I am glad to repeat it for you, with further comments.

In the question of the acceptance of a disciple, his karma plays the main role. Precisely, in connection with discipleship it is most essential to realize the law of Karma and to comprehend it in all respects. Thus, a person overburdened with karma cannot hope to become a close disciple. Only those whose earthly karma is almost completed can be accepted among the closest disciples. There are few who realize what a heavy burden the Teacher takes on by accepting a disciple. Therefore, the Great Masters, who are constantly watching and directing the world processes for the maintenance of its balance, and who lead in the gigantic cosmic battles, accept only those about whom They have no further doubts, those who have gone through and purified themselves through many fiery tests, and who in this life have again displayed their readiness, devotion and self-denial not in conditions of comfort but on the edge of the abyss. Precisely those whose high spiritual centers are not only open but are undergoing the fiery transmutation. Hence, the small number of the closest disciples.

You may ask what the burden of the Teacher is. I assure you that it is terrible. It is almost impossible to imagine the whole scale of this tension without knowing the occult laws. By accepting a disciple, the Teacher includes him in his consciousness and establishes with him an invisible but active bond. From that very moment, the Teacher knows at any instant what is happening to his disciple. He can even know his fleeting thoughts, and can direct him accordingly. Therefore, it must be understood how hard, how unbearable for the High Consciousness of the Teacher would be any disharmonious vibrations caused by unpurified thoughts of the disciple, how inadmissible under such a close, sacred bond with the Teacher would be any still-not-outlived lust. Every disharmonious vibration cuts into the current of this bond, and if repeated can break it altogether. But each severing of the thread, occultly speaking, is most painful and brings its consequences. Of course, the pain is entirely different for the Teacher from what it is for the disciple. But this is only a part of the burden; the other part cannot be discussed now. That is why the acceptance of the disciple is carried out with greatest caution and is considered the granting of the greatest privilege.

From the moment of acceptance, the disciple begins a new and also not an easy life, due to terrible inner and outer tensions. During these tensions, not only are all his energies awakening (this partially takes place during the preparatory stages), but there comes also their accelerated development and transmutation. A whole battery of invisible but powerful rays are directed toward the disciple. These rays become more and more intense and varied in their quality, according to the striving and broadening of the consciousness of the disciple and the refinement of his organism. The object is to transform the inner man and to refine and separate his three bodies for independent activity on the corresponding planes. Great is the tension of the disciple, his physical strength temporarily decreases, and without giving up the duties of every day the disciple must live according to a certain regime. Higher altitude, pure prana and certain isolation are necessary conditions of such regime. All these rays can be assimilated by the disciple only if the highest striving is manifested. Everything requires reciprocity, correspondence and harmony.

This harmony the Great Teachers find in the so-called destined disciples. Thus we designate those who, in their previous lives, were disciples of the Great Guardians, or were connected with Them by bonds of devotion and love. Such a disciple, in his present incarnation, from the moment of birth is under the High Guidance of the Teacher. The very conditions of his birth are determined by the Teacher, and the essential abilities are manifested in accordance with his mission. Such a disciple carries the full chalice. From the earliest days he knows the Teacher, knows his Image. Therefore, such spirits are unable to turn away, and the events of their lives, like an irresistible current, carry them toward the predestined shores. Blessed is the karma of those who in their previous lives united themselves, with bonds of devotion and love, with one of the Great Spirits, or with their nearest disciples; such karma is the shortest way to the goal. That is why the Hierarchic Chain is so sacred. Hence, in this life one should manifest love and devotion, those qualities which are the first conditions on the path of approach.

The second condition is striving and readiness to sacrifice self in the service of the General Good, as no one will be permitted to approach if he intends to obtain knowledge for personal aggrandizement, for such is the way of the black magician. When self-renunciation and striving are affirmed in the heart they will become as second nature. The application of the Teaching to oneself and in the life of every day will become joyous, and then progress and even achievement of the sacred aim is assured., But one must ask oneself, and answer with full sincerity, whether there is really such fiery striving and self-denial, or whether there is some secret selfish desire to achieve greater knowledge for covetous purposes. The slightest signs of such hidden desire will be the greatest obstacle on the path of spiritual progress. For success one must have understanding, as well as readiness to practise *podvig*—the great self-denial—in life.

One must seriously ponder the concept of *podvig* as the necessary condition. The profound understanding of all the qualities that are included in *podvig* is extremely important. Therefore, it is useful to write down from the books of the Teaching all the necessary qualities enumerated there, as well as all vices which are obstacles on the path. Verily, it is most difficult for people to realize that the foundation of discipleship and of all spiritual achievement is the striving toward the Highest Ideal and the fiery purification of all one's feelings and one's whole character.

I shall quote to you a page which I have just sent to one of my correspondents:

"It is much easier for people to give up certain excesses and to perform mechanically a pranayama than to restrain a single habit which is a stumbling block on the path of spiritual progress. But, as it is said, everything mechanical concerns only the outer man and cannot reorganize the inner man, and therefore is worthless; for the transformation of the inner man is the only aim of all true Teachings. Therefore, one must clearly remember that all the Great Teachers care for and deal only with the inner man, whose sphere lies in the realm of thought. Thus, not a single high Raja Yogi or Agni Yogi needs any mechanical or physical exercises. The only concentration allowed by them is concentration on the chosen High Ideal, performed with an unfailing and continual determination to reach it. And such concentration continues perpetually, regardless of what the Yogi or the disciple is doing. Everything is performed in the name of the chosen Image. Every moment he feels in his heart love and the presence of this Image. The prayer of the disciple is precisely this continuous striving of the heart and the presence of the chosen Image. When such a presence is established, when the guided spirit has become firmly fixed upon his chosen Image so that there can be no turning back, then the true readiness is manifested and the Teacher will not delay."

Also, for everyone who enters the path of discipleship and is not just studying the books on occultism, it is absolutely essential to decide in the depth of the heart which of the Great Teachers of the Brotherhood is the nearest to him, and then to surrender himself completely to this High Guidance, without any limitations or conditions. The beginner will not necessarily receive a message from the chosen Great Teacher, but hope must not be lost. Great patience and courage must be found. In spite of the silence of the Great Teacher the aspirant must continue to strive and to work in perfecting himself, applying his abilities for the General Good.

Unfortunately, in his desire for immediate progress and for greater knowledge, a person quite often throws himself into a search for other Teachings and other Teachers and divides himself, losing his place on the ladder of ascension. Let us remind ourselves of what is said in the Teaching about the selection of the Teacher:

"To be affirmed in the heart upon the Lord is the first condition on the path to the Fiery World. It is impossible to arrive at the ordained Gates without this fiery requirement. Of course, Guidance must be recognized in spirit and heart, for the acceptance of the Hand of the Lord is alone insufficient without devoting the heart to the Lord. One must understand that law which unites the Teacher with the disciple because without the manifestation of complete attachment to the Lord there can be no bond. A full acceptance of Guidance means a conscious relationship, for one must understand and feel in the heart the warmth which arises from the depths of the spirit. It is especially necessary to feel and to learn to discern that by which the nature of the Lord is linked with that of the disciple. Thus, one must remember that vibrations and karma are as connecting links on the path to the Fiery World." [Fiery World III]

Thus, the disciple must prepare his organism by refining his receptivity, for who knows except the Great Teacher whether the karma of the aspiring disciple is or is not conducive to his success? Therefore, apply all your efforts and aspirations toward a better understanding of the Teaching and its application in life, and leave the rest to your karma and to the great knowledge of the Lords!

I may cheer you up by saying that, although the path of preparatory discipleship is long and there are many obstacles and trials on this path, the mastering of these difficulties bring its own joy, achievement and revelation. Also, you must know that these tests are not artificially created but deal with the inner attitude and presence of mind of the disciple, giving him a chance to show how he will act in cases of sudden difficulty and amid general trying circumstances. In Theosophical literature seven years is usually mentioned as the first period of trial, followed by the next period of seven years. But these periods can be shortened or prolonged indefinitely. All depends upon the karma of the disciple and on his inner development and aspiration. For one must achieve the gradual opening of the higher centers; otherwise it is impossible to become an accepted disciple. But remember that until the age of thirty years is reached, not all the centers can be awakened without terrible harm to the organism. To force their opening is equal to suicide.

And now, I would like to warn you against psychism, as this condition is especially dangerous on the first steps of discipleship. Psychics have contact with the lower spheres of the Subtle World, and often they mistake the voices of entities from these spheres for the true Call and the Voice of the Great Teachers whom these entities are trying to impersonate. It is a mistake to think that these voices will always suggest evil acts, depravity, or crime. Only the most primitive and low forces act in this way. Much more dangerous are those who approach under the mask of the Teaching of Light. We know many cases of such "guiding" voices and "luminous" visions. Therefore, the Teachers always warn against psychism, which can be acquired by those who practise pranayama.

If one wishes to follow the path of true Light and yet possess a certain amount of psychism, one must treat this faculty with great discrimination, remembering that in ancient India and Egypt not a single born medium could be accepted as a disciple, and that they were not permitted to enter the holy of holies of the temple. But in our day, people possessing the lowest psychic abilities consider themselves especially advanced spiritually. Great is this delusion! Psychism and true spirituality are proportionally inverse. A strong manifestation of psychism retards the growth of spirituality. Therefore, all those who are so proud of their psychic manifestations should be most careful. It is said in the Teaching:

"The saints of Great Service have no psychism because they are always striving in spirit toward Hierarchy, and their heart resounds to the anguish of the World. Psychism is a window into the Subtle World, but the teacher tells the pupil, 'Do not turn so often to the window, look into the book of life.'

"Often psychism proves to be a weakening influence, but the Great Service is in straight-knowledge. Therefore We warn against psychism, against turning one's gaze backwards without a definite object for the future. The spiritually weak psychists are often a tasty dish for the satanists." [Fiery World II]

Therefore, try to realize the great difference between psychism and the lofty straight-knowledge. Try to hear the voice of the heart; purify and broaden your thoughts in order to refine all your feelings!

My first advice to you is to write down from the books of the Teaching all the qualities that are essential for the one who would be among the accepted disciples. Then, penetrate deep into your innermost, determine your worst faults, choose one of them, and try with all your might to get rid of it by replacing it with its opposite. After getting rid of one vice, start to work upon another, and so on. It is not at all easy, but then nothing easy is fitting upon the royal path which leads to the Fiery World.

I think it would be useful to quote to you one more paragraph from *Fiery World*:

"The ability is given to a fiery spirit to receive subtle energies. Only the fiery consciousness is able to conduct a current of subtle energies. Therefore the records must be scrutinized with a great deal of discrimination. It is because humanity has become accustomed to visualizing the Highest on a low plane that the Images of the Lords have acquired such distorted forms. Indeed, people have become used to the thought that the Higher should serve the lower, but they do not realize that only the understanding of Service gives one the right to a manifested link of the Chain. Thus, it is the distorted understanding of Sendings that produces the results which litter the space. ... Therefore, We shall warn everyone against all distortion and false records. ... But what does a medium or a recipient poisoned with imperil reveal? Thus, it is necessary to purify the profane human actions and to destroy these records in the future. In the Fiery World, only the fiery consciousness can be a true recipient of Our Sendings."

And so, read attentively my letter and question yourself honestly. Are you able to choose a life full of renunciation, courage and intensive labor for the General Welfare? Can you patiently wait for a message from the Great Teacher in spite of possibly years of silence? But if the path of the heart is close to you (it requires great steadfastness and devotion, this rarest of noble qualities), your path may be suddenly shortened and become beautiful. Everything is in the hands of the man himself. Let this truth cheer and inspire you.

Most sincerely I wish you to find in your heart the aspiring love for the Great Image and readiness for the great task. The time is so ominous that all those who have heard the Call must realize the significance of podvig and become true heroes. Thus, become a hero!

31

8 September 1934

We never force and we do not press the books of the Teaching upon anyone. All our institutions are first of all cultural and educational, giving lectures of all kinds, concerts and if possible classes on art, religion and the sciences. Precisely, an enlightened consciousness can better assimilate the concepts of the Teaching of Living Ethics. It is impossible for a primitive, uncultured and undisciplined mind to embrace and understand the cosmic all-comprehensiveness of the Teaching, coming from the remotest time, from the very Source of Knowledge and Light. The Teaching of Living Ethics embraces all domains of life, touching upon all manner of improvement. Therefore, apart from the constant moral self-perfecting, each one should study and practise at least one art or craft. The idea of a mission for women was my dream from early youth; I called it "The Community of the Heroine Sisters," and I imagined them bringing light and joy into the hard conditions of the life of our country. The various fields of action in life could be covered by this Community. That is, some sisters could devote themselves to medicine, others to agriculture, and still others could be teachers and lecturers in the various branches of knowledge, also covering social problems in a popular vein. Of course, the study and teaching of the arts would be most important in such a community, together with the investigation into the significance of color, sound and scent, and their influence on man's general living conditions. The function of the Living Ethics would be to beautify the whole benevolent movement of the Heroine Sisters. Such were my dreams, which of course grew with the growth of my consciousness. Now is the time to think of the near future and to strive to recruit pure souls who would be ready to undertake selfishly this task. A whole army of such sisters and workers will be necessary to satisfy the spiritual hunger of the people. It is time now to fill the ranks of capable women teachers. Therefore, if something like this program could materialize in your group it would be beneficial in many respects. In the books of the Teaching it is said very beautifully, referring to such sisters: "Let them endear themselves to people. Let people say, 'A dear one came to our village.'"

In the group which studies the Living Ethics, there should be inculcated first of all the idea of good deeds and self-renouncing service to one's neighbor and for the General Welfare. All pseudo-occultism, all exercises for the development of psychism, are strictly forbidden. The pupil must try to develop spiritually and to awaken straight-knowledge, which is possible only by purifying the heart and the thought of all prejudices and preconceptions; precisely when the consciousness is broadened and the heart is aflame with the desire to accept the great tasks. True, such a program is possible only for a minority, as few understand and appreciate true beauty and its companion—simplicity. The majority prefer to encumber the consciousnesses with complicated formulae which they scarcely understand and, most of all, to revel in psychic phenomena. They do not realize that all psychism, without the Higher Guidance, is an obstacle on the path of true spiritual development. I have already written about the dangers of psychism, and I shall return to it once more in connection with your strange experience, which you wish me to explain. But now I shall continue about the mission of women.

Taking into consideration the difficulties you describe, I would *select* for this mission of women a *special group.* I would accept into this group only those who are really firm in their thinking and who understand that devotion is the rarest quality. This group could continue to study the books of Living Ethics. As for the rest, it could be suggested that they first prepare their consciousnesses by gathering wider information and education, which could be achieved by lectures and study organized in accordance with a selected program at the Women's Mission Center. I do not think that one could expect anything productive or even useful from a religious group of church-minded people. Precisely, narrow dogmatism has distorted all the Covenants of Christ and is far from the evolution of the future! I thought that your priest was one of those enlightened (and alas, rare) souls who have realized that it is impossible to enter the current of evolution burdened with dead dogmatism. We personally have been fortunate enough to meet many enlightened priests. But sooner or later you are bound to have a conflict with the narrow ecclesiastics. There can be no doubt about it. Therefore, since there is so much unsteady and divided thinking, I would not establish a special religious group. The group which is studying the Living Ethics, however, I would separate from the rest, and would accept new members only with the greatest discrimination. Do not be tempted by quantity, but always think about quality! Always consider the consciousness of man. Even those who have entered the path of discipleship and who consider themselves advanced are surprised at the first new aspect of Truth manifested to them, and sometimes they even begin to scoff a things that are sacred. That is why the acceptance of a disciple is such a rare thing and, as it is said, there are too many fingers on one hand for counting them! Those who have entered the path of probationary discipleship must go through many tests before they can hope to be considered as eligible for real discipleship.

Dead dogmatism killed the luminous Teaching of Christ; that is why the church so easily came to ruin in our country. And in other countries also it is on trial. The difference is only in the fact that the representatives of other churches are much better educated, and they realize that they must consider the laws of evolution and the demands of our time. Therefore, some of the members of the Western clergy are abandoning the mental attitude of the Middle Ages and are even beginning to accept the law of Reincarnation. Recently there was a meeting of bishops at which it was decided to start the study of the works of Origen—that light of true Christianity and martyr to the ignorance of his contemporaries. Yes, great sin is committed by the church in holding back the thinking of the people entrusted to her, keeping them on the level of the ignorance and darkness of the Middle Ages. But for an unprejudiced mind that cannot be frightened by eternal anathemas (how can they be reconciled with the "all-forgiveness" of their God?) it is sufficient to read the history of the Church Councils and the history of the Papacy to lose entirely and forever all respect for most of the representatives of the church. Let us recollect the ages of the Inquisition! Let us think of all the great minds who suffered from it! Let us also not forget the terrors of the Night of St. Bartholomew! Let us read the biographies of the saints written by priests who describe the crimes of the church! The real documents, i.e., the epistles of the saints to the heads of the churches, are still available; and in those letters severe accusation of bloody crimes is made. But you may protest, you may say to me that the Western Church was guilty of those things but not our Orthodox Church! Then, I shall remind you of the times of the Patriarch Nikon, who introduced the tridactylous cross in place of the didactylous cross. This cross, by the way, was used by that true follower of Christ, the great Builder and Founder of Holy Russia, the revered St. Sergius of Radonega. Under Nikon those who used the two-finger cross were persecuted, tortured, and burned at the stake. Is it possible that the revered St. Sergius was also a heretic? Let us carefully read the history of the Church Councils, and we shall see many interesting things that are characteristic of the level of consciousness of those churchmen who dictated the dogmas which exist in full strength even today. Thus, we should find that the law of Reincarnation was rejected by the Council of Constantinople in the sixth century A.D., in spite of the fact that the Gospel itself contains *words of Christ that have obvious reference to the law of Reincarnation*. If people would take the trouble to study seriously the fundamental Teaching of Christ, and if possible in the original language of the Gospels *instead of being satisfied with the school textbooks, they would discover a new meaning in the words, and the true, great Image of Christ* would be revealed to their spiritual sight. Long ago it was said by all the Great Teachers that ignorance is the worst crime. And so it really is. What if not the darkness of ignorance bred the Inquisition? The Inquisition is the most frightful, ineradicable stain on the golden vestments of the Christian Church. The Inquisition was a terrible caricature of Divine Justice. It was instigated by the Prince of Darkness for the complete corruption and destruction of man's faith in the purity, clemency and justice of the church.

Let us think of all those great ones who suffered under the Inquisition, or who had to conceal their luminous knowledge under the mask of folly or under the most complicated symbols, the key to which—unfortunately for humanity—is almost lost. Let us remember also about those numerous great books, full of light and goodness, the loss of which is irreparable and was considered by the best minds of all later epochs as the greatest misfortune. It is an accepted thing to be indignant about the burning of the Alexandrian Library, but many hypocrites will prefer to be silent about the string of fires lit by the Inquisition which through centuries steadily consumed at the stake the pearls of human genius!

Long is the list of crimes against the welfare of humanity. Long is the list of martyrs of Knowledge and Light; and this list, to the shame of humanity, continues to lengthen in this our "enlightened" age.

It is mentioned in the Teaching that in every retort of the alchemist the priests saw the horns of the devil! And now also, they see the sign of Antichrist in the books of the Teaching of Light. Verily, everybody sees his own reflection.

Therefore, let us open and purify our consciousness by way of increased enlightenment. Of course, the misfortune was that all the light-bearers were anathematized in our country. Thus, our great compatriot, H. P. Blavatsky, was compelled to take the Light of the Teaching to America and Europe, as the consciousness of Russian society was not ready for it.

The International Government mentioned in the books is the Great Hierarchy of Light; and for us Christians, who take our religious terminology from the Jews, it is of course Jacob's Ladder, which is mentioned precisely in the second book of *Leaves of Morya's Garden.* And for the East it is Great Shambhala, or Shabistan, or Mount Meru. There are other names as well, for they vary according to the people and the country. As for Masonry, it was in the beginning a great and glorious movement often guided by Great Souls, and in such cases it was particularly persecuted by the representatives of the church.

But as the church has turned aside from the pure Teaching of Christ, likewise contemporary Masonry has turned away from the former greatness of its covenants. In both, only the form remains, the dead dogmas and rituals. Therefore, a revival of the spirit of the early church, full of the pure essence of Christ's Teaching, should replace the present decay. Precisely, a purification restoring the Covenants of Christ should take place.

One could ask the heads of the churches why they, being the representatives of the luminous Teaching, allow mutual dishonor and discord. Each church excludes the other. And who if not they should bring unity today? They should have practised the great enlightenment, I should say, a planetary enlightenment. If they did so, great tolerance would come, which would embrace all the multiform aspects and manifestations of the Almighty, the All-penetrating, Omnipresent, All-comprehensive Deity, which never excludes from Itself *a single world, a single son, a single manifestation.*

Thus, the Teaching of Living Ethics destroys nothing, does not cast down, but calls for the purification of the heart and thought. But ignorance, being of darkness, always furiously struggles against Light. The first impulse of the savage is to destroy or to kill everything that is not clear to him. *Intolerance is the sign of ignorance.* Tolerance is the Crown of the Great Knowledge. By this sign, you should determine the worthiness of your interlocutor.

And now I shall attend to your questions in consecutive order.

You ask how to understand the words. "Stand aside, Thou Flaming One. Why, O Thou Flaming One, dost Thou avert Thy

Face?" These words could be applied exactly to the cases you have mentioned. Do not these people become frightened by the Fire of the Light-Bearer? Do not they say, "Stand aside, Thou Flaming One! Hide not the Heavenly Gates"? And again, the answer of the Fiery Messenger: "My sight brings pain to thee; thy wings are not yet spread!" Verily, cunningly contrived are the snares of superstition and prejudice—these offshoots of ignorance which entangle the wings of the spirit. Dread falls upon the soul which knows not the path to the Light and is unable to see in the twilight that surrounds it. Precisely, "Knowledge comes not readily when the spirit is troubled." There are many such diseased souls. And no one can help them, for the cleansing must come from the bottom of the heart and the spirit. But let them for the last time read in the books of the Teaching about treachery and sacrilege, and then let them choose their own path.

And now, regarding the condition you mentioned. Of course, the vision of light formations indicates the beginning of the activity of certain centers. The advice is to be very cautious; brief, short pranayama, without overdoing breath control, should do no harm. But pranayama should not be performed in the manner adopted by some who have become acquainted with the instructions given in some of the books written by various pseudo-yogis and who also sometimes combine them with gymnastics. This sort of thing can suddenly lead to the most unexpected disastrous results! Therefore, I beg you to be very careful. I have never practised any exercises, not even simple pranayama. To tell you the truth, I have always instinctively revolted against all artificial methods when dealing with the sacred fires of the heart. Do not forget that intense pranayama develops the lower stage of psychism and mediumship—the two antipodes of true spirituality. In order to emphasize the harm of all artificial methods, I shall quote the words of H. P. Blavatsky from the third volume of *The Secret Doctrine*:

"Now, the science of Hatha Yoga rests upon the 'suppression of breath,' or Pranayama, to which exercise our Masters are unanimously opposed. For what is Pranayama? Literally translated, it means the 'death of (vital) breath.' ... Several impatient Chelas, whom we knew personally in India, went in for the practice of Hatha Yoga, notwithstanding our warnings. Of these, two developed consumption, one of whom died; others became almost idiotic; another committed suicide; and one developed into a regular Tantrika, a Black Magician, but his career, fortunately for himself, was cut short by death."

Therefore, do not exaggerate the importance of pranayama. The science of breath that is practised by the true Raja Yogis has little to do with pranayama. The Hatha Yogis are interested in the control of the vital breath of the lungs, whereas the ancient Raja Yogis understood it as mental breathing, for only the control of this mental breath brings a high state of clairvoyance and the restoration of the functioning of the third eye, together with all the real achievements of the Raja Yogi.

You know how much the Great Teachers are against the development of psychism. I quote:

"At a time when one sacrifices his soul for the good of the World, the other sits upon the water. While one offers his heart for the salvation of his fellow men, the other flounders in the manifestations of the Subtle World. The saints of Great Service have no psychism because they are always striving in spirit toward Hierarchy, and their hearts resound to the anguish of the World. Psychism is a window into the Subtle World, but the teacher tells the pupil, 'Do not turn so often to the window, look into the book of life.'

"Often psychism proves to be a weakening influence, but the Great Service is in straight-knowledge. Therefore, We warn against psychism, against turning one's gaze backwards without a definite object for the future. The spiritually weak psychists are often a tasty dish for the satanists.

"Verily, in the Great Service is the feeling of great responsibility. But one should become accustomed to this chalice, for there can be no shortest path without emptying it. The heart which aspires to Hierarchy feels how necessary and salutary is the Chalice of Offering. To some it is only the object of derision and condemnation, but to others it is a precious treasure. It is Our great desire that the true straight-knowledge be developed." [Fiery World II]

"The realm of psychism is so complex, so fearful, and it conceals many surprises for the self-deluded 'adepts.' There is much conscious, and still more unconscious deception in the visions of mediums and undisciplined psychics. Without the High Guidance, one cannot be safe in this sphere. Only a disciple who is under the direct guidance of the Great Teachers can discriminate regarding these visions. In order to see and understand correctly, one must learn to control the lower manas and not permit it to interfere. There are many examples of visions when the higher Manas manifested the great truth, but the feeling of selfishness called out the lower aspect of it; and the lower manas, by its interference, not only brought its own additions but distorted the whole sense of the manifested truth."

Thus, one must always point out the harm of psychic manifestations. In ancient India, fakirs and mediums *were not allowed into the holy of holies of the temples.* Likewise, the Hierophants of Egypt did not accept mediums and psychics as disciples. They even avoided lymphatic servants. Spiritual achievement is in the accumulation and development of straight-knowledge. I have written about mediumship before, but this question is so fundamental that it is necessary to deal with it from all angles and to return to it many times. One must realize that mediumship has nothing to do with the opening of the centers. Remember that in one of the books of the Teaching mediums are referred to as inns for disembodied liars! The same is true of psychism, which is far from the fiery transmutation of the centers. Therefore, let us strive toward the true discipleship and service, which are manifested in austere, continuous, heroic achievement, and in selfless work for the General Good. all else will come in due course, without any artificial methods, which can only retard our true spiritual development.

You wrote so touchingly about your being attracted to the idea of "Mother." That is why I feel like writing to you as a daughter. I am worried lest in your ardor, and due to ignorance, *you hurt yourself irremediably.* The striving of one's heart to the Great Image is above all physical exercises. Let us apply all our efforts not in artificial gymnastics but toward the actual service to the Fiery Heart of Him who in titanic strain is perpetually watching and who is now at the head of the Forces of Light battling against darkness. Armageddon is no longer a far-away fairy tale; it is a threatening, dreadful reality. Therefore, those who serve and fall into disunity are criminals. Is it possible that people are becoming entirely blind and deaf, and that they do not see all the ominous signs of the Great Battle?

The work of St. Yves d'Alveidre, *The Agarta,* is not a "remarkable" or a true record. In reality, he visited the Agarta of his imagination in the phantasmagoria of the Subtle World. St. Yves was a typical psychic and medium. That is why his descriptions are so contrary to truth. Precisely, his Agarta has no connection with the White Brotherhood. Full of deception is the realm of psychism. There are many in the Subtle World who like to impersonate the Great Teachers.

I must also tell you that I was greatly hurt by the lines you sent about H. P. Blavatsky. I sensed in them an echo of the vulgar opinions so characteristic of persons of a certain type. I must tell you that, definitely, H. P. Blavatsky was a fiery messenger of the White Brotherhood. Most certainly she was the bearer of the entrusted knowledge. Definitely, of all the Theosophists, only H. P. Blavatsky had the privilege of receiving the Teaching directly from the Great Teachers in one of their Ashrams in Tibet. She was the great spirit who accepted the bitter task of giving to humanity, lost in dead dogma and on its way to atheism, the impulse to study the great sacred Doctrines of the East. Precisely, only through H. P. Blavatsky was it possible to approach the White Brotherhood, as she was the link in the Hierarchic Chain. But some of those who surrounded her were very much beneath her fiery spirit and heart; yet in their self-conceit they thought of reaching alone the Heights, ignoring the Hierarchical link as well as her merit. In their jealousy, they slandered, criticized and inveighed against her, the one who had given them everything, who trusted them. But all those self-deluded, arrogant people achieved nothing, for the law of Hierarchy is immutable. For the benefit of the general work, the Mahatmas corresponded with some of her co-workers; however, not one of those people was admitted into discipleship. In the writings of H. P. Blavatsky, and in *The Mahatma Letters*, you will find the statement that H. P. Blavatsky was the Hierarchical link which, if neglected, would cause complete failure. And now the self-deluded ones who have passed into the Subtle World and are surrounded by their followers are probably even further away from the Stronghold of the White Brotherhood than ever. Whereas, our great compatriot, because of her fiery striving, was incarnated (in Hungary) almost immediately after her death, and now it has been ten years since she arrived in her physical body at the main Stronghold and under the name of Brother X is working for the salvation of humanity. *Thus acts Cosmic Justice.* H. P. Blavatsky was a great martyr in the real sense of the word. The envy, slander and persecution of the ignorant killed her, and her work remained unfinished. The concluding volume of *The Secret Doctrine* could not be given. Thus people deprive themselves of the highest.

I much revere the great spirit and fiery heart of our country-woman, and I know that in the Russia of the future her name will be fittingly honored. H. P. Blavatsky should truly evoke our national pride. Great martyr for Light and Truth! May Glory always be with her!

* * *

About the *Chalice of the East*, I have already written. Do you know that in the East "Mahatma" means Great Soul—a Soul which has fulfilled its earthly task and is now working for the welfare of the whole world? Therefore, it cannot be said that a particular Mahatma dislikes Christians, as a Mahatma who embraces all knowledge cannot be a sectarian.

Also, if you read attentively and objectively the "Letter about God": in *The Mahatma Letters*, you will see that the Mahatma repudiates the sacrilegious and anthropomorphic conception of a Personal god—cruel and unjust, chastising with eternal damnation all so-called heretics, and justifying all the crimes committed in his Holy Name! Verily, such a God cannot have a Mahatma's approval and respect. But it is impossible to call the book, *The Mahatma Letters*, atheistic, for how could They who proclaim the Immortality of the Spirit and who Themselves have attained it have anything to do with dead atheism? But people are not yet ready for this book—here you are quite right. But please point out that there should be no *utterance of condemnation* of the Mahatmas. Great will be the astonishment and, I might say, mortification of many when they find out who in reality is the Leading Mahatma. Great Images have many Aspects and Names.

In conclusion, I want to ask you not to be annoyed by my letter, which perhaps is severe; but my heart aches when I see how few there are who realize how threatening are the times we are experiencing. They do not seem to understand that, verily, the last chance has come for many; and they continue to creep in the darkness of ignorance, looking for contradictions where there are none, seeing the horns of a devil and the seal of the Antichrist, for their consciousness is bound to Earth. They cannot think independently, and blindly they jostle in the confines created by the phantom of the eternal anathemas of their "Merciful" God! Verily, as it is said, "All the waters of Urdar and Uruvela cannot wash the stains from the garments of Christ and Buddha left by sacrilegious hands." Believe me, the spirit of the Inquisition is still strong. If Christ appeared on Earth today, possibly he would escape crucifixion and the stake, but He would hardly escape severe life imprisonment, with the stamp of Antichrist upon Him. I suggest that you reread Dostoyevsky's "The Grand Inquisitor."

* * *

Humanity attaches significance only to those concepts which are stored away in a consciousness of mediocrity, for it arrays correspondingly each form in its consciousness. Why, then, have all the Higher Concepts not been inculcated? Why so many distortions? Why so many belittlements? Because, in truth, the essence of human quests and strivings has been turned downward. But the problem of the New World is to rouse the consciousness and to restore to the world the predestined Image of Beauty. Creativeness of the spirit must indeed be intensified in ascent. Precisely, not to lower the Higher but to allow it to rise. Therefore, the first requisite will be to create the Divine Image according to Divinity. When the human consciousness will cease to depict Divinity in an earthly way, then the attainments of the spirit will be fiery." [Fiery World III]

* * *

Let the women co-workers treasure the little flame of gratitude to you. You pointed out their path and connected them with the Teaching of Light, thus giving inspiration and joy to their spirits. Devotion is the rarest quality; it helps one toward the goal faster than anything else. Let them affirm themselves in the Teaching of Light, but if something is not clear to them, let them inquire. I shall be glad to explain what I can. It is most important to arrest the doubts at the very beginning. If the great concept of devotion is dear to their spirit, they should write down from the books of the Teaching all that is said about this regal quality. By rereading often these notes, they can strengthen within themselves this manifestation of true spirituality. It is said in the Teaching: *"Devotion is the foundation of spirituality."*

I am calling all those who are ready to bring their entire

abilities and energy to the service of the people. For the time is near when every intelligent helper will be indispensable. It is so important to infuse into people respect for knowledge and for every teacher, each of whom they should consider as a representative in life of light and progress.

32
12 September 1934

You think that the author of the "Letter on God" would be perplexed if he knew that Sergius of Radonega performed the austere achievements of his long life in the name of this "heavenly tyrant." May I answer you with a passage from the book, *Heart?*

"Besides, avoid arguments about that which is undeniable. Recently I wondered at the dissension between the followers of Joan of Arc, Sergius and Moses. Each one proclaimed that his Protector did not agree with the other. Whereas, knowing the truth, it was sad to hear these inventions, composed for discord."

Perhaps these words are not clear to you; therefore I shall try to explain them. One may and should select an individual Protector, toward whom one's heart is particularly drawn; but in choosing Him we have no right to belittle or deny another Teacher. Indeed, it can happen that different names can mean the same Person. The Great Images had and have many aspects and names. Do you know what great names are written into the Book of Lives of the Leading Mahatma? Verily, only the Mahatmas, and especially the Leader among Them, know the truth. Therefore, in your ignorance, beware lest you commit *blasphemy!*

And now, if you will read carefully and objectively the "Letter on God" from the book, *The Mahatma Letters*, you will see that the Mahatma rejects and speaks only a sacrilegious, too human, concept of a Personal God, a God cruel and unjust, chastising with eternal anathema every heretic and justifying all the crimes committed in his Name for his glorification. This is the God of ecclesiastical dogma, who, being propitiated by the sacrifice of his Son, allows into his Kingdom only those who believe in this sacrifice. Furthermore, if we consider the fact that humanity, from the very beginning of its existence, was and is still being born in multitudes outside the bosom of the Christian Church, we must admit that from this point of view the majority of humanity is condemned to eternal damnation. But then, can the fault be theirs that the "Merciful Father" chose to send his only Son at a particular time, to one particular country and people? Why punish the rest? Can it be possible that all these billions of souls are condemned to burn forever in hellfire only because they were deprived of seeing and hearing the Gospel of the Son? The Mahatmas know nothing of a God of this kind, nor could They esteem such. But it is quite impossible to call the Mahatmas atheists; for how can They, who proclaim and who Themselves have attained spiritual immortality, have anything in common with dead atheism? Read attentively—do They not even oppose agnosticism? "Pantheistic we may be called—agnostic never." And again: "Having found Gnosis we cannot turn our backs on it and become agnostics."

You are quoting the profoundly philosophical statement of the Great Mahatma: "As to God—since no one has ever or at any time seen him or it—*unless he or it is the very essence and nature of this boundless eternal matter, its energy and motion,* we cannot regard him as either eternal or infinite or yet self-existing. We refuse to admit a being or an existence of which we know absolutely nothing because (a) there is no room for him in the presence of that matter whose undeniable properties and qualities we know thoroughly well (b) because if he or it is but a part of that matter it is ridiculous to maintain that he is the mover and ruler of that of which he is but a dependent part and (c) because if they tell us that God is a self-existent pure spirit independent of matter—an extra-cosmic deity, we answer that admitting the possibility of such an impossibility, i.e., his existence, we yet hold that a purely immaterial spirit cannot be an intelligent conscious ruler nor can he have any of the attributes bestowed upon him by theology and thus such a God becomes again but a blind force. ... In other words we believe in *matter* alone, in matter as visible nature and matter in its invisibility as the invisible omnipresent omnipotent Proteus with its unceasing motion which is its life, and which nature draws from herself since she is the great whole outside of which nothing can exist."

You are indignant at this aggrandizement of matter. But do you not know that in esotericism matter and spirit are one—that matter is just the differentiation of spirit? Do you not know that matter is indeed energy, as one cannot exist without the other?

Therefore, matter isolated from spirit is regarded as illusion. Do you not know that all comes from the One Element, and that this Element is considered as the Divine Principle, triune in its manifestation? Do you not know that spirit divorced from matter is deprived of expression, in other words, of existence? Indeed we cannot separate ourselves from matter, neither in action nor in thinking. We deal either with the subtle or with the denser aspects of that same matter. I shall translate for you the same thoughts from the most ancient Hindu Scripture, the Agni Purana:

"This Nature is incomprehensible and it surpasses all dimensions and all comprehension. Endless are the embryos of worlds and systems being born continuously under the wing of Mother Universe. Puman, or the subjective element (Brahma of the Vedantists) in its potentiality, exists in the depth of Cosmic Nature, even as fire is concealed in a piece of dry wood and as oil exists in the heart of the kunjut tree. This Puman, or subjective element, lies hidden in Nature, as a psychic witness or spiritual element entirely neutral and free from any actions.

"This junction of Puman with Nature is brought about by a special force known as Vishnu-Shakti (Energy), which holds all the embryos and fundamental qualities of all beings and of Matter which must consequently issue from this union of Cosmic Nature with her consort Puman. The force discussed here is an active mediator for the fulfillment of their junction when they are in opposite states and are separated, or else it is a force which decomposes, destroys this contact from which the Universe was born, as a necessary result. ...

"Gods and other heavenly creatures are being born from this mutual action of Nature-Universe, and the dynamic action of Vishnu's force, which is put into motion by the impulse of the first."

You can find the same thought in the Hermetic philosophy, although in different terminology. Yes, the conception of Deity, the Incomprehensible Source of all beings, was majestic in ancient times. This Cosmic Law gave to each spark issuing from it all its qualities, permitting free choice in applying those qualities either for construction or destruction.

And now let us return to the statement of the Mahatma that "no man has seen God at any time." Of course, you realize that it is taken from the Gospel; that these are the authentic words of the Apostle John, whom no one has yet dared to call, or thought of calling, a heretic or an atheist. Thus, we read in the Gospel of St. John (1:18): "No man hath seen God at any time"; and the same words occur in his First Epistle (4:12). Precisely, by these words John gives us to understand that by His very nature, God cannot be seen. Again John says, "God is Spirit, and they that worship Him must worship Him in spirit and in truth." (St. John 4:24.) And yet again, "And the light shineth in darkness and the darkness comprehendeth it not." (St. John 1:5.) We know, however, that Light is matter plus motion. There are many indications in the Bible about the "Unknown God" and the fiery nature of this God. In Deuteronomy (4:24) Moses says, "For the Lord thy God is a consuming fire; even a jealous God." Thus, verily, "Blessed are the pure in heart, for they shall see God." (St. Matthew 5:8.) It is also appropriate to think of the words of the Apostle Paul in his Second Epistle to the Corinthians (3:6): "The letter killeth, but the spirit giveth life." Therefore, let us reject the dead letter and mediaeval dogma, and let us kindle in ourselves the fire of spirit whenever we commune with this most Sacred Concept. Let us say to ourselves: "God is limitless, boundless and intangible, otherwise He would not be God." The God of the Mahatmas is a Cosmic God, or rather, the Cosmos Itself. Is it not said that "He is Omnipresent, All-penetrating, Omniscient?" And also, "For in Him we live, and move, and have our being." (Acts 17:28) All this is said in the Bible. Likewise, in the Teaching it is declared that "people do not understand the meaning of God and Bodhisattva." Indeed they do not!

But, as the great Origen said, "Our mind alone is unable to comprehend God Himself, but can intuit Him as the Father of all beings from the *beauty of his creations and the splendor of Nature.*"

Likewise, the Mahatmas conceive God in the Divinity of Nature, both in its visibleness and in its spiritual invisibleness.

"A personification is always demanded for worship by the masses, and they create the Higher Image according to their own consciousness; whereas the Higher Ones aspire through all manifestations to the Principle."

And Origen continues: "Therefore, we cannot consider God as being a particular incarnation, or as incarnate at all. God is Uncompounded Spiritual Nature, excluding all complexes. He is intelligence, and at the same time the source and origin of all intelligence in Nature and Creation. God, Who is the origin of everything, should not be considered complex; as otherwise it might appear as though the elements that have created everything considered complex existed before their very origin."

Here is true philosophical thinking. It is close to, and I would say identical with, that of all the ancient philosophies.

Verily, if our church fathers would follow the example of certain of the Western clergy and study the works of Origen, that great light of Christendom, the symbols and sacraments of Christianity would be revealed in their true light, and the ecclesiastical dogmas would fall away like severed iron fetters, and the Church—the Body of Christ—would be resurrected. Even small children begin to think more logically than our grey-haired instructors!

Yes, the fathers of the Western Church have realized that the consciousness of their spiritual flocks requires a different food and can no longer accept the naive statements which perhaps were once necessary for the restraining of semi-savage tribes converted to Christianity. In order not to lose their influence, some representatives of the Western Church hasten to increase their knowledge and to abandon the erroneous concepts. Just think how many clear indications in the Gospel about reincarnation and the law of Karma were given by Christ Himself! But the clergy completely avoid this argument. It is hardly possible that they are not aware of the fact that *the law of Reincarnation was rejected only in the sixth century by the Council of Constantinople!* Can it be that their understanding has not advanced since that time? One of these Councils discussed also the subject "Does woman possess a soul?" One comes across many similar gems when reading these historic records of darkness and ignorance. And now, in view of the dreadful crisis through which humanity is passing by reason of the spread of the terrifying, all-corrupting atheism resulting from dead dogmatism and the fall of morality among the clergy—indeed, because of all this, the entire priesthood should make a renewed stand against every type of intolerance, ignorance and immorality. They should become true spiritual leaders and *be in advance of their* time, and should not creep along, laden with the chains of dark ignorance. As it is said in the Teaching, "The falsification of Christianity began to spread after Origen." And again, "Horror seizes one at sight of the religious superstitions of that time. Origen walked upon the still-hot coals of the Ancient World. Knowing the Covenants of Jesus, he suffered on seeing the ignorance of the crowd. Knowing the sacraments of Ancient Mysteries, he suffered on seeing the noncomprehension of the oneness of the Source. Knowing the simplicity of the Teaching of Jesus, he suffered on seeing the erection of churches. ...Being an apologist of knowledge, he was indignant at the decline of knowledge among the priesthood." [Leaves of Morya's Garden II]

It is important to remember that in all ages the most enlightened priests were persecuted by the ruling church. How much slander surrounded our contemporary, Father John of Kronstadt, slander spread by his own adherents! Let us recall the "Optina Pustin," that beautiful spiritual group—how many persecutions it suffered from those high ecclesiastic dignitaries! Let us remember also many other things that cannot be compressed into a mere letter.

And now let us deal with the words that made you so indignant. "I will point out the greatest, the chief cause of nearly two thirds of the evils that have pursued humanity ever since that cause became a power. It is religion, under whatever form and in whatsoever nation. It is the sacerdotal caste, the priesthood and the churches." This statement is completely true, as we shall see if we turn to the historical records. Precisely, for the student of the history of religion and the church in general, this is *the indisputable and shocking truth*. At all times, among all peoples, the question of religion has been and is most acute and fraught with fear, and no other human problem is so closely associated with bloodshed. No wars have been so cruel as those for religion.

Remember the militant fanaticism of the Moslems. Let us not forget that in India the Buddhists were persecuted and then destroyed by the Brahmins. Even today, fights involving bloodshed between Moslems and Hindus are not so rare. Likewise, in some Chinese provinces Buddhist lamas have been (and still are) cruelly persecuted. And you have to admit that the Inquisition is the most hideous blot in the annals of Christendom. The Inquisition was certainly not established just for the persecution of witches and sorcerers (mostly mediums and heretics) but for the annihilation of *all differently minded people, all personal enemies* of the representatives of the church, the latter having decided to obtain absolute power. First of all, among the enemies of the church were the most enlightened workers for the General

Good and the true followers of the Testaments of Christ. And the easiest way to destroy the enemy was by accusing him of being in league with the devil. The so-called "Guardians of the purity of Christian Principles" attempted to instil this devilish psychology into the consciousness of the masses by all possible means. Small wonder that in those days the visions of the nuns and monks bore the stamp of Satanic influence and were full of devilish images and all sorts of ugly temptations.

The persecution of the miserable witches, sorcerers, mediums and those who were obsessed, was just a screen. The Inquisition was created to establish unrestrained rule over the poor, frightened population. The most effective means of achieving this was robbery and the extermination of all those who aspired to bring light into the darkness of the Middle Ages, of all those who were too independent, who dared to talk about the General Good, who protested against this kingdom of the devil, personified in the representatives of the Inquisition. The establishment of the Inquisition was a horrible caricature of Divine Justice. It was inspired by the Prince of Darkness for the corruption and destruction of man's faith in the purity, goodness and justice of the Church.

It is edifying to recollect the times of the Inquisition, the Night of St. Bartholomew, and the whole history of the Papacy and the Church Councils, in which at times the reverend spiritual fathers are to be found boxing each others' ears and pulling each others' hair! There can be no respect for such a church and her dogmas—only indignation and horror over such unsurpassed crimes, such monstrous, self-seeking ambition, greed and ignorance committed in the name of Him *who was against all violence and who bade us love our neighbors as ourselves.*

Let us think of all those great ones who suffered under the Inquisition, or who had to conceal their luminous knowledge under the mask of folly or under the most complicated symbols, the key to which, unfortunately for humanity, is almost lost. Let us remember the mountains of destroyed manuscripts, works full of light and goodness, the loss of which is irreparable and is considered by the best minds of all epochs as the greatest misfortune! It is an accepted thing to be indignant about the burning of the Alexandrian Library, but many hypocrites will prefer to remain silent about the string of fires lit by the Inquisition which through centuries steadily consumed at the stake the pearls of human genius! Long is the list of the martyrs of knowledge and light, and such splendid names as Giordano Bruno, John Huss, and Joan of Arc will remain forever in the consciousness of humanity as of those who bore witness at the stake to the existence of the kingdom of the devil in the times of the Inquisition!

It is edifying to read the biographies of the saints of the Catholic Church written by its own clergy. There are preserved authentic writings of the saints to the heads of the church severely condemning their bloody crimes. To think that precisely these criminals created and molded the consciousness of the masses! The history of religion provides some of the darkest, bloodiest chapters in the history of humanity!

You may say to me that the Inquisition was created not by our Orthodox Church but by the Western Church. Then I would remind you of the times of the Patriarch Nikon, who introduced the tridactylous cross in place of the didactylous cross (which, by the way, was used by that true follower of the Gospel of Christ, the great Builder and Founder of Holy Russia, the revered St. Sergius of Radonega). Under Patriarch Nikon all those who crossed themselves with two fingers were persecuted, tortured and burnt. Should the revered Sergius also be regarded as a heretic? Let us carefully read the records of the Church Councils, and we shall see many interesting things that are characteristic of the level of consciousness of those Church Fathers who dictated the dogmas which still exist in full strength today. If people would take the trouble to study seriously the fundamental Teaching of Christ and, if possible, in the original language of the Gospels, instead of being satisfied with the school textbooks, they would discover new meaning in the words, and the true great Image of Christ would be revealed to their spiritual sight—that very Image to whom the revered St. Sergius devoted all his austere life and which was the cause of the enmity of the priests of that period.

And now, what is the greatest sin of the church? The fact that during the centuries the church has inculcated into its adherents a sense of *irresponsibility*. From childhood people have been taught that a person can commit the worst crimes and yet (if he goes to confession and the priest grants forgiveness) be relieved of all burden. This process of shedding sins for a fee can go on and on, save that progressively perhaps the sinner is charged higher and higher fees. Why not sin, when forgiveness can be bought with coin? How many churches have been built and founded on the tears of orphans! Precisely for the erection of the great cathedrals, from what sources has the money most often come? How many candles, lit in front of the Sacred Images, were placed there by the hands of traitors? Verily, as it is said, "Great would be the venality of Christ if He were ready to conceal treachery for a candle! Such candles are abominations. Christ does not need such devotees; do not their candles besmirch the sacred vestments?"

What lack of comprehension in the prayer "I, undeserving priest, by the power given to me by God, now forgive thy sins"! Yes, the forgiveness granted to the repentant sinner in exchange for his money is the greatest crime. The bribery of Divinity with gold—is it not worse than the worst forms of fetishism? This dreadful question must be discussed from every angle. Verily, this hideous ulcer is spread all over the world, in all religions. Thus, in Tibet, there is a gang of robbers called gollocks, who believe in lamaism, a religion just as distant from the Covenants of Buddha as our church is from the Teaching of Christ. These gollocks go to Lhassa annually on pilgrimage to pray for the forgiveness of their crimes. On this particular journey they abstain from robbing the helpless population because they hope to be received by the high priests of their sect. But after receiving full forgiveness for their crimes upon payment of money, they give full freedom to debauchery and return to their practices of robbery, with even more violence, whenever they can. Has not their guilt been taken from them, and may they not purify themselves again the following year? It is only a question of a fee! Also, in India, sinners will hasten to present a goat to their Brahmin as an expiation. Other valuable offerings are also made, according to the degree of the sin, and the transgressors receive absolution and purification just as easily. You may say that this concerns only backward races. But does not the same thing take place even among the highly intellectual classes of America and Europe? Even worse! Recently, the Catholic Church renewed the ancient practice of granting indulgences. And now Catholics need not even bother to make pilgrimage to Rome or elsewhere to do penance for their sins! All that is necessary is to send a certain sum for an indulgence, and thus the remittance of a fee will permit entrance into Heaven. Undoubtedly there must be a scale of prices for these indulgences, as sins vary so much. Verily, through correct estimating, a fortune might be made! Alas, can nothing put a stop to this? Are we not returning speedily to the darkness of medievalism?

Indeed, by instilling into the minds of children the idea that the church, as a powerful intercessor, can for a tear of repentance and a fee give passage to the erring through the gates of Paradise, *the church commits the greatest sin.* By removing from man the sense of responsibility, the church shuts him off from his *Divine Origin.* The church has discredited the great concept of *Divine Justice.* By losing the understanding of responsibility and justice, man will inevitably begin his devolution, for those who fail to follow the cosmic laws are destined to deterioration.

The whole Cosmos is built upon the law of responsibility, or, as it is more often called, the law of cause and effect, the law of Karma. And it is quite impossible to ignore this law and to neglect it without bringing on, in the long run, self-destruction. All the ancient Teachings, without exception, taught this law of great responsibility, this pledge of the *Divine in us.* This is clearly indicated in the words of Moses, "Eye for eye, tooth for tooth," misinterpreted and taken as an example of the revengefulness of the Jewish people. Let us, however, think of the words of Christ: "Ye have heard that it was said by them of old time, Thou shalt not kill; and whosoever shall kill shall be in danger of the judgment: But I say unto you, That whosoever is angry with his brother without a cause shall be in danger of the judgment: and whosoever shall say to his brother, Raca, shall be in danger of the council: but whosoever shall say, Thou fool, shall be in danger of hellfire." (St. Matthew 5:21-22.) Does not this appear yet more severe than the law of Moses, if we refuse to see in it the same inescapable law of Karma?

Without doubt, you also know the words of Christ: "Verily I say unto you, There is no man that hath left house, or brethren, or sisters, or father, or mother, or wife or children, or lands, for my sake, and the Gospel's, but he shall receive an hundredfold now in this time, houses, and brethren, and sisters, and mothers, and children, and lands, with persecutions; and in the world to come eternal life." (St. Mark 10:29-30.) How can one "now in this time" have more mothers and fathers, etc., if one does not admit the law of Reincarnation? Precisely, here is emphasized the contrast between "this time here" (a time of earthly existences "amidst persecutions") and life in the world that is to come.

And more: "And his disciples asked him, saying, Why then say the scribes that Elias must first come? And Jesus answered and said unto them, Elias truly shall first come, and restore all things. But I say unto you, that Elias is come already, and they knew him not, but have done unto him whatsoever they listed. Likewise shall also the Son of man suffer of them. Then the disciples understood that he spake unto them of John the Baptist." (St. Matthew 17:10-13.) Furthermore: And as Jesus passed by, he saw a man which was blind from his birth. And his disciples asked him, saying, "Master, who did sin, this man or his parents, that he was born blind?" (St. John 9:1-2.) Did not these questions of the disciples reveal that they knew of the law of Karma and that Christ also did not reject it? Likewise one must understand the parable of the talents. Why then, have the fathers of the church so persistently refused to accept the great cosmic law, which alone can explain all the seeming injustices, all the differences in the conditions of birth, and all the misfortunes which come to us? There is only one answer. Everywhere there is the one selfish motive—not to surrender power, and to increase one's material welfare and prestige. Thus, the ignorant masses all over the world, for long centuries, have been held between the fear of eternal damnation and hellfire and the hope of eternal peace with enjoyment in Paradise, while the keys to the Gates of Heaven, we are told, are given to the priesthood by God Himself!

But until man comprehends all the grandeur of his origin, that his being is an immortal part of the Divine Ego and is eternally changing its forms, and until man realizes his responsibility and that *there is no one who can forgive his sins or reward him for his merits, that he himself is the creator of causes and effects,* that he is the sower and the reaper of everything created by him—until he realizes all this, he will remain the disseminator and propagator of the insanity, criminality and corruption which threaten our planet with dreadful destruction.

The irresponsibility inculcated into the consciousness is already *hereditary*. In order to save man from perdition, it is necessary that great enlightened minds be united and that they vigorously awaken the obscured consciousness of humanity. It is necessary that the more advanced spiritual instructors start immediately the purification of the Covenants of Christ in the light of the Teaching of the last great apologist of Christ, Origen, the martyr. With this purification, the New Great Prediction will shine forth in all its glory, bringing synthesis, bringing tolerance and a transformation of all the Covenants.

In conclusion, I shall quote paragraphs from the Teaching:

"Humanity attaches significance only to those concepts which are stored away in a consciousness of mediocrity, for it arrays correspondingly each form in its consciousness. Why, then, have all the Higher Concepts not been inculcated? Why so many distortions? Why so many belittlements? Because, in truth, the essence of human quests and strivings has been turned downward. But the problem of the New World is to rouse the consciousness and to restore to the world the predestined Image of Beauty. Creativeness of the spirit must indeed be intensified in ascent. Precisely, not to lower the Higher but to allow it to rise. Therefore, the first requisite will be to create the Divine Image according to Divinity. When the human consciousness will cease to depict Divinity in an earthly way, then the attainments of the spirit will be fiery.

"Indeed, the very loftiest consciousness strives toward the Fiery Principle, while the lower one creates the Higher Image in its own likeness. The capacity of the small consciousness will determine the created Image, hence so many obvious distortions! How is it possible to fill a small consciousness with a Universal Concept, when all-comprehensiveness leads the spirit into a frenzy. I say—distressing, grievous is human thinking! A spatial horizon is accessible only to him who knows the Universality of the Principle, for the kingly spirit can merge with the Higher Principle precisely as the microcosm merges with the Macrocosm. Hence, a small spirit cannot merge with the Fiery Principle. Fiery power reveals the entire Furnace manifested to him who senses the pulse of the Fiery World. This life-giving Principle builds life upon Fohat. Thus, let us remember that only a small consciousness denies, but the fiery spirit is all-comprehending. On the path to the Fiery World let us remember about the great Principle." [Fiery World III]

Thus, people serve the God created in their own image, and attribute to him their own vices. But the Mahatmas serve the Divine Unutterable Principle, and revere that Principle by the purity of their lives and by their self-sacrificing service to the Good of the whole world.

And since I address, I hope a consciousness which is not alien but young and fiery, I shall quote one more paragraph from the Teaching:

"In this time of world obstruction there is only one path of regeneration of thinking. Precisely it is important to awaken the consciousness. Indeed, when the spirit can look back and know that yesterday's thinking has already passed, then takes place the transmutation bringing discernment. Indeed, the expiring time can indicate to the spirit how all energies pass on and are reworked. But woe to those who wish to encounter the future by looking backward! For the spirit overburdened with yesterday's remains is laden with a massive weight. With such a burden one cannot ascend the Mountain, one cannot pass through the Gates of Light, one cannot become associated with the luminous future. Thus, if the church fathers summon to the past, the Servants of Light summon into the future. Awakening of consciousness, clarification of the Teaching, and summons into the future will result in a great regeneration of thinking. On the path to the Fiery World, My Guiding Hand shifts energies." [Fiery World III]

Remember what was said in one of the first books: "Those who desire to reach the New Country must not only cast away all prejudices but also must enter by the new ways." Yes, it is impossible to build on the refuse of the past. A shifting in the consciousness of the masses has taken place and it must be considered. People are longing for Light, for spiritual food; but this food must be pure, and the chasubles of the new spiritual instructors must be truly stainless. The instructors must follow the path of the Lord Christ, even as did our great revered Sergius. Indeed, Sergius, who communed with Fire and received fiery baptism, knew and knows the nature of the Divine Element. Precisely, the great Sergius was not just a theologian; his whole life was a *powerful imitation* of Christ, both in his self-sacrificing service to his country and to the world. Yes, the venerable Sergius applied the Covenants of Christ, but not the dogma of the church. And as for his refusal of the position of Metropolitan, was it not because He knew how much the doctrines of the church conflicted with the Truth?

Many mysteries incomprehensible to the intellect *are revealed when one is in communion with the divine element of Fire.* But these mysteries the spirit treasures in the heart. "Give not that which is holy unto the dogs, neither cast ye your pearls before swine, lest they trample them under their feet, and turn again and rend you." (St. Matthew 7:6.) Thus, let us take heed lest we commit blasphemy; let us humbly bow our heads before the sacrament of the great Divine Element, which is revealed to us mortals in the glory of creation, visible and invisible. Let us worship this Divine Element by the purity of our lives and motives; let us fill our hearts with love and devotion to the One who gave Light to us, and let us devote ourselves to the service of humanity.

Father Sergius, Thou Wondrous One, with Thee we are going, with Thee we shall conquer!

33

15 September 1934

It is instructive to observe that people are asking for knowledge, are dreaming of all sorts of initiations, yet the moment they are introduced to a new aspect of the all-embracing Truth which does not quite agree with the concepts instilled into them they become most indignant and draw back. They are full of conceit and love to repeat that "man is the king of nature." However, if one tries to tell them that the destiny of man really is that of a divine creator—Man-God—they become furious and would rather stick to their old slavery, the name of which is fear, fear of the new and sublime.

It is said in the Teaching:

"Humanity attaches significance only to those concepts which are stored away in a consciousness of mediocrity, for it arrays correspondingly each form in its consciousness. Why, then, have all the Higher concepts not been inculcated? Why so many distortions? Why so many belittlements? Because, in truth, the essence of human quests and strivings has been turned downward. But the problem of the New World is to rouse the consciousness and to restore to the world the predestined Image of Beauty, Creativeness of the spirit must indeed be intensified in ascent. Precisely, not to lower the Higher but to allow it to rise. Therefore, the first requisite will be to create the Divine Image according to Divinity. When the human consciousness will cease to depict Divinity in an earthly way, then the attainments of the spirit will be fiery.

"Indeed, the very loftiest consciousness strives toward the Fiery Principle, while the lower one creates the Higher Image in its own likeness. The capacity of the small consciousness will determine the created Image, hence so many obvious distortions! How is it possible to fill a small consciousness with a Universal Concept, when all-comprehensiveness leads the spirit into a frenzy. I say—distressing, grievous is human thinking! A spatial horizon is accessible only to him who knows the Universality of the Principle, for the kingly spirit can merge with the Higher Principle precisely as the microcosm merges with Macrocosm. Hence, a small spirit cannot merge with the Fiery Principle. Fiery power reveals the entire Furnace manifested to him who senses the pulse of the Fiery World. This life-giving Principle builds life upon Fohat. Thus, let us remember that only a small consciousness denies, but the fiery spirit is all-comprehending. On the path to the Fiery World let us remember about the great Principle." [Fiery World III]

I have quoted these paragraphs for you, as you may have to deal with this subject. Of course, one must not force the consciousness. The growth of consciousness is slow. And as it has always been it is even so now; the various aspects of Truth are given by the Great Teachers according to the varying degrees of consciousness. This is done by reason of great compassion, as well as of great wisdom. The purification of consciousness and the regeneration of thinking, indeed, should take place, but we know that too great a dose of even an exceptionally curative medicine, without a proper preparation of the organism, may cause just the opposite result.

34

10 September 1934

Although you may not agree that the whole danger in the present governmental structure over the world is caused by the absence of synthesis in the spirit of the national leaders, I shall insist that it is so! What is so often taken to be leadership is in reality nothing but a crafty caricature of real guidance. The leaders elected by the masses usually lack synthesis, for precisely the masses themselves *do not possess it.* True leadership has nothing to do with this kind of pseudoleadership, and it certainly does not contradict the Hierarchic principle, being the foundation of it. The Hierarch is, first of all, a leader. What then, can exist without the leading concept or focus? Precisely, the idea of Hierarchy is a cosmic concept, a cosmic law. The whole Universe exists, is nourished, and is supported solely by this principle. In Cosmos each form has at its foundation a nucleus, and each center of striving lives by the principle of Hierarchy. The Cosmos acts by the attraction toward the affirmed powerful center. Precisely, in Cosmos, the lower principle is subordinated to the higher. Otherwise, what would be the foundation of evolution?

It is said in one of the books of Living Ethics:

"Of all principles leading to the broadening of consciousness, the principle of Hierarchy is the most powerful. Each manifested shifting is created upon the principle of Hierarchy. Whither can the spirit direct itself without the Guiding Hand? Whither can the eye and the heart be directed without Hierarchy, when the Giving Hand of the Hierarch affirms the direction of destiny, and when the Hand of the Hierarch directs a better designated date and the highest energies assume the closest Images? Therefore, the seed of the spirit is imbued by the Cosmic Ray of the Hierarch. Since a most powerful principle contains in itself the potentiality of fire, the pure fire of the spirit of the Hierarch is affirmed as the highest principle. Hence, let us remember our spiritual Leaders. Thus shall we reverence the law of Hierarchy." [Agni Yoga]

As an admirer of Hermetism, you will certainly remember the axiom "As above, so below." Infinite is the chain of the Hierarchy of Light, and it has its representatives and leaders on Earth; but they were never elected by the crowds.

Of course, such a democracy as you describe, "a democracy, vital and transformed, based on the realization of the responsibility of the individual toward his duties, on which responsibility his rights depend, a democracy consisting of the cooperation of all, together with the maximum of personal initiative for the sake of the General Good"—such a democracy, perhaps, we shall see toward the end of the seventh race (provided our planet will not have been exploded by that time). But now, being merely in the fifth race bordering on the sixth, we can only envision such a democracy in our best dreams. Thus the great Plato dreamed, and perhaps he is now actualizing it upon some higher planet. However, even such an ideal democracy would have to be led by someone; and such a leader would certainly need to possess spiritual synthesis. But the modern democracy that affirms the leadership which issues from the crowds fails all tests. Is it possible to expect that the consciousness of the majority will regenerate so quickly that everybody will understand at least his social responsibility and give elementary cooperation, to say nothing of the higher aspects of responsibility?

And is it possible to suppose that one can acquire the synthesized consciousness just in one life unless it was previously accumulated by the spirit during aeons of time by stubborn labor for the acquisition of spiritual knowledge and experience? Indeed, synthesis is the most difficult, the rarest, and the greatest achievement. Verily, this is the crown for those who are completing their earthly path. One may talk of synthesis, but to realize it completely is possible only if one possesses the great accumulations which inevitably raise one above the crowds. Therefore, there will always be leaders, as nothing can be entirely leveled out, especially consciousness and thinking. However, the leaders of the future will be selected not by the irresponsible masses but, verily, by the Hierarchy of Light and Knowledge. And much hard labor will have to be performed in order that the consciousness of humanity may be raised for the acceptance of this leading principle of the whole Universe.

Indeed, it would be inadvisable to bewilder a small consciousness by mentioning the concept of synthesis. Nothing but perplexity and detachment would result. The process of broadening the consciousness is a very slow and most dangerous one. Violation of the balance can result in insanity, enfeebling of the will, or obsession. The growing tree needs fencing about; the nervous and difficult horse needs blinders. And it is most difficult to broaden the consciousness of the average intellectual person, who is full of conceit and negation. The people, in the depths of their hearts, know now that "life cannot be joyous without heroes." But the average intellectual tries to prove his education and knowledge by repudiating with a superior air all things which his mind does not comprehend. Due to this attitude, his whole personality is a failure. Therefore, I think that the statement "In Russia there was always less lauding of personality than in the West" is not altogether correct. The people (as is clear from the above proverb) revere and treasure the concept of a bright and shining hero, who indicates the path to Light and Good. Just hearken to the various national epics! However, if you reread Dostoyevsky you will notice that the Russian intelligentsia at the end of the last century had really commenced condemning itself by a ruinous, corrupting denial of the great foundations of life. Self-abasement, self-humiliation is so obvious. Man so clearly destroys himself!

Yes, nothing provokes so much indignation in the average intellectual as the concept of Hierarchy. They are all so afraid to accept the Higher authority, and at the same time they are influenced every moment by the judgments and decisions of nonentities. This severance from the Higher and submission to the lower, in other words, equation with the lower, is the menace of our time, and it is leading toward the deterioration of our planet and its possible premature destruction. If all those who feel indignant about the Hierarchic principle could but realize what discipline of obedience reigns among the Hierarchy of Light, and what a schooling in obedience their close disciples have to go through! And this obedience is demanded not in order to control the disciple in the interest of the Teachers. It is only required of the disciples in order to enable them to enter the first steps leading toward the understanding and acceptance of the Cosmic Will. *Discipline is the beginning of all knowledge and power.* I shall conclude with a few more lines from the Teaching:

"The welfare of nations is constructed around a single personality. There are numerous examples of this throughout history, in the most diverse regions. Many will attribute this evident manifestation to the personality itself. But this is short-sighted; those who are far-sighted understand that such synthesis is nothing else but the manifestation of the power of Hierarchy. Actually in all such manifestations the Hierarchy selects a focus upon which the current may be directed. Besides, a personality of such order possesses a fire, realized or unrealized, which makes the communion easy. But indispensable also is a certain quality on the part of the people themselves—trust and the recognition of the power. Therefore, in different matters I so often reiterate about the confirmation of authority. This quality is needed as a link of the fiery machine. You yourselves see how nations progress by affirming a leader. You yourselves see that there is no other way. Thus, the link of Hierarchy must be realized. One should not be short-sighted." [Fiery World II]

* * *

Quite correctly, you have stated that "the fact that the books of Living Ethics are given in such numbers and with such revelations indicates the seriousness of the time." Precisely, we are approaching the decisive decennaries—"to be or not to be" for the welfare of our planet. The change of race, all displacements and reconstructions may be ended at this time far more tragically than in the days of Lemuria and Atlantis. Verily, man can become the exploder of the planet.

* * *

Also, it is true that a knowledge of the books of Living Ethics obliges a person to apply these indications in everyday life. Otherwise, karmically speaking, it is better not to approach the Teaching. As for the enemies, we do not worry about them, but we take them into consideration. Often, among them are disguised well-wishers who after personal contact become our most devoted friends, while others serve us by tensing our energies! The power of a stroke is measured by the power of resistance. Truly, obstacles and enemies sharpen all our abilities and tense the most precious energy; therefore, we know the value of enemies. Long ago it was said, "Blessed are the obstacles, by them we grow," and "without enemies, grateful humanity would have interred the most vital manifestations." Thus, Vivekananda used to say that "Buddha and Christ were impressed upon the memory of the people because they were lucky enough to have strong enemies!" In the Teaching, slander is defined as the torches of savages—but during the night crossing, each fire is of use!

As your say further, some people, having read *Illumination* and *Agni Yoga*, who until then were kindly and honest, suddenly begin to show their worst qualities, which formerly were hidden. This is a usual occult manifestation. By approaching the Teaching one increases the tension of all active energies, and the forces that were formerly dormant begin to awaken, manifesting one's real nature. Therefore, great care is always advised and no forcing is permissible. Proselytism is never advocated by the Teaching. Quality is essential, not quantity. The ability to give to everyone according to consciousness shows the true knowledge of an advanced disciple. Therefore, it is not necessary to spread widely the books of the Teaching, but rather to adhere in a broad way to a cultural and educational program accessible to everyone. The foundations of Living Ethics offered by the Teaching can be correctly assimilated only by a cultivated and disciplined mind. And how many such intellects are there, even among the so-called educated people? Without a foundation of culture and refinement, how can we expect a person to react to the most subtle vibrations? Is it possible to expect this from one who sees and yet does not see, hears and yet does not hear; whose eyes and ears are closed to the reception of the finest vibrations of nature; for whom earth is always black and mountains always green or grey; to whom all Hindus and all Chinese look alike, and all the sounds of waterfalls, rivers and forests are just noise! Can one expect from such a person the cognition of higher vibrations? The first requisite for each reception is an expanded consciousness. The consciousness is only the magnet that will attract and assemble our treasury. That is why in the books of Living Ethics the opening, purifying and broadening of the consciousness is so much insisted upon. The Teaching stays with those who strive toward it.

And now, with regard to the heart, one should understand the heart not as a symbol but as a great laboratory, where the transmutation of our consciousness and therefore of our whole being is taking place. The heart is the highest manifestation of the sixth principle. The heart is the abode of Brahma. One cannot separate the physical from the spiritual. All things are so interwoven and so interdependent. Precisely, this unity manifests its harmony. There are subtle and astral sensations, just as there are physical ones, but their flow is correspondingly subtle. It is impossible to treat them separately. It is always necessary to realize the complete correspondence between the subtle and the physical bodies. Hence, the formula "as above, so below" should always be remembered.

Without the development and refinement of the heart there is no progress. Therefore, in the foundation of each construction there must be laid the great magnet of the heart. Hence. the representatives of the new race will be known by the refinement of the heart—this key to all achievements.

You talk about "liberation from the slavery of personality,

sex and the flesh." But how differently, and I would say "out of true" in its abstractness and absence of reality, is this liberation understood by the majority! Begin to discuss it with those around you and you will discover the most unexpected things. For example, let us take the idea of liberation from sex. There are many who see liberation from this slavery in the repugnant hermaphrodite, considering this as humanity's "crown of creation." As a proof, they point our the recurrence of such cases, whereas in reality this means degeneration. In the liberation from sex there is a great cosmic mystery; the symbol of the Androgyne is so profound. And the great Plato, with his twin souls, was much nearer to this mystery than the modern thinkers.

The concept of personality is also distorted and vulgarized beyond all measure. The majority of people indeed are without personality, being suffocated from infancy by forced, ready-made concepts, dogma and every kind of convention. Their whole lives are spent as in a dream, without thought—like robots. Don't you think that it would be useful if such people could first of all affirm their "personalities"?

Similarly, the liberation from the slavery of the flesh is understood by many as fanaticism, asceticism and the complete neglect of the body; whereas the body is man's only instrument for the accumulating of the new spiritual possibilities. In the ancient Teachings the foundation of all achievements was wisely linked with the great Golden Path, or the Golden Mean. Doubtless you know all this, but as you will have to deal with the average mind, you should always remember that the concepts that should be most easily understood acquire the most unexpected twists! I know it from experience, and therefore suggest that you check and purify the consciousness of those who approach you.

What are teraphim? There is a great and complicated literature about teraphim. Teraphim have many forms and aspects. Broadly speaking, a teraph is a talisman or an accumulator of energies; thus, every article saturated with precipitations of psychic energy is a teraph. When saturated with the psychic energy of a specific command, the talisman or teraph conveys it to a person to whom it is sent. Often, in the past, teraphim acted as oracles. In antiquity the preparation of such teraphim was extremely complicated, and besides, the knowledge of astrology was widely applied. Of course there are also astral teraphim, but such teraphim belong only to highly developed spirits. The secret of the preparation of such teraphim is in the hands of the great Arhats. Through such teraphim it is possible strongly to influence a person, and also to guard his health. If you have read about the experiments in the exteriorization of sensitiveness, you can imagine the influence of such teraphim to a certain extent. In the book *Agni Yoga* the creation of a simple teraph is explained in detail.

In Sanscrit the word "Santana" means a stream. It is customary in Buddhism to compare the chain of our lives with a perpetual current, or stream. Therefore, the Teaching tells us to "go through Santana with your heart"; in other words, to go through all our lives with the tireless striving of the heart.

What is Armageddon? Armageddon is the great decisive Battle between the Forces of Light and darkness. It was predicted in all the ancient scriptures, and the name "Armageddon," as well as the description of it, can be found in the Apocalypse. The year 1936 is indicated as most significant. It is interesting to note that these calculations are also found in the pyramid of Cheops. Thus, today, we find ourselves in the midst of this Battle, which will increase. This Battle is still more fearful in the Subtle World, but eventually its reflections will be intensified on the earthly plane. Great is the tension of space, and the tensed fiery energies are surging in the subterranean and superterranean spheres, threatening an explosion. Verily, the planet is in convulsions. The time is most ominous. Verily, we are facing an incredible world catastrophe. As it is said, "The hostile elements of the race refuse to submit to destiny. The departing race seeks to destroy the chosen successors, but We must save them. Destiny may be eased and the battle ended sooner." So far, there are no signs of easement. But the ark of the sixth race is already being built. Let us trust that it will be larger than that of Noah.

Yes, the New Epoch requires spiritual cognition. The New Epoch must manifest due respect to the Mother of the World, to the Feminine Element. "The bird of the spirit of Humanity cannot fly with only one wing"—these are words of Vivekananda, who meant to affirm the great significance of the Feminine Principle. Man does not willingly give full rights to woman. However, this opposition but intensifies the forces; and woman, fighting for her cosmic rights, will acquire the knowledge of her power.

35
18 October 1934

The noble idea of the Banner of Peace must gradually enter life and, as one writer has said, "Every scientist, every creator, every teacher, every pupil, everyone who thinks about the meaning and purpose of history, must hasten to follow the call of N. K. Roerich, who raises the Banner of Peace over the entire world. Of course, we realize that this peace is also a struggle. But it is not a selfish struggle, a struggle for one's own welfare, but rather a *defense* against the dark forces, who are attacking the treasures of the spirit. ... It is not statutes that are important, but the will of the individual cultural workers. They are not yet united, but they must be merged into one current, one flowing river, surging toward the entrance into the great ocean of ideas."

The idea of defending the creations of human genius is so beautiful and so essential that it is imperative to put it into practice as soon as possible. Just think how many years will have to pass before the consciousness of the masses will be prepared to respect what the Banner proposes to protect! But time does not wait. In Spain there was recently destroyed a very ancient church, together with the paintings of some of the best masters. Long is the list of priceless treasures that have been destroyed. It is time to arrest this vandalism.

* * *

You are quite right that it is necessary to *purify the atmosphere*. Obsession is terribly infectious. "It is necessary to observe carefully the manifestation of obsession and to purify the atmosphere. Space is full of vampires and many attract entities from the lower spheres. It is necessary to purify the whole atmosphere." That is why it is so important to warn against the danger of psychism. I shall quote one more discourse about psychism:

"Much has already been said about psychism; nevertheless this scourge of humanity is insufficiently understood. Psychism blunts each aspiration, and higher attainment remains inaccessible. The sphere of activity of a man engulfed by psychism is limited within a charmed circle in which all the energies which retard growth of the spirit find their fitting place. Psychism embraces the manifestation of the lowest energies, and the fires of the centers are extinguished by these precipitations. With psychism there is inevitably to be found disorder of the nervous system. In addition, the breaking away from vital functions closes the path to self-perfectionment. Creativeness is blunted, and there is established a passive state which makes a man an instrument for the influx of all kinds of forces. By reason of relaxation of the will, control is weakened, and by this the attraction of various lower entities is increased. He who wishes to approach the Fiery World must battle with these forces of evil." [Fiery World III]

We have often met psychics who were so pleased with their astral visions and visitants, as they considered these to be high achievements, that they lost all impulse toward self-perfection, thinking that they were especially privileged persons who had reached the goal. This is dreadful, for the moment we imagine ourselves as knowing everything, verily the future ceases to exist for us.

And now, one more paragraph:

"Fiery energies, being drawn into tension by some center, can often cause enhanced actions of the energies of this center. Partial action of energies gives a center the power to manifest partially. These tensions lead to those partial manifestations which bring into error consciousnesses of small discrimination. With reason has Ur. pointed out those manifestations, evoked by the tension of one center, which lead to psychism. Truly, each opening, saturation or irritation of the centers gives a sharp direction to the fiery energy. But only conformity between the state of the organism and the spiritual awakening produces, as an inevitable effect, the opening of the centers in highest tension. A partial pressure will produce a partial attainment, which may prove to be a very dangerous manifestation. On the path to the Fiery World let us strive to realize the higher tension of fiery energy." [Fiery World III]

Few wish to understand that the highest achievement is not in psychism, not in astral visions, but in *synthesis*, in the development of one's own abilities. This is achieved by the scrupulous fulfillment of one's duties, or, as those of the East would say, by dharma. Truly, the manifested world is upheld and is developed by action, and only action gives birth to new energies. It is also said that the world is created by thought, or that thought engenders action. Therefore many, supposing that thought is higher than action, plunge into dreaminess, taking it for creative thought, forgetting that only that thought which is *saturated by fiery will* can create. But one can acquire such will only by *stubborn practice, and by the application into life and action* of one's own thoughts as well as the thoughts of others. Therefore, one must first earn the right to a purely mental existence.

In their earthly lives, all the Great Teachers applied their thoughts expressly to action, expressly to construction. Not one of Them tried to withdraw into anchoretic life. All of Them labored with human hands and human feet toward new achievements. Therefore, one must insist upon action, for air castles have no place. And at the present time this is more necessary than ever before, as humanity struggles against the gigantic attacks of the dark forces.

Hence, one must emphasize the significance of an active and as perfect as possible fulfillment of the *earthly tasks*, or, as it is said, of "one's dharma to the end." Only in this way is it possible to achieve the *true progress of the inner man.* "Man comes to perfection by the constant fulfillment of his dharma," says Krishna in the Bhagavad-Gita.

36

8 November 1934

I am so happy if my letter brought you the necessary explanations, as it is most important to have a clear understanding of what is meant by the path of discipleship and the path of Service. Without a realization of the difficulties and of the austere beauty of service, without the firm decision to choose precisely this path of achievement and self-denial, we may be drawn into the horrible snares of psychism, mediumism and black magic. I say horrible because, if once caught, an incredible effort of will power will have to be used in order to rid oneself of it. And how many possess such a will power? Therefore, avoid all mechanical exercises, which develop the projection of the subtle body and the acquiring of low forms of psychism.

In the Teaching a preparatory stage is indicated, wherein the organism is gradually prepared for the reception of the higher influences—but all mechanical exercises are forbidden. The quick results achieved by you, when the "methods of projecting into the astral" were applied, only prove that you are psychically and mediumistically inclined. Therefore, you should be especially careful. As I have to write very often on this subject I shall quote some extracts from my letters to other correspondents, thus saving time:

"You ask me how to perfect yourself psychically? There is only one answer: by applying the Teaching in your life—the rest will come in due time. First of all, the complete purification of your consciousness is necessary, with eradication of the slightest sign of irritability. The latter is most dangerous during the process of psychic development. High achievements are practically impossible for the organism polluted by imperil. It is clearly stated in the Teaching that *it is impossible to acquire the psychic technique without a Teacher*, as this technique is connected with dangerous processes. Therefore, we can only patiently prepare our organism, applying all the indications to daily life. The Teacher knows when it is possible to develop the hidden power.

"Believe me, the Teacher will not lose a single moment if He sees the disciple is ready to accept the first steps or the next degree corresponding to his spiritual development. There are many degrees of psychism, and the Great Teachers are extremely concerned about the increased manifestations of lower forms of it. As for the ignorant, dishonest or undeveloped consciousness, it often ends with mediumship and obsession. Therefore, the Teachers are so against all artificial exercises and methods which lead toward the rapid acquisition of lower psychic powers. The surest, the most natural way is the development of the heart and the purification of the consciousness.

"It is difficult even to imagine how the infection of lower psychism has gripped people. And how distorted have become all the great concepts and the great Images of the Lords! Some people imagine the Teachers in garments adorned with precious stones, or even as guardians of chests filled with gold and diamonds! How astonished such people would be if they could but grasp the true picture! Nothing is further removed from the lives of the Great Teachers than the concept of well-being and luxury. Their lives are full of beauty, but then, beauty and luxury are two opposites.

"It is always necessary to remember that lower psychism can

manifest itself only in the lower strata of the Subtle World, where there are quite a few pompous Olympians and plenty of impersonators of the Great Teachers of Light.

"Let us also remember that there is the very powerful Black Lodge, which tries in many ways to imitate the methods of the White Brotherhood. It is characteristic of them to use all means in order to entice into their camp those who are on the first steps of the Teaching, and whose convictions are not yet firm. Each hesitation in thought, each doubt can carry one away into the opposite camp.

"All this I write in order to warn against the terrible danger of artificial exercises. Only those achievements are valuable that come naturally, as then they manifest the inner, spiritual development. With such development, eventually all-comprehensive power becomes possible. Let us not forget that the forces developed by artificial methods are not lasting, whereas all that is acquired by inner spiritual efforts *cannot be lost.* All these hidden powers are developed in man gradually and, as a rule, by the man himself, in proportion to his mastering of his lower nature in the long course of his previous lives. Therefore, some people who approach the Teaching begin comparatively early to show signs of such development. For instance (and this is indicated in the Teaching), they may see stars of various size, color and brightness. Each such star has its own meaning, either warning or indicating or comforting. Sometimes there are light formations and sparks, either within oneself or near by. There are visions of flowers, whole scenes, and finally one begins to hear the Voice of the Teacher. But one can also hear the voices of friends, as well as the undesirable voices from the lower spheres of the Subtle World. One should subtly discriminate regarding these manifestations. Fatigue or an excessive tension of a center may cause inflammation and is most dangerous—it can even bring death.

"You ask whether or not you should continue with meditations. Everything that increases the power of concentration and thought is very useful, and clearness of thought should by all means be encouraged. There is now so much chaotic thinking that it is most essential to learn to marshall one's thoughts and to avoid an involuntary leaping. Clarity and sequence of thinking is very necessary in the process of the broadening of consciousness."

* * *

And now, regarding your statement that you do not dare to criticize the book, I must tell you that one must always be ready to express an unprejudiced and intelligent criticism, or rather to give an opinion on what one has read or heard. Otherwise, how would it be possible to develop one's consciousness and thinking? Exactly, if we choose the path of Service, we must develop our power of discrimination. True, we must have complete confidence in the wisdom of the Teaching we have chosen. Yet we are not asked to accept each indication blindly, just on faith alone. If something is not quite understood, it should never be repeated parrot-like, just because it is in a book of the Teaching. This would be the surest move toward fanaticism. It is our duty to increase the power of our thinking, in order that we may understand everything that does not seem clear. This will not be criticism, but rather issues from a sound motive to save the Teaching from distortion. Just think how much evil has been spread because of blind faith and the acceptance of the dead letter of scriptures! One must understand that not a single question can be answered totally, and the answers must be as numerous and varied as the consciousnesses of the inquirers. Hence, all the distortions of the Great Teachings. Thus, do not be afraid to analyze what you read about the Teachings and the Teachers. Too many distortions are spread throughout the world. There is no blasphemy in honest seeking and discussion, in the sincere desire to understand.

Now about your confession. It is very good that you yourself have come independently to the understanding of what is usually most difficult for those people to accept who have been brought up on church dogma, i.e., the realization of God as the One Impersonal Element of Be-ness. In spite of the fact that in books which people have accepted as true they read that "not at any time or anywhere has anyone seen God," they try to attribute to Him a form and a dwelling place! The independent perception of this truth always indicates previous spiritual accumulations, and regarding this, I sincerely congratulate you!

Referring to the vision you describe, I can only tell you that the Great Teachers never wear crowns! The crowns of the Lords are in their royally beautiful radiations. Only the cliche created by people's imaginations invests them with these astral symbols of earthly power. It is also wrong to understand the Advent so narrowly. The Great Advent predicted by all the ancient scriptures means the ending of Armageddon and the arrival of the epoch of the regeneration of the spirit, which is linked with the formation of the sixth race.

Of course, none of the Great Lords will appear in a physical body. But the spiritual power of the Three Lords will be manifested on the earthly plane at the crucial hour. Remember, it is said that the Son of Man will appear in thunder and lightning and in a trice.

* * *

You ask whether it is possible to trust the writings of Olcott. Indeed, much more than many others. His first works are the best, for by accepting the authority of H. P. Blavatsky he came under the Ray of the Great Teachers. You know about the immutable law of Hierarchy. Only through H. P. Blavatsky was it possible to approach the White Brotherhood.

You say that you feel lonely. But what about your intention of gathering young people around the Teaching and the concept of *podvig*? These young forces could help you very much in your own development, you would be forced to deepen your understanding of the Teaching, for by their questions they would make you crystallize your ideas. Indeed, we learn while we teach. Why do you not try to exercise the magnet of your spirit and attract the new young people who know less than you?

And so, if you decide to fulfil your first intention, let it be entirely on your own responsibility and initiative, and at the beginning do not join with the other groups already organized. Therefore, act very cautiously and apply discrimination, as it is easy to give entry to the dark intruders who are always especially anxious to infiltrate the pure organizations. If you are able to build up a really worthy group, you will have achieved something worthwhile. There are some young souls who should, by all means, be supported by the ways accessible to their consciousness.

Even the books of Kryjanovsky have played their good part. Parallel with a rather pronounced vulgarity, these books contain some real gems. The most important, the most responsible thing is to know how to give to each one *according to his consciousness*. The great error is to give more than the consciousness of your companion can accept. To give too much to a consciousness that is not yet ready is tantamount to giving a loaded gun to a child. Therefore, approach everyone with the canon "By thy God," and then carefully direct him and broaden his horizon. Thus, it depends on you whether or not you remain spiritually lonely. Act not by impulse but by the intelligence of your heart! The intellect and the emotions must be balanced in all the judgments and actions of a disciple. Do not confuse sentimentality with the kindness of the heart! Sentimentality has nothing in common with true kindness, which is based on higher knowledge and higher justice. The science of how to deal with people is a most complicated and most difficult one, as it requires a heart tempered and strengthened by many battles with the dark destroyers and betrayers, and affirmed by invincible patience and self-denial.

Thus, strengthen yourself upon the foundations of the Living Ethics, and verify your abilities and possibilities by helping the young seekers. Good Luck! Sincere striving will always bring results.

37

15 November 1934

Regarding the further development of the Pact, I shall once more remind G. G. so that he can inform you about all his steps, as this is quite essential for complete coordination. Only in this way can good results be expected. Also, he should keep you informed in detail about the past history and the present activity of the Pact in America and Europe, as well as about all the news that has appeared in the European and American press regarding this question.

During the last few months in America and France, there has been a great deal of talk about the ratification of the Pact by the United States of America. I shall therefore forward to you some clippings from the newspapers. I think it is just the right information for you. Also, I shall add a list of the Belgian Committees.

Yugoslavia was supposed to join in the ratification of the Pact, and in this connection King Alexander had promised G. G. an audience to be held on the day after the King's arrival in Paris. But a black hand cut off this beautiful heroic life. Also, in France this development was temporarily delayed because of a change in government.

You are quite right that people forget easily. Undoubtedly this is true regarding everything—from the smallest matters to the greatest. Everywhere, it is necessary to remind and to arouse interest. People who are busy with everyday affairs are often unable to grasp the significance of a great idea which is beyond the province of their routine actions.

There are very few whose thinking is broad enough to enable them to realize that the Banner of Peace expresses a new step in the development of the consciousness of humanity. Such consciousness will be built upon the conception and awareness of the great significance and sacred inviolability of the creations of human genius. The next step could be the acceptance of the Hierarchy of the Spirit.

Often we hear such remarks as "everything that pertains to pure art and to high abstract science is luxury." These statements are made not only by mediocre people but by quite a number of public leaders as well. We must fight against these absurd and harmful opinions. People are surprised that morality is lowered and that the flourishing prosperity of nations proves to be a mirage. But it is time to realize that if man is unable to exist without earthly bread, he is just as unable to exist without the spiritual sustenance which brings refinement of feelings and thoughts through the realization of Beauty and of the great laws of Nature. But how can Beauty and the higher laws be revealed to the minds of those who lower themselves to the level of consciousness of the masses?

Now I shall attend to your questions. In paragraph 25 of *Agni Yoga* the words "It is incorrect to think that the past experiment of My Friend could have been unsuccessful" refer to the attempts to create the Theosophical Society. As you know, H. P. Blavatsky was sent to the world to fulfill a great mission, i.e., to give the Secret doctrine to humanity—to shift the consciousness of humanity. She had to tell people the truth about spiritualism and thus try to prevent the many harmful consequences of this movement. The ignorant participants were infatuated, and had not the slightest idea of all the dangers connected with dealing with the communications from beyond. In those days spiritualism was spreading rapidly, especially in America, and was acquiring ugly and dangerous forms.

Because of the strong and persistent desire of the co-workers of H. P. Blavatsky to establish a society for the study of esoteric teaching, of all religions and philosophies, with the idea of introducing them to those who were ready, the Mahatma K. H. gave his consent to direct this society. And so, with the assistance of H. P. Blavatsky, Col. H. S. Olcott, W. Q. Judge, and several others, this work was started, and in the course of time it took the form of what is now known as the Theosophical Movement. One can read about the history of this movement in *The Mahatma Letters to A. P. Sinnet*, and in the volume of *Letters of H. P. Blavatsky* herself to the same A. P. Sinnett. The Teaching given to the world through H,. P. Blavatsky did its great work, in that it awakened numerous individual souls all over the world, and the Theosophical Societies everywhere were greatly responsible for this. Therefore, it is wrong to say that this experiment was not successful. Of course, if human nature were different, the results could have been much better. Even as it is, this work cannot be said to have failed, and such claims that it did fail definitely came from the dark forces. As it is said, "The steps of consciousness have been firmly built." Of course, in America this movement is connected mostly with the name of H. P. Blavatsky, and it continues to spread and enter life. The Mahatma K. H. made a great effort in establishing the Theosophical Movement, and even became ill from contacting the lower earthly strata and human auras. For a while the Mahatma had to withdraw and reside in one of the completely isolated and inaccessible (for ordinary mortals) "Towers" of the Tibetan Stronghold.

* * *

In reference to paragraph 277 of *Agni Yoga*, the year of the Earthly Dragon is the Tibetan designation for the year corresponding to 1927. In Tibet, all the years have names of animals. Thus, there is the year of the mouse, the pig, etc. In addition there is a strange adjective used, as for instance, "iron," "wooden," etc. Probably, these definitions also relate to the character of the coming year. The year of the Earthly Dragon began with the most intensive attacks of the dark forces.

In reference to paragraph 279 of *Agni Yoga*, and the legend about Indra, Indra is the chief God in the Hindu pantheon, and is equivalent to the Greek Zeus. According to the oral tradition, with the coming of a new cycle of Indra's manifestations, the heat of his throne rises until he has to leap off and send down the purifying lightnings (i.e., there is an accumulation of psychic energy and new manifestations of it are required).

In reference to paragraph 416 of *Agni Yoga*, Sarasvati is the feminine aspect, or the consort, of Brahma—the Goddess of Wisdom, Speech and Esoteric Knowledge.

* * *

You ask whether blood has a direct relation to the elements. Indeed it has, but so far science has not found the subtle methods necessary for such researches. Therefore, we must say that for the time being this definition is only approximate. It is correctly stated that there is one type of blood that will blend with all other types. And of course this type is nearest to the element of fire. But since even the blood of animals contains fiery particles (this being its main characteristic), when comparing the blood of various individuals we should remember that, as far as it is possible to say, healthy blood will possess the most particles of fire. But it will be possible to determine the relationship between the different blood groups and those of the elements only when the subtle emanations are thoroughly studied and explored. In the present stage of science, the definition and knowledge of the blood is insufficient, as our discoveries are incomplete, which explains why there are so many unsuccessful blood transfusions.

It is also not quite true that the father's blood is assimilated by the mother. In the fiery laboratory of conception, the creative forces of the mother produce the fiery affirmation of blood. The whole process of the development and formation of the blood and the child is in the mother. The most convincing proof that the ultimate processes take place in the organism of the woman is in the ape, since, according to all the ancient esoteric teachings, the ape, with its human appearance, came from the copulation of the human male with animal females. This breed, in spite of having received the spark of divine fire, remained just animal.

38

6 December 1934

The Mahatma Letters is a book which should be widely disseminated, as it is most essential to awaken the consciousness of humanity out of the impasse to which it has come. And you surmise quite correctly that it is especially difficult for conventional church people to accept this book. They are too much bound by their dogmas—created by the narrow sectarian minds of the Middle Ages. The consciousness of such bigots is indeed dreadful in its deadliness. In their frenzy (which equals that of the zealots of the Inquisition), they insist upon the distortion of the Covenants of Him whom they consider their God. In their blindness they refuse to see that precisely they themselves betray and crucify Him every moment. It is terrifying to encounter such static suffocation of thought, which has persisted over so many centuries! Let us hope that before long science will stretch forth its helping hand and will prove that precisely *thought nourishes life* and that where thought is arrested the process of decay commences.

Now, regarding a definition of the grades of Intelligence. Of course, what the Mahatmas call "an active Power, an immutable, therefore an unthinking Principle" (*Mahatma Letters*) is the principle of Life or Consciousness (and therefore the foundation of Intelligence), being infinite, eternal and absolute. The Cosmic Intelligence is the Hierarchy of Light or the Ladder of Jacob. In addition, the Crown of this Hierarchy consists of the Spirits, or Intelligences who have completed their human evolution in this or another solar system, the so-called Planetary Spirits, the Creators of the worlds. These Creators of worlds or planets are the Master Builders of the present and the future Universe. In the days of the Pralaya They are in charge of the great Vigil of Brahma and They mark the next cosmic evolution. Therefore, the crown of Cosmic Intelligence does not depend on the Manvantaras; *verily, They exist in the dimension of Infinity.* Thus, the Highest Hierarch of our planet is one of the most resplendent Gems in the Crown of Cosmic Intelligence.

The Cosmic Magnet is the Cosmic Heart, or the consciousness of the Crown of the Cosmic Intelligence—the Hierarchy of Light. Precisely, the Cosmic Magnet is the bond with the higher worlds in the order of Be-ness. The bond of our heart with the Heart and Consciousness of the Highest Hierarch of our planet leads us into the majestic current of the Cosmic Magnet.

I shall quote a paragraph from the Teaching which I think is appropriate here:

"If the consciousness of humanity could compare the eternal with the transitory, then would be made manifest flashes of understanding of the Cosmos because all the values of mankind are based on an eternal foundation. But humanity has been so imbued with respect for the transitory that it has forgotten about the Eternal. Whereas, it is demonstrable that form changes, disappears, and is replaced by the new. Transitoriness is so obvious, and each example of the transitory points to eternal life. Spirit is the creator of each form, yet it is rejected by humanity. When the fact is grasped that the spirit is eternal, then too will infinity and immortality enter into life. Thus, it is imperative to direct the spirit of peoples to the understanding of the Higher Principles. Mankind is engulfed in effects, but the root and principle of everything is creativeness—and it has been forgotten. When the spirit shall be reverenced as sacred Fire, then will be confirmed the great ascent." [Fiery World III]

It is quite correct, as you say, that nearly all the Greek philosophies were closely related to the Teaching. All the highest and noblest philosophies and religions issue from the one Great Source, and the Great Minds who brought Light and gave the impulse to the begetting of thought before the dawn of our humanity have continued to give it during the whole slow process of the evolution of human consciousness. Let us remember those Seven Great Spirits or Kumaras who are mentioned in *The Secret Doctrine*. Precisely these Seven, and among Them the Highest One, who accepted the Guardianship of the World, have appeared during all the turning points in the history of our planet. Their consciousness has nourished the consciousness of humanity with the One Truth, presented by Them under the guises of various philosophies and religions which suited the times. You put it so beautifully when you say, "The true sense of the Divine is revealed according to the level of our consciousness." Yes, the great Mysteries, and Beauty, are revealed to us when our consciousness comes into contact with the Light of the consciousness of Those who lead us. Indeed, so many beautiful accumulations, "resoundings and flashes of the spirit," arise in our being when contacting these powerful Sons of Light. I should be very happy to read your new works. I am so fond of your article on Beauty, and I appreciate your subtle spiritual understanding of the Teaching.

Many are writing about the greatest concepts. But if they lack a sense of beauty they do not hesitate to demean the highest concepts and make out of them apothecaries' formulae.

How majestic and beautiful are the myths of antiquity! How highly developed the sense of beauty! It is one of the calamities of our time that we deadened our sense of beauty by trying to lower and level everything to the consciousness of the masses. As one writer puts it, "The wonderful colors of the world are going, the prevailing color is a protective grey. How painful it is to live during our epoch! How hard it is to see the touches of the all-leveling hand!" Therefore, I say to you, write! Array the beautiful concepts in accordance with the "flashing and resounding" of your spirit!

The descriptions of your sensations are most characteristic. And it is quite correct that they issue from many causes. The anguish and heaviness in the heart may be from the dense atmosphere—remember that we are in the midst of Armageddon. The lower layers of the Subtle World also are being destroyed, and their decay poisons our earthly plane. In proportion to the refinement of our organism, we become more sensitive to all atmospheric pressures. Let all those who sense the heaviness and anguish of the heart note down the days and the hours of these sensations and then check them to see whether or not they coincide with any storms, earthquakes, typhoons, etc.

But one should not forget that parallel with the broadening of the consciousness these attacks of heart anguish are quite inevitable. These sensations are very familiar to me. I always know in advance when there will be earthquakes or other calamities. And I know it not only by seeing the red atmosphere and the outbreaks of red fire, but by the physical reactions as well. Pressure in the back of the head also can be attributed to the increasing sensitivity of the centers. At each sensation of tension or pain, it is best to take a short rest. Characteristic also are the sudden swellings, which just as swiftly disappear without leaving a trace. All this indicates the preparation for the opening and activity of various centers. I remember how my elbows used to swell and my shoulders ached painfully.

The intruding thoughts are becoming worse, and one must fight them by concentrating on some work and fixing the attention. Of course, the mental link with the Hierarchy and the sevenfold pronouncing of the Name of the Teacher usually frightens and drives away the whisperers. But such a repetition should be accompanied by the rhythm of the heart. The seeing of the black particles or sparks at the present time is quite correct, as just now space is full of dark explosions. Usually the black spots indicate the approach of darkness or of the chaotic energies. In such cases it is advisable to apply carefulness in everything. Thus, when I see the small dark spots I know that they often indicate the coming of trouble or are a warning regarding health. The larger they are and the more of them you see, the greater the care that should be taken. Sometimes one can even see big velvety black spots swimming in space. The purple, blue, silvery, and at times golden ones are always the good messengers, or are the signs of the closeness of the emanations of the Teacher. Yellow ones warn against possible danger, and red ones indicate extreme tension in the atmosphere; and then one may expect earthquakes, storms and even revolutions.

Usually, when I think of something or make a decision, or read something which should be confirmed, I see a bluish-silver spark, underlining and affirming the necessary concept or decision. Occasionally a whole section is crossed out by a shining line. And then I know that this part should be erased. and then again it happens that a whole page is illumined with an unusual bright silvery light. Yes, there are many signs sent by the Hierarchy of Light to those who follow the path of Light. Make a note of all the signs, and write down when and under what circumstances something unusual was sensed or seen. Thus, often the spots or sparks indicate the character of the newcomers. One can know the worthy person by the blue or silver star, and the betrayer by the black one. But in the latter case one should be rather careful, as the black star can also indicate the accidental approach of chaotic energies.

Indeed, it is most distressing when the Teaching remains as something abstract, unapplied in life; we know such cases too well. Few are those who realize what true discipleship and nearness to the Lords of Light means. The majority are interested only in those statements of the Teaching that enable them to develop their lower psychic abilities, and if they are mediumistically inclined they often achieve this, thus opening themselves to the obsessors. I have written much about the harm of psychism, and have quoted the appropriate lines from the Teaching. I suggest that all the newcomers be warned. You must tell them that by no means should they be tempted by mechanical exercises but that they should tense all their forces and work on the task of broadening and refining their thoughts, and on the outliving of the bad habits which stand as obstacles on the way toward Light.

I am happy that in broadening the program of activities you are creating new possibilities and contacts with wider cultural circles. Only in contacting the consciousness of people do we open new creative possibilities. I am very happy about the expansion of the cultural work.

And now, about your significant dream. No doubt this dream comes from a High Source. Our planet is going through a most dangerous time, indeed the most critical period. If humanity refuses to be spiritually resurrected before the approach of the fiery cosmic energies, the cataclysms which always accompany a change of race may result in the total explosion and destruction of our Earth. But before this final catastrophe of our planet happens, many children will have time to grow old. Undoubtedly, partial cataclysms will occur during the next coming decades. Therefore, the Lords of Light more than ever call humanity to the spiritual awakening, to the realization of the gravity of the approaching fiery reconstruction. All people of pure, unprejudiced consciousness shall be saved and led away into safe places, just as in the last days of Atlantis. Of course, each reconstruction of the world brings great possibilities as well, and although our time is threatening, it nevertheless can be beautiful and constructive. One should try most intensely to help lay the foundation for the coming luminous constructive age that is so near—in fact much nearer than many think, surrounded as they are with destruction and decay.

I am including a few paragraphs from the Teaching:

"The planet is completing a cycle which leads everything to summation. The time is coming when each principle must manifest its entire potential. These rings are looked upon in history as downfall or renascence. But these rhythms must be regarded as the triumph of Light or darkness., The time has come when the planet is drawing near to such a circle of summation, and only the most saturated tension of the potential will result in victory. The circle of summation awakens all energies, for in the final battle all the forces of Light and darkness will take part, from the very Highest down to the dregs. Sensitive spirits know why there is being manifested so much of the Higher, side by side with the guilty and the inert. In the conflict, before the circle of summation, there will the contentions of all spatial, earthly and supermundane Forces. On the path to the Fiery World the co-workers must remember the Ordinance of the Cosmos.

"The world is living through those stages by which have been signalized all the decisive moments in the history of mankind. Stages of destruction precede construction. Creativeness, having been tensed, calls all energies to life. That epoch into which humanity has entered will inevitably manifest all the potentials of forces, for this epoch is a decisive one, and a turning point in history is approaching. Surely, the condition of the planet has not come about by accident, and each tension bears witness to that current which is engulfing all spheres. If the conflict is inexorable, so will the victory be decisive. For all forces and spheres participate in this Cosmic Battle. On the path to the Fiery World one must take up the Sword of Light for the building the New Epoch.

"Waves which engulf nations arise out of the national karma. In cosmic construction each epoch leaves its waves in space. When the date draws near for magnetic attraction, all waves begin to act—thus karma is unavoidable. When in ancient scriptures it was said, 'All is from the Heavenly Father,' by that precisely the law of Karma was voiced. All is created according to these waves, which depart into space and preserve an everlasting bond with the planet. The bond between worlds, supermundane and earthly is conditioned by these waves. The records of space consist of these waves, and nations create their own historical redemptions. The realization that everything passes into the waves of space can awaken best aspirations. On the path to the Fiery World let us manifest a striving for the betterment of the national karma.

"Transmutation is inevitable, in the whole Cosmic Plan. Only fiery reconstruction will yield new creative energies. The Cosmic Magnet creates and intensifies all that exists, for dates are approaching which will compel everyone and everything to participate in the Cosmic Battle. Space is in need of a discharge. The Cosmic Scales affirm the process of agitations; throughout all space resounds the call to a final tension. I affirm that the transmutation of energies will produce new steps in evolution. Therefore one must strive with heart and spirit toward the Fiery World.

"If we but ponder upon just what suppresses the higher concepts, we inevitably arrive at at consciousness which compares everything with the lower manifestations. Bringing everything down to compare with the lowest is a labor of the dark ones, and humanity is indeed subject to these tendencies. Everyone instinctively has recourse to this destructive action. Therefore, the condition of the consciousness is the best indicator of all epochs and all human directions. Whither leads such error as the losing of connection with the Fiery World? Purification of consciousness will indeed give access to the higher energies. On the path to the Fiery World one must contend with the dark consciousnesses." [Fiery World III]

I want to tell you once more how happy it makes me to know that your thinking is not obstructed and distorted by prejudices and the ready-make formulae. What can be more dreadful than limited thinking? Verily, it is the death of the spirit.

39

12 December 1934

The ability of a leader to discriminate regarding people is very important. It is quality and not quantity that matters, and one should apply this principle always and in everything. I must also ask you to test and check all the newcomers. There are cases when even people who are not evil succumb to the influence of the dark whisperers, earthly as well as of the Subtle World, and become completely changed in their nature.

Also, it is necessary to understand that the unprepared and spiritually weak people who deal with spiritualism open themselves to all sorts of obsessions, and who can tell when that degree of obsession may be reached when the victim will be unable to rid himself of his obsessor? Exactly, the dark forces are using these obedient tools in order that through them they may gain entry into the spiritually pure groups and treacherously ruin them. Madmen! They do not understand the dreadful danger to which they open themselves by permitting the entities from beyond to enter their auras. The mediums and the weak psychics do not possess spiritual synthesis and often become victims of the dark whisperers.

Naive people usually presume that the dark forces are always brutal and criminal in their methods and intentions. This is a fatal error; only the small insignificant dark ones act in this manner. Much more dangerous are those who approach under the guise of Light and pronounce our formulae. The dark ones always act according to the *consciousness* of their victims, and one must give them credit—often they act very subtly and *cleverly, appealing to conceit and other weaknesses.* Usually such victims are chosen from among persons full of egotism and conceit, who aspire only for their own profit. The idea of self-sacrificing achievement is not likely to be understood by such people; consequently, true spirituality is impossible for them. Therefore, we can judge people only by the *fire of their hearts,* by their devotion and readiness to sacrifice and cooperate in every possible way. *There is no other measurement.*

Of course, there are also the ones who sacrifice everything in the hope of reward. Usually they are found among the fanatics, but they are also far from true discipleship and spiritual ascent. The destined disciple never expects anything; he proceeds joyously, bearing in mind only service, applying all his abilities and making use of all possibilities., It is a strange thing, and I would call it a law, that *usually the one who gives his utmost does not expect any reward.* But the one who brings only his burdensome karma considers that he is giving his life in sacrifice! This remarkable psychological peculiarity is noted and worked out in detail in the Buddhist Teachings.

Indeed, it was never advised to give away everything and to remain in poverty! Remember how this was expressed: "Who hath said that one must renounce madly? Madness doth so remain." Reread it in the first part of *Leaves of Morya's Garden.* Always and in everything, the great *co-measurement* is required. Without co-measurement, discrimination, honesty and devotion, it is difficult to progress on the Path. These are the four cornerstones that are the foundation of every construction.

Today, the ability to discriminate between people is especially necessary, as we are in the midst of the great Cosmic Battle. The forces of darkness are struggling for their very existence; fear unites them closely and makes them tenacious in their aggression. The majority of the "whitish" ones, however, are wearing the grey garments of nonresistance. Some do it in subconscious hypocrisy, others in faint-heartedness, still others in ignorance or fear. But the results of this nonresistance or lukewarmness are always the same, precisely the destiny predicted in the Apocalypse: "So then because thou art lukewarm, and neither cold nor hot, I will spew thee out of my mouth." But how few are those who think of the *scientific preciseness* of this pronouncement! But there is small reason to wonder, as from our very childhood we were not allowed to question or to ponder upon the great pronouncements of the Scriptures. Anathema threatens those who dare to insist upon the checking of the distorted Covenants of Christ! And the new, dishonoring stamp of "*mason*" is ready for them! But of course, such a shameful misuse of this word is possible only by the ignorant.

Many foreign words are curiously distorted in certain consciousnesses. Really, it is advisable to use cautiously certain terms that are strange to us! Generally speaking, it would be amusing, were it not so sad, to see how uninformed are certain circles about the role of Masonry in Europe and America. Apparently they are unaware that a large number of the aristocracy of England and of some other countries belong to various Masonic Orders. And even here in India, every year on a certain memorial day British officials who are Masons parade in the streets in their Masonic regalia. Everything is quite open, and the newspapers and magazines show photographs of kings, princes and noblemen in their Masonic robes, together with their lodges and gathering places. The Masons of America and England, besides their numerous lodges, have also in the large cities their own grandiose temples. Of course, as a result of the popularity of this movement (and even of its profanation) there are some harmful lodges as well. As is usual in all things, *anything beautiful is a rare exception today.* And the proverb "One diseased sheep is sufficient to spoil the entire flock" remains completely true. But the minds that pretend to be cultured should base their opinions on facts and not behave like parrots, who senselessly repeat what they hear. They should become better acquainted with the history of culture of our own country. Some of our most distinguished representatives, our best minds, as, for instance, Novikov, Prince Kudashev, Suvorov, Golenishchev-Kutuzov (Prince of Smolensk), Griboyodov, Pushkin, Khieraskov, Bakunin and others, were Masons. Therefore, why should such ignorance be manifested? And would it not be more fair and more scientific to study what Masonry was and what it is now? After becoming acquainted with the basic principles of Masonry, many would be astonished to learn of its *high moral code.* Yes, it is necessary to fight against inertness and ignorance, against limited thinking.

This is the most pressing and enlightened task. Life is nourished only by lofty thoughts, and therefore the *suffocation* of thought will inevitably result in *decay*. I shall quote some lines from the Teaching:

"Just as the consciousness can be a pledge of fruition, so can it be manifested as dissolution. Limited thought can prove to be a conduit for all dark manifestations. Therefore, thought can be developed into a great vital beginning or it can destroy each origin. Limited thinking shatters all possibilities, for the process of constructiveness is based upon the growth of consciousness. How can one aspire to the Highest Ideal without broadening the consciousness! Surely the Higher Image can be realized by the fiery and fearless consciousness, for there are no limits to a fiery consciousness." [Fiery World III]

Thus, it is so important and joyous to build into life the foundations of the Living Ethics based on the realization and acceptance of the Great Hierarchy.

* * *

"Yes, there can hardly be a heavier cross than to be born a Russian genius! The giants of Russian art, of Russian thought, all their lives drank from a cup of poison, being pursued outrageously and pettily by all save those who were indifferent. The bitter words of Pushkin—a slip of his tongue in a moment of deep despair—"The devil caused me to be born in Russia" have not lost up to this day their convincing sharpness and sarcasm as we are able to see over and over again how Russians look for every opportunity to belittle, to backbite one another, for the sole reason that the other dares to be better." So writes one of the most talented modern writers, A. X., and we fully join with him in his sorrowful words. Truly it is said, "More than half of humanity acts under the influence of obsessors." But the time of great changes is near, and a great purification will take place.

Let us keep the foundations entrusted to us in purity, let us remember the covenant we have received, and let us protect ourselves from all the crafty traitors. Reread paragraph 231 in the book, *Agni Yoga*: "Let few but firm trunks comprise the future forest. But small shrubs devour each other and engender malicious beings."

* * *

The Mahatma Letters to A. P. Sinnett has already reached about twenty editions, and—if I am not mistaken—is translated into other European languages, excepting of course the Russian. We must still be kept in kindergarten. We are not grown enough for freedom of thought. We are still in our infancy, needing fences and bridles. So our spiritual leaders think. But our self-abasement only confirms the immaturity of thought. However, long ago it was said that not the small-minded blasphemers will build the new country but the common sense of the common people. Precisely, "It is the hundreds of thousands of Ivans who will save their country." Verily, it is Ivan's turn, and to him will be given the possibility of expressing his potentiality. But this Ivan is not the same as he was of old. The new Ivan will demand a new, strong faith that does not contradict real life. And those who will tell of this faith will have to apply it in life, by personal example; otherwise, it cannot be affirmed. The consciousness of a people who have suffered much, who have lost their faith in the mercy and justice and protection of the Heavenly Father, could not possibly return to the dead chains of former times. If any spiritual ascent is possible, it will have to be entirely different in its meaning and quality than it appears to some minds. And in order that it should materialize, new theses based on reason and logic will be necessary. One cannot blind oneself to the fact that the consciousness of the people has greatly advanced. Surely, suffering is a great teacher and transmuter. Enlightenment cannot come to us if we are in the midst of greyish comfortable life.

It is necessary to prepare one's consciousness toward the solution of many problems. It will be difficult for the consciousness that stagnates and has not outlived the old prejudices. A new church in the full glory of the understanding of the beauty of the Great Sacrifice of Jesus must replace the old one. It will have to call a great oecumenical council to reexamine, with a new, unprejudiced consciousness, all the rulings of the former councils and to study the works of the earliest Christian philosophers and Fathers of the Church closest to the times of Jesus. Then the whole beauty of the sacrifice of Jesus, the broad sweep of his Teaching, will be understood in its true spirit and not just in the dead letter of the often-distorted Scriptures. And only then will a new religion be established. "Neither in this mountain, nor yet at Jerusalem, worship the Father. But the hour cometh, and now is, when the true worshipers shall worship the Father in spirit and in truth: for the Father seeketh such to worship him. God is a Spirit: and they that worship him must worship him in spirit and in truth." (St. John 4:21-24.)

I must also remind you that all the Archangels and Angels had to go through human evolution. And the Archangel Varahael, or Uriel, was and is a *Man*. Likewise the Archangel Michael, though ranking amongst the Highest Archangels, nevertheless walked on our sinful Earth, bringing salvation. If these greatest Spirits who gave the impetus to the creation and development of thought at the dawn of our earthly physical humanity and who continued to impel the evolution of the human consciousness throughout the entire span of this most difficult and lengthy process had not done so, our earthly humanity, even up to this day, would have remained at the caveman stage. Precisely, the great Archangels are those Seven Kumaras, who, including the Highest One among Them, are spoken of in the Eastern Scriptures and in *The Secret Doctrine*. They came from the higher worlds, and They made the greatest sacrifice by incarnating as the great Founders of religions, kingdoms and philosophies, during all the turning points in the history of the planet, in order to quicken the evolution of humanity. So, the Archangel Michael is now guarding the destiny of our planet. He is destined to fight the last Battle with the Prince of this World. (This is also stated in the Bible.)

40

12 December 1934

You write, "Your letter was read to us, but we did not completely understand it; I am one of those who did not." I was surprised to hear it! It seemed to me that my statements were fairly complete, especially when we consider that you have already some of the books of the Teaching, in which the line of demarcation between spiritual achievements and the manifestations of so-called psychism is clearly indicated.

Probably this obscurity comes from the misunderstanding of the term *psychism*. No doubt you know that the word "Psyche" is of Greek origin, and originally it meant just the vital breath and the animal soul (precisely something belonging to the animal nature,). In its next transformation this term was given to the rational soul (the human soul), and finally it became applied to the highest, the spiritual synthesis, the crown of the human being. Thus, by "psychism" the Easterners as well as the Westerners mean the manifestation of the lower degrees of this energy, precisely those powers which are exhibited so strongly in mediums and psychics. This latter term is given in the West to those whose powers are somewhat higher than those of the usual medium. But in both cases the *higher psychic energy* is absent, as this quality can be manifested only when the centers are open and are fierily transmuted. Many misunderstandings occur, and many peculiar interpretations and applications are made, because these psychic happenings are wrongly determined.

The psychic realm is vast, and it includes an endless diversity of manifestations, from the highest to the lowest. All which has no connection with true spirituality, that is, with the planes of the higher Manas and Buddhi, is called psychism. All that is performed or achieved through the aid of mechanical exercises pertains to the realm of low psychism, as such methods can never bring the opening of the higher centers, least of all their fiery transmutation. Such attempts result in insanity.

Contact with the lower spheres of the Subtle World is easy for mediums as well as animals. Certainly, animals see, sense and hear much more than we do. As Luke Berk says, "Clairvoyance is a common faculty; dogs, idiots and men are equally disposed to it." It is curious to note that the vast majority of mediums and psychics (with the rarest exceptions) do not possess high intellectual abilities. Precisely, in mediums it is a certain peculiarity in the organism, and in psychics a lack of balance, that hinders the correct development of the higher centers and sometimes even completely paralyzes them. That is why we do not like mediums but feel rather sorry for them. Due to the peculiar structure of the organism, a medium from birth is opened to all external influences. The will of a medium easily submits to the obsessors, who are so numerous in the lower layers of the Subtle World, and the danger is that a medium does not realize his subjugation. Indeed, for a medium it is a most difficult thing to strengthen the will and thus resist the obsessors and whisperers. Many have mediumistic tendencies; however, these tendencies being yet nascent, they are unrealized, and lucky are those who do not develop them until spirituality is completely awakened.

That is why all instructions regarding the development of

certain siddhis are so dangerous. Until a spiritual synthesis is created, such siddhis can give nothing, and in the end almost always lead to disorders of the nervous system, obsession, and spiritual, if not physical death. Thus, all books that broadcast these mechanical exercises for obtaining psychic manifestations should be considered most harmful. At least, it would be better if these books also mentioned the dangers that await the ignoramuses who dabble in this science, which demands a careful, subtle, and precise scientific method. Exactly, as it is said in the Teaching, "Without the Teacher it is impossible to develop the psychic energy, as this process is linked with great dangers." Would you permit children to enter a physical laboratory without a guide!

One should welcome every scientific method, every bold research. Indeed, the most dangerous experiments with unknown energies are being performed. But for this purpose precautions are taken and special conditions are created; and not only are crowds not allowed and not informed but even people who possess some knowledge are not permitted into the laboratories. Can we then give people entry into a laboratory far more subtle, more complicated, and therefore far more dangerous? In the kind of literature we mention, any ignorant, any spiritually impure (and therefore unprotected) person is invited to participate in these investigations. All the books that treat of these subjects without explaining the grave consequences of wrong methods and motives are not given out with the blessing of the Great Teachers.

It is true, correct breathing, i. e., the ability to breathe rhythmically and deeply, is a great healing means for the restoration of our forces, both spiritual and physical. But you know that the pranayama suggested by these books does not mean only correct breathing but also breath control and concentration on the rotation of the centers, and all the rest of such gymnastics. Whereas, an honest and progressive physician would prescribe for each patient a dose of medicine precisely according to the individual needs. Arsenic, for instance, is very beneficial in small doses, but if taken excessively it can cause poisoning or cancer. The wide publishing of such sensational manuals for the broad masses I consider equivalent to the legalizing of the open sale of poisons. No, it is even worse; for poison destroys only the physical body, whereas the violation of the subtle centers leads to spiritual death.

I have read the books of Atkinson, or Yogi Ramacharaka. Before the Great War his books flooded the Russian market, which was unfortunately poor in literature dealing with Eastern philosophy and its psycho-physiological teachings. At the time, I found nothing wrong with them, but neither did I enthuse, as I always preferred the original sources. Thus, the luminous image of Ramakrishna and the clear mind of Vivekananda resounded in my heart as a powerful call to spiritual synthesis. If I were to read Atkinson now, I might perhaps form a different opinion about his books. Certainly, no one could object to advice dealing with the development of attention, will power and the elimination of defects; but only so long as all this runs parallel with our spiritual aspiration and intellectual discipline. Exactly, all that which is discussed so all-embracingly in the books of the Teaching.

And now it is my turn not to understand how you can compare the extracts of the writings of N. K. regarding the development of attention with the instructions given in the books we have just mentioned. The development of attention is one thing, but the concentration on the centers and their rotation, as well as breath control, is something quite different. Of course, all the experiments connected with the development of attention and recommended by N. K. cannot be considered artificial or mechanical. If it were so, learning by heart might just as well be considered harmful!

Further on, you again quote from N. K.'s book: "We try to study and to translate into everyday life the so-called abstraction." Well, only ignoramuses would think it could be otherwise! But again, I do not see what this has to do with an ignorant approach to these most dangerous experiments which we are now discussing. We are not against the investigation of phenomena as such, but against an *uncultured, unscientific* approach to them; certainly, we are against ignorance. One does not allow children to play with radium.

Further, you give this quotation: "The newest schools must have laboratories dedicated to the natural sciences." And this one: "The best minds are in various ways directing human thought toward the broadening of consciousness, which is the only true prophylaxis and vision for the future luminous and constructive life." Neither here do I see any contradiction of my statements. Nobody can argue against the advantage of a good education for children. If from the earliest possible age they are taught to understand the various unfoldings of nature revealed before them, eventually they can discern the subtlest manifestations; verily, *not in ignorance, but with full perception of all the necessary scientific conditions.* All this is mentioned in the books of the Teaching. Besides, is not the whole Teaching directed toward the broadening of consciousness? But merely to concentrate on the tip of one's nose or on one's navel, without striving to spiritual synthesis or a building up of spiritual accumulations, will lead to idiocy or obsession.

Likewise, nobody would argue against the necessity for institutions for psychic research, but as things are going now, these researches reveal nothing new. Although the Society for Psychical Research was founded in 1882, most of its records of phenomena are still unsettled and open to dispute. We have the books on these subjects, and if you read the final summary of all these investigations, you will see that psychic research has reached an impasse. We know an outstanding professor who is at the head of a psychical research society, and he has confessed quite frankly that in the way these researches are being conducted now they can offer or reveal nothing that is lofty or inspiring. All their experiments do not advance beyond the previous achievements. Being a highly cultured man, he realizes very well that this ineffectiveness is due to the ignorant, unscientific methods of the researchers themselves. There is a lack of understanding of the fact that experiments of importance require a few select persons possessing a high degree of spiritual synthesis. But is it possible to find this synthesis among ordinary mediums? It is equally rare among the scientists who devote themselves to these researches. But without these requirements the psychical research societies will only drag on a banal existence. Thus, there are many books concerning psychism in our library, but I very seldom look through them—only perhaps occasionally for specific information. I do not praise myself, but I must say that I am not for a moment sorry that I have spent no time or effort on breath control, or on concentrating on the tip of my nose.

You say that you do not want to be a medium. But how can a person want or not want to be a medium? Do not forget that mediumship is an *inborn* faculty, a peculiar condition of the organism which has nothing to do with the unfolding of the *higher* psychic energy. There are many mediums who do not practise their faculty, and they are especially numerous among the lower classes. Sometimes, as I have mentioned already, this peculiarity remains dormant, which is extremely fortunate. But woe to those who awaken this energy while still being of small consciousness or poisoned by egotism; nothing but deterioration will be the result. That is why in ancient times, in the East, mediumistic children were isolated in order to bring them up in spiritual purity, so that they could be protected from harmful astral influences. But despite their purity, not one of them could hope to become an Adept or Arhat, or to be accepted into the holy of holies. *The Power of the Great Teacher of Light* can help a medium conquer his mediumism and raise him to the degree of a mediator, but only provided there is a stubborn and constant aspiration on the part of the medium himself toward the Source of Light. The slightest deviation from this path of striving will ruin the previous achievements.

Hence, let us strive to lofty manifestations because it is not only foolish to contact the lower spheres of the Subtle World, it is extremely dangerous as well. I shall quote some more paragraphs from the books of the Teaching:

"Much has already been said about psychism, nevertheless this scourge of humanity is insufficiently understood. Psychism blunts each aspiration, and higher attainment remains inaccessible. The sphere of activity of a man engulfed by psychism is limited within a charmed circle in which all the energies which retard growth of the spirit find their fitting place. Psychism embraces the manifestation of the lowest energies, and the fires of the centers are extinguished by these precipitations. With psychism there is inevitably to be found disorder of the nervous system. In addition, the breaking away from vital functions closes the path to self-perfectionment. Creativeness is blunted, and there is established a passive state which makes a man an instrument for the influx of all kinds of forces. By reason of the relaxation of the will, control is weakened, and by this the attraction of various lower entities is increased. He who wishes to approach the Fiery World must battle with these forces of evil.

"Fiery energies, being drawn into tension by some center, can often cause enhanced actions of the energies of this center. Partial action of energies gives a center the power to manifest partially. These tensions lead to those partial manifestations which bring into error consciousnesses of small discrimination. With reason has Ur. pointed out those manifestations, evoked by the tension of one center, which lead to psychism. Truly, each opening, saturation or irritation of the centers gives a sharp direction to the fiery energy; but only conformity between the state of the organism and the spiritual awakening produces, as an inevitable effect, the opening of the centers in highest tension. A partial pressure will produce a partial attainment which may prove to be a very dangerous manifestation. On the path to the Fiery World let us strive to realize the higher tension of fiery energy.

"Psychism and mediumism turn man away from the higher spheres, for the subtle body becomes thus so saturated with lower emanations that the entire being is altered. In reality a most difficult process is contained in purification of consciousness. Man does not precisely differentiate between the fiery state of spirituality and psychism. Thus, we must overcome the terrors of psychism. Actually, the ranks of those instruments are filled by the servants of darkness. Thus, on the path to the Fiery World one must contend with psychism." [Fiery World III]

These paragraphs, together with those I sent in my previous letters, clearly indicate the point of view of the Great Teachers.

"The time now is so threatening, so dangerous because verily it is the last Battle between Light and darkness., Therefore, everyone must honestly and firmly decide on which side he signs his name. Everyone must check his spiritual baggage and definitely join either this or that side. The choice must be taken, otherwise one may expect nothing but deterioration. Our path is the path pointed out by all great Sages—the path of spiritual transfiguration, the path of the development of the heart, without magic and forcing. Verily, there can be no lukewarm middle way when the Sword of Light cleaves the darkness."

I know that many will consider me severe. But I must say that only the dreadful danger, to which some good sensitive souls open themselves through communication with other worlds without proper knowledge, compels me to talk so firmly and emphatically. Every wrong advocacy and every instance of light-mindedness is now criminal. The spheres nearest Earth have become extremely overcrowded, due to mass killing through war, revolution, etc. And now these victims are longing to get in touch with a vital force in order to receive an illusion of life. Undoubtedly the fact that there are such a great number of ill-balanced people at the present time is the result of such vampirism or obsession.

Therefore, please hold to the purity of the Teaching in your life, and the most beautiful and joyous will come to you in due time. But the organism polluted by contact with the lower spheres cannot assimilate the higher energies.

41
12 December 1934

The Call has been sent and you have hearkened to it. You love the books of the Teaching and thus you have accepted the Call. But besides the acceptance of the Call, the one who is ready for the heroic service is obliged to work hard toward self-perfection. Why should it be thought that great deeds have to be performed not where we live but somewhere else under different conditions? Verily, great is the deed of bringing the Teaching into our daily life, giving joy and knowledge to those who surround and who meet us. As Krishna says in the Bhagavad-Gita, "Man achieves perfection by the stubborn fulfillment of his dharma (i.e., duty, karma)." Is it not a great achievement to work for self-perfection, for the benevolent influencing of our surroundings, together with a constant readiness to apply one's forces whenever the need arises?

Karma, or cosmic justice, puts everyone into conditions where they can either learn or atone for something. But for the fulfillment of heroic self-denying service, the spirit must be greatly strengthened. That is why the path of discipleship is never easy. Many obstacles have to be conquered, as how otherwise can we test our strength and temper our spirit? Without this tempering of the spirit, we really cannot perform a life of achievement and become co-workers of the Great White Brotherhood. Great should be the renunciation in all true aspirants. In ancient Egypt the neophytes had to pass through fearful, artificially created, dangers and temptations, and only a very small number of them were able to stand the trial. In our days all artificial tests are abolished, and the disciple must be able to face the difficulties and obstacles of everyday life. And of course his inner motives are always taken into consideration, together with his alertness, his courage, discrimination, caution, honesty and devotion. And likewise, as of old, very few succeed to the end.

But those disciples who possess a great potential of accumulations from former lives are able to welcome all difficulties. Thus, the nearest disciples learn to walk on the edge of an abyss. When the extreme limit of endurance is reached the miraculous Help always comes. Great trust, devotion and gratitude to the Hierarchy of Light dwells in the hearts of true disciples, and this is the main reason why it is possible to give such miraculous Protection and Guidance. When the silver thread linking the heart of the disciple with the Teacher is intact, nothing seems to frighten, and whatever is necessary is granted. However, the Help comes at the last moment, when all our abilities and efforts are tensed to the extreme. For in what other way could our energies be transmuted into the higher fires? Even according to physical law, all energies are transmuted only at the limit of their highest tension. The transmutation of our energies into the higher fires is indeed the aim of our existence. And only by the attaining to this transmutation does our organism become worthy and able to assimilate the subtlest energies sent by the Hierarchy of Light. Therefore, let us accept the heroic beautiful service and apply it to the work of every day. Let the possibility of approaching the Lords of Light become our daily joy; verily, this possibility is within ourselves and we alone can hasten its realization.

All misery as well as all happiness is within us. The Great Teachers are always ready to stretch forth a Helping Hand, but one must know how to accept it. Remember the way it is expressed in the Teaching regarding those who are praying for Highest Help yet are not able to accept it. "Each person who yearns for assistance has already decided selfishly the direction and measure of it. Can an elephant find room in a low cellar? But the seeker of help cares about neither its proportion nor its suitability. For him, lilies should flower during wintertime, and in the desert a spring must burst forth; otherwise the Teacher's merit is small. ... 'My spring of pure water remained unnoticed and you did not turn to regard My flowers. You encumbered your way with selfishness and found time only to protect your precious feet from the thorns that you yourself grew. My help therefore took flight like a startled bird. My messenger returns in haste. ... My help is rejected.' But the traveler continues blindly to call for help, while wending his way to the site of his future destruction. We always advise alertness, flexibility, and open-mindedness, without which one cannot keep in step with reality." [Agni Yoga]

Thus in complete confidence in the wisdom of the Leading Hand let us continue to refine and perfect our inner instrument. We can achieve it only by way of the purification and broadening of the consciousness, and then the heroic service will be gloriously revealed to us in all its beauty. Indeed, the books of the Teaching are full of the most complete indications, if only we will learn how to apply them! Is not each indication applied in life a step closer toward the Great Teacher? There comes a crucial moment in everyone's life! Verily, we know neither the day nor the hour! Thus, I send the flaming wish of my heart to you; work amicably, take care to preserve a harmonious atmosphere in your meetings and communions. Let these meetings be not too numerous but illuminated by and inspired with the flaming love to the Teacher who called you.

The time is so threatening that only great devotion and solidarity will help you to endure until the great day of the predestined New Era. Unity and mutual respect among the most enlightened minds and hearts will facilitate greatly this task.

42

20 December 1934

Do you really wish to fall into narrow sectarianism! Of course, if one wants to regard the Teaching of Life from the Christian point of view, one should be perfectly welcome to do so, as indeed there is certainly a great deal in the Teaching that can be explained from the experiences of many of the Christian Mystics. Is not the source one? However, the achievements of the Christian Mystics and the narrow dogmatism of the church are two opposites. The one who wishes to follow the path of the Mystics and the early Fathers of the Church may do so parallel with the deepening of his understanding of the Teaching of Life. Let each one choose the most suitable individual approach, but let him beware of blasphemy against other aspects of the same great Truth. Therefore, encourage all to travel their own individual path.

Least of all do I care for those articles on practical occultism that fail to mention the importance of a lofty purification of the heart before commencing the experiments with dangerous energies. I cannot tell you how I dislike all these mechanics that lead to nothing but destruction. Verily, if instead of concentrating on the tip of one's nose, or the navel, all efforts were put into striving toward spiritual synthesis and the task of building up one's mental body, the achievements could be significant and beneficial; certainly much greater than the exuding of the scent of violets, which can be obtained from any perfumery!

* * *

For your information, I must tell you that occultly speaking it is wrong to say that "one energy becomes a part of another." It is more correct to say that the qualities of energy may be transmuted with the aid of a binding element, the stimulus of a third power, or a new ingredient, which transmutes one quality into another. Thus, the reciprocal action of the energies of space is established. Indeed, everything in space is reciprocal. I would advise you to read the *Diary of a Physician*, by the eminent Dr. Pirogoff. I myself have not read it, but in her time H. P. Blavatsky highly approved of his works and often quoted him in her books. His unprejudiced mind, following the path of scientific research, brought him into the realm of the occult.

* * *

The reconstruction of the world cannot take place without collisions and calamities. All efforts of the Great White Brotherhood are concentrated on holding back the tide of madness until the time when the combination of the luminaries will be more favorable, thus facilitating a more extensive salvation. Occultly, it is most harmful and dangerous to cast precise formulae and dates into space. Indeed, the precise dates are particularly guarded by the Forces of Light. That is why it is said: "The ways of the Lord are inscrutable," and, "Watch therefore, for ye know neither the day nor the hour," and also why miracles are always unexpected. The servants of darkness have many ears, and so much of the predicted welfare has been ruined by ignorant and light-minded announcement of dates.

I shall quote a page from the Teaching:

"The planet is completing a cycle which leads everything to

summation. The time is coming when each principle must manifest its entire potential. These rings are looked upon in history as downfall or renascence. But these rhythms must be regarded as the triumph of Light or darkness. The time has come when the planet is drawing near to such a circle of summation, and only the most saturated tension of the potential will result in victory. The circle of summation awakens all energies, for in the final battle all the forces of Light and darkness will take part, from the very Highest down to the dregs. Sensitive spirits know why there is being manifested so much of the Higher, side by side with the guilty and the inert. In the conflict, before the circle of summation there will be contentions of all spatial, earthly and supermundane forces. On the path to the Fiery World the co-workers must remember the Ordinance of the Cosmos.

"The world is living through those stages by which have been signalized all the decisive moments in the history of mankind. Stages of destruction precede construction. Creativeness, having been tensed, calls all energies to life. That epoch into which humanity has entered will inevitably manifest all the potentials of forces, for this epoch is a decisive one, and a turning point in history is approaching. Surely, the condition of the planet has not come about by accident, and each tension bears witness to that current which is engulfing all spheres. If the conflict is inexorable, so will the victory be decisive. For all forces and spheres participate in this Cosmic Battle. On the path to the Fiery World one must take up the Sword of Light for building the New Epoch." [Fiery World III]

Thus, the time is very tense and great events are approaching. But how can those who have entrusted themselves to Highest Guidance, whose consciousness is *undivided* and who *in full readiness* are prepared to offer everything to the service of humanity, have any fear? Verily, the devoted ones shall be saved. So one must irrevocably decide whether one is serving the Forces of Light all-embracingly or, by reason of narrow sectarianism, serving the forces of darkness. There is no lukewarm middle way where the Sword of Light is striking. The time is most menacing.

For the time being, the sacred dates must be concealed. If all that is destined is announced prematurely, people most assuredly will furiously condemn it.

Yes, one must be extremely careful in contacting so many organizations. It is not difficult to imagine what a variety of people enters them. The founders of these organizations may be good people, but the followers, because of their great numbers, may surprise you in many ways. *Therefore, be cautious.* Examples of the unreliability of such followers are not far from you.

The Great Covenant is, and always was, "not quantity but quality." *The Sacred is entrusted only to the most devoted ones* who have been tested during thousands of years.

The faces of many reveal their true selves, and it is important to know how to discriminate among them. For those who have chosen the path of Great Service for humanity, *discrimination is a touchstone*; it is the first requirement and condition on the path of true discipleship. Thus, at a certain stage of spiritual development we are able to see occultly the sculpture of the spirit of those who surround and approach us. Without acquiring this ability, it is vain to hope to be accepted; for how can a disciple be trusted if he is unable to discriminate Light from darkness or friend from betrayer? The whole constructiveness of life would be ruined by such ignorance. Certainly, straight-knowledge is most helpful in discrimination. But how many possess it? Surely, it is the rarest quality and comes as a result of aeons of tireless striving toward Knowledge and Light. I really do not think that we can count even a hundred of such fortunate ones! It was once said that there were no more than one hundred spirits over the entire expanse of our planet who had knowledge of the Truth. And to think—this out of two billion human beings! For those who declare themselves able to discriminate without error this is not at all encouraging.

Also, many think that they possess cosmic consciousness, that they have been through the highest degrees of initiation, etc. etc. *The self-conceit of people is a most tragic page in the history of humanity.* And only when people are able to see the true records of the history of the planet will this tragedy become clearly seen. The time will come when they will realize that if it were not for the great self-sacrifice of a small group of the Highest Spirits who, through aeons, have incarnated among the people at the great turning points in the history of the planet in order to give a new impulse to the human consciousness, and if their efforts had not been continued on by a small number of their disciples and the co-workers of these disciples, our humanity would even now be on the level of the troglodytes!

Thus, one may see how the same Ego of the Greatest

Individuality has appeared in a whole series of Great Images. Truly, very few significant incarnations are left to the earth-dwellers! Verily, to these Bodhisattvas, as They are called in the East, we are obligated for all that is most precious, most high, most essential in the world, for They have nurtured the human consciousness and thus transformed and prolonged our lives.

I shall quote a few extracts from N. Rokotoff's *Foundations of Buddhism*, pertaining to Bodhisattvas:

"The word Bodhisattva comprises two concepts: Bodhi—enlightenment or awakening, and Satva—the essence. Who are these Bodhisattvas? The disciples of Buddhas, who voluntarily have renounced their personal liberation and, following the example of their Teacher, have entered upon a long, weary, thorny path of help to humanity. Such Bodhisattvas appear on earth in the midst of the most varying conditions of life. Physically indistinguishable in any way from the rest of humanity, they nevertheless differ completely in their psychology, constantly being the heralds of the principle of the common welfare. ... What qualities must a Bodhisattva possess? In the Teaching of Gotama Buddha and in the Teaching of Bodhisattva Maitreya, given by Him to Asanga, according to the tradition in the fourth century, the maximum development of energy, courage, patience, constancy of striving and fearlessness were first of all underlined. Energy is the basis of everything, as it alone contains all possibilities. Buddhas are eternally in action, immobility is unknown to Them. Like the eternal motion in space, the actions of the Sons of Conquerors manifest in the worlds. ...

"Mighty, valiant, firm in His step, not rejecting the burden of an achievement for the General Good. ... There are three joys of Bodhisattvas: the joy of giving, the joy of helping and the joy of eternal perception. Patience always, in all, and everywhere. The Sons of Buddha, the Sons of Conquerors, Bodhisattvas, in their active compassion are the Mothers to the all-existing." (*Mahayana—Sutra.*)

Are not these Bodhisattvas leading that hundred who are to be found on our planet? But the burdensome is the law of these Bodhisattvas; no one has endured (and They continue to endure) so much slander and persecution as these true Saviors of the human race. From among their number came the Founders of great kingdoms, great religions and philosophies, many alchemists and several saints. But do not look for Them among the narrow dogmatists! They are Founders of the living religion of the Heart, but not of enslaving dogma. They are the Founders and the Fiery Purifiers of religions. Now I must halt. I have digressed too far and I must return to your letter.

You ask about the deniers of the Hierarchy of Light. In India, those teachers who reject the succession of the Hierarchic Chain are considered "rootless trees," and no one heeds them.

You may tell your interrogators that the true Teaching never repudiates the foundations of the most ancient Covenants, and that these foundations are based on reverence to the Great Hierarchy. Without the bond with the Hierarchy of Light, our destiny is that of a kitten at sea. What can exist without the Leading Concept? Verily, the Concept of Hierarchy is a Cosmic Concept and a Cosmic Law. The whole Universe is nourished and sustained under this Fiery Law. Therefore, every teaching that denies this Principle is a false teaching.

Regarding initiations, I may say that in life there are many degrees of initiation, and each one who knows a little more than his neighbor is already initiated into something. Also, please distinguish thoroughly between the White Brothers, Members of the Himalayan Community, and the ordinary white brothers, who are people following the Teaching of Light.

The majority of the Great Brothers are now using densified subtle bodies. And Those who are still in their physical bodies are gathered now in the main Stronghold. All the Ashrams in Tibet are hidden in closed, impassable defiles. The dreadful effluvia of the earthly atmosphere does not encourage the presence of the Great Teachers among people. Moreover, at the moment their work does not require their physical presence. Such terms as "Initiate," "Adept," "White Brother" are terribly profaned! It would be a good thing to ponder upon the words of the Great Teacher K. H.: "An Adept is the rarest flower of a whole series of generations of seekers." Yet indeed, how many times this flower has been born among the host of these self-sacrificing Sages! Thus, let us manifest here the highest care, and let us not profane the greatest concepts! It is truly impossible to imagine the entire majesty of an Arhat of the Hierarchy of Light! It cannot be comprehended by our limited minds and imagination. Only the tremor of the heart will indicate the spiritual exaltation of a devoted disciple, who feels the approaching Ray of the Teacher of Light!

In conclusion, I shall quote a paragraph that affirms the necessity for discrimination:

"The manifest Battle summons to discernment of the paths which lead to Light and to darkness. During the cosmic tension of all forces, this discernment is indispensable, for space is saturated with fiery arrows. Every consciousness must be imbued with affirmation of the fiery Battle. Verily during such fiery tension of manifested arrows humanity must urgently accept that direction of salvation which has been indicated to it by the Forces of Light. To the assistance of the planet are sent fiery currents; they must be received with spirit and heart. On the path to the Fiery World it is especially important to realize the power extended for the salvation of mankind. [Fiery World]

Part III

1935

1

9 January 1935

The process of outliving the accumulated karmic results is painful. But precisely this very process brings us quickest of all to the path of Service to humanity. Answer yourself honestly: was it not these blows of fate that made you seek the path of the true Light? Did not the contact with the horrible ulcers of reality broaden your consciousness and enable you to emerge from the conventional ways of thinking? I think you will bless this life of yours that opened to you the source of spiritual rebirth. Do you not experience joy when your consciousness ponders upon Being? Is this not the joy of a new comprehension of the purpose of existence, the joy of spiritual creativeness?

Likewise, the attraction and love between the opposite Elements should be regarded as a manifestation of Cosmic Law. Verily, spiritually dead is the one who lacks this divine fire of inspiration and creativeness, given us by the Cosmic Law of existence. Unfortunately, even up to the present time there is no true understanding of this powerful foundation of cosmic structure. People have forgotten, or rather do not want to admit, the great cosmic significance of love. The materialism of our age puts love on the level of a purely physiological function. At best, love today is treated as a psychological process. But if the cosmic significance of love could be realized once more, people would see in love its highest function, i.e., the awakening of all the highest emotions and creative abilities. Precisely, this awakening is the chief purpose and the true keynote of love. Love is a unifying creative power. On the higher planes of Being everything is created by thought. But for the fulfillment of these thought forms, there must be the two Elements united by Cosmic Love. There is a great deal of misunderstanding surrounding the fundamental concept of the dual Element. Religions are to blame for this, and especially Christianity. The church profaned the greatest Cosmic Mystery by demeaning marriage and degrading the woman, by its contempt of love and its vows of celibacy and monasticism, and by declaring this spiritual impoverishment to be the highest achievement of the human spirit. This frightful fanaticism brought about terrible consequences, among which the mortification of the flesh was and is not the worst. Let us recall the criminal hypocrisy, the dreadful sexual perversions and crimes that resulted from these prohibitions and condemnations, which are completely against Cosmic Law. Likewise, the words of Christ, "But I say unto you, That whosoever looketh on a woman to lust after her hath committed adultery with her already in his heart" are entirely misinterpreted. These words should be understood in the light of the Cosmic Law, which has in view the affinity of souls and the true lawfulness of marriage. (I have written about this before.) The science of correct marriage will give to humanity the necessary equilibrium. Precisely, most unions which constitute marriage today are, from a cosmic point of view, adulterous, and they threaten to ruin the whole planet. The right comprehension of this great mystery, and the giving of due respect to woman can regenerate the world. People should understand love in its highest manifestation, and should look for its reflection here on Earth. And, indeed, the posterity that would result from this love would be much higher than that which issues from chance unions. Marriage entered into just for the sake of progeny is an ugly and sacrilegious manifestation. We should always remember that man is a destined creator of the world. Therefore, all types of creativeness should be manifested by his spiritual substance, which is possible only if he becomes kindled by the highest love. Love alone reveals all concealed fires. Thus, in the foundation of each creation is laid the great Attraction, the great Love. All that is in the world depends on love and is sustained by love. Love must lead to the higher comprehension.

How beautiful is the Image of the Mother of the World! So much beauty, self-renunciation and tragedy is in this majestic Image! Aspire in your heart to the Highest, and joy and exultation will enter your soul. The whole creativeness of man, all mystic exaltation, is the result of that same Love, be it expressed or concealed. And we should remember that for the pure, all is pure.

Some day, you will write beautiful hymns, dedicated to the Raiment of the Mother of the Universe, which flashes with all the colors of the rainbow and with all the joys of Be-ness and great creativeness. For there is no life, no expression of spirit, without the Mother of the Universe, the Great Matter of All-Being. The placing of spirit and matter into diametrically opposing positions bred in the ignorant consciousness a fanatical conception of matter as something inferior, whereas in reality spirit and matter are one. Spirit without matter is nothing, and matter is but the crystallization of spirit. The manifested Universe, visible and invisible, from the highest to the lowest, reveals to us the infinite aspects of Radiant Matter. Where there is no matter, there is no life.

Be aflame in your spirit and heart!

2

11 January 1935

The statement that "on the highest planes of Existence matter can be so subtle, so transparent that we may see only the life which is enwrapped in it, but not the matter itself" is most vague and erroneous. How can life be seen without seeing the matter which covers it? It is wrong to imagine matter on the higher planes as something transparent. Materia Lucida, which is the substance of the forms of the higher spirits, is entirely visible to the person whose centers are open. This matter, Materia Lucida, although most subtle, is not invisible. It is a luminous substance, a matter which radiates with colors ranging beyond those known to our physical plane.

* * *

You want to say, do you not, that consciousness develops perpetually and is infinite in its achievements? Of course, in principle, this is correct, but in life here on Earth we often witness how the consciousness of a person reaches a limit and is unable to proceed further. Rather, it does not wish, or is afraid, to do so. But, in these cases, as nothing in reality can remain static, the consciousness is retreating. By this process, the consciousness may deteriorate to such an extent that the seed of the spirit, being unable to obtain sustenance from the higher sources, dies off. We call such people "walking corpses." At the present time, a vast retrogression is taking place in the human consciousness, and hence all the calamities which come to our planet.

You say that "the continuity of the consciousness is a necessary condition for its development." May I add to your statement? Certainly, the continuity of the consciousness is necessary for its development, but the idea of such a continuity is very relative. Do we not observe this relativity of the continuity of consciousness here on Earth in the periodic conditions of sleeping and waking? The number of people who preserve vivid continuity of consciousness when passing into the Subtle World, even into its middle strata, is not so overwhelmingly large. Upon arriving there, many fall asleep or drag out a semi-conscious, miserable existence. Variations in the degrees of consciousness are infinite. There are as many stages of consciousness as there are steps in Infinity. There is complete consciousness in the Subtle World only for those who created the bond with the higher worlds while still living, by reason of the aspirations of the heart toward evolution, and by persistent attempts to preserve such consciousness. Thus, even though he possesses an intellect developed to its utmost, a materialist who denounces spirituality and the possibility of existence in the higher worlds may remain without a conscious life in the higher spheres of the Subtle World; for, having not created or affirmed the higher attractions, he will be drawn almost immediately into the whirl of the attraction of the Earth, and in a semi-conscious or unconscious state he will await a new incarnation. Of course, one can well imagine what kind of incarnation it will be. Such immediate returns to the Earth, with the exception of those of very high spirits, are not desirable. As you know, the stay in the Subtle World has a great significance in the way of nourishment and intensification, and toward transmutation of the accumulated energies into spiritual forces. Therefore, one can well imagine what a deterioration of the spiritual substance takes place in the cases of long deprivation of such nourishment.

In the Teaching of Life it is said: "People have their subtle bodies almost formed; but the mental body is created only by a select few." Therefore, a semi-conscious existence in the higher strata of the Subtle World or else a temporary interruption of consciousness is, in the majority of cases, still inevitable.

Reaching a state of conscious continuity of existence, or of the preservation of a complete consciousness in all the bodies and in all the spheres, is the greatest achievement of the Arhat. This is what is called Amrita, or true immortality. That is why all the efforts of the Great Teachers are directed toward the broadening of the consciousness of humanity, the development of the mental body, and the awakening of the higher aspiration for the creating of the magnetic current which uplifts the spirit into the higher spheres.

The development of consciousness is the longest and most difficult process in the Cosmos. Thus, if people could reach the state of continuity of consciousness in their subtle bodies or in the higher planes of the Subtle World, they could considerably accelerate evolution.

The spiritual entity passing into the Subtle World continues its conscious or semi-conscious existence in proportion to the development of its higher Manas, or spirituality. Are there many even here on Earth who live an entirely conscious life? As below, so above. But there is the difference that in the above everything is more vivid and more clearly defined, i.e., more intensive, whether experienced in a conscious or an unconscious state. Let us understand clearly that whatever is not realized here on Earth will not be realized in the Subtle World. You remember that it was said that it is almost impossible to acquire a new consciousness in the Subtle World. Therefore, in earthly life we must sow the seeds of aspiration which in the Subtle World can be transmuted into knowledge. Were it otherwise, we should not have to return to Earth.

* * *

The star of the Mother of the World is the planet Venus. In 1924 this planet for a short time came unusually near to the Earth. Its rays were poured on Earth, and this created many new powerful and sacred combinations which will yield great results. Many feminine movements were kindled by these powerful rays.

* * *

It is incorrect to call the fire of space Cosmic Reason, for the fire of space is the Source of Life. Consequently, it is the potential consciousness or the basis of Mind. The Cosmic Mind is the manifested Mind or the collective Mind or Reason of the Hierarchy of Light. The fire of space is an arouser, a kindler, but also an exploder and burner of useless refuse.

* * *

Only the Highest Spirits can have astral teraphim. Verily, only the Teachers Themselves, and their nearest disciples.

3

16 January 1935

I suggest that you avoid overdoing the mental exercises. In the polluted atmosphere of cities such concentration will merely lead to errors. Recall these lines from the Teaching:

"I consider the schools of concentration dangerous in a heavy atmosphere. Men persist in their chosen desires, but the current is too weak and they create only an image in their brains. For powerful visions there is needed an atmosphere charged with electricity and a consciousness in repose." [Leaves of Morya's Garden I]

Therefore, do not be in a hurry to impress upon the third eye the Image of the Teacher. It is better if you are able to fill your heart with a constant memory of and love for the Great Image.

You must display gratitude for every joy in your life. And if your feeling is sincere and aspiring in its devotion, it will reach its destination. Perhaps you aspire toward the Image of the revered Sergius of Radonega. Indeed, the Great Teachers have many Images, and each nation chooses the one that is closest and most dear.

With the broadening of the consciousness and the refinement of all the feelings of the whole organism, the assimilation of the subtle energies will become possible. But this refinement cannot take place as quickly as you expect. *Many years* of stubborn work of self-purification and self-development will be required. And once again I warn you that mediumship and psychism have nothing to do with the true refinement of the organism. Only the broadening of the consciousness and the opening of the higher centers and their subsequent fiery transmutation will bring true achievement. But this does not come suddenly—years are required. Furthermore, at a certain stage of refinement it is necessary to dwell in the pure prana of the mountains. The fiery transmutation cannot take place in the poisonous atmosphere of a city. Therefore, all exercises are *extremely dangerous* in cities and may lead to obsession and even death. Remember this and fight against psychism. Think about the spiritual perfecting of the heart and temporarily stop all mental concentrations.

Likewise, the refinement of the heart is not characterized by a sweet sentimentality, but by valor and a sense of justice.

Sentimentality and justice are two opposites. I shall quote from the Teaching:

"Receptivity to subtle energies is always accompanied by refinement of the organism. Besides, it must be remembered that the consciousness assists first of all, for the subtle energies can be perceived only through refinement of the organism. This principle must be thoroughly understood because usually there results a mixture of concepts. And this misunderstanding and jumbling leads to very dangerous errors. During purification of the consciousness it is very necessary to discern these processes, for people are always disposed toward affirmation of psychism instead of the higher fiery concepts. The spirit who falls into this extremity may find himself so surrounded by psychic fluids that he cannot succeed, even though he may so desire, to be enwrapped by other, higher energies. And in this also let us point to the consciousness as to the salutary agent. Thus, on the path to the fiery world it can be affirmed that the fiery consciousness will bestow the key to discrimination." [Fiery World III]

Moreover, one must bear in mind that the approach and the visitation of the High Images to the earthly plane is always accompanied by a terrible shock to the organism of the one approached. The tremor which shakes the whole being is so awful that the heart may be unable to endure it. That is why some who saw just the light of such an approach almost fell dead from shock. Recollect the visions of the great saints. Let us take, for example, St Sergius' vision of the Holy Mother. A great tremor shook Him, his hair turned grey, and his disciple present at this moment was prostrated and near death! And we know of the almost inaccessible loftiness and greatness of the spirit of the revered Sergius. But the earthly body, even if most refined, cannot contact and assimilate the subtlest energies without a shock. Therefore, when people tell you about their visions of the Great Teachers, treat such tales cautiously. Remember that "if the Highest Images and the highest spheres were of such easy access to a small consciousness, the world would have been destroyed long ago." Only the lower spheres, and the personators who dwell therein, are of easy access; that explains why there are so many distortions and such conceit, as well as why the mediums err so much.

Many of those who insist upon their visions are neither honest nor discriminating. Take this into consideration and refine your consciousness by the aspiration of your heart! Ponder deeply upon the Teaching, reason and *co-measure*: learn the art of *discrimination* regarding the experiences of life. For discriminating between people, discrimination about reality, is a *primary condition*, the first *demand* on the path of true discipleship. Without the acquiring of this faculty there can be no spiritual advancement or approach toward the Teacher. Can a disciple be trusted if he knows not how to tell truth from falsehood, light from darkness, friend from betrayer? All achievements would be ruined by such ignorance. Therefore, sharpen your attention and observation; develop the ability of right judgment in everyday life. You may meet many people who will talk about their high achievements, about their initiations and about the cosmic consciousness which has illumined them, etc. Do know that, barring some rare exceptions, they all are either mistaken or deceived by personators from the Subtle World—or else, still worse, they are simply dishonest people. The self-conceit of people is the most tragic page in the history of our humanity. This tragedy will be revealed in its full proportions when people will be able to look into the true records of the history of our planet. But this time is still very far off, and before that bitter moment we shall see plenty of destruction caused by this plague of humanity. Self-conceit is a deep corrosion of the consciousness. Beware of it as of infection. *The one who truly knows, or an Initiate, will not announce his initiation in the bazaar.*

And now regarding erroneous concepts which you have read and adopted. We read in the Teaching the following:

"Also, let us clear up the confused conception of a group soul. The spirit of concordance is expressed with especial force in animals, before individuality has been manifested. But it is incorrect to term the concordant soul a group soul. Translations and commentaries have produced this confusion. But Plato's conception of twin souls not only was closer to the truth but was expressed beautifully. Then let us not use this erroneous term, group soul; let us replace it with the term *spiritual concordance*. ..." [Fiery World I]

To me, it seems so clear. If animals possess a group soul, why then all the diversity of their characters? In the same herd, in the same conditions, cows, for instance, show entirely different peculiarities of disposition and habit. Quite possibly of course, in a moment of sudden stress or danger they may act similarly;

but then, people of small consciousness act likewise in times of panic, and no better than cattle. Does it mean that such people have a group soul? The spirit or monad always remains in its primeval purity whether in an animal or a man. But only the precipitations which accumulate from contact with other energies build individuality, or, if you prefer, a soul. From all this, it is clear that there can be no group soul. Each monad, while gathering its own accumulations or supplies, follows a *definite* evolutionary course, for the magnetic attraction that lies in the foundation of each vital focus acts with precision. Some writers have confused the conception of the divisibility of spirit with that of a group soul. There are many mistakes, but they are inevitable in view of human dishonesty. Likewise, the popularization of great Truths has added to their distortion. The unprepared or small consciousness is unable to understand the profundity of an entirely new conception, and in trying to grasp it with the old consciousness it distorts it at times to such an extent that it becomes completely unrecognizable.

Many see themselves in previous metamorphoses on Earth—as an elephant, a dog, deer, cat, tapir or tiger—but few ponder whether this could really have been possible. Are not the aforementioned animals either later developments or degenerates of prehistoric types? But even if certain sections of present-day humanity were in the animal stage in the early cycles of the development of our planet, this animal type was entirely different from the contemporary counterpart. The remains of the man of the animal type which was the link between the animal and the human will never be known to our scientists, as that type existed in cycles previous to ours and it is impossible to find those remains. Likewise, all the present animals will not become humans on this planet. Therefore, if you and I do not represent the evolution of some dinosaur during this cycle, or even on this planet, probably at some time our monads animated similar elegancies on some other planet!

* * *

Being awakened for the human physical evolution, the spirit commences a new task: the development of intelligence. For that purpose, the spirit unites with manas. The manas at this primitive stage cannot, of course, guide the human being. So, such a man-animal is impelled for a long time by its impulses, or instincts, or by the lower aspects of the manas. Millennia and aeons of incredible length are passed before the higher faculties of the manas are able to unfold and, thus, to create a true human being, the crown of this manifested Cosmos. Were it not for the self-sacrifice of the High Spirits, we would be even now in the state of troglodytes. Our earthly humanity owes its accelerated evolution to its Elder Brothers and Sisters, the Great Teachers.

The spirit must direct its evolution, and the efforts of the Great Teachers are directed toward the acceleration and awakening of the consciousness in man. But how often the spirit remains silent, and how rare are the cases of continuous uninterrupted development! So many soulless people fill the space! So much regression in the development of humanity! The spirit can manifest itself and truly guide only in cases of highly developed consciousness or unusual purity of heart.

I must confess that to me the following questions of yours are not clearly formulated. I shall try to answer them in the way I understand best. You ask, "Does not on a certain plane the chain of planets become an undivided whole, the same as one whole planet on the physical plane, and on the plane which is still higher does not this occur with the whole solar system, etc?" I shall remind you that in all the ancient Teachings the Cosmos was always considered as a total organism, and it was likened to the human organism. Therefore, from this point of view, all the solar systems may be considered as smaller units or groups within the totality of the Cosmic, even as blood corpuscles in the single human organism. What do you mean by the chain of planets? Perhaps there is again a misunderstanding. The chain of planets mentioned in *The Mahatma Letters* and *The Secret Doctrine* should be understood as various phases of the same planet, including all the spheres visible and invisible to us, which surround it, but not as independent physical planets.

Further on you say, "Suppose in the state or on the plane of Nirvana there is matter: purusha of this state spreads infinitely over the entire planetary chain, and the matter of a still higher state spreads infinitely over the entire Solar System." (I hold to your text, and use exactly your punctuation marks—colon after the word "matter.") It is even more difficult for me to follow your thought here, but I shall answer as best I can, and if my answer does not satisfy you, try next time to formulate your thoughts more clearly. For "if we take two interlocutors who are at the same stage of mental development, they still may not be able to understand each other. Only a complete attuning will bring the unification of consciousness. Often, an improper definition may give an entirely wrong idea. One must affirm oneself in precise understanding of many definitions, as people often use definitions in their reverse meaning without noticing it."

Now I shall give my answer. Space is filled with fundamental cosmic matter, or cosmic substance—Spirit-Matter, or the substance Purusha-Prakriti. Take the definition which is closest to you; they are all synonymous. This matter or substance is the basis of our Universe in its visibility and invisibility. As a *foundation*, as a *potentiality of all existence*, this substance is everywhere *one*, but its differentiations are infinite. Thus, each body, each luminary, each solar system has its own atmosphere, with all the qualities characteristic only of it. The tension of this atmosphere, as well as the degree of its development and refinement, or perfection, will differ from that of the atmospheres surrounding other bodies or systems, but the *cosmic substratum of these differentiations will be the same one, in the span of infinite space*. Even so is the monad one in its essence, be it embodied in a mineral, plant, animal or man. One must ponder deeply upon the concept of the fundamental *Unity in the Cosmos*.

Each divine monad-spark in its fiery origin is unitary with all other monads, but the combination of energies which come in touch with it manifest its distinct potentiality, giving it the color which corresponds with this particular combination; thus are created all diversities. In the Teaching there is given a beautiful explanation:

"The spirit remains inviolate. The fiery seed of the spirit remains in the primary consistency because the essence of the elements is immutable. But the emanation of the seed changes, depending on the growth of consciousness. Thus one may understand that the seed of the spirit is a fragment of the elementary fire. And the energy accumulated around it is consciousness. ... You may add any chemical ingredient to a flame and thereby change its color and size, but the primary nature of the fire will remain unchanged." [Agni Yoga]

Remember that the condition of Nirvana is the condition of the highest manifested perfection *corresponding to a given cycle of evolution in each kingdom and species*. Likewise, the consciousness, i.e., instinct, of plants and animals during Pralaya will have its corresponding Nirvana. There are as many degrees of Nirvana as there are cycles of perfection in Infinity. But the Nirvana will always be the expression of the maximum achievement of perfection corresponding to the particular stage of evolution. But as regards the Cosmic Foundation or Substance, we may say only that it remains in the condition of potential Paranirvana. The Cosmic Substance, Spirit-Matter, which is spread throughout Infinity, is the Divine Foundation or the Potential of All-Being. In its endless manifestations, differentiations and changes of forms, it strives toward infinite perfection and self-consciousness in these particular forms. Whether or not this will satisfy your inquiry, I do not know, but this is how I understand it.

And now, as regards your group. Of course, I have pictured this as a number of aspiring people who are young in the true sense. Certainly, youthfulness of spirit is the main condition—youthfulness in the sense of mobility and aspiration of the consciousness.

The simple spiritual discourses on themes from the Teaching are much more useful than any lectures or rituals. Build up a group of flaming hearts who do not need husks or superficialities but the life-giving grain. Often a talk of three minutes gives more than a two hour lecture. However discriminate between the newcomers and act as you see fit, using your own initiative.

I am sending my best wishes to you. Strengthen your thoughts along the path of austere practical achievement, of beauty of service for the General Good, of joy of cooperation with the Forces of Light, and the light and beauty will enter your life. Without the bond with the Higher World there is no progress, neither is there true joy.

Just before mailing this letter to you, I received your second letter, and as there is still some space on this page I will fill it with my answers.

Tara is a goddess, the feminine equivalent of the *Arhat*, or a Sister of the White Brotherhood. But please do not be too much interested in the names of various initiations; this will not lead you anywhere. In ancient times, each religio-philosophical school, or sacred brotherhood, had its own gradations or degrees, and had special names for them. But you may be sure that the true degrees were not designated by the names we now see in books. If you are interested in this, take the beautiful definitions of the degrees of spiritual advancement given in

Agni Yoga. Indeed, among some who study occultism, there are those who are convinced that the Sun-initiation takes place on the physical sun! All degrees of initiation are in ourselves. When a disciple is ready, he receives a Ray of Illumination, which corresponds with the degree of purification he has achieved, as well as of the broadening of his consciousness and the fiery transmutation of his centers.

For your satisfaction, I shall give you the names of some ancient Egyptian degrees of initiation in their Greek equivalents. The first degree was called Pastoforis; the second, Neokoris; the third, Melaneforis; the fourth, Christoforis; the fifth, Balahat; the sixth, Astrologos; the seventh, Propheta or Safknaf-Pankah. I question, however, whether the knowledge of these relative terms can help you in your spiritual development. Also, I must mention that we must not move along the Path as a smoking torch but as a light which purifies and pierces the darkness.

And now, regarding the photographing of the auras. Great expense and patience are connected with this. And it is quite essential to maintain conditions for the favorable currents, for the purity, peace and harmony of the whole atmosphere. People participating in these experiments should all be well harmonized. One must remember that not a single scientific experiment succeeds without great labor and patience. In aura research, there is also a mechanical procedure, with the assistance of a chemical preparation. This preparation is placed on the glass through which the person is observed. However, this preparation is very injurious to the eyes, and of course the method is quite imperfect.

4

1 February 1935

You write that in *Chalice of the East* you came across a complete repudiation of not only a personal but also an impersonal God. This cannot be quite so, for nowhere in the teaching or in the Letters of the Great Teachers is there a rejection of an impersonal God. Possibly the misunderstanding comes from a wrong terminology. What is this impersonal God? Is He not the Divine Immanent and Infinite Principle, or the Inconceivable Cause, of all Existence, who, according to the Apostles John and Paul and the works of the first great Fathers of Christianity, is "the Invisible and the Unknown God"? Do we not read in the Bible (St. John 1:18), "No man hath seen God at any time"? And the same words are repeated in the First Epistle of John (4:12). There are many references in the Bible to "God the Unknown" and about the fiery nature of this God. In Deuteronomy (4:24) Moses says, "God is a consuming fire."

I strongly recommend that you read the works of the great Origen, that brilliant expounder of the true Teaching of Christ. Incidentally, the Western Church has now commenced to study his works, as the more informed clergy now understands that the church with its dead dogma has come to an impasse and can no longer maintain its influence with the new consciousness of the broad masses, who, first of all, demand logic and flexibility of laws. Origen, in his treatise on *First Principles*, says:

"Therefore, we cannot consider God as being a particular incarnation, or as incarnate at all. He is Uncompounded Spiritual Nature, excluding all complexes. He is intelligence, and at the same time the source and origin of all intelligence in Nature and Creation. God, who is the origin of everything, should not be considered complex, as otherwise it might appear as though the elements that have created everything considered complex existed before their very origin."

Is it possible to affirm more clearly the concept of God as the purest first Principle or Element of Be-ness than in these words expressed by the great Greek philosopher and Christian Father?

Likewise, is it not said that God is Omnipresent, Omniscient and Omnipotent, and that "in Him we live and move and have our being"? All this is given in the Bible. Therefore, if we cast away the dead letter of the Scriptures, so often distorted by wrong translations, and if we rid ourselves of the prejudiced ideas, created by slavish thinking of minds held for centuries in bondage by Christian dogma, we shall see that all the religions and all the Teachings of antiquity had as their foundation the majestic, eternally-inconceivable Cause of All-Existence—that all religions have worshipped this One Divine Element under various names and aspects in accordance with the individual peculiarities of different peoples and different countries.

* * *

The Christian world selected the term *God* for the Highest

Concept. Therefore, why look for a new appellation for this Majestic Concept? Truly, through the centuries, the Christians have associated with this term all that is of the highest and most beautiful according to their understanding. That is why in the books of the Teaching this Incomprehensible and Infinite Principle or Element is often designated by the word *God*. It is said, "God is spirit, and they that worship him must worship him in spirit." It is also said, "My Father and thy Father." In truth, this Divine Element, Incomprehensible and Invisible, spiritually exists in and around us. Therefore, the God of the Mahatmas is a Cosmic God, rather Cosmos Itself, in all its Visibleness and Invisibleness. Verily, "in Him we live and move and have our being."

Likewise, it is said in *Agni Yoga*, "People do not realize the meaning of God and Bodhisattva." Indeed they do not! But, as the great Origen said, "Our mind alone is unable to comprehend God Himself but can intuit Him as the Father of all beings from the *beauty of His creations and the splendor of Nature*."

It is impossible to express this thought better. Yes, in ancient times the conception of Deity, the Incomprehensible Source of all beings, was majestic. This Cosmic Law is, verily, a just Law. It gave to each spark issuing from it all its qualities, permitting free choice in applying those qualities either for construction or destruction.

Let us also bear in mind that all the ancient religions, without exception, were divided into esoteric and exoteric. Indeed, much has become complicated in our Christian religion due to the fact that the clergy lost, or rather rejected, the key to the understanding of Christ's Teaching. This Teaching is full of esotericism, as is continuously confirmed by the words of Christ Himself.

Returning to the definition "impersonal" God, I must add that if we attach to the idea of God what is usually meant by the vast majority of people, this definition of God as an impersonal Being becomes simply a monstrous absurdity—completely nonsensical. Therefore, only by accepting God as the Inconceivable Element, as the One Law of All-Existence, may we speak of Him as being impersonal. Furthermore, if it is said that God is Infinite, how can it be possible for Him to have a form and an image? How, being Infinite, can God become finite and limited? Thus, only the idea of God as the Divine, Unchangeable,

Omnipresent, Infinite and Inconceivable Principle really answers all problems and explains the many perplexities.

Just think how the idea of God differs in different consciousnesses, according to the stage of human evolution. It grows and broadens in proportion to the growth of the consciousness, but people usually forget to consider the evolution of this concept. For the sluggardly majority always trail in the rear and follow the dogmas as they are established. Let us recall the beautiful saying in the Bhagavad-Gita: "I am that thread upon which all these ideas are strung, and each one of them is as a pearl." Verily, one may say that there are as many conceptions of God as there are consciousnesses.

If we accept the possibility of the existence of an Omnipotent, Omnipresent, Omniscient, All-Loving, All-Merciful God as a Person, would it not be logical to ask why such an All-Powerful and All-Loving Ruler of the Universe allows so much terrible cruelty and injustice? Why does the whole of nature exist by mutual devouring? No one can deny that the world at its present stage is horrifying, is indeed hell itself! We should not conceal from ourselves that if a man who is satisfied by merely material pleasures is unhappy, the man who dares to protest and to demand justice and something higher than the animal, material pleasures is, unfortunately, much more unhappy.

Does not the All-Seeing God behold how milliards of his creatures—humans and others—are constantly being destroyed? Can we even sigh, or take one step, without destroying thousands of infinitesimal lives? Each moment of our life, each breath, brings death to millions. Why should they die? Why is their death necessary? No doubt there are people who will try to prove that everything is created by God for our benefit, and that evil leads to good! But such childish ideas can by no means satisfy a thinking person, for we know how contagious is evil, and if it were not for the exalted souls of great individuals, the waves of evil would engulf the whole world. Can it be possible that apart from these few high consciousnesses, who became victors in this cruel and incessant struggle, God wants the perpetual suffering through endless centuries of these billions of other souls?

Why is there such injustice in the conditions of birth, which leaves its trace for the rest of our lives? Where, then, is all-mercifulness, all-knowledge and all-power? Could not God, possessing these attributes, create a higher and more perfect Nature?

Why does He need this endless destruction and the survival of the fittest? No, it is quite impossible to reconcile the existing conditions with the providence of an all-merciful, all-knowing and all-powerful God, such as the church would present to us. Thus, all the concepts regarding the nature of God should be thoroughly analyzed. It is time to turn to the Teachings of the East, and to the Minds that gave these Teachings. It is time to accept these Minds as our Teachers. Indeed, the East left the idea of the monotheistic God, Ruler of the Universe, and came to a higher concept of Divinity. In the Inconceivable Absolute was found the unity of the whole Universe. For this Absolute includes in itself all the finite and infinite, all the manifested and the latent, and beyond this all-unifying Concept the human mind is unable to reach.

That explains why all the greatest Teachers of humanity never encouraged arguments about the Unknown Cause. It was accepted as the Greatest Mystery, forever unknowable. For if we begin to limit the Absolute by our own perception, it will cease to be the Absolute and will become limited. Therefore, the Absolute cannot be conceived, for it includes in itself also the concept of Infinity. But who will ponder upon the majestic and awesome idea of Infinity? Therefore, we can perceive only the various aspects and manifestations of this Absolute. But, since we are particles of the Absolute, and since each particle of the One Whole potentially possesses all the qualities of this Whole, we can gradually unfold this potential within ourselves during the span of countless incarnations and the millennia that reach into Infinity.

The Vedas say, "He is the substance of thy soul. He is the Truth. He is I; Thou art That. " Examining all the concepts about God, should we not say that the Manifested God could be only humanity itself? But in its present stage humanity is nearer to the shadow of God—the image of Satan.

You probably will also point out that the Mahatmas, in the *Chalice of the East*, affirm that They believe only in matter. But in all the ancient esoteric Teachings of the East, Matter and Spirit are considered to be one and inseparable. That is why the exoteric Gods have their Consorts personifying Matter and its Power. Thus, Parabrahman is imperceptible and has no manifestation without the finest veil of Mulaprakriti, or Matter, slipped over Him. But of course, the Matter spoken of is sublimated to such a degree that it is inaccessible to our gross senses. As you know, there is a definition that matter is crystallized spirit. Truly, spirit is energy, but we know that energy cannot manifest itself without matter. The light visible to us is a kind of very subtle matter in motion. On all planes, in all actions and thinking we cannot be separated from matter. We deal either with the higher or the denser aspects of the very same matter.

The Subjective Element (God) is spoken of in the Agni Purana. "It exists potentially in the depths of Cosmic Nature, even as fire is hidden in a piece of dry wood, and as oil exists in the heart of the kunjut tree. This subjective element rests in Nature, hidden as a psychic witness or spiritual element, entirely neutral and not acting. The fusion of this subjective element with Cosmic Nature is effected by a force known as Fohat (cosmic electricity). This energy holds all the embryos and fundamental qualities of all beings and of Matter, which must consequently issue from this union of Cosmic Nature with her consort Puman (Spirit, Subjective Element, God)."

Modern science rapidly approaches the great Truth as laid down in the Teachings and religions of the East; soon, very soon, they will meet and shake hands with each other. Let us hope, too, that our church will also become enlightened by the new consciousness and will not remain a mere witness of this new union. Thus, science already understands that there is no matter as such, but only energy, and vice versa. And in this way science approaches the spiritual understanding of the One Element. Likewise, progressive minds begin to study the power of thought, and there are even attempts at photographing and measuring it physically. Thus, the spiritual unites with the material. And how can it be otherwise, when Matter is but a quality of Spirit!

Further on, you write about the Cosmic Reason. Indeed, the whole *summum bonum* of Reason in its convoluted or involuted state in the Unmanifested Universe, we may call God. But it is necessary to establish the difference between the Cosmic Foundation, or the Potential Mind, infinite in its absoluteness, and the Manifested Cosmic Mind. Thus, the Highest Reason and the Great Heart, mentioned in *Chalice of the East* and in the books of the Teaching, is precisely the Collective Mind and the Heart of the Great Hierarchy of Light. Precisely, the Mind and the Heart of these Highest Spirits who have completed their human evolution for this Manvantara (either here or in other worlds or systems) direct the lower forces subordinate to Them, together with the destinies of various humanities in various worlds. Without invading the karma of humanity, They nevertheless give the evolutionary direction and lay the foundation of consciousness. Without this Leadership, human evolution would be retarded for millions of years, and at times would completely collapse.

I have also had to write to others of my correspondents who, like you, were indignant about certain statements in the book, *Chalice of the East*. I shall give some extracts from one of my letters, together with quotations from a still-unpublished book of the Teaching:

"Let us remember that the consciousness of the masses always demands an Individuality for worship and creates the High Image in the likeness of one of its own, whereas a high consciousness always aspires to the Principle in all manifestations. ..."

"Humanity attaches significance only to those concepts which are stored away in a consciousness of mediocrity, for it arrays correspondingly each form in its consciousness. Why, then, have all the Higher Concepts not been inculcated? Why so many distortions? Why so many belittlements? Because, in truth, the essence of human quests and strivings has been turned downward. But the problem of the New World is to rouse the consciousness and to restore to the world the predestined Image of Beauty, Creativeness of the spirit must indeed be intensified in ascent. Precisely, not to lower the Higher but to allow it to rise. Therefore, the first requisite will be to create the Divine Image according to Divinity. When the human consciousness will cease to depict Divinity in an earthly way, then the attainments of the spirit will be fiery.

"Indeed, the very loftiest consciousness strives toward the Fiery Principle, while the lower one creates the Higher Image in its own likeness. The capacity of the small consciousness will determine the created Image, hence so many obvious distortions! How is it possible to fill a small consciousness with a Universal Concept, when all-comprehensiveness leads the spirit into a frenzy. I say—distressing, grievous is human thinking! A spatial horizon is accessible only to him who knows the Universality of the Principle, for the kingly spirit can merge with the Higher Principle precisely as the microcosm merges with Macrocosm. Hence, a small spirit cannot merge with the Fiery Principle.

Fiery power reveals the entire Furnace, manifested to him who senses the pulse of the Fiery World. This life-giving Principle builds life upon Fohat. Thus, let us remember that only a small consciousness denies, but the fiery spirit is all-comprehending. On the path to the Fiery World let us remember about the great Principle." [Fiery World III]

Thus, people serve the God of their own reflection and worship Him through their vices. Whereas the Mahatmas serve the Divine Unalterable Element and worship it through the purity of their lives and through their self-sacrifice for the Good of the whole world. Therefore, in our ignorance let us not accuse of atheism Those who are so immeasurably high, whose Essence, being sublimated by the pure fire, is verily a manifestation of the Divine.

All the greatest minds held always to a high impersonal concept, but there is no harm if, at a certain stage, the developing consciousness requires a Personal Being for the concept of God. The most important thing is that this Personal Being should not be the reflection of oneself, but a true likeness of the Highest Hierarch on the Ladder of Light. And you will be justified in accepting the "Highest Hierarch upon Jacob's Ladder" as your God. Verily, the One who heads the Chain of the Hierarchy of our world is in his power actually the manifestation of God for us.

Let us also recall the beautiful lines in the immortal Bhagavad Gita: "By whatever path you come to Me, by that path will I bless you." Again we see that the outward form is not important; only the highest aspiration toward the Ideal is essential. Many repeat the formula that has become an axiom: " The Macrocosm and the microcosm are identical," but how ridiculously few are the number of those who understand the profound meaning of it!

And so, the words of the Teaching which you quote: "There is no way without God," are quite correct. For God is the Original Cause and the Spiritual Foundation of the whole of life; and if we deny this highest power which is in us, we verily commit blasphemy against the Holy Ghost. By losing the path and union with the Highest, the leading Element, we fall into the abyss of chaos and become cosmic refuse till the time of a new universal rebuilding.

* * *

Now returning to your questions, there is no mistake in the translation, but rather it is incomplete. Firstly, the letters were meant for several persons, at various stages of consciousness; secondly, in most cases they were answering certain questions and were not independent treatises.

The book you mentioned has no particular test in view. But it would be quite right to say that any book can test the level of the reader's consciousness. That is why it is so useful to reread books that were read three or more years ago and discover to what extent our consciousness and understanding have changed.

The analogy you have accepted for solving the question regarding God is not bad. But I would add that the complex which directs the whole organism is the Hierarchy of the Forces of Light, which is manifested and concrete; whereas, the Unutterable Element, in this complex will be that highest Fiery Principle which gives life and foundation to all manifestations and unites the whole complex with the visible and invisible Cosmos.

And so, do not feel unhappy about the loss of the anthropomorphous God. Instead of an Inaccessible and Incomprehensible Image, since "no one at any time has seen God," there will rise before you the Majestic Chain of the Hierarchy of the Forces of Light, which directly guards and guides the whole of humanity toward the Good. And one more thing of which I wish to remind you is that even our church, after it had made God out of Jesus, recognized the Archangel Michael, the Leader of all the Hosts of Heaven, as the greatest after this God. Moreover, in the most ancient Jewish scriptures, the Archangel Michael is called "Godly reflection of God" and even God; whereas Satan is his adversary or his shadow. Hence the image of the Archangel Michael destroying the dragon. Why then have we who have taken our religion from the Jews and who have accepted the Bible, the Prophets and the Tablets of Moses, forgotten about so many remarkable lines and details in their most ancient Scriptures? Christ Himself said: "Think not that I am come to destroy the law, or the prophets: I am not come to destroy, but to fulfil. For verily I say unto you, till heaven and earth pass, one jot or one tittle shall in no wise pass from the law, till all be fulfilled."

Christ spoke as a true Initiate who knew of the One Law given at the dawn of our earthly physical humanity by the Greatest Spirits who came from the Higher Worlds. And so, choose that Light-bearing Hierarch who is nearest to your spirit and surrender yourself to his guidance, for, verily, each Great Hierarch of Light is the reflection of God upon Earth. In the joy of service for the Great Welfare and the evolution of humanity, let us give all our thoughts and strivings of the heart to the chosen Hierarch.

It may comfort you to know that in the East it is said that "there are only two sorts of people who do not worship God as a Person: man-beast, who has no religion at all, and the liberated soul which has risen above human weaknesses and has transcended the restricting limits of its nature. It is this latter soul only who can worship God as He really is." As always, the extremes meet. This explains the great reverence shown by the Hindus toward a spiritual Guru. They see in the Guru a manifestation of the Higher Element, precisely a crown of creation—Man—who has reached the higher perfection through the revealing of the Divine Potential Knowledge stored in him. Let us follow this noble example of reverence and devotion, and, after finding our Guru, let us give him the flaming veneration and devotion of the heart.

I shall end with words of the Teaching: "The grandeur of the Cosmos is so little realized! At best, people speak of the warmth of the sun. But is not our solar system within the Cosmos comparable to an atom in the sun?"

When science is discovering every day billions of worlds and systems exceeding in scope our solar system and the Milky Way, how is it possible to limit this immense Grandeur? Ponder upon the principle of Infinity and Immensity.

You are quite right: the subtleness of the Eastern metaphysical conceptions is rather difficult for Western minds to assimilate.

Thus, the East knows and believes in the Divine Principle, ineffable and eternally cognizable—which amounts to inconceivable—the One Element, eternally manifesting Itself in a visible and invisible Universe. This Element is also known as the Absolute, as It contains in Itself *Everything*. In Its manifested form, It is *Spirit-Matter*, as *Matter* in reality is only Its differentiation or *Quality*. Pure Spirit may be manifested or perceived only through the cover of Matter. That is why it is said that without *Matter* pure *Spirit* is *Naught*.

The mystery of differentiation and fusion into one is the greatest *Mystery* and *Beauty of Be-ness*.

5

28 February 1935

You write, "There are about fifty or sixty people attending the group meetings with satisfactory interest." This is excellent. If eventually six or seven of them prove to be firm in consciousness, devoted to the Teaching and able to write articles and give lectures on the Foundations of Living Ethics, I would consider it a great achievement.

You noticed that some of the members are tired because most of them are working people. I think the main reason is that most of them have already been through the first steps of enthusiastic approach to the Teaching and, according to the occult law, they now begin to show their real nature. Always remember that on the first steps and in the first months of approaching the Teaching, each one burns with eagerness and hopes for the immediate development of his dormant spiritual powers. Many do not realize, or forget, that only in extreme tension of all forces does the awakening of the inner man, and the further degrees of transfiguration, take place. Such people, in most cases, do not find in themselves enough spiritual strength to resist the plungings of the spirit, which inevitably follow every transport of enthusiasm. The law of alternation of rhythm is everywhere the same.

From experience, I know that at the first touch of the spirit's depression many people lose their enthusiasm and often give up the Teaching entirely. All such people are souls with small spiritual accumulations. Verily they are *ignis fatuus*. Thus, it is so important to have a profound understanding of the significance of the approach to the Teaching and a constant striving to self-perfection for the transfiguration of the inner man, the true bearer of immortality. This transfiguration reveals an inexhaustible reserve of spiritual power and leads to complete mastery of one's spiritual will—this crown of achievement. If one attains such mastery of spiritual will, one becomes a real co-worker of the Forces of Good. Much labor is required for such transfiguration, but the time must come when one sets forth.

Those exceptional persons who have developed within themselves spiritual balance, or self-discipline, and who firmly follow a single chosen path, may truly be called the pillars of the world. If we have realized that broadening of the consciousness is most essential, we will conquer fatigue; we will not miss a single moment for the filling of our treasury of the spirit with the jewels of knowledge and experience. Verily, many are called but few are chosen.

I can well understand how difficult it is to direct adults of varying levels of consciousness and education. I suggest complete freedom in selecting the themes for lectures, and I would not insist upon regular attendance. Everyone should understand the foundations of an elementary self-discipline. What spiritual progress is possible without discipline? And how right you are that a careful approach is necessary, and no invasion into another's karma. Verily, forcing is impermissible. The way can be indicated, warnings may be given, but that is all.

There is no doubt that many spiritually developed people, and especially the disciples of the Great Teachers, work during the night on the astral and even on the mental plane, helping their dear ones and friends, or fulfilling the missions of the Teachers. But one must bear in mind that the mediumistic natures remember better their nocturnal adventures because of the peculiar structure of their organism. The reason even spiritually advanced people comparatively seldom remember their activities on the other planes is because there is too great a difference between the vibrations of the two planes. The physical brain cannot so easily reflect these finest vibrations, and if these vibrations were to be artificially raised the organism would inevitably be destroyed. It is possible more often for those who have achieved a certain degree of Agni Yoga to retain in memory their nocturnal activities. But for this, too, certain cosmic and physical conditions are required. Purity and harmony in the surrounding atmosphere, as well as a considerable altitude, are essential. Only a full Adept preserves complete consciousness in all his three bodies, and is not limited in his actions. But for this purpose, even He has to be in a special environment.

Some occult books give a detailed account of visions and adventures in the Subtle World, and often those who have read them see these brain impressions and mistake them for reality. Our main task is to warn people about the harm of forcibly developed psychism (which may result from the following of pseudo-occult books) as well as about the harm of spiritualism. It would be much more useful to study the symbolism of dreams. Indeed, each consciousness has its own symbols, which often have the reverse meaning for another consciousness. Dreams are so little studied, whereas correct research in this field could yield most valuable findings. But, as in everything else, honesty (this rarest of qualities) is necessary. And alas! on the spiritual plane—or rather on the psychic—it is still rarer.

Furthermore, not many realize that development of the heart means first of all the broadening of the consciousness. Verily, the heart is the throne of consciousness but not of sentimentality, this surrogate of benevolence. It is significant that the Easterners, when speaking of the highest and most sacred concepts, always lay a hand upon the heart, for they regard it as the abode of consciousness.

* * *

Yes, the horoscope of the personality rarely coincides with that of the true individual. Often the spirit has in the horoscope of its personality all fiery signs while its fundamental substance belongs to the opposite element, and vice versa. The fiery substance is determined precisely by the fundamental seed of the spirit.

As regards the passion for teaching, it is most characteristic of beginners. I myself remember that in the beginning I longed to share the joy which lived in my heart! But then, experience taught me how carefully one should spread the seeds of the Teaching.

6
5 March 1935

It is splendid that you accept all those practically unavoidable burdens of earthly life so cheerfully. Regarding your fiery congestions, it is rather difficult for me to diagnose the real reason, not knowing the condition of your organism. In certain occult manifestations the nerves are especially discordant with the blood. The Advice is given: "During such discordance of the nerves with the bloodstream, one should maintain a special calmness and not overburden the stomach, as these congestions may be so strong and painful that they may even cause fainting." Indeed, when the higher centers begin to work, a reverse of polarity often occurs and is frequently revealed in such fiery manifestations. But one should not direct this wave downwards toward the lower centers. Try to preserve serenity, and particularly avoid any kind of irritability. Valerian is excellent, and in some cases one should take it twice or thrice daily, but of course not so strong.

In the ancient Eastern pharmacopoeia musk was regarded as the remedy for restoring the balance, but obviously a great deal depends on the dose. Various organisms react to it differently. Many people simply cannot take musk, as even with a very small dose blood congestion and the pulse are increased. Therefore, in your case, I would rather advise taking five or six drops of tincture of strophanthus three days in succession, once a day, and to repeat this fortnightly.

* * *

The equilateral triangle with the apex uppermost is one of the signs of the White Brotherhood, and most likely you have seen it as an affirmation that your prayer has been heard. Each sincere prayer is accepted, but the answer does not necessarily come immediately. Sometimes it is delayed because of certain cosmic reasons.

* * *

You would like to know how to liberate a certain girl from mediumship. It is extremely difficult, as mediumship results from a certain structure of the organism that enables the etheric double (the *lower* astral body) to effuse most easily and without the least control of the will. Most of the phenomena at the spiritualistic seances are performed through this etheric double, which, so to say, forms a means of connection between the soul and the physical body. This can be compared with the ether waves which work between wireless telegraph stations. Of course, in all such mediumistic manifestations, the high psychic energy does not participate. *It is quite impossible to change the structure of an organism.* One can develop one's spiritual will and thus gradually conquer with it the involuntary projections of one's double. Most undesirable inhabitants of the Subtle World may take advantage of such ethereal emanations and use them for their own purposes. For the control of these involuntary projections, it is necessary primarily to direct the thoughts toward the Highest, trying to surround oneself with an atmosphere of purity in order to preclude any intrusion of dark entities. Thus a medium must develop a strong inner resistance against all dark influences, but precisely this is most difficult for him or her. As it is said in the Teaching, "a medium is but the inn for disembodied liars." Therefore, all you can do is to advise this girl to purify her consciousness and to strive firmly and consciously toward the Highest—there is no other way. However, much depends upon the environment. If the family is sufficiently intelligent, it may be possible to influence them and to make them realize the condition of the girl; this would help a great deal.

And now, regarding the young man who, after some mechanical exercises, began to feel the movement of his centers. There is no doubt that he might have felt them, as mechanical exercises stimulate particularly those nerve plexuses that are easily accessible. Of course, such irritation can cause the most unexpected results; first of all, the loss of nervous balance which may even lead to insanity. Moreover, if there is some predisposition to a particular disease, the predisposition may become even stronger. Thus, in case of weak lungs, often consumption results; in cases of pronounced sexuality, sexual perversion may occur, etc. But I quoted to you some time ago extracts from H. P. Blavatsky's writings on the consequences of such exercises.

In spiritual development, the opening of the centers comes quite normally. The opening and acting of these centers should first be manifested in their psychic or spiritual aspects. With a constant inner striving toward the Highest, and a broadening of the consciousness, the acceleration of the opening of the centers is quite possible. It comes either with the help and guidance of the Great Teacher of Light, or sometimes from contact with the purified fiery aura of a high disciple. Everything must come from higher to lower, from spiritual to physical, but not vice versa. Indeed, only the higher can raise the lower, and here the Hierarchic principle is powerfully affirmed.

I also must warn that a sensation between the eyebrows does not necessarily mean the partial opening of the third eye; it may be simply the result of muscular strain. There is a belief that the organ which corresponds to the third eye is the pineal gland. This gland, together with the pituitary, is now considered very important in the correct functioning of the organism. In ancient India they were also known as the channels for all spiritual-manasic manifestations.

In true clairvoyance, one cannot say that one sees with a particular organ, as the visions may arise above one's head, or behind one's head, or behind one's back, or from the side, or in front, or in the circle of the third eye, or in the solar plexus, etc., etc., and one can see them all equally well. Let us recall the image of the Goddess Dukkar—the circle of her aura consists of numerous eyes. Let us remember that the nerve centers have their subtle counterparts. Therefore, any abnormality and imbalance in the development of these physical conductors inevitably reacts throughout all the bodies. Thus, let us be careful not to evoke any imbalance.

* * *

I welcome sincerely your article about the Pact. The idea of the Pact is advancing. Public opinion responds strongly to this noble concept. I hope you have received the booklet on the "Proceedings of the Washington Convention." Of course, not half of the greetings that have been received were published in this book, but we may have a possibility of publishing a second volume. The complete history of the Pact will make a most instructive book, in which both sides, that of Light and that of darkness, will be distinctly revealed, and the nations will see the value of and the need for the ratification of the Pact and the acceptance of the Banner. Verily, the Banner of Peace is the great requirement of the future. It is essential as a great touchstone for the development of the consciousness of humanity.

* * *

Now, to take up your questions. Regarding the paragraph from *Heart* about "a new form of the subtle body," this deals with the new attempts to densify the subtle body almost up to the point of the physical. In the future, this will give to some high spirits the possibility of appearing among the earth dwellers at a comparatively low altitude, and for longer periods. Moreover, such bodies will be entirely visible and even possible to contact physically without the aid of a mediator.

In the Tibetan language, "Rigden" is a part of the title of the Lord of Shambhala..

"Kalachakra" (the Wheel of Time, or the Wheel of the Law) is the Teaching ascribed to the various Lords of Shambhala. Traces of this Teaching can be found in almost all the philosophical systems and teachings of India. At the present time, it is perhaps more known in Tibet. But in reality this Teaching is the Great Revelation brought to humanity at the dawn of its conscious evolution in the third race of the fourth cycle of Earth by the Lords of Fire, the Sons of Reason who were and are the Lords of Shambhala.

"Uruvela" was a sacred grove on the bank of a river where the Lord Buddha, according to legend, reached His Illumination.

Keeley was an American inventor at the end of the nineteenth century—from Philadelphia. He was interested in the problem of the molecular vibrations and the disintegration of matter. With the aid of sympathetic vibrations, he attempted to liberate energy locked within the molecules and atoms. He found success, but he was the only one who could demonstrate it. According to the explanation of H. P. Blavatsky, this was due to a personal power of his own. Many fraudulent speculators and financiers tried to make fortunes out of Keeley's discovery, and this besmirched his reputation. As a result, he was condemned by the scientific authorities and was declared a charlatan. This, however, was officially pronounced only after his death. It is of interest to note that today his writings are extremely difficult to obtain, and as usual are probably read secretly. Keeley is one more victim of human ignorance and baseness.

"Ahamkara" means here the high condition of consciousness during the opening and unification of the higher centers. This concept is the opposite of that of the lower condition of selfhood which is also sometimes called "Ahamkara."

"Preta-Loka" corresponds to the purgatory of the Catholic religion.

"Marakara" is a very gloomy locality in the lowest strata of the Subtle World inhabited by the spirits of darkness. Mara is the Prince of Darkness. He is also called the "Destroyer" and "Death" (of the soul).

"Golem" is a legend from the Middle Ages. This legend has

much in common with the famous novel *Frankenstein*. Here in brief is the story of Golem. There was a learned rabbi who was an alchemist in Germany during a time of persecution of the Jews. In his revengefulness, he wished to punish the persecutors of his people. So he decided to create artificially a giant possessing enormous strength who would be under his complete control and would do his bidding. With his unusual knowledge, he succeeded in creating such a giant and implanting in him a spark of animal life. After many magic rituals, the great mystery of the formula of life was discovered by the rabbi. It took the emblematic form of a star, and the rabbi placed this upon the chest of the giant, who immediately came to life and was dispatched by his creator to fulfil his destructive mission. Golem stalked along, heedless of obstacles, obedient to the will of his maker alone, destroying everything in his way. Many calamities and deaths were caused by Golem among the persecutors of the Jews. Finally, after destroying one whole village, he marched from there out into a field, where he saw a little girl plucking flowers. The animal life had given animal instincts to the giant and he was attracted by the child. He lifted the little one, but was hesitating to kill her. At that moment, the child noticed the star on his breast and plucked it off, and at once the vital spark left the giant. According to the legend, only a pure hand could remove the star, the symbol of the great formula of life.

* * *

Well, I think I have answered all your questions. I am very glad to hear that you love action. Indeed, this is a most valuable quality, and unfortunately one of the rarest among people, who love to talk much and do little. The majority love to dream and to lean upon others, and so very few desire to create and build. Therefore, I particularly welcome you on the path of active cooperation for the General Good.

7

7 March 1935

You accepted the Call, which fills the first book of the Teaching of Life, and you know that the call of love brings the answer of the Beloved. This answer indicates the need for austere achievement in life. In the succeeding books of the Teaching are indicated all the steps that must be gone through which lead to the Beloved.

There is so much beauty and joy in a life dedicated to cooperation with the Forces of Light for the General Good! And, first of all, this joy is a result of a great liberation from attachment to the trifles of life. It comes inevitably if our consciousness treasures unwaveringly the chosen Ideal and the heart is aflame with devotion and gratitude to the One who called. The true devotees not only cast away the burden of attachments but also learn to love all the obstacles and sufferings which they encounter on their path. Verily, these obstacles become our teachers; they initiate us into the further mysteries of the opening of the flower of spirit. Those who declare that it is possible to attain spiritual growth without suffering speak a great untruth. But these sufferings are transformed into joy, into a new spiritual ascent, provided there exists the fire of true love. Easy and speedy is the path of heart and devotion, which transforms all the thorns into a blossoming garden; but difficult, twisted and painfully long are all other ways. That is why the Call of the Great Teacher is the Call of Love.

Once chosen, this path should be continued. Be sure not to turn away, as nothing will result but destruction. There are many people who, in their desire to grasp the utmost, rush from one Teaching to another. And this pursuit of novelties becomes like a disease, a kind of mental lapse or religious intoxication. They want always to hear something new, only for a temporary nervous excitement, and as soon as one exciting influence is exhausted they are ready for a new passion. This reveals a certain mental intemperance, and here all their achievements end. But there are souls who remind us of the pearl in the Eastern tale. "This oyster lives at the bottom of the sea and comes to the surface in order to catch a raindrop at the time of the ascent of the star Svati. It floats on the surface of the sea, with its shell wide open, until it succeeds in catching a drop of rain. Then it submerges once more, and there it remains, resting on its sea bed, until out of this raindrop a beautiful pearl is formed." True disciples should be as this oyster; they should first accept the One Image, and then create out of his Teaching a beautiful pearl of spirit.

This striving to One Image is particularly essential on the

first steps. Only after the foundation is firmly laid should we try to add to our temple ornaments found in other Teachings.

Furthermore, we should not imagine that the achievements of the spirit must necessarily be performed in some special environment and not where destiny has placed us. Verily, great is the deed of applying the Teaching in everyday life, of giving joy and enlightenment to those who come near us. It is said in the Bhagavad-Gita: "Man reaches perfection by constant fulfillment of his dharma." Hence, let us temper our spirit in the tireless work of self-perfection, let us transmit our benevolent influence to those around us, and let us joyously apply our abilities wherever it is possible.

8

8 March 1935

You insist that "the Hierarchic Principle is as utopian as the Ideal Democracy." I cannot agree with you. To begin with, neither of these concepts do I consider utopian, but, of the two, "Ideal Democracy" is the more difficult to achieve. And then, if the principle of Hierarchy is the primary foundation of Creation, the Ideal Democracy is its natural crowning. How then can the effect come before the cause? You certainly will not deny that it is easier to gather a few people who are ready to be directed by the Great Hierarchy of Light than to raise the vast majority of humanity up to the level required for the Ideal Democracy.

You say, "I know that the spiritual leadership is essential, but I also know that the pyramid must be built from the bottom. ... The foundation of the pyramid should be built upon the sound principles of a renewed democracy, and people should be brought up on this. ... Only in this way will the nations that are prepared be able to react to the spiritual leadership. Only if there is a foundation can there be a summit of synthesis to the pyramid." Here again, I do not quite follow you. You seem to affirm the Hierarchic leadership, but at the same time you think that first of all the foundation of the understanding of this leadership must be laid, and that only then, after this, can the Hierarchic structure or leadership be accepted. But how can people build the foundation and continue with the construction if a certain guidance will not be given them? Each building is erected according to the plan of an architect, and the plain workers lay the stones of the foundation, without knowing the whole plan of the architect. Verily, many workers participate in this task, from the lowest to the highest, but they all fulfil the plan of the creator. Without the Hierarchic Principle the "earth dwellers," as you call them, will verily build, again and again, not a pyramid of synthesis but rather a Tower of Babel. Does not our disintegrating modern civilization exemplify with amazing clarity this eternally living symbol?

Further on, you make another stand: "In order that there could be a possibility of creating what you call a focus, through which the ray of Light can be sent, it is first advisable to coordinate the periphery." But the focus or nucleus is always built before the periphery. Each circle takes for granted its center. The periphery grows in proportion to the growth of the focus and with the intensification of the ray of Light which it receives and which pours out along its radius, but not vice versa. Likewise, let us remember that in life, in the Cosmos, nothing is isolated—everything is built *concurrently*. All the constructive elements are always present and impelling forward progress. Wherever the focus appears, there forms the periphery, although often this periphery cannot be defined exactly according to earthly measurements.

* * *

You say that ideals are not reached on our Earth. Here, too, I cannot agree with you. Certainly, the ideals are understood differently, and one may even say that there are as many ideals as there are degrees of consciousness. Yet we have the ideals which are actually embodied in the great Teachings. We have had and still have these ideals, personified in human beings. Thus, is not the existence of the great White Brotherhood on our Earth the fulfillment of the highest ideal accessible to human imagination? We are much richer than we think, and only our blindness prevents us from seeing many splendors of life.

You insist that "Russians are more capable of perceiving the synthesis than Western Europeans, as Russians do not limit themselves to their small earthly personalities." True, the potentiality of the Russian soul is great; but even so, at the present time it is still slumbering. So far, we have encountered ignorance and terrible mutual spitefulness—this first sign of a low level of consciousness, lacking the capacity for synthesis. No doubt Ivan (in hundreds of thousands) is very gifted, but if he fails to awaken his gifts in time we may as well say that there is no hope for the salvation of our race and the "ark" of the new Noah will not be utilized. True, the destruction of our planet would be an inexpressible, unparalleled disaster, but then, being so cruel and eager to exterminate one another, does humanity on the whole deserve a better destiny? What do they care if the advancement of the masses is retarded for a million centuries? The imagination of most people does not go beyond tomorrow anyway!

You protest against my affirmation of the significance of personality. But how can we ignore personality, when precisely it builds individuality? I assert that it is very useful to express one's personality as intensely as possible, but not in its negative aspects. Certainly, the true conception of personality and individuality is possible only to a matured consciousness. But in a small consciousness this conception can take the following complacent, hypocritical, conceited form: "My individuality is so great that it can hardly be expressed through my present personality, inherited from my physical forebears. Therefore, I would rather concentrate on my real individuality, regardless of my present outward semblance." We used to encounter such "profound" declarations. These ignorant and destructive notions make the conceited hypocrite gloat over his illusory former achievements. No, we must each strive to make our present personality more beautiful than the preceding one. We must think about the beauty of our present life and look upon it as the cutting of the finest diamond for the necklace of life wrought by our spirit. Hence, let everyone affirm his personality, as how else can he express his individuality?

Indeed, all the foundations of the Living Ethics must be applied in life, as otherwise life is impossible. With the new combinations of the planets, there will be a favorable radiation of spiritual rays, which will enable people to awaken their dormant energies. And verily, the feeling of reverence and highest devotion must again be sensed by humanity, if it is to continue its evolution. Likewise, cooperation between all the branches of life is becoming more and more possible. Precisely, science will stretch out a helping hand to religion, and the Indications of the

Great Teachers will assume the radiance and power of the rays from the laboratories.

* * *

Indeed, human disunion with the Cosmos, as well as all human divisions, push the consciousness into chaos. Yes, you understand quite correctly this acute moment in the planet's life. The Teaching and many signs are poured forth lavishly, exactly, in view of the threatening danger which faces humanity.

"Is it indeed possible that a tocsin is not heard in each movement of the planet? Is there not an anguished cry in every movement of all beings? Does not rebellion ring out with each movement of the spirits levelled to the ground in servility?...

"It is better if an abscess be cut open, and it should be possible afterward to close the opening. But first it is needful to draw out the pus; therefore, "We do not take halfway measures. We expect broad actions, and at the time of a tocsin it is impossible to think about a piece of yarn." [New Era Community]

Also, you have understood rightly the lines from *Infinity* about the fiery energies issuing from space which, not finding a sufficient number of conductors upon Earth, become destructive.

* * *

You claim that self-discipline is often the harder kind. But, truly speaking, every discipline finally leads to self-discipline. Discipline imposed by someone else is purely external, and of course does not lead to any spiritual attainments. Although it is usually assumed that it is easier to tread the Path with the Teacher (and, as you write, "we have before us a concrete and glorious example"), nevertheless, if we turn back to history, we face an amazing fact: the greater the Teacher, the smaller the number of disciples. Do not the facts of today strongly confirm this law of Correspondence in its inverse ratio? Does not this fact prove that it is hard to follow the Teacher? Verily, the path of discipleship is not easy! Of course, an earthly teacher, possessing the fiery and purified aura, can accelerate the advancement of a disciple by his very presence. But for this a complete harmonization of the consciousness is essential, as well as the profound devotion of the disciple to his teacher. Then, verily miracles are possible. But, as one great Teacher said, "There are too many fingers on a single hand for the counting of the number of disciples."

The aura of our Earth is very murky. If at one time it was yellow, now it is nearer to a slate color. It is dreadful to watch this atmosphere, especially the spreading of an absolute darkness. I was for several days in a state of nervous tremor after this experience. I painfully sensed the calamity which threatens our planet. But now I have overcome it, and I almost quietly accept all the signs which indicate how, under the assault of the dark forces, all the anchors of safety of the ship of humanity are one after another being destroyed.

* * *

You should not think that the problem of the twin souls was not solved by Plato. The great Plato was initiated into the mysteries of Be-ness; that is why he could not lay before unprepared minds this great knowledge, and only hints on Truth were given out. As it is said, "He who discovers a precious formula cannot cry it out of the window because the resulting harm would obliterate the best usefulness."

* * *

You write that the karma of woman is well deserved. It is hard to say that the humiliation of woman is merited by her. Of course, everything comes in cycles, and in ages when brute force dominated, woman was unable to express herself. Only when the higher psychic energy revealed itself once again in humanity did the feminine principle demand its legitimate rights. The path of woman has been full of self-sacrifice and perpetual giving. As it is said, "Those who affirm their rights do not necessarily possess those rights." The equilibrium of the elements is a foundation of Life, and the violation of this law leads to destruction. And now the Great Teachers will affirm the rights of woman. Therefore, the coming epoch will be not only an epoch of great cooperation, it will also be the epoch of Woman. Woman will have to be armed with courage, and first of all, she will have to restrain her heart from unwise giving, for there must be the Golden Balance in everything. Woman must affirm herself, and that is why the Sword of Spirit is given precisely into the hands of woman. In the East this epoch is noted as the epoch of Maitreya, the epoch of Great Compassion, and the epoch of the Mother of the World.

* * *

In conclusion, let me say that it is quite possible that the "misunderstanding between us," as you write, "comes only from a difference in terminology." Indeed, only a complete understanding gives a unification of consciousnesses. As it is said, "If we take two interlocutors equally developed, they still may not be able to understand each other if the consciousness of one of them lacks even some slight unimportant links. This small difference may reflect in a different motion in the cog-wheels of thinking and result in the movement of entirely different levers."

9

12 March 1935

I have seen in a Hindu magazine an announcement about a yoga center in Europe. Now in India also there are similar groups, on a European pattern, in which the members are openly trained in the development of lower psychism and of innate mediumistic abilities. In these magazines they widely advertise courses for the development of the dormant forces in man, with the idea of obtaining profitable jobs, promotions, etc., etc. This is terrible! In this connection, just recently I received a letter from an American (it was forwarded to me), in which he told some of his experiences. He attended one of these schools established by a Hindu in America, and he accurately followed all the required exercises until his health became entirely ruined. This is what he writes: "I did not know of any other approaches to yoga, and I had no other contacts. Thus, I did not realize the dangers to which I was actually exposed. But after two years of practising, having entirely lost my health, I was obliged to stop the whole thing. Afterwards, I tried many times to undertake some work or to take up some job, but every time I failed because of my ruined health. But at last a whole chain of inexplicable events brought me to the house of Mrs. S. She told me about Agni Yoga, and instantaneously I realized that I had at last found what I had so long been searching for." Further on, he describes his spiritual state, and he ends his letter with the following words: "After having given all my strength to the Great Service, I have found myself for the last few months entirely well, both physically and spiritually." As you can see, in this case, the dark ones had succeeded in ruining the health, but could not extinguish the fire of the spirit.

Yes, there are many such schools spread all over the world, and they are most successful as far as their finances are concerned. I myself knew of one such school in New York. The head of it was also a Hindu, and it was arranged most luxuriously, as he catered to bored millionaires of both sexes. Every student had a suite of rooms with all the necessary equipment for the exercises. They paid five hundred dollars a month and more, according to the number of rooms occupied. I knew personally a woman who had studied there, and she used to demonstrate to me her achievements; for instance, she could stand on her head! However, circus acrobats are able to perform much more difficult tricks, and yet they remain only acrobats. Of course, fundamentally, all these exercises are intended to increase the flow of blood to the brain centers and thus to stimulate them. But we know cases where people have lost their sight from attempting to stand on their heads. One should be able to regulate carefully the blood pressure when performing these mechanical exercises. All sorts of troubles occur because of these irregular pressures. In order to avoid the excessive blood pressure which follows the opening of some centers, real Yogis spend this period in the mountains. Thus, it is not hard to imagine how dangerous are all these forced exercises undertaken in big cities where the essential pure prana is so lacking.

There are a few informed persons who are aware that all the Yogas are fundamentally based on fire. Agni Yoga is a synthesis of all Yogas. In all the ancient Hindu scriptures the approaching Fiery Epoch has been predicted. It is said that Agni—the Fire that is found in varying degree at the foundation of all Yogas—will saturate the atmosphere of our planet tremendously, and all the branches of Yoga will be fused into a fiery synthesis. Verily, Agni Yoga is a fiery baptism. As usual, small knowledge tends to negate and is exceedingly dogmatic in its assertions. One should always have this in mind. In the Vedas, Agni is the God of Fire, one of the most ancient and revered of all the Gods of India. Thus, one of the sections of the most ancient Hindu Scriptures—the Puranas—is called the *Agni Purana*. Therefore, the Hindu realizes what the term "Agni" means; it resounds in his heart.

There are many who, after having read the *Raja Yoga* by

Vivekananda, consider the practising of Raja Yoga quite simple. But they forget one very essential point: Vivekananda, while discussing the aids for developing certain centers by way of breath control, *first of all insisted upon the complete purification of thought and of the heart*—in other words, upon the *regeneration of the inner man*. Only after this did he consider it possible to begin the mechanical exercises. But are there many who, while performing these exercises (which are, after all, Hatha Yoga exercises), would consider this fundamental condition laid down by Vivekananda? The practice of Raja Yoga without the inner transmutation is *quite impossible*. Moreover, the science of breath, which is practised by the *true* Raja Yogis, has little in common with the popular pranayama. The Hatha Yogis are preoccupied with the control of the vital breathing of the lungs, whereas the ancient Raja Yogis understand such breathing as *mental* breathing. Indeed, only the achievement of this mental breathing leads to the higher forms of clairvoyance and to the restoration of the functions of the third eye, as well as to other achievements of Raja Yoga.

And now, regarding thought messages. Indeed, one should send only the purest thought which comes from the heart, as otherwise the most unexpected results may take place.

It would be excellent if you could arrange special classes in your groups dedicated to the development of organized thinking. This should be based not on abstract psychology but on practical foundations, such as the cultivation of observation, attention, memory, concentration, etc. In all the ancient schools of India, the development of observation was required first of all. Only those disciples were accepted who possessed this quality in large measure. It would be most advisable to establish such tests of observation and attention. This can be practised in the most ordinary environment and with the most common objects. Any object can teach much, and a most versatile sense of observation can be developed in people. Of course, there are certain instructions on this subject in Theosophical literature. Perhaps, for a beginning, you could use Ernest Wood's little book, and then life itself will show you the best examples.

* * *

It is useful to become acquainted with the historical development of human thinking. I should also recommend the study of the pamphlet on "Symbolism," by H. P. Blavatsky. The similarity of the symbols of the various religions is most instructive.

* * *

Yes, the atmosphere around H. is extremely stagnant and heavy, for many reasons. But, as was said, "It is necessary to disclose the true face. The unveiling of faces is in itself a purification of space." It is absolutely necessary to open the abscesses and let the pus come out. "Surely, the New World has new conditions and requires new actions. It is impossible to enter the New World by old ways. Therefore, I emphasize so much the regeneration of the consciousness. Only the manifestation of a new consciousness can save the world." Indeed, this regeneration of the consciousness is the chief aim of the Teaching of Living Ethics. But let it be understood that it cannot come about by concentrating on the tip of one's nose.

I would like you always to point out the particular book and the paragraph in which you find any obscure meanings. Often a sentence may have more than one meaning, and then a student can be instructed to keep the one which is intended in that certain paragraph. For instance, "the density of the astral" may mean the density of the layers of the Subtle World near our Earth, caused by forcibly disembodied souls, or it may also mean the densification of the elements of the subtle body.

10

22 March 1935

The answer of Jesus to Salome was truly wonderful. She asked Him, "When will Thy Kingdom come?" And Jesus said, "When two will be one, and male will be female, and when there will be neither male nor female." The Teaching of Life preaches the same: the necessity of the equilibrium of the twin Elements, their equal rights and correct unions. This would be the salvation of humanity, and would bring the Kingdom of the Spirit. Verily, the Kingdom of the Spirit will not come without the true understanding of the Foundations of Be-ness.

* * *

All the Great Teachers, who have appeared in various nations and countries under different Images, are the Gates to the Spirit.

Each of them is the Alpha and Omega, and it is even so with each person who has found and affirmed the principle of Christ within himself. You remember the expression "the microcosm is as the Macrocosm." We all know that the term "Christ" was taken from the pagan dictionary and originally meant "Initiate" or "Hierophant." The Christ is our purified and highest Ego. I shall quote a verse from the Epistle to the Galatians (4:19): "My little children, of whom I travail in birth again until Christ be formed in you." From this statement it is clear that the term "Christ" in those days signified an especially high state of consciousness. An explanation of the concept "Christ" can be found also in the books of "Dobrotolubye." Also, the words, "I travail *in birth again*" affirm the law of Reincarnation.

* * *

The departing race harms the selected successors not only by hindering their birth but also by the action of the dark forces, who fight against the Forces of Light and all their undertakings in everyday life. Indeed, only an uncultured mind thinks that the Great Spirits have an easy existence; a refined consciousness knows that the opposite is true. Verily, the greater the spirit, the more difficult is his path. It is said, "A saint is threatened by demons, but the Archangel contends with Satan himself!"

* * *

But in spite of all the difficulties on the path, each victory increases the new spiritual joy. It is customary in Buddhism to judge the good quality of a person or his work by the number of his enemies and obstacles. Likewise, in the wonderful books of "Dobrotolubye" enemies are praised, as nothing can evoke our hidden abilities and qualities more than they. The enemies also have been called "Christ's cauterizers," as in ancient days many diseases were treated by cauterization.

One may be quite sure that the conventional religious instruction, without the knowledge of the One Source, without the comparative history of the religions of all nations, gives only a false concept of the spiritual evolution of humanity and develops a sense of religious intolerance. Intolerance is a terrible scourge of the human race, and it contradicts all the Covenants of the Founders of the existing religions. As to the children, Eastern philosophy may be too difficult for them, but the biographies of the Great Teachers and Saints, and their practical counsels, will always find an echo in the heart of the child, and will affirm the necessary respect for spiritual values and for the accomplishments of other nations.

* * *

It is necessary to point out the harm of the widely growing craze for sports. Undoubtedly it is accompanied by a vulgarization of tastes. Sport of course has its place, but within limits and when co-measured with beauty. But all varieties of boxing can only evoke a profound disgust.

It is most essential to develop from earliest childhood the ability to think. Precisely, as it is said, "It is necessary to establish the science of thinking in schools, not as an abstract psychology but as the practical foundation of memory, attention, concentration and observation. True, apart from these four fundamental branches of the science of thinking, many other qualities require development; for instance, accuracy, resourcefulness, quickness, synthesis, originality and others. If even a part of the effort used in schools for sports were applied to the art of thinking, the results would be astounding." But indeed, at the present time, this divine ability is a thing that frightens the mediocre. Most of all, people dread thinking. Small wonder that the leaders of the Mediaeval Church, in their cunning awareness, hastened to declare this awakening ability as a "gift of the devil." They knew their "paradise" would become poor and empty as soon as intelligence manifested itself. And who would then lay at their feet the wealth of the earth won by the sweat of the people?

Likewise, it is essential to point out one of the chief evils of modern religious instruction, i.e., the instilling into the human consciousness a sense of irresponsibility. Precisely, a degenerating church, during the centuries, instilled into the consciousness of its flock an animal sense of irresponsibility. From childhood, people are allowed to believe that they may commit most terrible crimes because the priest, by the power given to him, can free the person of sin through confession and remission. Then, after this liberation, what is there to prevent the erring one from again committing the same sins and once more receiving remission, for perhaps a yet higher fee?

Remember how it is said, "Is not the forgiving of a repentant sinner for a fee the most heinous crime? Is not the bribery of Divinity with gold worse than the first forms of fetishism? This frightful question must be discussed from every angle." Frightful indeed, as this ulcer is spread all over the world, in all religions. Recall the papal indulgences of the Middle Ages. But even now the old law is coming to life once more, and a Catholic does not have to bother to make a pilgrimage to Rome to do penance for his sins. All that is necessary is to send a certain sum for the indulgence, and the remission will permit entrance into Heaven.

I have written all this to one of my correspondents, and therefore, in order to stress fully this evil, I shall quote from that letter of mine:

"Indeed, by instilling into the minds of children the idea that the church, as a powerful intercessor, can for a tear of repentance and a fee give passage to the erring through the Gates of Paradise, the church commits the greatest sin. By removing from man the sense of responsibility, the church shuts him off from his Divine Origin. The church has discredited the great concept of Divine Justice. Losing the understanding of responsibility and justice, man will inevitably begin his involution, for those who fail to follow the cosmic laws are destined to deterioration.

"The whole Cosmos is built upon the law of responsibility, or, as it is more often called, the law of cause and effect, or the law of Karma. And it is quite impossible to ignore this law and to neglect it without bringing on, in the long run, self-destruction. All the ancient Teachings, without exception, taught this law of great responsibility, this pledge of the Divine in us. This is clearly indicated in the words of Moses, 'Eye for eye, tooth for tooth,' misinterpreted and taken as an example of the revengefulness of the Jewish people. Let us think also of the words of Christ, 'Ye have heard that it was said by them of old time, Thou shalt not kill; and whosoever shall kill shall be in danger of the judgment: But I say unto you, That whosoever is angry with his brother without a cause shall be in danger of the judgment: and whosoever shall say to his brother, Raca, shall be in danger of hellfire. ...'"

* * *

Also, the significance of labor should be emphasized even more, as it is the most important factor—the cornerstone—of our existence. It is appropriate to recall this wise interpretation of a Biblical legend:

"Let us see how distorted is the legend about the departure of Adam from Paradise. God condemned him by commanding him to work by the sweat of his brow. Strange God, who punishes by giving work! An Intelligent Being would not consider work an evil, work being the path to Light. What then, lies at the foundation of this legend? When man, with the help of woman's intuition, achieved the power of mastery over the forces of nature, the Divine Instructor gave a viaticum. The principle viaticum was concerned with the significance of intensive work. This is a blessing rather than a curse. The mention of 'sweat' is given as a symbol of tension. ..."

"It is absurd to think that perspiration is only a physical manifestation. During mental work a particular emanation valuable for the saturation of space issues forth. If bodily perspiration can fertilize the earth, then that of the spirit restores prana by being chemically transformed in the rays of the sun. Labor is the crown of Light. It is necessary that school pupils remember the significance of labor as a factor of world-creation. As a result of labor there will be steadfastness of consciousness. ..." [New Era Community]

* * *

Someone says that "after passing into the Subtle World, man does not find the hell which he so dreaded before leaving the Earth. ..." It would be necessary to add the adjective "average" before the word "man." Verily, hell does exist. In the Subtle World, not only do criminals suffer terribly, but also those who have permitted in themselves spiritual deterioration, or who are full of any kind of lust. This is taught in the scriptures of all peoples.

11

25 March 1935

I was very happy to read your letter. Most of all, I value people with self-command, people who take karma into their hands and who, through honest searching, achieve liberation from all forced dogmas and prejudices. I therefore welcome you on your chosen path of bringing light into the consciousness of people. Quite correct is your approach; one should never force but should give only what can be assimilated. All teachers, from the smallest to the greatest, had and have disciples of various degrees. In order to succeed, one first of all should consider the consciousness of listeners.

So many souls are longing to comprehend the Teaching of Christ in a new light. Therefore, if the works of Origen are not available, I suggest the remarkable books of "Dobrotolubye." Reading the vital counsels and explanations of the Gospel by the great spiritual workers of the first centuries of Christianity, one sees clearly how full of confusion is our modern mind. By the term "Christ," those great Sages meant precisely the highest divine principle in us, just what it really meant originally in the Great Mysteries of antiquity. The terms "Krestos" and "Kristos" were taken from the dictionaries of the pagan Mysteries. Krestos, or neophyte, who went through all the sufferings and passed all the tests in the last ritual of Initiation, after the anointing became Christ, "the purified." His finite personality was fused with his infinite individuality, and he then became an immortal Ego. The same conception of the word "Christ" one finds also in the Epistle to the Galatians (4:19) and in the First Epistle to the Corinthinans (3:16), as well as in The Gospel of St. John (15:4) and The Gospel of St. Luke (17:21).

The books of "Dobrotolubye" were sent to me from Athos, but I am sure that some of our "Old Believers" may have them. Some pages are very similar in spirit to the Eastern Teachings, and to the Teaching of Living Ethics. Remarkable are the statements of the great Antonius regarding the Royal Path or the Path of Balance. This Middle Way, or Golden Mean, was also advocated by all the great Teachers of humanity. How beautiful is the task or purifying the Teaching of Christ in the spirit of the earliest great Christian workers in the spiritual realm, and of expounding it in a new understanding! It would be excellent to examine the history and all the resolutions of the early Church Councils, and to learn how in the course of time the majority of the representatives of the church turned away from Truth. Yes, of course, it would be most valuable to obtain the work of Origen, *On the Elements*. There are so many commentaries on all the obscure parts of the Gospels and on the Old Testament. The task of the purification of what is accepted as Christ's Teaching, and the proper way of correlating it in spirit and unity with all the other great Teachings of the East, would be a most precious contribution to our either poor or inaccessible religious literature. The fire of the heart can be smothered by ploughing through the modern theological works. This is true not only of Christian theology, but of other religions as well. Only by returning to the original sources is one able to discover the beauty and unity of the great Revelations.

* * *

Your question regarding animals is rather complicated. Certainly, the killing of harmless animals for the sake of food, when the whole of nature provides us with plenty of other sustenance which is bloodless, cannot be excused in principle. But then, life is so complex! It is impossible to bring to Earth immediately all the conditions of the higher worlds. Our Earth and its population are not yet ready to accept higher laws and higher conditions. Therefore, one is obliged to tolerate the present customs and circumstances, striving at the same time to improve and ennoble them as much as possible. But in order not to be entirely lost in this labyrinth of most complicated and at times almost insoluble problems, we have to bear in mind the following rule, which should become our guiding principle: "From two kinds of evil, select the lesser; from two kinds of good, the greater."

Thus, our first concern should be for people, with concern for animals secondary. I quite understand your feelings, but remember that only gradually, with the broadening of the consciousness and with the refinement of the human organism, will many concepts find their true application. Also I remember that when I once reminded that plants do not react to pain as much as fishes I was told, "Not necessarily so, as the consciousness of some flowers is not below that of many fishes and insects." After this statement, we can hardly insist that a plant or vegetable does not feel any pain when cut or plucked. This is proved on the basis of modern scientific experiments with plants, conducted in the Calcutta Institute of the Hindu scientist, Jagadis Bose. These experiments have shown that the sensitiveness of the nervous system of plants is amazing.

We can do nothing but accept the great law which is laid in the foundation of the life of the entire Cosmos, the law of the Great Sacrifice. Indeed, everything in Nature lives at the expense of something else. But with the growth of the consciousness, this sacrifice becomes subtler and loftier, at the same time remaining a sacrifice. And only in the highest worlds is this giving and renouncing transformed into a source of highest joy. Do not the Greatest Spirits sacrifice their forces in sending forth their spiritual emanations, which sustain us in the truest sense of this word? Do They not sacrifice their well-deserved joy of permanent, immutable creation in the spheres that are rightfully theirs, and remain instead in the earthly spheres for the sake of directing the evolution of humanity? At its present stage, humanity is a dreadful vampire, draining and robbing the forces of the Great Spirits who are on eternal watch, as well as the energies of everyone who is a trifle higher in spiritual development than the majority. Often this causes complete exhaustion, and sometimes even premature death. But without the flow of this spiritual power, which is sent by the Highest Spirits, humanity would have been lost long ago. Therefore, first of all one must think about human beings and help them *not to exhaust and not to kill each other.* By *improving* people, we shall improve the destiny of animals.

Hence, let us love and be compassionate to animals, but let us not make idols of them, and let us not place them above man. Let us accept the law of the Eternal Sacrifice, this eternal churning and whirling of exchanging energies which, in the Furnace of Cosmos, transmutes everything in its eternal striving toward perfection.

* * *

You may point out to the true seekers that the Stronghold of the Great Knowledge has existed since the remotest days and guards tirelessly the evolution of humanity, observing and directing the current of the world's events into a salutary channel. All the Great Teachers are connected with this Abode. All of Them are its members. Manifold are the activities of this Stronghold of Knowledge and Light. The history of all times and peoples has witnessed this Help, which was never promulgated but which for each country is always given at the turning point in its history. The acceptance or the refusal was invariably followed by either the flowering or the downfall of the country.

This Help, in the form of warnings or advice or even complete Teachings, was manifested under the most unexpected and diverse aspects. Such warnings mark history with a red letter. With a few exceptions, all such warnings remained unaccepted. Thus, let us recall the Swedish King Charles XII, who received a strong warning not to start war with Russia. But he did, and that ended for long the development of his country. The publishing of the diary of the Countess d'Ademar, a lady-in-waiting to the unfortunate Marie Antoinette, revealed the fact that many warnings had been given to the Queen. The warnings were transmitted either by letter or through personal meetings arranged by this same countess. The message always emphasized that the country, the royal family and many friends were in danger. And every one of these warnings came from Count Saint-Germain, an envoy of the Himalayan Brotherhood. But all his salutary admonitions and advices were considered insulting and fraudulent. Saint-Germain was persecuted, and more than once was in danger of the Bastille. The tragic consequences of these rejections are quite well known.

We may also recall Napoleon, who, in the first years of his glory, loved to speak of his Guiding Star. But his mind became clouded by too much success, and in his pride he did not accept the whole Advice and violated one primary condition by invading Russia. The collapse of his armies and his sad end are also well known.

We also know that Washington was advised by a mysterious professor, whose counsel he applied in life with historic success. At the time of America's Declaration of Independence, when preparing to separate from England, a remarkable incident took place. During the proceedings at this historic convention there came a moment of hesitation and uncertainty. Suddenly, a tall stranger stepped out from amid the Assembly and delivered a fiery speech, which he ended with the words "Let America be free!" The enthusiasm of the Assembly was kindled, and the Declaration of Independence was signed. But when the delegates sought to greet the person who had helped them to make the great decision, the stranger had disappeared. Thus, through the whole of history is seen the Helping Hand of the Great Community of Light. In the twelfth and thirteenth centuries the Western Christian Church was aware of the existence of a mysterious Spiritual Abode in the heart of Asia headed by Prester John, as this great Spirit called himself. This Prester

John from time to time sent to the Popes and other heads of the Western Church admonishing and warning notes. We know as a historical fact that one of the Popes sent an embassy to Prester John in Central Asia. One can well imagine the purpose of such an embassy! And, of course, after diverse misfortunes and vicissitudes, this embassy returned, unable to find the Great Abode.

Yes, history knows a number of outstanding persons whose destiny it was to play an important role in the advancement of human evolution, who had previously visited this Stronghold of Great Knowledge. Thus, Paracelsus spent a certain period of time in one of the Ashrams of the Trans-Himalayan Stronghold, obtaining great knowledge. Later, Paracelsus wrote many volumes, but often he had to use the most obscure language in order to escape the persecution which in those times was powerfully directed against any illumined bearer of knowledge. Dreadful are the crimes of ignorance against knowledge! Dark the pages of true history! Let us also not forget Cagliostro, who escaped execution only through the intercession of a mysterious stranger. When the latter appeared before the Pope at Rome the execution was stopped, and later Cagliostro disappeared from his prison. Let us also not forget our own H. P. Blavatsky, who was so slandered. She spent three years in one of the Ashrams of Tibet, and then returned to the world with great knowledge and resplendent evidence regarding the Mahatmas. Had there not been so much malice and envy around her, she would have written two more volumes of *The Secret Doctrine*, in which she would also have included an account of the lives of the Great Teachers. But people preferred to kill her, and her work remained unfinished. Thus history repeats itself, and that is how the karma of humanity is built. And so, do work on the path you have chosen, and the blessing of the Hierarchy of Light will be with you. But please take this advice—continue as wisely as you have started.

12

12 April 1935

In answer to your letter, I can only repeat my affirmation which still stands in its original strength and truth: the Great Advent cannot be manifested in an ordinary way, and it cannot take place in the physical body. One should understand that the Great Lords take on or maintain this or that Image, according to the needs of the world. Why is it so difficult to imagine that a Great Individuality does not require a physical body to manifest very close to us? Moreover, the facts of the past, with examples in modern times, show how strangely the appearance of Great Spirits is taken by ignorant humans. At best they have been given the epithet of charlatan or spy, or both. Generally, people attribute their own vices to others. It would be most edifying to read the historical facts of the life of Count Saint-Germain, the envoy of the White Brotherhood. But even if Christ Himself appeared now among us, would He be able to escape imprisonment, or even execution? Please reread Dostoyevsky's "The Grand Inquisitor." One must realize that the Greatest Individuality cannot be manifested now, in the midst of chaotic thinking and the vibrations of depraved crowds. The Great Lords apply in everything the great *Law of Goal-fitness.* Please realize that in view of the level of contemporary humanity, the Advent in a physical form is entirely impossible and would be only disastrous for the whole of evolution. The Great Individuality—invisibly visible—will rule, equipped with the Rays of the powerful but invisible *Laboratory.*

It was equally strange to read in your letter that "if the Lord Maitreya should become a Buddha, He most probably will manifest Himself in a physical body." That Individuality which, in the Eastern conception, took on the Image of Maitreya, became a Buddha long ago. Therefore, the reason brought by you for his physical incarnation also falls away. I could again confirm all the prophecies mentioned in the book, *Shambhala.* Of course, the year 1936 was indicated as a year of great foundations and great changes. But the reign of the Lord of Shambhala does not imply that He will come and take part physically in the last battle; this is the mistake that the most ignorant of Buddhists make. The Lord of Shambhala, according to the most ancient chronicles, will fight the Prince of Darkness himself. This battle, first of all, takes place in the subtle spheres; whereas, here the Lord of Shambhala acts through his earthly warriors. As for Himself, He can be seen only in the most exceptional cases, and certainly would never appear in a crowd or among the curious. As for his manifesting in a Fiery Image, this would be disastrous for all and everything, as his aura is charged with energies of tremendous power. In the Gospel of St. Matthew (24:27-39) the Advent and the Judgment Day awaiting our planet are described fairly accurately. However, you will have plenty of time to grow old before this event, but partial catastrophes may take place sooner.

I would not advise you to start with Volume III when you begin to read *The Secret Doctrine*. Nothing but perplexity will result. The third volume was put together after the death of H. P. Blavatsky, and there are some uncertainties. The statement that the Teacher Shankaracharya used the body of the dead maharaja should be taken as an exoteric one, i. e., something based on folk stories rather than on real facts. That H. P. Blavatsky allowed her body to be used as a vehicle by some Teachers is described in *Old Diary Leaves*, by H. S. Olcott. But a real disciple knows well how such phenomena should be understood when it concerns the Great Teachers. Indeed, this phenomenon has nothing to do with either the possession or obsession of the body. The Great Teachers strongly disapprove of any such violations or similar phenomena. Likewise, there is much misunderstanding around the concept of the Avatars.

* * *

And now, in regard to one's incarnations, a premature knowledge is extremely harmful for the growing spirit. That is why Nature, which acts always according to the law of goal-fitness, wisely conceals it. Often, an untimely knowledge of one's previous incarnations can stop further ascent, as the spirit may either fall into the abyss of despair (upon discovering some evil of the past) or into self-conceit, one of the most serious impediments on the path of discipleship. Therefore, one should really bless this wise veiling of the past. Moreover, in due time and with gradual advancement the spirit itself will be able to remove this veil and see and understand the significance of its previous incarnations. Often, one encounters dishonest or conceited people who assign great incarnations to themselves. That explains why there are so many Julius Caesars, Tamerlanes, Aspasias, Semiramises, Cleopatras, etc., simultaneously visiting our Earth.

* * *

And now, regarding the chakras. As you know, there are forty-nine chakras, or centers, altogether. In *Agni Yoga* twenty-one are mentioned. The opening and transmuting of these twenty-one centers causes a kindling of the rest, as many centers have double branches. For a high spiritual development, not only the opening of the centers is essential but their transmutation also, as the mere opening of one or two centers leads to nothing more than a low psychism and to many dangers. In general, without the help of the Teacher the correct opening of the centers is quite impossible. Of course, I mean the Highest Teacher, as only such a Teacher is able to know the true condition of the organism in all its envelopes. Only He can regulate the blood pressure, which becomes so dangerous during the opening of the centers, to say nothing of their fiery transmutation. Therefore, in the books of the Teaching there is indicated a long stage of preparation of the organism first of all, precisely a physical and spiritual prophylaxis. Absolutely essential is the purification of the thoughts and heart. Then comes the broadening of the consciousness, refinement of all the senses and cultivation of the heart, which is the organ of synthesis. It can give us spiritual development, and thus not only can it cause the opening of the centers but it possibly can attract the attention of the Great Teacher, who would then watch us. Eventually, if our spiritual quality would permit this dangerous test, He may even permit the next step—the fiery transmutation of the centers. Without a purified spirituality, we can go through all the known exercises for the stimulation of the nerve centers but, at best, achieve a pitiful psychism or develop mediumship (if the potentiality exists)—and then we can easily become a victim of any obsessor. You are interested to know where the chakras are located. It is customary to mention as the seven main chakras:

1. Maludhara-Kundalini, located at the bottom of the spine.
2. Svadhisthana-chakra, in the abdomen between the base of the spine and the navel;
3. Manipura-chakra, or the solar plexus;
4. Anahata-chakra, or the Chalice;
5. Vishuddha-chakra, or the center of the throat;
6. Ajna-chakra, or the Third Eye;
7. Brahmarandra-chakra, or the Bell, on the top of the head.

But, of course, the brain alone has more centers than this. The centers in the shoulders, cheeks, lungs, wrists, kidneys, etc. are seldom mentioned. Even in Hindu literature there are disagreements regarding the location of the third eye. Some associate it with the pituitary gland; others with the solar plexus, etc. Upon personal experience, I may say that when one reaches the state of real clairvoyance, one sees most of all through the center of the Bell. It is possible to see with the center of the solar plexus, and we can really say that each center can see. We can even see the inside of our own organism. All this is possible with a sufficient accumulation of spirituality, together with the required conditions of prana and altitude.

In the ancient pictures of the Mother of the World (in the Tibetan language, Dukkar the Many-Eyed), her aura consists of eyes. Each ray terminates with an eye. Thus, the ancients knew much that is concealed from us.

Likewise, among Great Teachers, the manifestation of the Eye of Dangma is especially valued. This is not clairvoyance, as generally understood, but the straight-knowledge accumulated in the Chalice during thousands of lives and self-sacrificing experiences. The goal of this accumulation is to achieve a great destiny and become a full Arhat, or Man-God.

* * *

What is Aryavarta? It is the northern part of India, the valleys in the Himalayas where the emigrants of Central Asia established their homes after the disaster of Atlantis. Translated, it means "The Country of the Aryans." Thus, our Ashram is located in the most ancient and sacred mountain valley of Aryavarta.

* * *

It would be must useful for you to write down, from the books of the Teaching, the qualities essential for discipleship. You will need them.

Also, I may add that if it is said in the Teaching that the dark forces are by their very nature unable to practise unity, in the same Teaching it is mentioned that the dark ones hearken to their Hierarchy much more than do the so-called "fireflies." No doubt it is so now, as the dark ones are acting under the impulse of fear. They know that darkness is their only salvation. Thus, although by nature one may be far from unity, fear is a great unifier. The panic which compels people to rush in one direction is a well-known fact. "The dark ones do not slumber. They maintain a far stronger contact with their Hierarchy than the so-called warriors of Light. The dark ones know that their only salvation lies within darkness, but the fireflies flit about a great deal, argue much and love their Hierarchy but little.

"It is necessary to know and to understand the Teaching in its all-embracingness. It is necessary to learn to *perceive* the opposites, as otherwise no progress is possible."

* * *

I have already expressed my opinion regarding the written article you have mentioned. However, we do not intend to force anyone's ideas. We give, we direct—that is all. Everyone absorbs as much as he wants and can.

The Fiery World is one of the highest gradations of the worlds, or spheres, in the chain of our planet.

Certainly, the Monad corresponds to the idea of spirit. But when it is spoken of as spirituality and the spirit in life, in manifestation, it is always meant as the highest Ego. The Monad, in reality, consists of the sixth principle and of the universal seventh and is not a conscious entity on the planes of manifestation. In order that we reach a conscious manifestation on all planes or in other words, that we reach the real immortality (i.e., become an Arhat, Buddha or Dhyan Chohan), we must unite the three principles, fourth, fifth and seventh, while here on Earth, and fuse them in the sixth principle. The seventh principle is just an eternal vital force, which is spread through the whole of Cosmos. Also, do not forget that each principle has its own highest and lowest manifestations or qualities. Thus, the subtle body, which clothes the high spirit, corresponds to the highest feelings. That is, all the passions and desires are transmuted by pure fire into the subtlest feelings and perceptions. Thus, there are many degrees of subtle and mental bodies.

* * *

I was glad to know that you are not alone; that you have found a co-worker who, in addition, is connected with art. Give him my greetings. Certainly you may allow him to copy from my letters all that concerns discipleship.

* * *

Yes, I should not forget to advise you not to be against the Theosophists. Indeed, in their consciousness they are far above many, many people. Often, just from their ranks come the followers of Agni Yoga. Therefore, we should not really object, but should try to find something good everywhere. But the obviously harmful should be noted and stopped. We did not meet many Russian Theosophists, nor did we hear much of them. But I must say that an openly hostile attitude was exceptional. Likewise, one should not condemn all the works written by the followers of H. P. Blavatsky. Amongst those writings, there are good and valuable pages. Life is so complex; therefore, be cautious in your criticism.

Your last letter I shall have to answer somewhat later, as there are certain points that need especially clear-cut answers, which might take more time than I have at present. Neither have I the time to attend to your translation. I shall have to postpone it. I shall be very happy if you are able to apply the Teaching in everyday life. Indeed, I advise you to think more about spiritual perfecting than about cosmogony. Without the purification of the heart and the broadening of consciousness by the methods of Living Ethics, no true knowledge can be obtained. Thus, the elimination of one of your undesirable habits will bring you more benefit than learning by heart all the existing systems of cosmogony. Indeed, true understanding comes to us through closeness to the Hierarch and the unification of our consciousness with the consciousness of the Hierarch. But such unification may take place only when our inner essence is purified to such an extent that it is able to perceive and respond to the vibrations sent by the Great Teacher. I shall never tire of repeating about applying the Teaching in daily life, and once more I suggest that you attend to the work of self-perfection. As it is said in *Agni Yoga*, determine your three worst vices and try to rid yourself of them. A tremendous victory will be yours.

Do not allow yourself to become submerged in illusions. Every disciple, first of all, should rid himself of all sorts of illusions, especially those created by his own will. Illusion is our destroyer. Illusion or Maya is sometimes understood in Hindu Literature as the equivalent of Mara; and Mara means darkness. Therefore fight vain illusions with all your might.

And so—strive, perfect yourself, and rejoice!

13

18 April 1935

I want to touch on an extremely delicate and complicated matter: the listening to so-called mutual condemnations or offenses. In principle, of course, any kind of slander should be disapproved; but a teacher must know all the peculiarities of the thinking of his pupils. Often by allowing a disciple, or a member of a group, to express the accumulated bitterness of feelings, we help him to discharge harmful energy. There is nothing more dangerous than a hidden offense or anger. It is said: "Listen and do not condemn. Often, exactly this discharging of poison liberates a person for a new path. The Teacher renders help not by negation but by attraction." Thus, by careful touches it is possible to bring order into unbalanced thinking. The desirable course is not to encourage condemnations but to clear up unfounded offenses, suspicions and slander. The task or, as I like to call it, the art of creating the proper relations between people is one of the greatest of all arts. There is no more noble activity than peace-making; but it is also a most burdensome and difficult one.

My life was such that from childhood I was surrounded by people who brought their troubles to me, and almost always I was able to solve the real as well as the imaginary offenses. I always tried to remember everything or anything good that the accuser had ever spoken about the accused. And this simple method almost always brought the best results. People very often utter the most terrible things without even realizing what they have actually said, besides immediately forgetting their words! By listening patiently to these grievances, we can explain many things and help people to acquire a new understanding. Gossip for gossip's sake amongst the co-workers is an awful thing. But a teacher should be able to discriminate between mean, ignorant, idle talk and that which is more serious and requires his kindly, heartfelt interference. After all, confessions arise from the necessity of the soul to rid itself of all the accumulated energies that hinder progress. Better to confess to a teacher than to strangers. From experience I know how terribly difficult it is to guide people, and what diverse methods one has to apply to keep in accord with the consciousness and character of each individual. But in most cases, friendliness and warmth of the heart bring the best results. Thus, do not be afraid to listen. This will not be an encouragement of gossip and slander but, rather, a psychological operation on those who trust you, or a mental prophylaxis for them. In many cases you will find the needed explanation and give a warm, encouraging word; and in other cases you will find the words of severity that are necessary...

* * *

Asceticism, or rather abstinence, which is sometimes required by the Teachings, came about as a protest against a frightful looseness of morals, which became characteristic of humanity. Moreover, there is no doubt that those who dedicate themselves to practical occultism must practise abstinence, as all energies have to be preserved for the development of special abilities. But one can also contribute to the Great Service without being an ascetic. Many think that for spiritual growth a monastic celibate life is absolutely essential, and is required for the approach to the Teacher. However, that is not quite so. By purity of life, there is understood primarily purity of thoughts, intentions, fearlessness, steadfastness, independent activity, etc. As for the needs and functions of the body, *they should not be considered impure, for they are natural,* and only excesses are harmful, destructive, and therefore vicious.

It is a great happiness, a great privilege to have the confidence of the Teacher; and if Indications coming from Him require for their fulfillment that the disciple pass through the most poisonous spheres of life, upon completion of this the disciple will find himself on the height of achievement (provided his whole being strives toward the best fulfillment of the given task). Whereas, the overrighteous ascetic may torture his body, but if his heart remains silent he will live in a spiritual desert from which there is no outlet to the radiant Stronghold of Life Eternal. Precisely, we should not run from life; rather, we should transform all our emotions into the highest beauty. Wonderful are the feelings of love and friendship toward one's family and all near ones; indeed they teach us the most beautiful and the highest. They are the necessary steps that lead us toward Cosmic Love, and everyone who realizes his great destiny may approach this Love. I shall quote a few lines from the Teaching, which indicate how distorted are many sacred concepts:

"The World is molded in beautiful Principles. The expression about the renunciation of the World is incorrect. One cannot renounce the heavenly beauty. The whole World has been given to man. Therefore it would be far truer to speak about the discovery of the meaning of things. When the manifestation of renunciation arises, it concerns the most perverted concepts, the most harmful actions, but it is inadmissible to misuse a beautiful concept, the World, to describe a generalization of these abominations of ignorance! Worldly matters do not have to be unworthy and shameful. Great consciousnesses have taken great pains over the World. It is unfitting to attribute to them the distortions of ignorance! In studying the foundations of the Fiery World, it is first of all necessary to have an agreement over the understanding of many concepts. Is it at all possible to call gluttony, or depravity, or theft, or betrayal, *worldly* matters? They are even beneath the actions of animals. Animals know the measure of need, but if man has forgotten the measure of justice, it is only because he has abandoned the World and has fallen into darkness. Whoever does not reflect more worthily about the World, is not able to distinguish right from wrong. How could he comprehend the Blessed Fire? He would shudder at the very thought of the Fiery World. Let us advise friends to gradually differentiate the World from chaos. I advise friends to begin discourses about the fiery element as the subject of *forthcoming* revelations." [Fiery World II]

14

20 April 1935

It is the separation of God from Manifested Nature that causes all the mistakes and terrible contradictions. So very few ponder upon the Immanence of God and realize that this first of all implies that man is empowered by God.

Then why should you be so sure that "it is impossible to lose qualities that have been acquired and developed"? Indeed, the Cosmos embraces both evolution and involution; and if something that is manifested in the Cosmos can again deteriorate into chaos, even so this can happen within man, the microcosm. This occurs if the best feelings of man are transformed into ruinous energies by being mixed with and overwhelmed by the lowest manifestations of egotism. The greatest and most tragic example is the fall of the Prince of this World. Such falls are possible even on the high degree attained by this Spirit.

One must seriously think over the concept of the *Absolute* and its synonyms, Infinity, Absolute Reason or Wisdom, Absolute Consciousness and Absolute Be-ness, and then ask oneself whether it is possible to reach them. When a fusion with the Cosmos is spoken of, this must be understood in its complete *relativeness*; otherwise it will contradict Infinity. The spark of Divinity, or God, in us can be developed by the striving of the heart that it may fuse with the highest fire of space. Then it can reveal by its Light all the accumulated spiritual treasures in us, these very high energies which manifest as majestic *Straight-Knowledge*. But the degree of this illumination will correspond completely with the accumulations of the Chalice of the individual. Therefore, with every new improvement, with each higher evolution of humanity, with each succeeding cycle of our planet, these illuminations will be higher and more beautiful, and so on into Infinity.

It is wrong to regard the primary Matter as without spirit. Primary Matter is the first stage of the manifestation of Spirit, consequently it is the highest one. Spirit without matter is naught. By "matter deprived of spirit" we mean the condition of matter on the lowest planes, when the highest energies have left it and it maintains only the animal life. Precisely, when matter becomes waste it is fit only for cosmic reworking.

Likewise, it is wrong to call the condition of Pralaya "death," as in the Cosmos there is no such purely human concept as death. There is only an infinite change of forms. Even so, Matter in the times of the Great Pralaya remains in its highest condition, and therefore is not deprived of spirit; for the Great Breath does not stop even during the Maha-Pralaya. The small Pralaya leaves all the worlds in status quo.

No doubt there are many imperfections in the manifested Cosmos. Otherwise, there would have been no manifestations, as the life of the Cosmos is in eternal movement out of which flows the whole evolution, the whole process of perfection. Although it is quite true that many calamities in the long run prove to be not disastrous but rather beneficial, nevertheless, one must understand that all these disasters correspond with the condition of human consciousness. Therefore, when the consciousness of humanity improves, then not only will the everyday disasters change their character, but the cosmic cataclysms will also change their aspect of terror. For the consciousness of man will be better adjusted to withstand both. Indeed the great law of Goal-fitness rules the Cosmos.

And only man himself, by degrading and betraying the divine gift of free will, constantly violates this law and thus involves himself and his planet in dreadful disasters. Great is man's influence over all cosmic conditions and vice versa. Indeed, it would be wise to study most attentively and urgently this great mutual influence of cosmic and human forces. The whole life of man would become so much broader, so much easier and more beautiful!

And now, I will only add that the Teaching is accessible to everyone who has sufficient spirituality and the needed qualities—qualities essential for those who wish to approach the Great Teachers. But without the basic qualities mentioned in the Teaching no one can hope to be accepted as a disciple, even if he possesses *great* intellectual abilities. Indeed, the Teaching is *accessible*, for in all times that part of Truth which humanity could assimilate was always given to the world. But it is quite impossible to force the truth upon anyone; each one must find it for himself. All that can be done is to point out the direction.

* * *

As for the experiences in levitation, materialization, projection of the astral, etc., all this has been demonstrated many times in psychical research institutes, and it has nothing in common with spiritual achievements and the approach to the Teacher. On the contrary, quite often it is only an obstacle on the path of ascent. All the Great Teachers are very much against such phenomena and, with rare exceptions, They do not accept as disciples people who are mediumistically inclined. Of course, the experiments with the high fiery energies are something entirely different, and they are beyond the capacity of a medium.

Likewise, there is much misunderstanding regarding paragraph 185. And often such misunderstanding is based on something more serious than simple-mindedness. Fundamentally, it is the unrealized revolt of selfhood against the authority of Hierarchy. This paragraph indicates clearly the necessity of choosing an earthly teacher who could eventually become a link with the Higher Teacher. Surely, the Teachers are unable to direct everyone who approaches Them. They are occupied with cosmic tasks, and are now engaged in a terrific battle with the dark forces, who are trying to destroy our planet. Therefore, They give the Teaching through a main channel, and then watch the numerous group movements around the Teaching. However, They can direct individuals only if the latter can meet certain requirements. Many of those who approach the Teaching are in such elementary stages, and their consciousness so infected by prejudices and subconscious preconceptions, that it is essential for them first to have an earthly teacher. This teacher can purify their thinking and prepare their consciousness for that further degree which can help them to assimilate the approach to the Great Teacher. Indeed, it is most rare to hear the voice of the Great Teacher. Great spiritual accumulations are necessary for this! And how often it happens in their self-deceit many people who have just glanced through the books of the Teaching have mistaken the voices from the Subtle World for the voice of the Teacher! Only the spiritually strong, those who possess spiritual balance and discrimination, can approach and study the Teaching of the Great Brothers of Humanity. Many delusions and all sorts of temptations from the Subtle World attack the one who is on the path. The only true measure, the only light that directs to the goal, is the pure flame of the heart. Precisely, the pure heart and the clear consciousness will reveal the right path. That is why the Teaching puts such stress on the purification of thought, the broadening of consciousness, and cultivation of the heart.

* * *

Not a single Great Teacher of Humanity has left our solar system. Moreover, They have not even left the spheres which surround our planet. On the contrary, They are now nearer to us than ever, as the fury of Armageddon requires the tension of all the Forces of the Hierarchy of Light. But even if there were no Armageddon, all these Highest Spirits would continue their perfecting on other higher spheres and planets still within the boundaries of our solar system. Earth is not the highest planet in our solar system. The High Spirits come to our planet from a higher planet for the acceleration of the evolution of our humanity. But since their planet has not as yet completed the entire cycle of its evolution, They will remain there when the cycle will be in conformity with their spiritual state.

There is so much misunderstanding and fallacy around the concept of the Great White Brotherhood. Perhaps it is to be expected, for our literature is very poor as far as this knowledge is concerned, and often is distorted by hands that are neither honest nor beautiful.

* * *

What do you mean by "the choosing of the Teacher is also meant for the local disciples, who can choose one of the Brothers"? If you have in mind the local Hindus, or those who live in India itself, they are in the same position as yourself! As for the Stronghold of the White Brotherhood, the number of disciples who live there in their physical bodies is extremely small; moreover, all of them are already Adepts. No more than one or two in a century join the White Brotherhood while still in their physical bodies. Thus, in 1924, our compatriot, H. P. Blavatsky, joined them (in a male body of Hungarian nationality). Ridiculed, slandered, persecuted, she has taken her place among the Saviors of Humanity. So history repeats itself, and thus acts cosmic justice.

* * *

Fohat is the subtlest fiery energy, and if it contacts an unprepared organism it may burn and cause torturous fiery death. I myself saw Fohat with my physical eyes, and was full of wonder at the splitting of the sun rays into millions of luminous sparks of Fohat. Afterwards I suffered a slight singeing of the centers. Likewise, I saw the crystal of Materia Lucida. All this was shown to me by the Great Teacher. I also was twice on the verge of fiery death, and was saved by the Rays of the Great Teacher. But this degree of experience is rather rare and one has to go through the preparatory degrees of fiery manifestation, otherwise an inopportune death would result. When the right moment comes for the assimilation of the higher fiery energies, the events of life are so arranged that the disciple comes to the right place where such experience can be given. If a disciple is ready, nothing can prevent him from receiving what is well deserved. As it is said in the Teaching, "each one will allot to himself his share."

Your sparks are an excellent sign, and I suggest that you take them seriously and hopefully. Note and write down under what circumstances you saw them. Besides purple, blue and silver, there can be black ones with circles of light, plain black, also yellow and red. All have their significance. Thus, we are used to taking the black ones, and the black ones with circles of light, as threatening signs, often signifying danger to health and the presence of enemies. The yellow ones warn, indicating caution. The red show tension in the atmosphere, and one may expect earthquakes and hurricanes. The rest are all good omens. The spots of various colors which you have seen signify the beginning of the opening of the centers. Of course, such colors may be attributed to a certain stage of manifestation of Materia Lucida. Likewise, seeing yourself, so to say, as divided into two images is a good omen. I shall quote a paragraph from the Teaching:

"Sometimes you see yourself in an exact replica, as if alive before you. Such a vision demonstrates that the eye is only an accommodation, and that sight is in the nerve center. Such a tension of the center can also be regarded as a fiery quality. In the Fiery World there is a vision of the spirit, which is not in need of ocular adaptions. It is easier to become possessor of the fiery eye if already in the earthly state one has been able to have flashes of such spiritual insight." [Fiery World II]

* * *

Thank you for sending me the answer regarding the discussion at the local university. The interest expressed in the problems of life is most pleasing. Yes, science, in its best representatives, approaches the ideas expressed in Eastern philosophy. Thus, I have recently read an interview with an eminent American physicist, Professor Pupin, concerning the same subjects. When asked how he pictured heaven, he answered, "It is what the scientists call the true world, whereas our earthly world is only its reflection. All scientific researches and explorations are directed toward the further unfolding of the world beyond the boundaries of the physical."

"Where do you think the abode of the Divine Intelligence exists?"

"In the soul of man. In this great world within us Divinity dwells. The soul of man is the greatest evidence of Divine creativeness. If we would realize that God spent endless ages in the creation of man, endowing him with a soul that reflects his Creator, we would find it hard to believe that a human being lives on this earth only a short period and then disappears without a trace, and that his soul dies together with his physical body—that the soul's existence was in vain."

Of course, for the East these are elementary questions and answers. However, for the broad masses of the West they are full of interest and hopes. Likewise, in America, Professor Rhine, of Duke University, has for a number of years experimented with his students on thought-transference at a distance. He has achieved significant results. It has been proven that it is possible to transfer to a human antenna in another city long quotations from poems, complicated problems, etc., which were immediately written down with the greatest precision. True, from many thousands of students the professor selected only thirty, who were the most sensitive individuals. And they, over a period of several years, unified their consciousness. Nevertheless, considering our present times, the results were quite satisfactory.

15

30 April 1935

Your letter discloses many beclouded perceptions. Naturally, this vagueness results from the fact that you have not yet assimilated the first volume of *The Secret Doctrine* but have been concentrating on the third. The latter is full of concealments. I shall try to clarify briefly some misconceptions, following so far as is possible the order of your questions and assertions.

1. The Absolute is the Parabrahman of the Hindus. Likewise, Mulaprakriti should be looked upon as the Absolute, as it is the abstract Divine Feminine Principle. In the highest concept, Spirit and Matter are one; the two principles are joined together and make the One Element. Therefore, we can treat all things from the point of view of the spirit alone or matter alone, but we must embrace all the infinitude of their manifestations or gradations. And if we can say that spirit without matter is nihil, we can also say that there is no such thing as matter but that there is energy only. Parabrahman's equivalent is Brahman, whereas Brahma is already divinity, periodically appearing and disappearing. This Brahma, as the manifested Divinity, has two aspects, masculine and feminine, the two polarities—or again it is the

eternal manifestation of the Cosmic Fundamental Thought in visible Nature.

2. Atman and Atma are also often mentioned as synonyms. Exoterically, they manifest the seventh principle, which is the eternal vital force spread throughout the whole Cosmos. But esoterically, Atma often means the World Soul.

3. The Planetary Chain consists of all those spheres of the Subtle and Fiery Worlds which surround our planet, and they correspond to the principles in the human structure or organism. Of course, Mars and Mercury are in the chain of planets which belong to our solar system, as well as many others not yet known to our astronomers. The distortion in Theosophical literature was not done on purpose, but rather it was due to ignorance and also perhaps due to the lack of a precise terminology in those days.

4. It is impossible to say that our Earth, or even the manifested world, is the *opposite of the Absolute,* as otherwise one would have to admit that something is possible *outside of the Absolute,* or that there are two Absolutes, which of course is absurd. Precisely, the Absolute embraces everything; finite and infinite; manifested and unmanifested; visible and invisible. And since it is All, it is not only the Cause but also the Effect. Beyond this all-embracing concept, the human mind is unable to reach. If we begin to limit the Absolute with our own conceptions, it will cease to be the Absolute and will become finite. Thus, the Absolute cannot be grasped. Consequently, we are able only to perceive the various aspects and manifestations of this Absolute. Being particles of the Absolute, we possess potentially all its qualities; therefore, we are able to unfold this potentiality gradually during the myriads of incarnations and millenniums that flow into Infinity.

5. It would be wrong to say that matter is passive, as matter does not exist without spirit; just as, strictly speaking, there is no such thing as a "passive element." In the manifested world, everything is passive and active *concurrently.* Do not forget the law of relativity. Also, remember that the stages or degrees of manifestation of spirit-matter are infinite! In the second volume of the Teaching, it is said that "Matter is a condition of Spirit."

Therefore, I suggest that you think over your statement and ponder deeply upon it. You say, "The Earth is only matter, a passive element in its relation to all that exists, and it is by no means a spiritual or an active element." But as we know that not a single atom in the whole of the Cosmos is without life and consciousness, i.e., spirit, then how much more filled with these must be the powerful heavenly bodies, including our own planet. But it is rather difficult for people to realize this, as they can scarcely imagine the presence of consciousness even in the forms nearer to them. Often in ancient philosophic works we find the comparison of Earth to a huge animal with its own special life, which means that it has its special consciousness or spiritual manifestation. There is no such thing as a "passive element" in the Cosmos. And then remember that *the Cosmos exists only through the interpenetration and reciprocal action of the energies of space which emanate from the countless billions of focuses or centers which fill it and are perpetually formed in it.*

6. The Monad, being a particle of the Divine Monad, or the Absolute, when surrounded by the energies peculiar to its manifestation on this or that sphere of a planet, nevertheless remains always a divine particle of the Absolute, or sublimated spirit-matter. Thus, in the manifested world, it is possible to speak only of one or the other stage of manifestation of spirit-matter. Spirit is energy, and we know that no energy is able to manifest without matter. Precisely, on all planes, in all actions and thoughts, we cannot separate ourselves from matter. We deal either with the highest or with the crudest forms of this same matter. Spirit, the subjective element or energy, dwells potentially in the depth of Cosmic Nature. Of course, differentiation causes multitudinous stages or degrees of manifested spirit-matter; that is how the concepts of relativity and counterpoise came into existence. But indeed, relativity and counterpoise are the foundations of our knowledge.

7. Now regarding your statement about "the blending with Atman in the realization of the Absolute," I will bring to your notice lines written by me on this subject to one of my correspondents:

"One must seriously think over the concept of the Absolute and its synonyms, Infinity, Absolute Reason or Wisdom, Absolute Consciousness and Absolute Be-ness, and then ask oneself whether it is possible to reach them. When a blending with the Absolute or with Cosmos is spoken of, this must be understood in its complete *relativeness*; otherwise it will contradict Infinity. The spark of Divinity, or God, in us (the Monad) can be so developed by the striving of the heart that it may fuse with the highest fire of space. Then it can reveal by its Light all the accumulated spiritual treasures in us, these very high energies which manifest as majestic *Straight-Knowledge.* But the degree of this illumination will correspond completely with the accumulations of the Chalice of the individual. Therefore, with every new improvement, with each higher evolution of humanity, with each succeeding cycle of our planet, these illuminations will be higher and more beautiful, and so on into Infinity."

8. Buddha, in literal translation, means "the Illumined." In principle, the process of perfecting is perpetual; therefore, when talking of perfection we must remember the many gradations of perfection meant for particular cycles of the planet and planets, etc. In the case of Buddha, this perfection is immeasurably high, as He, together with several other Spirits, came to Earth from the highest planet in the third race of our cycle for the acceleration of the evolution of our humanity. Therefore, He will not incarnate again on our Earth, but only in the last race of the last cycle of the highest planet of our solar system.

9. The words of Buddha that "in every bikshu there are six bikshus and one Buddha, and in the Buddha—seven Buddhas," precisely mean that all the principles, or centers, or fires, have reached in Buddha a complete fiery transmutation in their synthesized spiritual development and equilibrium—that is, of course, for a certain cycle. But, as it is said in *The Mahatma Letters,* even Buddha will have to incarnate within the boundaries of our solar system.

The Great Individuality of Buddha, His Fiery Ego clothed by Materia Lucida, is now in the spheres close to our planet. In view of the threatening period of Armageddon, a number of the Fiery Dwellers are in the spheres not far from our Earth. The approach of the fiery energies makes their presence possible. You can well understand how threatening is our time and what Forces participate in the salvation of our planet.

10. The Manas of the Buddha remains always with Him, as, let us hope, yours and mine will remain with us. There is no conscious life without the Manas. As I have already written to you, in order to become an Arhat, or Buddha, it is necessary to unite the three principles (the fourth, fifth and seventh) and fuse them in the sixth principle.

Indeed, the chapter "The Mystery of Buddha" is written obscurely and should not be taken literally. It is necessary to become thoroughly acquainted with the metaphysical concepts regarding the Avatars and the partial incarnations of the Greatest Spirits, in order that one may correctly comprehend this chapter. The matter or energy which enwraps a High Spirit is invincible; in some special cases it can, by the law of attraction, or affinity, serve as a basis for a subtle body which has to be formed for the use of this or that High Spirit. Recall the following from the second volume of the Teaching: "The matter which has garbed a lofty spirit affords the greater usefulness because nothing is wasted."

I can assure you (and my words are based on the statement of the Great Authority) that Buddha, after his incarnation as the Prince Siddhartha, has not incarnated again. Some incarnations of the Great Spirits must be understood metaphysically. For instance, it can be understood as a partial intensive, or even a constant sending of the ray of the Great Spirit to a chosen receiver. That is, a High Spirit who is karmically close to a newly incarnating bearer of a definite mission, can send to him his ray, so that this ray can accompany this soul throughout its entire life. The newborn soul assimilates this ray together with the rays of the luminaries under which it was born. The soul grows under the influence of this ray, and in the course of its spiritual development the soul assimilates this ray completely. Then occurs what we call an "incarnation of the ray," or "hiero-inspiration."

11. Sri Shankaracharya, the founder of the Vedanta philosophy, was an incarnation of the ray of one of the Great Teachers of the White Brotherhood.

And now I am sending a few more paragraphs from the still unpublished volume *Fiery World*. It is well to know them.

"Not magic but God-inspiredness was ordained in the ancient Covenants. When Higher Communion began to be interrupted, people themselves compiled magic from the earthly world, as a means of forced communion. But, as everything which is forced, magic ends up in the darkest manifestations. The very boundary line between black and white magic becomes elusive in its intricacy. Therefore, on the path to the future one should eschew all magic. It must not be forgotten that the old methods of magic were connected with other forms of life. Of course, magic is based on precise fulfillment of technical conditions, but if all the formulas of life have been altered, then too all magical effects must be correspondingly changed. This is why contemporary magic has sunk into necromancy and the other low manifestations. All those who study the mechanics of formulas fail to take into account the fact that they were written down for a completely different application. In addition, they completely forget that the higher formulas, and all the conditions, have not been written down altogether; if they have been noted at all it is in such symbols that now their meaning is quite obscured. Thus, contemporary studies of magic either amount to senseless scholastics, or else, flowing down, they lapse into the black mass. Therefore We speak much-needed words, in advising the abolition of magic. Let it be left to the dark necromancers. There is too much obsession on Earth. The sole path to the Higher Communion is through the heart. Violence must not stain this fiery path.

"Can people possibly think that the invocation of lower entities can go unpunished! And what sort of improvement of life could result from such evocations? No one can point to a benefit resulting from necromancy, nor to a heart which has been uplifted through necromancy. One must turn to the short and higher path, which will bestow health of spirit; and thence comes the bodily health. The abolition of magic will be a white stone on the path of the world.

"The expulsion of magic does not mean interruption of the manifestations of the Subtle World. On the contrary, the bond with the Higher World can be but strengthened through the abolition of all violence. Precisely, ignorant compulsion can violate the harmony of combinations. Nature, both in the small and the great, is opposed to any violence. To study and to cognize the marvelous approaches to the Subtle World and to the Fiery World will not be magic. Prayer of the heart is not magic. Aspiration of the spirit toward Light is not magic. One must guard against all forms of ignorance, for it is a source of falsehood, and falsehood is the entrance way to darkness. Be able to find in your heart the truth of turning to the one Light. Terror fills the world. Do not follow the pathway of terror. One may be fortified by examples of former times. The saints themselves were in contact with the Fiery World through the heart, the same heart which has been given to everyone. Ability to hear the voice of the heart already leads to truth.

"Hiero-inspiration descends through a single basic condition.

Neither concentration, nor command of the will, but love for Hierarchy produces direct Communion. We do not know how better or more precisely to express the guiding law than as a flow of love. Therefore, it is so opportune to put aside compulsive magic, in order to become imbued with love in one's entire being. As a result, one can easily approach the principle of Existence by a sense of beauty. Precisely, amidst the dissolution of the planet, one must turn to the most health-giving principle. And what can more strongly unify than the mantram 'I love Thee, O Lord!' In such a call it is easy to receive a ray of cognition. Observe this!" [Fiery World II]

In conclusion, I advise you to concentrate more on spiritual perfecting, rather than on such abstract concepts as the incarnation of the subtle rays of Lord Buddha, etc. Put aside the third volume of *The Secret Doctrine* and try to study thoroughly the first two; they will give you enough work for years. Do not obscure your consciousness by fragmentary, unsystematic studies! Do not rush to various sources, without studying first the foundations.

* * *

I really do not see why you should not continue your gymnastics, since you have done them before and they do not tire you. It all depends on the kind of gymnastics, and how you feel afterwards.

Continue courageously to perfect yourself, and do not become absorbed too much in cosmogony. Now is the time of the great and threatening Battle, and all the warriors of Light must stand their ground in order to repulse the assault of the dark forces against the Hierarchy of Light. On Earth, this assault is manifested in opposition to all enlightened undertakings.

All in this world is built by human hands and feet.

16

8 May 1935

I was extremely happy to learn about your independent attempts to establish a spiritual community. Indeed, only that which is *nursed by the spirit and heart* can be successfully established. So much strength is necessary for the laying of a healthy, constructive foundation for the benefit of the whole of the human family, this family which has suffered for such a long time! Verily, a colossal task, considering the fact that it will be necessary to re-educate not a nation, but *nations*!

The idea of "The Community of the Heroic Sisters" was my dream from an early age! I imagined these women bringing light and joy into the most remote corners and into the hardest conditions of the life of our country. Of course, my dreams grew together with my consciousness, and now I think of all the different aspects of life that could find their reflection in such a Community. Thus, some Sisters could devote themselves to medicine; others to agriculture; others could be teachers or lecturers in the various branches of knowledge and on social problems, expounding them in a way close to the people's understanding. The study of the arts and crafts and the teaching of them would be most important in my Community, together with an investigation into the significance of color, sound and scent, and their influence on man's general condition. The function of the Living Ethics would be to beautify the whole useful movement of these Sisters. Small groups of this Community could be widely scattered, and the Sisters could organize little tours for investigation and observation of those districts which were under their supervision. A whole army of such women workers would be necessary to supply all present needs and to satisfy the spiritual and physical hunger of the people. Schools could be established by the Central Community, as well as universities, laboratories and an institute for research in psychic energy. Furthermore, all sorts of workshops, sanatoria, cooperatives, model farms, etc., could be built up—in short, a whole city of knowledge! The Great Teacher, speaking of these Heroic Sisters, said so beautifully, "Let them endear themselves to people. Let people say, 'A dear one came to our village.'" Indeed, my Sisters would have to learn first of all to be close to the people. I know that it is not at all easy to find selfless heroines; nevertheless, I do not lose hope, as I know that even a small group devoted to this task could work miracles. Now you understand my joy when I find new souls that resound to my innermost thoughts. It seems to me that the coming epoch will attract souls full of aspiration to fulfil the beautiful, active, self-sacrificing deeds. Not long ago, I received a letter from an author. He writes, "We passed through many countries, worked in many lands, but the seed we planted did not grow and yield; no matter how much we sowed, the weeds choked everything!" Yes, we also have encountered such barrenness, but let us not be disturbed by this.

Great numbers were never a guarantee of success. Precisely, in the Teaching of Living Ethics it is constantly emphasized that a small group of people unified in consciousness and heart can perform miracles. Therefore, let us treasure our sacred thoughts in our hearts, and when the right moment comes we shall be fully armed! Already, the idea of the Community of Heroic Sisters is molded in the Subtle World, in the form of a beautiful teraph. And the co-workers of its earthly counterpart are already on this Earth. As it is indicated, we must strive to accumulate knowledge and experience, so that we can utilize them in the countries that are moving forward. Thus, if you feel strong enough to devote yourself to self-sacrificing labor, apply all the flame of your heart for the better assimilation of the foundations of the Teaching. Verily, a physician ought to be able to treat first of all the spiritual causes of diseases, as all diseases nestle in the subtle body. It is good that you are familiar with astrology; for a physician this is most important. A horoscope of a patient may give a clue to many diseases and to their treatment. And so, continue to work, having in mind a great goal.

Now I shall attend to your questions.

The Cosmic Magnet is the Cosmic Heart, or the Consciousness of the Cosmic Mind of the Hierarchy of Light. The Cosmic Magnet is the bond with the Higher Worlds in the plan of Be-ness. Our inner bond with the Heart and Consciousness of the Great Teachers of Humanity brings us into the powerful current of the Cosmic Magnet.

Straight-Knowledge is knowledge and experience accumulated in our Chalice. It is the so-called intuition, but of an extremely high quality.

Spiritual knowledge here means that there is both spirit and its manifestations. In the schools of the future, it will be essential to teach the physiology of the spirit.

Mulaprakriti is the abstract, divine, feminine principle. The feminine aspect of Parabrahman. Undifferentiated Substance. Literal translation: "The root of Nature or Matter."

Tactica Adversa is the tactical exhausting of the adverse. Precisely, when the Light Forces wish to fulfil some plan of Earth, They make allowances for all possibilities, envisioning even the worst conditions. Then every betterment of the conditions is already an unexpected plus. Thus, from the worst is derived a benefit. When such tactics are applied, the enemies often contribute to the success. Remember the praise to the enemies: "If it were not for the enemies, grateful humanity would have interred long ago the best beginnings." Indeed, are there not times when people are loathe to speak good of their friends, fearing to be accused of partiality? Verily, such abject feelings are not yet outlived by many humans. Thus, they either attack all the manifestations of Light or ignore them.

Materia Lucida is the degree of the Primary Matter on the astral plane, and it is still attainable for investigation, but of course having its own degrees or gradations. Materia Matrix is beyond the astral plane, and is an equivalent of Mulaprakriti, Akasha, Primary Substance—the subtlest, super-sensous, ethereal substance, which fills the whole of space—the Mysterium Magnum of the alchemists.

I do not know of any better remedy against astral entities than the oil of eucalyptus. Before retiring you can add a few drops to a cup of boiling water. Of course, the oil of deodar is just as good but is not commercially obtainable.

* * *

In order to receive a thought or an answer from space, it is necessary to reach a complete correspondence of vibrations—the same principle as in the radio. People catch thoughts from space much more often than they think, but these thoughts are not always lofty. Space is filled with all sorts of mental messages, and we receive exactly what is in correspondence with our own mental receiver. That is why the Teaching insists so much upon the purification of the heart and thought, so that we may resound with the thoughts from the higher world. The so-called inspirations often are from nothing else but this harmony of vibrations.

I shall be glad to render spiritual help, and shall never tire of answering questions. Was it not said that "without questions there is no teacher"? But each plan of spiritual work must be entirely individual. Therefore, I shall be better able to advise you after becoming better acquainted with you. Meanwhile, I wish to say that your striving toward spiritual community and your love of action are truly beautiful. So, nurture within yourself this striving. Make it the main task of your life. Write down from the books of the Teaching all that is said regarding heroic achievements, and follow them! Indeed, the time has come when everyone should speak of heroic deeds in everyday life. Without this understanding of heroic deeds in daily life, all our knowledge is nothing! The high knowledge is open only to the one who strives to life's achievements. No withdrawal from life, nor intensive study of the occult science, will give the highest illumination, which comes only to the one who gives his heart and soul to the service of the world. Thus, your mantram should be: "Let me achieve in active service to the world." Likewise, repeat to your pupils about heroic deeds! In our threatening times we need spiritual, self-sacrificing workers, we need enthusiasts, we need heroes!

I shall quote a few paragraphs from the second part of *Fiery World:*

"People usually have absolutely no idea how to use the given Teaching. When they hear some formula which seems familiar, they haughtily exclaim, 'Again the same thing, known to everyone!' They do not attempt to verify the extent to which this familiar formula has been realized by them. They do not stop to think that the useful Teaching is given not for the sake of novelty but for the upbuilding of a worthy life.

"The Teaching of Life is not a compilation of unheard-of utopias. Humanity is of very ancient origin; in the course of ages multifarious sparks of Wisdom have been poured upon Earth, but every cycle has its key. If someone can recognize the present key as a familiar one, then let him rejoice and be thankful for the indication which is close to him. It seems simple, but in reality it proves to be very difficult. People love to listen to news and to receive toys, but few are ready to refine their consciousness.

"It cannot be that one of the elements has not been stressed in the Teaching. Fire has been mentioned a thousand times, but now the stressing of Fire is no longer a repetition, for it is a warning about events which concern the planet's fate. Most people will not be able to say that in their hearts they have been preparing for the Fiery Baptism, although the most ancient Teachings forewarned about the inevitable epoch of Fire.

"Raj-Agni—thus was called that Fire which you call enthusiasm. Truly this is a beautiful and powerful Fire, which purifies all surrounding space. The constructive thought is nurtured upon this Fire. The thought of magnanimity grows in the silvery light of the fire of Raj-Agni. Help to the near ones flows from the same source. There is no boundary line, no limitation for the wings radiant with Raj-Agni. Do not think that this Fire can be kindled in an evil heart. One must develop in oneself the ability to call forth the source of such transport. At first one must prepare in oneself the assurance that the heart is offered to the Great Service. Then one should reflect that the glory of the works is not one's own but belongs to the Hierarchy of Light. Then it is possible to become uplifted by the infinitude of Hierarchy and affirm oneself in the heroic attainment needed for all worlds. Thus not for oneself, but in the Great Service is Raj-Agni kindled. Understand that the Fiery World cannot stand without this Fire.

"You have been writing today about physical remedies, but for crowds even barrels of the most precious substance will be useless. One may urge all physicians of the world to start upon a mission of spiritualization of the heart. Each physician has access to different homes. He sees various generations, and his words are listened to with attention. When giving physical instructions he can so easily add the most valuable advice. He has the right to be acquainted with all the details of the moral conditions in the home. He can give advice which will compel the occupants to reflect over and above the actions of the stomach. He can even command, for behind him stands the fear of death. The physician is a most sacred person in the household where there is a sick one. And since humanity has taken care to collect a sufficient quantity of diseases, the physician can give many valuable warnings. If we but had enlightened physicians! At present there are so few! The more do We esteem enlightened physicians, since of course they are always under the threat of expulsion from the medical societies. Heroism is needed wherever Truth is.

"The consciousness directed to Us is continually being refined. The process of refinement becomes a code of every day. Could it be admissible that the subtlest energy be turned into chaos? Everywhere it has been said, 'Whoever comes unto Me shall also abide in Me.' This must be understood literally. The subtlest energy cannot be turned into amorphousness; therefore I am so concerned about refinement of consciousness. Complication by grossness only demonstrates that the heart energy has not reached a level where it is no longer threatened with drowning in the waves of chaos. One must hasten with the refining process. Each ulcer begins with the smallest decomposition of tissue. A drop of resin can make healthy the ailing tissue, but for a neglected ulcer not even a pot of resin can be of help. Create a manifestation of refinement in the very midst of life. Why only in words, or in glances, when heart energy is multiplied precisely in thoughts? The collecting of the most precious is only for the purpose of returning it. Who, indeed, would not wish to give something of the best quality? Only a cheat will try to give something unfit or useless. One must keep watch over one's thoughts, in order to send those of the best quality. I am not speaking in the abstract.

"It is right that you do not forget the significance of soda. Not without reason has it been called the ash of Divine Fire. It belongs to those widely given remedies which have been sent for the usage of all humanity. One should remember about soda not only in sickness but also in health. As a bond with fiery actions, it serves as a shield against the darkness of destruction. But one should accustom the body to it gradually. Each day it should be taken with water or milk, and in taking it one should, as it were, direct it into the nerve centers. Thus can one gradually acquire immunity."

* * *

In conclusion, I wish to say that truly the women must sacredly guard the chalice entrusted to them: the moving of the consciousness and the saving of the world. The Epoch of Maitreya is the epoch of woman.

Let our every day be dedicated to the service of the Great Movement.

17

21 May 1935

There is no doubt that everyone who is able to indicate the direction inevitable for evolution becomes, by this very ability, a teacher to those whose consciousness is immature and who have not reached even a primitive understanding of social problems. But such teachers cannot be placed alongside the Teachers of the Great Himalayan Community—such comparisons are simply out of proportion. Do not forget that the Mahatmas of the Brotherhood include those Seven Greatest Spirits who, at the end of the third race, came to Earth from the higher planets for the acceleration of our evolution. Their Spiritual Strength, Their Greatness cannot be compared with that of any recognized human geniuses except those in whom They Themselves were incarnated. Therefore, the comparison which you make is simply an ignorant misjudgment, even a blasphemy. The teacher you mentioned may be a very pure and striving spirit—he might even be a candidate for discipleship of the White Brotherhood—but he certainly cannot stand equal to these Great Lords of the Planet.

And now, with reference to the book you mentioned, you can see for yourself, especially so after the issuance of your book, how little certain consciousnesses of our time differ from the consciousnesses of the times of the Inquisition. And even if the authors of such books as yours are not in danger of the stake, they are often persecuted and ostracized. Likewise, the alchemists of the Middle Ages, as you know, had to conceal their great knowledge under intricate allegories and various symbols, so that they would not have to join their ancestors too soon, but could preserve their lives for their self-sacrificing work for the good of humanity. Of course, today the much-ridiculed alchemists begin to draw serious attention, and the works of the great Paracelsus can already be found on the shelves of great scientists and physicians. Thus, the Truth always had to be given under a certain cover, and the Great Teachers often had to use a "grey cloak" in order not to blind people by their Light; so that at least people could accept Them and some fragment of the Truth prepared for them in this cycle.

Likewise, Christian Rosenkreuz, the founder of the Order of the Rosicrucians, upon his return from Asia was compelled to introduce the teaching of the East in a semi-Christian form. Otherwise, his disciples would have been persecuted by the fanatics and bigots. Today, the level of humanity is such that every great Revelation has to be protected by *eternal shields.* The vast majority of humanity remains as intolerant and cruelly fanatical as in the past. Both materialists and those who accept the Spiritual Element frown equally upon all those who do not think as they do. Until the unity of the twin Elements is realized, humanity will not be able to emerge from this impasse.

You are quite right in surmising that in the plan of evolution there are some ungrateful roles which have to be played by someone. Often these roles are performed by spirits not so utterly bad as they are usually thought to be. And these roles are distributed by the great impresario, the law of Karma. Very probably, even these concepts are not easily assimilated by the unprepared consciousnesses, who never think about the grandeur and inevitability of the law of cause and effect. If we look without prejudice for the reasons for this or that calamity, we shall come to the most amazing "revelations."

And, truly speaking, is the difference so great between those persons who for personal profit involve whole nations in disastrous wars and the kind of individual you mentioned and condemned? Do become acquainted with the true history of many, or rather *most,* wars. What overweening greed, ambition, envy and revengefulness of individuals drove the countries into these desperate, dreadful destructions! Life is so complicated that before making a final verdict we must come to know the true reasons that have caused this or that ruinous result. Of course, the trouble with humanity is that for the most part the strong characters, even when they believe in a good idea, understand this idea *one-sidedly and intolerantly.* Hence, all the destructive actions. The history of all peoples is full of bloody and revolting pages. So much blood has been spilled for every new construction, every new teaching or religion! That is why humanity urgently must learn the two great concepts—*Tolerance* and *Cooperation.* On these two foundations the New Epoch will be built.

So my words, "perhaps an ark will not be necessary," made you unhappy? I quite understand this, as I myself was very depressed at the idea that perhaps our Earth will not endure all this and there may not be enough fiery subtle energies to prevent the final explosion. However, now I have already overcome this weakness. The Great Spirits are so anxious to help humanity, and it is possible that the formation of the new rays will enable us to revive spiritually and to manifest the essential powers of the spirit, which will discharge the dangerous energies; then the inevitable catastrophe will be, as it was before, only partial. Verily, in great strain, on ceaseless watch, the Great Spirits dispel by their Rays the destructive energies. Few, very few, helpers are there on Earth for this self-sacrificing work. It is a fact that when such "Dispellers" place themselves in the localities that are in danger of earthquakes, the calamity is considerably mitigated, and sometimes entirely prevented, and similarly all sorts of epidemics are being warded off. As it is said, "The Dischargers of the spheres are most powerful Servitors of the Cosmos. Most subtle threads hold in unity these great Servants of the Cosmos. But this work also takes place only during fiery unification. Fiery equilibrium can save the planet. Only fiery might can at the last moment bestow new life." [Fiery World III]

Hence, these Servants must have centers that are fierily active. For your consolation I may tell you that all who are truly devoted to the pure Knowledge and to the General Good will depart for higher spheres. Sad will be the destiny of those who are left on the fragments of the wrecked ship or shifted to Saturn. But naturally, this destiny will be only for those who have lost every vestige of human value. Therefore, do not feel sad, but strive with all your heart to the Hierarchy of Light. The Lords of Light are verily the Keepers of Heaven and Earth. Truly, one should know about the coming partial catastrophes, which will be so much more dreadful if humanity continues to saturate space with hatred, greed, intolerance, and all sorts of divisions and negations. The decisive hour is not so far off, but still there is time for many children to grow old. Please speak in accordance with the consciousness of those who approach you. Do not overburden those who are not ready; *great may be the resultant harm.*

The Great Teachers have had to use and are using lesser Images for approaching people so that the hardened hearts could hear them. Greatness is very difficult to accept, or rather, to forgive!

So please do not be sad. And meanwhile let us intensify all our energies and forces in order to build not a new ark but a special aeroplane, which will be more timely and more useful for the Astral World, as there are many who will have to be saved.

18

31 May 1935

1. It would be more correct to say that the cycle of Kali Yuga is approaching its end on our planet and that we are now going through a transitory stage. Satya Yuga must begin with the affir-

mation of the sixth race, individual groups of which are already appearing on Earth. But the true era of Satya Yuga on our planet can begin only after the planet is purified of its unfit material and new continents are formed. As usual, the presages of the epoch appear much earlier, but the continents that are predestined to accept the majority of the sixth race can manifest many signs of the coming New Epoch.

2. I would not assert that "woman was burned in the fires of the Inquisition for the crimes she committed because of her weak and enslaved position.". Such an assertion would be one-sided and unjust. The real criminals were seldom executed by the fires of the Inquisition. The victims were the inquisitors' personal enemies and harmless individuals with mediumistic and psychic proclivities, which are often more strongly expressed in women.

It is unfair to blame woman because of the humiliating position in the social order that she occupies, even among the so-called civilized nations. Those of low intellectual and spiritual development are inclined to belittle the lofty. Unbiased history proves to us that in ancient times those nations flourished which revered the feminine element. As it is said, "All those who assert these rights do not necessarily possess them." Verily, the seizure of rights through brutal force is against the Cosmic Right. Otherwise we could easily declare that the machine surpasses the subtle apparatus of man. Such thinking is rather widespread, and it is ruinous for the social and world order. In the higher worlds the Feminine Principle is greatly revered, for woman is the personification of self-sacrifice and of eternal giving on the path of difficult human evolution. "Woman went by way of achievement," it was said. Let us not forget how the Hierarchy of Light reveres the Mother of the World!

3. Wrong are the assertions found in books that all religions and teachings discuss the low level of woman. Such discussions as do appear are the distortions and additions made in later times by those holding power through avarice and ignorance. Verily, the Great Founders of religions and teachings are not to be blamed for this crying ignorance. Let us consider how many dishonest and avaricious hands have handled these teachings during thousands of years!

Buddha held woman in the greatest esteem, and stated that she could achieve, as well as man, the highest degrees of

Arhatship. Verily, the same fire of spirit, the same monad is aflame in woman as in man; the psychic apparatus of woman is more subtle than that of man. That is why in ancient Egypt the high priestesses of Isis transmitted the orders of the Goddess to the Hierophants, but never vice versa. If our Christian Church has humiliated woman to the extent that during the marriage service the minister proclaims "the wife shall obey her husband," in ancient Egypt it was entirely different because there the wife was the head of the household. Many curious things are still to be revealed. Truly, we dwell in the Maya of our ignorance. This is due not only to a meagerness of tangible proofs and facts, but to the inherited ailments of prejudice and negation. From very early childhood this malady eats into our thinking like a cancer.

True history, and especially true knowledge, will reveal many astonishing pages and real facts. Let us recollect these great words: "It could be said that not a single Covenant has reached us without distortion. Endless are the alterations and distortions which have appeared in the translations of the great writers." How terribly distorted are the works of the first Fathers of Christianity. Let us take, for instance, the great Origen. Do we not have an example of such distortion in the preface to his works written by his disciple? Verily, the deeper we ponder upon the origins of all the Teachings, the more clearly is their oneness and grandeur manifested. Therefore, in our ignorance, let us not accuse the great Founders of the Teachings who assuredly knew about the great law of the Equilibrium of the Elements. In antiquity the last and highest Initiation was connected with this illumination and knowledge. The entire mystery, the whole beauty of Be-ness was revealed to the soul illumined by the highest Light. Even in distorted Hinduism there are preserved some hints of the significance of the Feminine Element. And even up to the present day, the most sacred ritual cannot be performed by a Brahmin without the participation of his wife.

Christ also asserted the equality of the Elements; but dark were the followers of his disciples, and this darkness increased, so to speak, not in arithmetic but in geometric progression.

Likewise, Zoroaster highly esteemed the Feminine Element, and in his Covenants one may find remarkable hints as to the grandeur of Cosmic Love.

4. It is said in the Teachings, "Lingam is the vessel of wisdom," meaning that its vital substance possesses important

properties. Precisely, by sparing this substance vital forces are accumulated, and thus we sustain creative power within ourselves. Therefore, complete continence is expected of everyone who studies practical occultism. Only later did this knowledge take the form of ugly phallic cults. This explains why the Arhats lead a life of complete continence.

5. One should not speak of perfection of man in the first two races, as this perfection was only potential. If in the second half of the third race the civilization of our planet was so high, this was due only to the fact that at that time the Great Elohims came to Earth. (Esoterically, among them were spirits of both sexes) They were incarnated as Divine Leaders and Rulers, and their progeny received a spark which awakened the mental abilities. In these descendants the centers began to function, whereas in the majority of humanity they were still inactive. These Elohims, who came from the higher worlds or planets, were incarnated into the then existing human forms and became the kindlers of the consciousness and mental abilities of humanity. Thus, even if spirituality was predominant in the early races, they could not be considered perfect, inasmuch as they lacked the ability to think. Thought is the crown of world-creation, as only conscious thought is able to create. Therefore, the thinking man illumined by the light of spirituality is called "the crown of creation" and "creator." Only the spirit who has gone through endless forms and existences can accumulate that experience, that foundation of feelings and imagination, without which there is neither discrimination, thought, nor creation. Thus, mind illumined by spirituality is verily a gift of God. As all the Eastern Teachings declare, "There is no God who was not man at one time," and also, "All gods must undergo human evolution."

6. Twin souls, if separated over centuries, do not recognize each other when they meet. Precisely, only those souls which have been united for thousands of years on the earthly plane by great spiritual and heartfelt feeling may reach cosmic union in the higher worlds. The unification of consciousnesses and hearts does not take place in one life, nor even in the course of several lives. Indeed, thousands of years are necessary, in order to accumulate the energies capable of uniting these inseparable bonds. The highest beauty cannot be so easily accessible!

7. Verily, all spirits in whom the spark of striving toward the Beautiful and the Highest has not been extinguished and

are and will be resurrected in forms which correspond to their spiritual condition or the accumulation in their Chalice.

* * *

Vulgarity of imagination corresponds completely with the low moral level of man. Therefore, we are particularly responsible for the special guarding of the Highest Images from all sorts of abasement, blasphemy, and sacrilegious interpretation.

It is essential to know that the Cosmic Crown is possible only in the higher worlds, where the problems of cosmic fiery creativeness have little in common with their earthly equivalent. This Crown bears no resemblance to the earthly interpretation of it. It is necessary to keep in mind that here, in the Earthly Stronghold of the Brotherhood, the Arhats remain in solitude, as the service to humanity demands. Each one of Them undertakes his specific mission and carries out most difficult tasks. The souls nearest to Them, who are karmically connected with Them, incarnate on earth during the fulfillment of a new plan of evolution; and they, while moving the human consciousness along the new evolutionary lines, preserve the bond with the Arhats and fulfil their Will. The manifoldness of the tasks requires various conditions. Therefore, some of the Arhats remain in the densified astral form, and only a small group of Them, because of special missions, preserve their physical bodies. Verily, the burden of their work for the General Good is beyond imagination! The principle of self-sacrifice in all its grandeur and beauty is completely adopted by these Servants of Truth and of the General Good. In tremendous tension, on eternal vigil, in great patience, and at the cost of terrible strain, They direct the course of the ship of humanity. They sacrifice their lives for their fellow men; They straighten the heeling of the ship and steer it along the right channel. Here is a paragraph in the Teaching of Life:

"What more nearly compares with Our Community—a choir of psalm-singers or an armed camp? Rather the second. One can imagine how it must conform to the rule of military organization and leadership. Is it possible to establish the paths of advancement of the Community without repulse and attack? Is it possible to take a fortress by assault without knowing its situation? The conditions of defense and attack must be weighed. Needed is experienced knowledge and keen vigilance. They are wrong who consider the Community a house of prayer. They are wrong who call the Community a workshop. They are wrong who regard the Community as an exclusive laboratory. The Community is a hundred-eyed guard. The Community is the hurricane of the messenger. The Community is the banner of the conqueror." [New Era Community]

I should add that the Community is the lighthouse and the sole anchor of humanity. Thus, the best people are under obligation to ease their unbearable burden. And how immense should be our gratitude to these High Spirits who for centuries have sacrificed Themselves and who continue to sacrifice their well-deserved higher happiness so that They may ease the destiny of humanity and save the planet from destruction!

* * *

Can we draw a clear-cut line between monotheism and polytheism. Can we mention even one religion which proclaims a strict monotheism? Verily the whole meaning of life is unity in multiformity. In the Christian religion there is the most obvious polytheism. The concept of God the Father and his incarnated Son, Jesus Christ, cannot be considered monotheistic. Is not the pagan Trinity laid in the foundation of the Christian religion? And what about all the Angelic Host, and the Ladder of Jacob? Verily, it can be repeated here that those who see the mote in their brother's eye do not see the beam in their own. One certainly has the right to assert that the Christian Church took the benefit of heredity from the despised pagans but distorted and diminished a great many lofty concepts.

* * *

Who can tell where woman's rights—rights given to her by Nature—begin and where they end? The same question could be asked about man's rights. Only evolution gives the answer and points out the direction. There is no indication in Nature that woman should be restricted to her hearth! Verily, she is the Mother and Custodian of the World. Hence, there is not a single domain of life where man could rule alone. *It is precisely this domination of the one Element that has created the dark epoch.* Creativeness is given equally to both Elements. In man it is more pronounced at the moment only because woman has been deprived of equal education and has not had the same possibilities for exercising her creative forces on a broad scale. Even today an ignorant belief prevails that the brain of the woman is lighter and smaller than that of the man, and that therefore woman is more stupid, etc. I remember how amazed were the scientists when, after the death of the brilliant writer, Anatole France, his brain was weighed and was found to be amazingly light—almost like a child's brain! Likewise, when someone once said that the more developed is the animal the bigger its brain, I remember that the Teacher pointed out that some insects are cleverer than animals. Take as an example the ants or the bees. A heavy weight of brain signifies great physical endurance, but not refinement. Entirely different are the signs of great intelligence. The convolutions of the brain have great significance. However, here also, only a partial conclusion may be reached, as very little is known about the mysteries of the inner man. There was another, still more ridiculous, theory of the anthropologists that the bigger the skull is, the more intelligent is the man. Here again, Nature proved the contrary, as it was found that the size of the skull of the island savage is larger than that of the average witty Frenchman. Today, many have come to the conclusion that there are no grounds for considering the mental abilities of woman below those of man.

The dark epoch tried to make out of a woman a concubine and a nurse. But if woman stands high as a mother, it is not only as mother in the family, but as Mother and Great Teacher of the consciousness of nations! Thus, as it is said in the Teaching, "Woman, who gives life to people, has the right to govern their destiny. We want to see woman taking part in government, in the councils of ministers, in all constructive activity." But it is said at the same time that "the struggle between the two Elements will be hard, and woman herself will have to recapture her rights which she voluntarily relinquished."

But the violated equilibrium has had such a terrible effect on the life of the whole planet that it is now in danger of destruction! And cosmic justice and goal-fitness once more come to the rescue by bringing forward more and more talented women. In the younger countries destined for evolution, one may observe the way in which woman expresses herself. Thus, in America, there are already women ministers, women diplomats, ambassadors, state governors, directors of the largest firms, aviators, lawyers who win the most complicated cases. Also, a trusted personal secretary of the President is a woman. Indeed, in America women are the main promoters of education and culture. Even most of the "wunderkinds" are to be found among little girls. All these are good omens of the coming epoch.

And now ponder deeply on the following: In the process of evolution Nature will remove the imperfections of physical conception, birth and helpless babyhood (this eventually will depart into the realm of the legendary); for the formation of the body of the incarnating spirit the forces of both mother and father will be necessary and will participate in this process of densification, and nourishment in general will not require a smoky hearth. Could it then be possible that the sphere accessible to woman may become still narrower until she is limited to the role of "amuser" of man? No, it is time for the best people to think about this and to be ashamed at the poverty of imagination that has been revealed thus far.

19

6 June 1935

You express a hope that I will write "without such long intervals." But frankly, I fear that my letters may disturb someone's peace, as I ignore superficial evidences and follow the reality shown to me by the Teacher. It is therefore very likely that my definitions and unexpected conclusions will not be accepted by those who see a scarecrow at every turn of the road. But I am sure that you will not read my letters to such individuals. Always speak according to your listener's consciousness.

I cannot agree with your statement that "outwardly, the clergy has practised complete tolerance, and there has been no open demonstration by them of any kind." I am in possession of just the opposite information. Did not, for instance, a certain priest threaten the members of the Community of Saint Sergius with anathema when they had come merely to ask his blessing? This is recorded and witnessed. Did not this priest confess that he himself gave information to the newspaper, which created confusion among the citizens? And when asked why he did it, did he not reply, "Just because I wanted to give that information"? No, the practice of such "tolerance" is defined differently in our dictionary! I could mention some other facts, but probably you know them better than I do. Therefore, let us drop all this discussion about the clergy; moreover, when I say "clergy," I do not mean only the priests, but in general all fanatics and hypocrites who cover their dark doings by rituals, genuflexions and kissing of the cross—like Mr. X. and his lot.

As you perhaps remember, I have always tried to keep away from the church and her representatives because I wanted my sons to preserve respect for their religion until their consciousness became strong enough to enable them to judge quite maturely what is beautiful in their church and to realize wisely what is negative in it, precisely so that the latter would not injure their attitude toward religion as such. And I think that I have succeeded because both my sons are deeply religious and in spirit they have their own church.

None of our co-workers would ever condemn any temple, but rather would light a candle in each one. But it is quite certain that fanatics and hypocrites do not travel the same road with those of enlightened consciousness.

The threatening time has come—*very threatening*—and a great sorting out is taking place. There is a shifting in the consciousness of people, an awakened striving toward the reconstruction of life, on a new basis and on a large scale. Nations are realizing that "life is wearisome without a hero." Everywhere one can see this longing for powerful leadership, in cultural, in social, in governmental life. Is it possible that one would want to miss the glorious daybreak by being busy with self-destruction and the betrayal of one's spiritual values? Yes, I would say that by the Living Church I mean a church which follows the true Covenants of Christ, in all their tolerance—a church which has in mind unification and not disunification—verily, where the love of Christ is built into the foundation. But where there is even a trace of intolerance or fanaticism, there is no Christ. I have read about the Patriarch Tikhon. Much in his personality indicates that he understood that "The New Heaven and the New Earth are coming to replace the old." Christ was living in his heart.

Have you asked yourself why the clergy are so much against the many religio-philosophical societies? It is because they fear that the truth may be revealed that all the symbols of our Christian Church are exact copies of ancient pagan symbols. The more educated Western priests *know it very well.* But one cannot conceal truth forever, and it is now beginning to proclaim itself loudly. I saw recently in a newspaper a photograph of a Greek Patriarch in full attire, with a crosier in his hand. This crosier is an exact copy of the caduceus of Mercury; it represents a two-headed serpent. One may ask, "How in the world could the image of a serpent—this symbol of a seducer, according to Christian dogma—be on the crosier of a Patriarch of the Greek Church?" Had I not known the truth, I could have thought that someone had sacrilegiously distorted the image of the holy patriarch.

Therefore, with regard to the case you have mentioned, I would say: let us put aside ignorance, and instead let us pay attention to a true interpretation of the facts. Let us ask ourselves who deserves more blame—he who according to his belief has surrounded the revered person with the best symbols, or he who in ignorance and malice not only has slandered an innocent person but also has blasphemed against high symbols whose significance he could not even imagine? Are not all those who are bringing the light of knowledge, who are raising ethical and cultural levels, are they not brothers and sisters of the great Brotherhood of Humanity? Verily, N. K. and I call each one who brings Light "brother" or "sister," by Christ's covenant. In India there is a custom to greet every unknown person by the word "brother." And it is so beautiful!

Indeed, in the magazine you have mentioned you would never come across the shameful abuse, the ignorant and vulgar judgment that I found in the articles sent to me from the H. and T. newspapers. I was sad when our foreign co-workers, after reading these shameful vilifications, wrote to me that they could never have imagined that certain groups of émigrés are still so ignorant—"One cannot help believing the tales that the Russian Cossacks eat tallow candles, and that on the city streets one can see bears," etc.

It is time for the best minds to understand that the consciousness of the whole world is being broadened and with gigantic steps is approaching new constructions. It is impossible to enter the New World with the junk of yesterday! Beautiful is the future but one must know how to accept it. The New Epoch bears on its Banner the sign of great cooperation in the whole of life, comprehensively based on true knowledge and tolerance. But cooperation in ignorance and fanaticism is not possible.

I have been sending and continue to send the articles of N. K. to all those who are longing for the word of Light, and I do not differentiate between pagans and Christians, sectarians and the orthodox; the word of Light can sound everywhere, and under any circumstances. If Mr. X. and his kind remain in the memory of the people, it will be in association with their predecessors, who executed all the differently minded!

And now I would like to know how the book *Sacred Vigil* is getting along. I think it might be possible to publish it in another country. It is interesting to note that this book was forbidden by Harbin's censorship. I wish that someone would point out to me which particular articles are frightening the censors. It is most curious! And this is the age of education! No, we live not in an age of education but in an age of subtle inquisition and irresponsible espionage, wherein the slaves of the spirit become true robots which soon can be ruled by any ape! It is time to realize that where the spirit of courage has gone, replaced by non-resistance to evil, faint-heartedness and fear, there is no place for renascence and progress. There is profound wisdom in the proverb "God helps the brave."

It is too bad, but to a certain mentality the words of Christ could now be applied in their full strength: "But Jesus said unto them: 'A prophet is not without honor, but in his own country and among his own kin, and in his own hours.'"

Likewise, in connection with discrimination of the Great Spirits, I cannot help thinking of an Eastern parable: "Once, a great Rishi, or Sage, was questioned by his disciples as to how to recognize the Avatars, the divine incarnations. And he answered, 'A certain greengrocer was given the opportunity of purchasing a beautiful diamond. He looked at it and declared that he could offer for it ten pounds of eggplants and not a quarter more!'"

Characters like J. L. and V. I. have proved to be even worse than this grocer.

The outrageous slander from H. and T. was spread in other countries, and someone, using the pen name "Mahatma," has reprinted the whole filth in his local newspaper. Certainly, this newspaper "Mahatma" came up against strong opposition from our friends, and in the same newspaper the slanderer had to admit that he accepts N. K. as a great artist and that he only meant that a great artist should not attempt to correct the religion of our forefathers—and that now he is stopping his polemics. As always, here too, "Tactica Adversa" was triumphant! Many articles were then published in newspapers and magazines about the Pact, the Institutions, and about all the cultural activities of N. K. Slander kindles the flame of great deeds, and sparks from this intensive fire are thrown into the most distant and unexpected corners, kindling new aspirations, new abodes of the spirit.

And now, I should like to ask those who accuse N. K. of "correcting the religion of our forefathers," what, properly speaking, are the dogmas of our church which we should consider so unchangeable. Thus, do we not know from the history of the Church Councils about the many changes introduced into the dogmas by the Church Fathers themselves? It would be useful to recall all the arguments between the priests during these Councils. Therefore, would it not be more logical to accuse these "most educated" priests and their blind followers of "correcting our forefathers' religion"? However, they are probably of the opinion that "Quod licet Jovi, non licet Bovi!" And against this self-conceit many examples from the Teachings of the great Antonius could be cited. However, I do not want to make my letter too long.

I am writing all this with pain in my heart, for I love my country and I suffer for its shortcomings. Much was given to the Russian people, and it deserved its name "God-seeker." It gave us such luminaries as Saint Sergius of Radonega, who not only laid the foundation for the Russian State, but who really molded the whole character of the people. By his labors, by the magnet of his spirit, as well as that of his co-workers, spiritual fires were kindled which for centuries nourished the consciousness of the people. But the successors have allowed the inherited treasure to go to waste. As they drew away from the God-given Leader and his Hierarchic Principle, the consciousness of the people became impoverished and incalculable calamities have overtaken them. The priests have no right to lay the blame for the fall of the church at the door of the worldly and intellectuals! They should blame themselves primarily, as they are the custodians of the spiritual treasures entrusted to them by Saint Sergius. Where is that spirit of valor, that austere abstinence and purity, and where the true achievements of life illumined by love for one's country, which were characteristic of all true disciples of the revered Sergius?

Furthermore, what did the Western Church achieve by selling indulgences and establishing the Inquisition? What extreme ignorance there was behind the condemnation of Galileo and other martyrs of Light and Knowledge! By burning at the stake Giordano Bruno and Joan of Arc, did it adorn itself? And now Joan of Arc has been pronounced a saint by the same church! And is not the Night of St. Bartholomew now considered synonymous with mass-murder? Ought we to continue insisting upon the infallibility of the church?

Great are the crimes of the church against the Covenants of Christ. It is time to peruse the bloody pages of true history and, in the consequent indignation of spirit, to acquire enough energy to cast away all encumbrances of ignorance and greed and return to the purity of life of the early Fathers of Christianity. The power of spirit of such heroes in the spiritual realm would be enormous, and they would be greatly honored by the people, who are looking for Light and for the leadership of the spirit. But no gilded surrogates can tempt the long-suffering soul of the people. They expect the true Light of Christ, true deeds in Christ's name, in all austerity, purity and simplicity!

Thus may our compatriots become revived in spirit, although some of them may be ashamed of their moral corruption. Let all those whose spirit has been revived gather under the Banner of Saint Sergius, the God-given Leader of the Russian Land. This is the only salvation. All the previsions given to me *have taken place and are taking place most accurately.* That is why I say that the threatening hour has come and it is time to become united in spirit; as otherwise instead of a forest there will be only sticks and chips, and the first wind will carry the sparks of their destruction.

I beg of you to ponder more deeply over the events and to perceive the Leading Hand. Let us take part in the great promised resurrection of the spirit. Great assurance for the victory of Light over darkness has been given. The significant year of formidable Armageddon is at hand. Let all the warriors of Light unite under the indicated Banner! The Great Guarantee of victory is in our hands.

I am sending to you wonderful chapters from the new monograph on N. K., written by the poet Richard Rudzitis. Many will benefit from the refinement and purity of heart of this writer, who responds so strongly to the luminous image of N. K. But the hearts of many have become graceless and their vocabulary has descended to a very low level. Let us learn to appreciate each talented worker. It is time to stop this senseless wasting of people who are real focuses of the highest energies and in whom is contained the entire significance of evolution—who are the *life* of the whole nation and country. It is time to change our thinking. Indeed, we stand on the edge of an abyss! And only a "Miraculous Banner can carry us across and put us at the Gates of the Miraculous Castle." May we not turn away from the predestined! Let us accept the Benevolence which is sent to us!

Father Sergius, the Wondrous, with Thee we go, with Thee we win!

And once more, I beg you not to be annoyed by this letter. *We love you and we would like to work together with you harmoniously and successfully*, but this requires a certain unity of consciousness and that is why I give you my credo. I suggest that you reread the article by G. Grebentchikoff, "I Protest." "Russia's Roerich leads his co-workers of all nationalities, creeds and positions, who are ready for any sacrifice that they may fulfil his ever-beautiful call to Light. *Could it be possible that Roerich does not deserve to have the Russians themselves—no matter how they each believe or where they live—turn away from his slanderers and stop this pollution of the atmosphere?* Roerich is our national pride, one of the luminaries of today's culture, one of the very few who has constantly maintained a high position, both spiritual and cultural."

And here is another statement of the poet, Richard Rudzitis: "Nicholas Roerich is known not only as an artist but also as a cultural leader, one whose name is spoken with respect both in Western and Eastern cultural circles. Verily, a universal amplitude characterizes the intelligence of his spirit; the field of his activities and ideas is amazingly broad and harmonious. We are especially impressed by the fact that he is not just a philosophical preacher, nor a dreamer, but that *there is not a single idea of his which is not possible to realize*. And he lays firm foundations for the fulfillment of his ideas. He has created a large number of powerful cultural movements, institutions and societies which in their monumental construction *bring to mind the great builders of history.*"

These are the voices of close witnesses of the activities of N. K.

20

11 June 1935

A few days ago I received the wonderful chapters of your new work, and a little later the complete book arrived. My heartiest thanks for this wonderful gift. The very appearance of the book is a joy to the eyes. I rejoiced reading it; the more I read the more I delighted in it, and this is an excellent sign. My heart indeed filled with joy as it resounded to the sensitive strings of the soul of a poet. The recognition and sensing of Beauty is such a high and rare feeling! How highly we should value the people who send these fine vibrations into space! Truly, only he who loves art can appreciate all the finest nuances of the human soul.

It is most gratifying to me that you have emphasized so strongly the universality of N. K.'s personality, and that you regard his creative work as harmonious with the rhythm of cosmic constructiveness. How right, how excellent is this estimation: "From the Beauty of the world he gathers the sacred dew of the spirit into his heart, until finally it is brimming like the Chalice of the Grail." Verily, N. K. is a carrier of the chalice of heroic deeds in the name of Truth and Beauty. Likewise, you have subtly pointed out his ability "to mark and greet in each one the positive creative aspirations, to affirm in him every spark of Light, and to preserve and fan it into still brighter flame."

Indeed, this "benevolent eye" is basic in his relations with people and in his efforts to give them hope of success and joy of creative work. This "eye of the heart" actually helps him to embrace the whole beauty of the creative life and to apply it simply and clearly, without conventionalities and limitations, so that it can resound in sensitive hearts. His constant deep sense of Beauty and his enthusiasm make his creativeness inexhaustible.

I was also happy to see how your creative work is saturated with the ideas of the Teaching. Such assimilation of the Teaching is valuable, but is very seldom met. I know that some people read the books of the Teaching for many years without assimilating in their consciousness a single great idea. One can recite the thoughts, but the important thing is not mere repetition but assimilation after passage through one's own prism! But for this, one needs to be a poet and to be able to think independently, and how many are so equipped?

That is why I want so much to see you writing on the themes of the Teaching. Your heart will create a whole beautiful symphony. The strings of your lyre can express all the beauty of subtlest nuances, which often are missed and not understood because of the depth and brevity of the formulae.

Thus create! Express your whole being in the joy of creativeness. This is the sole meaning and sense of our existence!

21
11 June 1935

I shall try to answer your question regarding the spirit and the soul. In occult literature, due to incomplete explanations, this question remains complex and vague. The Eastern Teachings differ as to the number of principles and their subdivisions and combinations that have to do with the definition of the spirit and the soul. But in truth, it is difficult to separate the soul from the spirit, as all these divisions are actually varying aspects of one fundamental energy, which manifests itself on different planes and through various nerve centers or vehicles. In all the Teachings one finds the subdivision of the human being into three fundamental principles: spiritual, psychic, and physical—or spirit, soul, and body. In the Eastern Teachings there is extension of these three basic principles, *for special purposes*, and we find the fourth, fifth, sixth and seventh principles. This development was approved by the Mahatmas in *The Secret Doctrine*. Thus, the highest or fundamental principle, which contains potentially the synthesis of all the others, is the fiery energy of life or spirit, which is spread throughout the entire Cosmos. For its focus it requires the sixth principle, or Buddhi (often called "the spirit soul" as distinct from the human-animal soul). Thus the monad is formed, which is the primary, unconscious, incarnated Ego. Then follows the fifth principle—the Manas, self-consciousness, "the thinker" (higher intelligence). These three principles form the higher triad, or the conscious, immortal Ego. In Devachan, this Ego survives after the dissolution of the other principles which form man's earthly personality, or, as the Easterners would put it, man's *lower ego*, or self. In the Teaching, this *Higher Ego*, or the triad, is often treated as the *seed of the spirit*, which is unable directly or independently to manifest itself on earth. In order to manifest, this triad needs a fourth principle, called Kama, through which desire is expressed in two aspects: Kama-Manas, or the lower intellect (literally, the intellect of desires), and Kama-Rupa, or subjective form (the form of mental and physical desires and thoughts). This is the thinker in action. Kama, in connection with Manas (the higher) and Buddhi, forms the higher Subtle Body (the astral body, in order that it be not confused with its etheric double, is often called "the lower astral") or the spiritual soul of the spiritually developed man. Kama-Manas is a sort of bridge which connects the higher Manas with Kama-Rupa, thus connecting Manas and Form to make the Kama-Manas body, or *human soul.* When this bridge between Manas and its lower aspect, Kama-Manas, has been established, i.e., when man begins to receive the impressions from the higher Buddhi-Manas, we can say that man is spiritually developed and approaches immortality. Thus, for the achievement of true immortality, in other words, of the maintaining of consciousness on all four planes of existence, and for becoming an Arhat, it is essential to connect, precisely *in the physical body,* the fourth, fifth, and seventh principles and fuse them in the sixth—Buddhi. All the qualities of the basic energy, being separately transmuted by its fire, must be harmonized and expressed in the highest quality of psychic energy.

In the East, the technique of communication between the lower and the higher Manas is called Antakarana, or bridge, or path. By this path, the lower ego, in its turn, extends to the higher Ego all those impressions and thoughts which can be assimilated (due to their high quality) with our external beings, thus becoming immortal accumulations of our Chalice.

Hence, the true individuality of man is his causal body, or spiritual soul, whereas his lower soul is his *personality,* i.e., the changing earthly manifestations. It is clear, then, that soul is a *growing concept* and *subject to changes.* In connection with all this, I am forwarding to you some extracts from the book, *Foundations of Buddhism.*

Thus, the personal or lower ego, or human soul, consists of five principles; whereas the spirit, or higher Ego, the true individuality, or spiritual soul, forms a triad of the seventh, sixth, and fifth principles.

The role of personality in the development of man is most important, as this is the foundation of his whole evolution. Only this manifestation in various combinations, and in perpetually changing conditions, gives us a chance to develop, refine and harmonize all our energies or principles through the activity of our nerve centers. Thus, the fourth principle plays an enormous role, for in it lies desire, the stimulant of life. If one has successfully gone through the ordeals of life, it becomes transmuted into perpetual fiery striving, or will, without which there is neither progress nor creativeness. Thus, let us appreciate each earthly manifestation, as it gives us a chance to improve something and to add to the accumulations of our Chalice, which gathers for us the Amrita.

An intelligent person can easily recognize the people with great accumulations. Thus, a rich individuality will always possess a mind of synthesis, whereas spirits of scant experience will often be met among the narrow specialists. The spirit possessing a well-stored Chalice easily perceives the substance of things. Of them one can say verily that they eat the fruit while others merely count the leaves, which change each year.

Into each new incarnation man brings those accumulations which one can define as "character" or "tendencies." The purely technical or physical abilities are often hereditary, which is also a result of karma. It can happen that a spirit with great accumulations, due to karma not necessarily personal but perhaps group or even national, incarnates into an unsuitable body, one which does not correspond with the magnitude of his spirit. Such lack of harmony sometimes manifests itself in idiosyncrasies which people cannot understand. Even in children, one can encounter strange things; for instance, crying and weeping without any obvious reason, and this can be explained by the inadequacy of the vehicle the spirit has received. This "vehicle," i.e., the body of man, is molded by the collective efforts of humanity, and since humanity has remained on a low level it is understandable that high spirits find it difficult to express themselves in the unsuitable bodies. Therefore, it is important to raise the general level of humanity in order to give a possibility to the high spirits to express themselves in full measure. Under present conditions, it is very difficult to discern the real value of a man. The photographing of auras therefore is essential as it can reveal the true nature of a person. Such certification would make many people think, and would compel them to improve their "passports."

Yes, the law of Karma is most complex; only an Arhat is able to perceive all its actions. Truly speaking, there is nothing but karma! The whole of Be-ness is an endless chain of causes and effects, each effect becoming the cause of the next effect, and so on, ad infinitum. Man ends his karma on this planet in order that he may continue it in other worlds. The end of one cycle of karma comes to man when all the elements or energies which form his being have achieved all the perfection possible on this planet.

The idea of a Personal God, who saves humanity, is absurd for Buddhists. Here are some pages from *Foundations of Buddhism*, by N. Rokotoff:

"The idea of God has its own interpretation for Buddhists, in accordance with the law of Karma and with the understanding of the necessity of personal efforts for one's own liberation. ...

"'Who is it that shapes our lives? Is it Īsvara, a personal creator? If Īsvara be the maker, all living things should have silently to submit to their maker's power. They would be as vessels formed by the potter's hand; and if it were so, how would it be possible to practise virtue? If the world had been made by Īsvara, there should be no such thing as sorrow or calamity, or sin, for both pure and impure deeds must issue from Him. If not, there would be another cause besides Him, and He would not be the self-existent One. Thus you see the thought of Īsvara is overthrown. ...

"If the eternally changing existence of man excludes the hypothesis of a constant, changeless entity, then the Universe, this complex of complexes, may be explained entirely without the necessity or even the possibility of introducing into it an unchanging and eternal Being. ...

"Two doctrines were especially condemned by Buddha: (1) the eternal unchanging soul, and (2) the destruction of the soul after death. Both these doctrines were denied by the law of causal conception, which establishes that all dharmas are at the same time causes and consequences. Buddha denied the existence of a changeless soul in man and in all, as He saw in man and the whole universe only inconstancy and the transitional.

"The thesis of continuity of the stream of phenomena and the formula of the causality of conception exclude the existence of the eternal unchanging soul, individual as well as universal.

"The connotation of the word 'soul' is absolutely inadmissible for the Buddhists; because the thought that man can be a being separate from all other beings and from the existence of the whole universe can neither be proved by logic, nor supported by science. 'In this world no one is independent. All that exists depends on causes and conditions.' 'Each thing depends upon another thing, and the thing it depends upon is, in turn, not independent.' (*Bodhicaryavatara*, v. 6, pages 26-31.)

"Buddha constantly taught that there is no independent 'I' and that there is no world separated from it. There are no independent things, there is no separate life—all are only indissoluble correlatives. If there is no separate 'I' we cannot say that this or that is mine, and thus the origin of the understanding of property is destroyed.

"If the understanding of a permanent and independent human soul is to be rejected, what then in man gives him the sense of a permanent personality? The answer will be—trishna, or the craving for existence. A being who has generated causes for which he is responsible and who possesses this craving, will, according to his karma, be born anew.

"Of one and the same complex of elements (dharmas) are born infinite combinations of skandhas of elements, which are manifested at the given time as one personality, and after a definite period of time appear as another, third, fourth, etc. ad infinitum. There occurs not a transmigration, but an endless transformation of a complex of dharmas or elements, that is, a continuous regrouping of the elements—substrata which form the human personality.

"Upon the quality of the new combination of skandhas—elements of the new personality—the last desire before death of the previous personality has a great influence: it gives direction to the liberated stream.

"In Buddhism a man is regarded as an individuality, built by numerous existences, but only partially manifested in each new appearance on the earthly plane.

"The individual existence, consisting of an entire chain of lives which begin, continue and finish in order to begin again, ad infinitum, is compared to a wheel or a year of twelve months, invariably repeated. The chain of the twelve nidanas becomes no longer a chain but the wheel of life, with twelve spokes. Once set in motion, the wheel of life, the wheel of the Law will never stop: 'The wheel of the benevolent Law in its unchangeable rotation crushes untiringly the worthless chaff, separating it from the golden grain. The hand of karma directs the wheel, its revolutions marking the beat of its heart.'

"All these changes of forms or of existence lead toward one goal—the attainment of Nirvana; it means the full development of all possibilities contained in the human organism. But Buddhism teaches the cognizance and creation of good, independent of this aim, as the contrary would be absolute egoism, and such speculation is foredoomed to disappointment. As it is said, Nirvana is the epitome of disinterestedness, complete renunciation of all personal for the sake of truth. An ignorant man dreams and strives to Nirvana, without any realization of its true Essence. To create good with the view of gaining results or to lead a disciplined life for the attainment of liberation is not the noble path ordained by Gotama. Without thought of reward or achievement life must be crossed, and such life is the greatest. The condition of Nirvana may be attained by man in his earthly life. ...

"Buddhism admits no difference between the physical and the psychic worlds. Reality attributed to the action of thought is of the same order as reality of objects cognized by our senses.

"Buddhism regards all existing phenomena as one reality. Physically and psychically these phenomena are dharmas, objects of our cognizance. Within us and without, we come in touch only with dharmas, as in us and outside us exist but dharmas. The word 'dharma' is one of the most significant and most difficult to translate in the Buddhist terminology. Dharma is a manifold factor, a factor of consciousness, with an inherent property of definite expression. Our organs give us sensations which are transformed into dharmas through the action of cognizance. Ideas, images and all intellectual processes are, first of all dharmas.

"As color, form and sound are to the eye and ear, so dharmas are to the consciousness. They exist for us by their effects. The blue color exists only as we receive the sensation of blue.

"It is customary to call the Teaching of Buddha itself Dharma, since dharma also signifies *law*. Subjective and objective phenomena are continuously changing. They are real; but their reality is momentary because all that exists is but part of an eternally unfolding development—dharmas appear one moment in order to change in the next. This doctrine of eternal flux of all things was so fundamental a characteristic of the Teaching that it was even named 'The Theory of Instantaneous Destruction.'

"Dharmas (transcendental bearers of definite qualities) are drawn into the stream of eternal change. Their combinations define the specifications of objects and individuals. Only that which is beyond combinations is unchangeable. The ancient teaching knew only one concept which was integral, unconditioned and eternal—Nirvana.

"Every dharma is a cause, for every dharma is energy. If this energy is inherent in each conscious being, it manifests itself in a twofold way: outwardly, as the immediate cause of phenomena; inwardly, by transmuting the one who has engendered it and by containing in itself the consequences revealed in the near or distant future.

"We find that the physical and psychic organism of a man is but the combination of five groups of aggregates or skandhas, which are divided into physical qualities: form—rupa; sensation—vedana; perception—samjna; forces—samskara; consciousness—vijnana. All five are equally unstable and dual. Samskara are the inclinations and creative powers, explaining the present dharmas by the previous and indicating which of the present dharmas prepare those of the future.

"'Samskara are accumulations left by former sensations and lending their fragrance to future sensations.' From this definition of samskara (skandhas) it is clear that this group of elements appears as the one absorbing all peculiarities of other skandhas. Vijnana-skandha, and partly samjna, lend their coloring or character to the other combinations, and therefore appear as the cause, defining the next existence, in the sense of strivings and inclinations.

"Rupa is like a plate; vedana is like food contained on the plate; samjna is like a sauce; samskara is like the cook; and vijnana is like the eater.

"No element carries from one existence into another, but not one attains a new existence without having had its cause in the previous existence. When the old consciousness ceases to exist—it is death. When consciousness returns to existence, a new birth takes place. One should understand that the present consciousness is not born of the old consciousness, but that its present state is the result of causes accumulated in the previous existence.

"From one life to another there is no transmission, but there is a seeming reflection, solidarity.

"The man who sows is not he who reaps; yet he is not also another man.

"The content of consciousness consists of dharmas. Dharmas are thoughts. These thoughts are as real as the four elements of the organs of sense because from the moment a thing is thought, it already exists. Man is a complex of combinations and at each moment his nature is defined by the amount and quality of the particles of which he is composed. Each change in his combination makes a new being of him. But this change does not exclude continuity because the motion of skandhas does not occur accidentally or beyond the law. Drawn into the eternal ebb and flow, the aggregates change in one direction or in another, as the conditions of each new combination are defined by a cause; and this cause is the quality of the preceding cause. Each successive combination harvests the fruit of former combinations and plants the seed which will bear fruit in the future combinations.

"Man is a complex of combinations and at the same time he is the link. He is the complex because at each moment he contains a great number of skandhas; he is the link because between the two successive conditions there is at the same time the difference and solidarity. 'If there would be no difference, milk would not turn into curdled milk. And if there would be no solidarity, there would be no need for milk in order to have curdled milk.'

"Let us explain by one more example: Physiologically, the human organism completely changes every seven years. And yet, when the man A. is forty years of age he is absolutely identical with the eighteen year old youth A; nevertheless, on account of the constant destructions and rebuildings of his body and changes in his mind and character, he is a different being. A man in his old age is the precise consequence of the thoughts and deeds of the preceding stage of his life. Likewise, the new personality, being the previous individuality, but in a changed form, in a new combination of the skandhas of elements, reaps justly the consequences of the thoughts and deeds of his former existence.

"The consciousness and its eternally changing contents are one. There is no permanent 'I' which remains unchangeable. It is necessary that the embryo should die in order that a child may be born; the death of the child is needed in order that the boy may be born, and the death of the boy produces the youth." (Ciksshasamuccaya, page 358.)

"It is customary to compare human existence with a necklace—each bead is one of the physical manifestations. But perhaps it is clearer to conceive of this evolution as a complex mixture into which, with each new embodiment on the earthly plane, a new ingredient is being added which naturally changes the whole mixture.

"Each new manifestation is limited by physical elements, rupa-skandha. ...

"The energy striving to create a new being and directed by karma is called 'trishna'—the stimulus, the craving for existence.

"And this stimulus, when imbued with the essence of the Teaching, rises before us not only as the greatest cosmic principle, but also as the greatest and most beautiful cosmic mystery. And Gotama Buddha, who unceasingly pointed out the eternally rushing stream of our lives, has thus asserted the cosmicality and therefore the infinity of this stimulus, which many misquoters of the Teaching try to suppress in themselves; but the fiery spirit of the Teacher could only destroy small conceptions, broadening them into Infinity. And Nirvana is the Gate which introduces us into the rhythm of the highest, fiery, creative and eternally expanding stream of infinite Existence.

"The Teaching of Buddha is an untiring fiery call to the realization of the beauty and unity of the great creativeness of infinite Existence."

* * *

Contemporary scientific data support the theory of karma expounded in Buddhism. Contemporary science teaches that each generation of man is heir to the distinctive characteristics of preceding generations, not only in the mass but in individual cases.

Psychology is fully associated with that intense and particular attention which Buddhism gives to the thinking process, to the purification and expansion of consciousness of the disciple. Buddha indicated thought as the primary factor in evolution, and in Buddhism the psychological processes are closely connected with physiology.

"The philosophy of Buddhism may be termed the analysis

of separate elements attracted into combination by the formation of a definite individual stream." The individual stream is accumulated and fed by numberless manifestations of man on Earth, in other planes, and other worlds. Absorbing all the characteristics of each manifestation, this stream swells in possibilities, transforming and remaining eternally self-containing. True individuality, true immortality is contained in the realization of the true "I," which is constructed by innumerable combinations of human manifestations. In Buddhism, man is not a pitiful pigmy, as he is in the representation of the Western mind, but the Lord of the Worlds. Being part of the Cosmos, like It he is limitless in his possibilities.

22

18 June 1935

I was happy to receive your letter. What can be more beautiful than the infinite feeling of love for the Great Image of the Teacher! Indeed, this flame nourishes us and sees us safely over all the abysses. There are no limits for the heart aflame with love. Therefore, I welcome so much that powerful resounding of the heart within you. Follow this most beautiful and shortest path. In due time, the necessary manifestations will come. But do not feel disappointed if you have not yet noticed certain signs mentioned in the Teaching. You should realize that the hardest battle is now being fought between the Forces of Light and the forces of darkness. That is why these manifestations of the Subtle World are delayed. However, one should be extremely careful because of the poisoned atmosphere of Earth, and even of the nearest subtle spheres, for there could be a too great stress on the heart. Thus, the Forces of Light always consider many conditions, and primarily the condition of the human organism. Therefore, all approaches to a person take place during a time most suitable and safest for his health. Indeed, during this trying time it is vitally necessary to carry one's "lamp" for safety in the darkness. As it is said in the Eastern Teachings, "Verily, excellent is the Kali Yuga (black Yuga), as it offers us a possibility of hastening our approach to the Light. All difficulties are possibilities, and a victory achieved is a step in the ascension."

The theme of your address is most vital. It is excellent that you have treated the question of the posthumous condition in the spirit of the Teaching. It is necessary to awaken thought by sudden but careful touches. Most definitely, true Christianity does not contradict the Teachings of the East and the Teaching of Living Ethics.

I realize that you must give consideration to the tendency toward nationalism, and even chauvinism. Sometimes it is needful to protect the little growing tree by means of a fence, and the only extra precaution to take is to make sure that the fence is not so close to the little tree as to interfere with its normal development. One must give it room at the right moment. Thus, let us outlive with patience this transitory period. The Teaching of Living Ethics does not bear the stamp of any definite nationality; therefore, it is applicable everywhere and at all times. Some Eastern terms could be easily replaced by their Western equivalents. It is essential to be able to express the new conception of the problems of life and of the immutable laws of Be-ness. But here, as usual, only the unprejudiced and open consciousness can assimilate the breadth of the new world outlook. Therefore, work in full conformity with the possibilities of your audience. In everything apply *goal-fitness*, that great ruling law of the Universe. Do not force the consciousness of people who approach you. I do appreciate how difficult it is to give to everybody exactly in accordance with his consciousness. I know how the heart is longing to share its wealth, and to give the joy of broad contemplation of the world. Yet we must be wise in disseminating the seeds.

I welcome the idea of your friends and yourself to publish the magazine. Try to make it popular and interesting. Alongside topics from the Living Ethics, perhaps you will be able to stress the widely growing interest in the realm of the Subtle World. Indeed, all progressive countries are making attempts to approach scientifically the psychic and parapsychic phenomena. I have just read in the newspapers that in one of the universities of Sweden there has been established recently a course for the study of spiritualism. They are investigating the psychic phenomena which lately have become so prevalent. In Italy, one of the most popular newspapers has a special section devoted to occultism. It would be of interest to maintain in your magazine a review of the records of psychic phenomena of the past and of the present, as they are now on the increase. People could learn a great deal from such evident proofs, and, as most of them like mystery, an interest toward further research might be awakened. Of course, parallel with this, one must point out the harm of mediumship and explain what precautions should be taken in order to protect a medium, as well as those near him, from the danger of obsession. In view of the increasing number of cases of mediumship and obsession, all such articles could bring much benefit.

By exchanging material with other magazines, you could collect much interesting information. So many scientific investigations are now being conducted which bring us to the edge of the beyond!

* * *

And now, I shall answer your questions. The divine Monad is to be found in every mineral, every plant, in every manifestation, as without this fiery grain there is no life. And gradually, ascending from the simple to the more complex organisms, the monad, or seed of the spirit, remains unchanged in its primary wholeness. But the emanations from this seed change according to the growth of the consciousness of the organism which has been animated by the seed. Consequently, the more complicated and refined is the organism, the richer and more subtle are the emanations of the monad.

Intellect began its development on the physical plane during the fourth root-race of our fourth cycle, when complete immersion into matter took place. But the impetus for its development was given by the Great Spirits, the Sons and Daughters of Wisdom (Elohims) who came from the higher worlds and were incarnated at the end of the third race. Of course, They were of the Diving Dynasty of Spiritual Teachers, of whom accounts are abounding in the most ancient mythology and legends. Precisely, through their incarnations and their direct progeny They transmitted to humanity an organism far more refined, capable of responding to higher vibrations. Likewise, contact with their high fiery auras kindled fires in those who were near Them. Thus, following the current of the natural law of development, humanity, in the majority, is not able to become perfect and have its seven principles or forth-nine fires opened before the seventh race in the seventh cycle.

To be sure, all these principles are latent in man from his

very birth. Also, according to the evolutionary law, the fifth principle (Manas) is not to be completely developed until the fifth cycle. Thus, all prematurely developed minds (on the spiritual plane) in our race are abnormal beings; they are those whom the Great Teachers call "people of the fifth cycle." Even in the coming seventh race of our fourth cycle, while our four lower principles will be fully developed, still the principle of Manas will be developed only in proportion. However, this limitation concerns only the spiritual development or the higher intelligence. Always bear in mind the difference between the highest Manas, or the spiritual mind, and the Kama-Manas, or the intellect. Thus the development of the intellect (Kama-Manas) was achieved in the fourth root-race of our cycle.

Likewise, the assertion that the divine Monad is not within the man is correct to a certain degree, as the seventh and the sixth principles form the so-called magnetic field or auric egg. Thus, by the width and emanations of the aura it is possible to determine the high standing or quality of the spirit. That is why it is so important to accelerate the discovery of methods of fixing or photographing auras. Such a snapshot would be a true passport for a man!

It is extremely important to move the consciousness of mankind. What a great achievement it is gradually to awaken the consciousness of the best people to the necessity of going back to the sources of Christianity, to the early Church Fathers who lived during the first three centuries after Christ! How beautiful are the teachings of the great Antonius! Thus, achieve your great work by wise and careful awakening and kindling of the consciousness of your listeners. Always remember the canon "by thy God," i.e., speak according to the consciousness of everyone. It is indeed hard! As it is said, "If it is hard to put a small sword into a large sheath, so much the harder is it to put a large sword into a small sheath."

May the blessings of the Forces of Light be with you in this great deed of purification of the true Covenants. Do not forget the prophetic words of St. Antonius about the condition of the churches and the monasteries of the future, quoted in the books of "Dobrotolubye."

"And so forward, forward, forward—without looking back!"

23

18 June 1935

I have no objection to my letters being read, with the quotations from the books of Living Ethics, to pure souls who possess an open consciousness. For my heart also longs to share the treasure with everyone able to appreciate it. However, one should be most cautious in the distribution of the entrusted seeds of the Teaching, and one should always apply the Indication "He who has discovered a precious formula will not shout it through the open window, for the harm would be greater than the benefit." I myself was much at fault in the beginning as regards cautiousness, and even now, by nature, it is rather difficult for me to keep anything concealed just for myself. That is why I understand so well your desire to share with others, to give them hope and joy. But personal experience and black betrayal gradually teaches us to be more cautious. Yet even now, at times (though only partially), I disregard the wise warning "Know how to safeguard that which is entrusted," a warning that is given to everyone who enters the path of the Teaching of Light. The most difficult trial for me is to live among people and not to trust them! But we must go through this as well. One should learn not to overburden others with excessive confidence and, at the same time, to be free of dreadful suspiciousness. Human nature is a sealed book! As a wise proverb says, "If you want to learn about a person, eat three stone of salt with him." So please be careful.

It is necessary to remember that by approaching the Teaching and the Elder Brothers of Humanity we unfold (due to unfailing occult laws) our true nature much more quickly. Certain characteristics come to the surface which otherwise might remain dormant until the next incarnation. Remember what is said in the *Chalice of the East*: "As the shower cannot fructify the rock, so the occult teaching has no effect upon unperceptive minds; and as water develops heat in caustic lime, even so does the Teaching awaken every unsuspected potentiality latent within the disciple."

This is an immutable law in the domain of the occult; the more serious and sincere the aspirant and the more he realizes the significance of his task, the stronger is the action of this law.

The ancient occult axiom "know thyself" must be familiar to

every disciple. But so very few understand the real significance of this wise saying of the Delphic oracle. All this I write to you in order to make it clear why some of those who have approached the Teaching suddenly display certain peculiarities. I want you to be well prepared. To a certain extent, this law explains why so many betrayers are uncovered around each enlightened undertaking. The free will of man is the highest divine gift, but this implies that one should use this gift, indeed, divinely! I am writing about this because just now my soul is wounded by a betrayal. But as the Teaching says, "We must learn to sleep in the same tent with a betrayer." Verily, one must train one's heart, and learn not to overburden people with an excessive confidence. Take this as a friendly advice and, as you may see, an advice of experience.

Now to your questions. Of course, the "Mother of the World" is at the head of the Great Hierarchy of Light of our planet. Read in the *On Eastern Crossroads* the narrative about the Mother of the World, and accept it as the highest reality. Behind each symbol stands a High Individuality, and each symbol covers a great reality. Each Great Individuality has its deputies, or personifiers, who are nearest to its Ray, and sometimes one of these Great Individualities personally incarnates—hence, the concept of the Avatar.

Even so, the Mother of the Universe, or of the manifested Cosmos, can be accepted as one of the figures of the Holy Trinity. Indeed, there is no religion, except later ecclesiastical Christianity, in which the Feminine Element is not included among the Primates of Be-ness. Thus, the Gnostics also considered the Holy Ghost as a Feminine Element. In the most ancient Teachings, the manifested Trinity of Father, Mother, and Son was considered as an emanation of the highest, eternally hidden Cause; and the latter, in turn, as that of the *Causeless Cause*.

This Causeless Cause is the Parabrahman of the Hindus. However, Parabrahman is not a Personal God. He is "That" of the Vedantists. Parabrahman is simply the Reality which has no equivalent—the Absolute, or rather, the infinite abstract Space, which contains the potential space, also called Aditi.

Precisely, the first differentiation in the periodic manifestations of eternal Nature, sexless and infinite, is Aditi in "That," or the potential space inside the abstract Space. In its next manifestation it appears as the divine immaculate Mother-Nature within the all-embracing absolute Infinity. Thus, Space is called "Mother" until its cosmic activity begins, the Father-Mother in its first stage of awakening.

As it is said in the Ancient Teachings, "From the beginning, before Mother became Father-Mother—in Infinity the Fiery Dragon moved. ...

"Thus, in the Cabbala—Ain-Suph is Space, Darkness. And from it, in due time, issues forth Sephira—the vital element. Sephira, when manifested as an active force, takes the image of Creator and becomes the Male Element. Therefore, it is the Androgyne. It is the Father-Mother, or Aditi, of Hindu Cosmogony and the Sacred Teaching. Thus, Darkness is Father-Mother; Light is Their Son. Darkness is the eternal womb in which the source of Light appears and disappears. ...

"Father and Mother are the masculine and feminine principles in the Root of Nature, or the opposite polarities in all things, in each plane of the Cosmos. They are Spirit and Substance, whose result is the Son. ...

"Thus, when Mother manifests from her undifferentiated state she becomes the sinless Virgin, who is adorned with the Universal Mystery ('That'), but is free from conception. Hence, comes the idea of the *Immaculate Conception*: She effuses out of Herself Her Consort. Thus, in the Eastern religions, one often comes across the definitions, given to all the highest Gods, 'The Consort of His Mother' and 'The Son of the Immaculate Conception.' In every religious system, the gods fused their functions of Father, Son and Consort into one function. In each cosmogony, the Son was considered 'The Consort of His Mother.' The title of the Highest Egyptian God, Amon, is 'Consort of His Mother.'

"When the Son separates from the Mother, he becomes Father. Therefore, it is said that in the world of Be-ness the One Point or Ray impregnates the Virgin Womb of the Cosmos, and the sinless Mother gives birth to the Form which generates all other forms. The Hindu Prajapati (Brahma) is called 'the first generating Masculine Element' and 'the Consort of His Mother.'"

I shall quote from *The Secret Doctrine* the description of Pralaya found in the book, *Stanzas of Dzyan*, which was its basic source.

"STANZA I. The Eternal Parent, wrapped in Her Ever-Invisible Robes, had slumbered once again for Seven Eternities. ...

"The 'Parent,' Space, is the eternal, ever-present Cause of all—the incomprehensible Deity, whose 'Invisible Robes' are the mystic Root of all Matter and of the Universe. Space is the one eternal thing that we can most easily imagine, immovable in its abstraction and uninfluenced by either the presence or absence in it of an objective Universe. It is without dimension, in every sense, and self-existent. Spirit is the first differentiation from 'THAT,' the Causeless Cause of both Spirit and Matter. As taught in the Esoteric Catechism, it is neither 'limitless void' nor 'conditioned fullness,' but both. It was and ever will be.

"Thus, the 'Robes' stand for the noumenon of undifferentiated Cosmic Matter. It is not matter as we know it, but the spiritual essence of matter, and is co-eternal and even one with Space in its abstract sense. Root-Nature is also the source of the subtle invisible properties in visible matter. It is the Soul, so to say, of the One Infinite Spirit. The Hindus call it Mulaprakriti, and say that it is the primordial Substance, which is the basis of the Upadhi or Vehicle of every phenomenon, whether physical, psychic or mental. It is the source from which Akasha radiates."

From these extracts quoted from *The Secret Doctrine* you can see how significant was the Feminine Element in the ancient cosmogonies. Only the profound ignorance of the Middle Ages could discard the Feminine Element from the construction of all Being. Verily, in their origin both Elements, Male and Female, are united, and one cannot exist without the other. The belittling of one is the belittling of the other.

And so, there is only one Substance, one Element—whether you call it God, Spirit, Fire, That, etc., or Parabrahman, Ain-Suph, Space, Absolute, etc.—which in potentiality has both polarities, or is the Androgyne.

I feel that I must quote one more extract from *The Secret Doctrine*:

"From the beginning of man's inheritance, from the first appearance of the architects of the globe he lives on, the unrevealed Deity was recognized and considered under its only philosophical aspect—Universal Motion, the thrill of the creative Breath in Nature. Occultism sums up the One Existence thus: 'Deity is an arcane, living (or moving) Fire, and the eternal witnesses to this unseen Presence are Light, Heat, Moisture'—this trinity including, and being the cause of, every phenomenon in Nature. Intra-Cosmic motion is eternal and ceaseless; cosmic motion—the visible, or that which is subject to perception—is finite and periodical. As an eternal abstraction it is the Ever-present; as a manifestation, it is finite both in the coming direction and the opposite, the two being the Alpha and Omega of successive reconstructions.

"Kosmos—the Nuomenon—has nought to do with the causal relations of the phenomenal World. It is only with reference to the intra-cosmic Soul, the ideal Kosmos in the immutable Divine Thought, that we may say: 'It never had a beginning nor will it have an end.' With regard to its body or cosmic organization, though, it cannot be said that it had a first, or will ever have a last, construction; yet at each new Manvantara its organization may be regarded as the first and the last of its kind, as it evolves every time on a higher plane."

* * *

We can say the Trinity is Atma, Buddhi and Manas; or Spirit, Soul and Intelligence; or Spirit, Substance and Light; or Spirit, Matter and Force, etc., etc.

* * *

You should not hesitate to put questions to me. I am always glad to give you certain hints, although to write in detail is rather difficult for me, as I have no assistants and yet have so much to write. But, apart from that, hints are more beneficial, as they give an impulse to thought.

* * *

And now regarding other matters. Do not be disappointed that the signs become rarer and not so prominent; rather consider the threatening Armageddon and the consequent poisoning of the entire atmosphere. Indeed, not only the terrestrial layers which directly surround us, but even the distant spheres of the Subtle World (to say nothing of those nearest to Earth) are polluted by decomposition. Precisely, all the subtle manifestations during such a period may *very seriously* affect the organism. The Forces of Light are acting in complete conformity with existing conditions and with the forces of our own organism. Moreover, after each victory there comes a period of *silence*, a sort of rest, in order that the organism may the better assimilate all that which has been received and prepare for further perceptions and refinements. All the symptoms described by you are very characteristic of the partial opening of the centers. Therefore, I suggest that you be extremely careful with your health. First of all, do not overwork, and avoid colds. Then I suggest that you take bicarbonate of soda twice daily. Do not forget that there is no better remedy for pains in the lower part of the chest than bicarbonate of soda. And, in general bicarbonate of soda is a most healthful preparation. It is preventative against all sorts of diseases, including cancer. But you must make it a rule to take it daily and regularly. Especially does it help to relieve the pains and the movements in the solar plexus. Likewise, for sore and burning throats hot milk (but not boiled) with soda is most helpful. The usual dose is one coffeespoonful to a glass. You should recommend soda to everyone. Also, take care that the stomach is not overloaded and that the bowels are kept free. Twice daily take valerian tea or valerian tincture thirty to forty drops of the latter). Bicarbonate of soda is absolutely necessary during a conflagration of the centers. It discharges the fiery energies and prevents consuming fire.

I was especially glad to learn about the sensation of the hot currents in the heart.

Thus, pay attention to every manifestation, and make it a habit *to write down* daily, and most precisely all your sensations and visions. Such notes may become a most valuable adjunct to the study of the subtlest energies. So—good luck! Create, write and observe! And above all, treasure that divine fire of love toward the Great Image of Him who pointed out to us the path of Light, Beauty and Joy.

24

24 June 1935

Folk wisdom says, "Righteous labor does not build one a palace of marble." Indeed, great beauty lies in the concept of independent effort. One should apply in life the great covenants by means of one's own labor. One should sacrifice not just from surplus but by giving it all, leaving only the most essential for oneself.

If it were not for difficulties and betrayals, where would be the achievements and service to Light? The entrusted ones and the disciples of the White Brotherhood have never led a prosperous and luxurious life like the magi in the books of Kryjanovsky! The path of comfort and luxury has never been advocated by any Teaching. The indication everywhere was toward the great Middle Way, but remembering high quality. This implies that a disciple does not have to starve, and can even have reasonable comfort in accordance with the mission given to him, but that at the same time he should be able to sacrifice this comfort if circumstances require it. The material obstacles on the path of Service are not the most difficult ones, although the dark ones are very fond of attacking thus the vulnerable spots of so many, bringing forth their hidden qualities. More difficult is the fight against the obscured human consciousness. Human nature is unpredictable, and it is awful to be surrounded by all sorts of betrayals, the number of which has increased greatly in this time of mass obsession. And yet, the hardest, the most stubborn fight is that against our own habits and shortcomings. Through the action of immutable occult laws, our true nature is revealed, and the qualities which would otherwise have remained hidden and dormant in us until subsequent incarnations come to the surface. One should reread often the last letters in the *Chalice of the East*. Apropos, I shall quote here a page from the writings of H. P. Blavatsky. It is entitled "Warning."

"There is a strange law in occultism which has been confirmed by experience over many thousands of years. Likewise, during all the years of the existence of the Theosophical Society this law was undeniably confirmed in every case. It is that the moment someone enters the path of probation, certain occult results are sure to manifest themselves. That which was previously dormant comes out: vices, habits, hidden desires and qualities—good, bad and indifferent.

"For instance, if a person, due to atavism or karmic heredity, is vain or sensual or conceited, all these vices will inevitably come out, even if until now he has succeeded in hiding and suppressing them. They will come out irresistibly, and a person will have to fight them with a hundred times more strength than before, until he succeeds in eradicating such inclinations.

"On the other hand, if one is kind, magnanimous, chaste and abstinent, or has some other dormant virtues, all these will be manifested as well as the rest. [In the realm of the occult, this is an immutable law.]

"The more serious and sincere is the desire of the candidate and the more profoundly he realizes the significance of his duty, the stronger is the action of this law.

"The ancient occult axiom 'Know Thyself' should be learned by every disciple."

I quote this because I want to remind you how often the followers of the Teaching begin to manifest, as it were, quite unexpected peculiarities of character. "Verily, a contact with the Source of Light is a touchstone for everyone."

And now something else. Do you not know that a sincere, ardent call of the heart and the consequent deeds act as a most powerful radio and inevitably reach the Great Heart? Therefore, if your friend is ardently striving toward Light, this very fact makes him known to the Great Teacher. Not that I want to belittle P. D.in the eyes of your friend, but I must tell you that the difference between the Great Teachers of the Himalayan Stronghold and every disciple here on Earth, is immeasurable. H. P. Blavatsky used to say that only in several Manvantaras would her spirit reach the degree of the Great Spirit of Lord M. Remember what I wrote you regarding *this Image*! Verily, only the *most high is connected with Him*, with this Hierarch. Only the very highest concepts are embodied in this Great Image.

Of course, one cannot reveal the whole Truth at once to the unprepared consciousness. Throughout the ages of the past, only that part has been given which could be assimilated by humanity. Therefore, the Great Images have had and still have to use a grey cloak, so that their light will not blind the dim consciousness. Let the consciousness of your friend gradually open toward the Truth. I think he is a pure soul. Therefore, his own heart should decide and should be illumined by the inner light of his Chalice of accumulations. Do not force him; let him choose *his own path*. In this spiritual battle, he *himself* must become the victor. I shall quote a paragraph from the Teaching: "Beware of zealotry, not only regarding the calls from others but lest you yourselves become missionaries. It is impossible to describe the harm done by missionaries, and it is impossible to observe without contempt how the Teaching is sold in the bazaar at a reduced price. Try to understand that the Teaching which realizes its significance will not advertise itself in the bazaar."

Do you remember that at one time you felt like unifying all existing spiritual groups? But now, through personal experience, you can see that this is impossible in view of the present state of humanity. Human nature is not yet ready for even the most primitive cooperation! We have had some experience, and therefore we never beg and never force anyone. However, if someone accepts our Sign, we are obliged to be on guard to make sure that there be not introduced under this Sign something completely contrary to our fundamental principles and rules.

Furthermore, the zealotry of followers destroys all the foundations laid by the Founders of the Teachers. So it was, and so it is. Therefore, I would not believe particularly the stories concerning the punishment meted out to the renegades by the person you have mentioned, as this would have been pure black magic, and certainly would contradict the spirit of the booklet you have forwarded to me.

Undoubtedly, there are cases when a dark spirit directs black thoughts toward a pure spirit and receives a return blow. But in such a case he punishes himself, for what can be done if the luminous aura does not accept the projected poisonous gases? We and our friends have witnessed many times such return blows, but I can assure you that in no case was there the slightest desire to return the blow. Forgiveness is a primary quality of the true Teacher. He can be indignant but will never send consciously a deadly arrow. Only the Great Teacher, the Lord of Karma, has the right to send consciously a fatal Ray. Thus, the Teacher is one thing and the followers are something entirely different! Therefore, let us treat such stories with caution. True, the evil will of any strong person can bring some harm if one's aura is weakened by fear or disease. The best panacea against such poisonous arrows is devotion to the Foundations of the Teaching, love of Hierarchy and complete serenity. We must accustom ourselves to the idea that we are dwelling in a poisoned atmosphere, in which numerous poisonous arrows are flying about, and that only our heartfelt bond with the Forces of Light helps us to preserve our protective net. But if we ever doubt the power of the Hierarchy, or if we allow faint-heartedness in the face of the enemy, we paralyze immediately our emanations and thus destroy the protective net woven out of them.

* * *

I sympathize sincerely with your friend, and I do hope that he is a striving soul able to comprehend the seriousness and the significance of the test he is facing now. Therefore, I ask you not to conceal from him that the path of Service, the path of achievement, is very, *very* difficult. He who chooses this path should be prepared for every self-sacrifice. The obstacles and difficulties grow proportionately as one progresses along the path. It is true that a disciple receives greater knowledge. But in life this does not bring much joy, there being no one with whom to share it and no way of applying it, for *responsibility* grows also in proportion to knowledge. Moreover, this very knowledge creates around him envy and betrayal. Indeed, the surrounding darkness is tragic.

Hard is the path of achievement, and it cannot be alleviated until the human consciousness stirs with a new impulse for the next step. There are hard periods on the path, when the disciple is left to himself, when he must display independently all his alertness and his abilities, when even the voice of the Teacher temporarily is not heard. But the heart of the true disciple is full of joy and striving, for he knows that it is but a new step. The joy of fulfillment of his duty stays with him, and with all the power of his spirit he strives to fulfil the task *even more perfectly*. Verily, in this is *his entire joy*.

Hard is the path of Service. Nevertheless, those who receive the possibility to join the path of Service while in life will not give up this crown for any of the treasures of the world. For no other joys can be compared with those spiritual exaltations which are experienced by the true disciple. The richer were his former accumulations, the more beautiful is his achievement. Certainly, there are many moths and butterflies around the Teaching, but the benefit from them and for them is proportionate to their fleeting flutter. In talking to you and your friend, I hope I am speaking to mature consciousnesses, unafraid of difficulties. Verily, the experienced fighter is full of heart tremor and enthusiasm before a new fight; so let your hearts be full of the new flame of light of the Abhidharma, before the possibility of new achievements and victory. Thus, let not your friend consider this as a pressing call, but rather as a heartfelt warning.

Who is ready for the great deed of self-sacrifice? Verily, only the complete giving of oneself is valued, and only this leads to the goal.

I am not at all surprised at the fact that certain ones among your intellectuals cannot understand the *Fiery World*. Was this so-called intellectuality ever the sign of true knowledge or of accumulations of the Chalice? Intellect is not the higher Manas. The higher intelligence is wisdom, the fruit of many years of accumulation. One may possess a brilliant intellect and at the same time not have the great synthesis which gives perception of the true nature of things. Often, narrow specialists are intellectually brilliant but reveal a complete absence of synthesis. And no explanations can help them, as nothing accumulates so slowly as the synthesis. Indeed, the majority of true "receivers" of the Teaching may be out of the cradle but still too young to be able to read. We are living among the disappearing fifth race and are watching the birth of the coming carriers of Light of the sixth race.

And now, I shall answer you very briefly.

"Abhidharma" is Buddhistic metaphysics. In this case, the light of Abhidharma signifies the highest consciousness, Buddhi-Manas.

"Dukkar," the many eyed and many-armed, is a Tibetan Divinity of the Feminine Element. She is an equivalent of the Hindu Kali and Lakshmi, the symbol of the Mother of the World. Usually, on Tibetan tankas, She is represented under an umbrella, which symbolizes the gathered drops of Highest Bliss.

The "rays of the shoulders" are the radiations from the centers of the shoulders. Every nerve plexus is the hearth of rays.

The energy "Kamaduro" corresponds to the subterranean fire.

"Uraeus" is a sacred symbol depicting the head of the cobra. It was used as a headdress by the Initiates and Pharaos of Egypt, and it also adorns the Gods of India. Thus, Uraeus is a symbol of Initiation and hidden wisdom. The serpent has always been a symbol of wisdom, and the ancient sages of India were called Nagasa. "Nag" means serpent. Uraeus also means cosmic fire.

"The densification of the astral" is the densification of the subtle body (almost up to the physical)—the state of most of the Great Adepts of the Himalayas. I cannot give you more explanations about densification, as I have no permission to do so.

25

24 June 1935

Your letter has reached our mountains, and I shall try to deal with your questions as far as possible. But before I do so, I should also like to ask you a question. Do you not think that there is a profound reason for the fact that the books of Living Ethics often contain not ready formulae but only hints? Precisely so. There is a rule in the foundation of the Teaching (or rather a law) that "all must be performed by human hands and feet." This formula expresses the full value of independent achievements, the kind of achievement that is our own and inalienable.

And now to your questions.

1. The essence of Moru, or Balu, is made from a plant which is to be found all over the Himalayan slopes at or above eight thousand feet. It belongs to the rhododendron family. In Tibet it is used as incense in temples and homes.

2. By "densification of the astral," one should understand the densification of the subtle body almost up to the state of the physical. For many centuries the White Brotherhood has experimented along this line, and now wonderful results have been achieved. But certainly, no details of the apparatus nor any of the necessary chemicals or ingredients can be given out, as the greatest harm might then result. In due time, the appearing of such densified bodies will destroy all doubts regarding the existence of the world beyond, and thus a visible bond with the Subtle World will be established.

3. The design of the apparatus which collects the psychic energy will belong to the one who has the karmic right to it. The same may be said about the apparatuses which will measure the tension of the fire of space. Even if I were to describe them to you, you would hardly benefit from it. But everyone is entitled to search and find. Indeed, hints are given, and all these discoveries are already fixed in space. All these apparatuses are used not only in the Subtle World but even in the physical, in the Stronghold of the Great Brotherhood.

Each one can intensify his vibrations in unison with a definite idea fixed in space and receive the so-called illumination, or inspiration—or at least a glimpse in the desired direction.

4. Consciousness is the fundamental energy, and the psychic energy is its highest quality.

5. The rhythms Mahavan and Chotavan are the rhythms of the Cosmic Fire. At a certain degree of achievement of the Fiery Yoga our organism begins to perceive these rhythms (which come from space) and to resound to them. But their mere repetition, as everything mechanical, will bring no results. In order

that this rhythm be of significance it is essential to possess a supply of psychic energy. Without the assistance of the psychic energy these rhythms remain dead. In connection with this, I give you a paragraph from *Agni Yoga*:

"The Teaching disintegrates because of soulless repetition. Hence, the quality of rhythm must be understood. Of course, at the foundation of each crystal lies attraction and pulsation. But pulsation—otherwise rhythm—is the manifestation of the life principle. Therefore, the given rhythm may be more or less alive or dead. The living rhythm, spiritualized by the effect of consciousness, will effect correlation of subtle energies. But the rhythm of the lips gives a dead beat which disturbs the wise silence and hence brings only harm. Beware of repetitions devoid of spirit! Verily, they dissolve the most precious gems of spirit! If its action is based only on fear or covetousness, then even a skeleton could rap out a more useful rhythm. In this case, the army drummer would be the most successful rhythmist. Could one expect the manifestation of fires from the raps of the tail of a dog awaiting a bone? Remember this when you are dealing with the finest energies, when you intend to approach and call to life the evidence of fire.

"When I gave you the rhythms of the fire of space, I certainly expected the application of a spiritual consciousness and striving without base motives. Long since it was told about the two fires: the creative fire and the destructive one. While the first shines and warms and exalts, the second reduces to ashes and sears. But I directed you only to the creative fire. You have seen upon yourself how the approach of fire is possible, and even daylight did not prevent you from seeing the messengers of space. And the stars became surrounded by signs. One must guard these fiery signs and learn to collect the best offerings of the consciousness.

"Not the blow of a fist, nor threats, but the light-winged ascent carries one to the Gates! Beware of everyday soullessness!"

When you have thoroughly pondered upon the given Teaching you will realize why I answer so briefly your questions. The Teaching attempts to develop first of all a high quality of psychic energy, without which the most precise and subtle apparatus will remain useless. Mechanics are now reaching a new phase where every apparatus will need the help of psychic energy; and the conductor of this energy is man. This realization will bring forth respect for the carriers of this sacred fire. Such people will be looked upon as the real treasures of their country.

Thus, only the one who has a supply of this energy and who is in contact with the Guardians of the reservoir of this power may hope to approach the discovery of the helpful conductor apparatus. That is why the Teaching puts such stress upon the purification and the broadening of the consciousness, and upon the refinement of our feelings. Without this, neither the accumulation of the high psychic energy nor correct communication is possible.

26
6 July 1935

All those full of fear should be reminded of this paragraph from the Teaching:

"Fulfill Our Message. Know to carry the Light. And understand how to manifest the grandeur of Beauty. To the wings that have touched the sun, to the courser before sunrise, to the song that fills the midnight, the way is not a terrible or cruel one." [Leaves of Morya's Garden I]

The fiery calls to the new consciousness, to the new constructiveness, are repeated in the Teaching in many different ways. Only with a new understanding and new ways, and with a regenerated spirit, can one enter the New World. Indeed, a great shifting is taking place now. "I create a New Heaven and a New Earth, and the Old World will be mentioned no more and will not enter the heart."

Each builder must know the material at his disposal. Whatever has deteriorated or is unsuitable should be rejected. Not crowds, but a few chosen ones are required. Crowds have never created; their destiny has been to destroy.

As the great thinker Nietsche says, through his Zarathustra, "And so my eyes have opened; I need followers and living ones, but not the dead. ... Opened are my eyes; not to the crowds shall speak Zarathustra, but to the seekers. Zarathustra must not be the shepherd and the dog of the flock. The one who creates is seeking for those who will follow, not for the dead ones; also not for flocks and not the orthodox. ... The one who creates looks for those who are able to create—precisely those who will inscribe the new values on the new tablets. ... I desire to join the builders and those who reap the harvest and rejoice; I wish to show them the rainbow and all the steps which lead to the Superman."

I am very fond of this book. Of course many become indignant upon reading it. But, precisely, they are the ones who will have difficulty in entering the New World. The time is too threatening now for sentimentality. All who can strive, who can be strong, persevering and courageous, should gather together. True warriors of spirit are needed, ones who are not afraid to raise the sword for the Light and for the Common Good. Thus, the Saints and Bodhisattvas of Tibet are pictured with a sword—the symbol of fearlessness, of valor of the spirit. If one is timid, he had better leave, for verily he will not be able to stand the fire of the New World. The Teaching is not for the weak and the cowardly. The regeneration of the spirit and the true comprehension of Life, illumined by the complete rainbow of Infinite Beauty, is at hand.

Yes, the revolutions and shiftings of the consciousness are needed; otherwise, there comes death and decomposition. Such is the Cosmic Law.

It is said that the true faces of people will be revealed because the purification of space must take place. But you should not be terrified by any such revelation. Long ago it was said that "Ivan" (in hundreds of thousands) will save his country! Tragedy occurs from lack of understanding, as many do not want, or rather fear, to realize that the consciousness of the people has changed—that a whole new generation has grown up, entirely separated from the old one. If our thinking differs so strongly from that of our parents, in spite of the slow tempo of the last century, what can be said of the psychology of the generation reared in a revolutionary environment! How utterly different must their psychology be! Verily, lack of imagination is a great impediment and a drastic limitation of possibilities. Therefore, meet calmly the attacks. "To be afraid of wolves means to avoid the forest," and "God leads the brave." The experience of life confirms these wise proverbs. The cultural constructiveness of the New World needs people of a brave and firm consciousness, who are devoted to the Service of the Good and who are ready to defend at every instant the Great Hierarchy of Light. I shall quote fragments from my favorite book, *New Era Community:*

"Not needed to Us are well-meaning Nicodemuses who come

by night and keep silent by day in the Sanhedrin. Each one must guard the secret entrusted to him, yet he must have ready a word about Us. Firm words can stun the adversaries. Say that it is curious to see one speaking about that which he knows not. If they speak against the hidden treasures, say that even the sea is full of sealed bottles. If they speak against the Community, say that he who reveres Christ, Buddha or Moses does not dare to speak against the Community of Good. The worst thing is to bring false accusation, for in it is falsehood, and slander, and betrayal, and ignorance. Say: 'Since the Teacher exists, why not make use of his wise counsels? You do not make use of them for you know not how to receive them. Hasten to become aware of the Mahatmas not in history but in life, and in the meantime keep your ignorance to yourselves.'

"We drive out all fear. We throw to the wind all the many-colored feathers of fear: blue feathers of frozen terror, green feathers of trembling betrayal, yellow feathers of secret crawling away, red feathers of frenzied heart-beat, white feathers of reticence, black feathers of fall into the abyss. It is needful to repeat about the multiformity of fear; otherwise there remains somewhere a small grey feather of complaisant mumbling or even some fluff of hurried bustle, but behind these will be the same idol of fear. Each wing of fear bears one downwards.

"The Blessed 'Lion,' garbed in fearlessness, ordained to teach the manifestation of courage.

"Swimmers, if you do everything possible within your strength, whither can the most destructive wave carry you? It can only bear you upwards. And thou, sower, when thou wilt distribute the seeds, thou mayst expect a harvest. And thou, shepherd, when thou dost recount thy sheep, thou wilt kindle a manifest light." [New Era Community]

Thus, you should continue your beneficial work, applying wise caution—but never give way to faint-heartedness. Do not fear scarecrows. Oh, these shadows of fear! So much beauty is destroyed because of them. And of so much do we deprive ourselves. I do realize how essential are the gifted co-workers, but unfortunately they are so scattered now!

* * *

In the last issue of the magazine *Occultism and Yoga*, I paid attention to the review of the book, *The Foundations of a New*

Contemplation of the World. I was surprised at the protest against the definition of "THAT" as the Incognizable, Infinite and Eternal! Here again appears the shadow of anthropomorphism. Of course THAT, as the Unutterable, the Inconceivable, or the Causeless Cause, Rootless Root, Absolute, etc., cannot be considered an Individuality, as each individuality is limited to a certain degree, whereas the Absolute is limitless. Likewise, I could ask the objector, who states, "God is Love, but only a 'somebody,' only an individuality and not an impersonal principle or law, is capable of love," whether he ever pondered on what Cosmic Divine Love is and how it is revealed in the billions of endless manifestations, how it is expressed in the various states of consciousness, how the infinite potentiality of THAT is being perpetually unfolded. The East holds sacred the Divine First Principle and hesitates even to use a name for It, pronouncing just the word "THAT" or "Unutterable." All discussions about the First Principle are forbidden in the East, but the whole power of perception is concentrated on the majestic manifestations of this Mystery of Mysteries. The Universe stands on Mystery.

Many of those who consider themselves competent in the occult are still dreadfully under-estimating the great Mystery of the Universe. They have learned to use the word *Infinity,* but very few realize fully this most grand and awesome concept. They continue to limit their God by all the finite attributes created by their own limited thought.

I wish you most sincerely to become a real warrior, and to temper your spirit under the rain of the hostile arrows. There is a peculiar joy in receiving these hostile arrows. Thus, at this moment a betrayal has been discovered where I least of all expected it. My heart was wounded, but somewhere in the depth of it joy is already rising. It is the joy of a warrior, the joy of a possibility of fighting for Truth, and above all the joy of one more liberation!

27

9 July 1935

You ask whether it is right or wrong to forgive sins. I have answered this same question in another of my letters, where I have quoted the words of the Teaching. "To absolve a repentant sinner for a fee—is it not the most heinous crime?" In the same letter I stated that such remission is one of the most terrible evils of modern spiritual upbringing, precisely because being able to obtain such forgiveness under the powerful and sole protection of the church has thrust into the consciousness of people from early childhood the ruinous sense of irresponsibility. Due to certain considerations of local conditions I would suggest that from school age the importance of personal responsibility be advocated in simple and reasonable words. Children in school should be taught to be responsible for every motive, every thought, every deed. They should be given also a clear idea of the meaning and significance of their existence. From this will come the understanding of the necessity to fulfil the obligations of life. Such concepts should be laid into the foundation of the upbringing of the young generation.

I suggest that you do not criticize too much the concepts which are still not outlived, as otherwise, under the existing circumstances, your book might not appear! Why was the image of a serpent chosen as a symbol of wisdom? One of the many explanations of this emblem is that the serpent always holds its head erect and moves in a straight direction, only its body curving according to the obstacles encountered. Thus, let us be as wise as serpents. Following our aim, let us choose the best path.

In order that one may correctly understand the words of Christ, "Verily I say unto you Whatsoever ye shall bind on earth shall be bound in heaven; and whatsoever ye shall loose on earth shall be loosed in heaven," one should carefully read the preceding verses in the same chapter (St. Matthew 18:15). Indeed, the 18th verse is, so to say, a summary which issues from the above parable, and it fully explains the action of the law of Karma. Verily, if we do not resolve our arguments with our near ones here on Earth, they will not be settled in the Subtle World either. For we reap in the Subtle World what we sow here. That is why we should always try to neutralize karma as much as possible or, in other words, to settle our relationships with others while we are on Earth. Why should the word "you" in the 18th verse apply only to the apostles and not to people in general? Certainly, it is not difficult to understand why these words were interpreted as being the right given by Christ to the apostles to "bind and loose," or in other words, to punish and forgive. By the way, the whole parable is far from the kind of non-resistance to evil that is so persistently attributed to Christ.

Indeed, strictly speaking, even the Greatest Spirit is unable to forgive sins that have been committed, as it would contradict the law of Karma. He could ease karma to a certain extent, but that is all. If man is the only creator and recorder of each of his motives, thoughts and deeds, who then can alter anything at all in his being, and therefore in his destiny, without his direct will? The High Spirit can do no more than help us in our efforts to reform our inner beings. Precisely, cooperation is necessary in everything.

Thus, the true meaning of the words "thy sins are forgiven" is that the Great Teacher could sense the aura of the sufferer. He saw that the aura of the sufferer, due to aspiration and faith in his High Power, had heightened its vibrations, and that his healing rays could now be assimilated, thus bringing liberation from the bad results accruing from bad deeds or thoughts. Therefore, He had reason to say "thy sins are forgiven."

Thus, to forgive or to redeem the sins means to eradicate their consequences. In this process of eradication or redeeming of a misdeed, there comes first of all the neutralization, so to say, of those currents which have arisen in the aura of the man due to the liberated energy used by him for committing the wrong. Just as one chemical ingredient is able to change the whole character of a substance composed of several others, so is the action of a high impulse or quality able to neutralize and overcome the results of an action arising from the base qualities in human nature, and thus to change the entire character of the man, transforming his nature.

From this, it should be clear that no one can forgive or redeem the sins of another, but that he certainly can help him, at a specific time, to open his heart toward his higher Ego, thus awakening within himself latent divine forces. In turn, these divine forces will benefit the aura of the one who has helped, and he will become a participant in the good results caused by his helpful awakening of the divine forces in another. Cooperation always, everywhere and in everything.

Christ the Redeemer certainly abides in every one of us. You know already that for the first Christians, as well as for the whole Ancient World, the word "Christos" or Christ, was synonymous with our higher Ego. In this sense, one should understand that

Christ is the Redeemer of sins. Thus, the redemption of personal sins is performed by the soul—the conductor and the messenger of Christ—perpetually, during the long chain of earthly lives of our individual Ego. "The crucified Christ is represented in every human being, who, after the achievement of a certain degree of evolution, must descend into hell and bring back to the higher or normal state the soul fallen there through the lawless deeds of its lower ego. In other words, the Divine Love must reach the heart of a man and must conquer and regenerate him before he is able to realize the monstrosity of his sins against Divine Law. This can be achieved only through a complete fusion and unification with the higher Ego or with the Divine Law of Love."

The same meaning is in the words of Christ to the sinner, Mary Magdalen, who poured myrrh on his feet. The power of faith, the power of love is that fire which transmutes all our feelings. The latter are energies which are transformed into qualities of thought and deed.

Thus, only the transmutation of energies, i.e., feelings or qualities of thought, can take us out of the magic circle of karma. Hence, let us uplift our vibrations through high emotions. It is most important to cultivate in children the aspiration and love toward everything beautiful.

In this heightening of the vibrations, the help of the Teacher is most significant, as He can transfigure by his mere touch a disciple who has attuned his receiver to the rhythm of the vibrations of the Teacher. Precisely, the emanations of a pure earthly teacher raise the vibrations all around him, sometimes over a tremendous area. Thus, not only is space purified, but sometimes even the fires of the individuals who surround him are kindled. That is why, in ancient times, it was considered a great privilege to live near a Teacher and serve Him, as this provided the possibility of contact with his aura. The East knew then and deeply revered the sacred Laws. And in present-day India it is considered a blessing if a holy man chooses to live in one's vicinity.

As to your fear that no one will believe statements which are not confirmed by reference to some well-known authorities, I should like to say that I personally, would prefer to hear either intelligent and clear statements from the authority himself or quotations from entirely new sources, since the very eminence of these authorities often contravenes the new, the forward-looking—in other words, the evolutionary thinking.

By the way, do you know the works of Edward Carpenter? He wrote some fine pages about Cosmic Love, and also about the training of the young generation. He was a pure writer.

Thus, confirm by all kinds of historical examples and stories from life the necessity of realizing the responsibility in fulfilling the duty of bringing up the new generation. In the Bhagavad-Gita also you can find beautiful passages for a chapter dedicated to the education of the young.

* * *

There is nothing higher than creativeness, and there is no greater joy. Therefore—create and rejoice! I send you my best thoughts and courage. Be daring in creative flight. In spite of my own numerous practical warnings to you, I sometimes feel like whispering, "Create courageously!" Let thought undistorted and unrestricted be impressed into space and in the inner records of your being. Let it be free from the shadow of the censor's scalpel. To be sure, it is never too late to cut, to mutilate, to bring down to the level of the crowd. But when you are alone or with those spiritually close to you, create and speak freely.

CONTENTS

Preface   vi

Part I
LETTERS TO AMERICA
1929-1932

1 – *1929*	11
2 – *1 March 1929*	13
3 – *19 October 1929*	16
4 – *13 October 1929*	18
5 – *11 February 1929*	21
6 – *17 December 1929*	25
7 – *11 September 1929*	26
8 – *15 January 1930*	29
9 – *24 February 1930*	32
10 – *24 June 1930*	36
11 – *17 August 1930*	38
12 – *7 October 1930*	43
13 – *13 October 1930*	45
14 – *3 December 1930*	50
15 – *17 December 1930*	55
16 – *7 January 1931*	58
17 – *15 January 1931*	60
18 – *21 January 1931*	64
19 – *13 May 1931*	67
20 – *29 May 1931*	71
21 – *3 June 1931*	78
22 – *11 June 1931*	84
23 – *17 June 1931*	85
24 – *30 June 1931*	89
25 – *20 July 1931*	93
26 – *21 August 1931*	95

27 – 7 October 1931	101
28 – 21 October 1931	104
29 – 8 November 1931	108
30 – 12 December 1931	109
31 – 5 May 1932	112
32 – 28 June 1932	113
33 – 7 July 1932	115
34 – 6 October 1932	116
35 – 12 October 1932	119
36 – 10 November 1932	120
37 – 17 November 1932	123
38 – 10 December 1932	124
39 – 29 December 1932	126

Part II
LETTERS TO EUROPE
1931-1934

1 – 24 April 1931	133
2 – 28 August 1931	133
3 – 26 December 1931	137
4 – 15 January 1932	138
5 – 24 November 1932	140
6 – 1933	141
7 – 27 January 1933	143
8 – 10 May 1933	148
9 – 19 June 1933	150
10 – 8 February 1934	156
11 – 17 February 1934	158
12 – 17 April 1934	164
13 – 11 April 1934	171
14 – 26 April 1934	173
15 – 5 May 1934	177

16 – *6 May 1934*	183
17 – *25 May 1934*	190
18 – *26 May 1934*	192
19a – *2 June 1934*	197
19b – *7 June 1934*	206
20 – *14 June 1934*	213
21 – *30 June 1934*	219
22 – *6 July 1934*	224
23 – *21 July 1934*	226
24 – *1 August 1934*	235
25 – *8 August 1934*	240
26 – *11 August 1934*	245
27 – *12 August 1934*	249
28 – *17 August 1934*	250
29 – *23 August 1934*	258
30 – *29 August 1934*	260
31 – *8 September 1934*	267
32 – *12 September 1934*	279
33 – *15 September 1934*	292
34 – *10 September 1934*	293
35 – *18 October 1934*	301
36 – *8 November 1934*	303
37 – *15 November 1934*	308
38 – *6 December 1934*	311
39 – *12 December 1934*	318
40 – *12 December 1934*	323
41 – *12 December 1934*	330
42 – *20 December 1934*	332

Part III
1935

1 – *9 January 1935*	341

2 – *11 January 1935* 343
3 – *16 January 1935* 346
4 – *1 February 1935* 353
5 – *28 February 1935* 363
6 – *5 March 1935* 365
7 – *7 March 1935* 370
8 – *8 March 1935* 372
9 – *12 March 1935* 377
10 – *22 March 1935* 380
11 – *25 March 1935* 384
12 – *12 April 1935* 389
13 – *18 April 1935* 396
14 – *20 April 1935* 398
15 – *30 April 1935* 404
16 – *8 May 1935* 410
17 – *21 May 1935* 416
18 – *31 May 1935* 419
19 – *6 June 1935* 426
20 – *11 June 1935* 433
21 – *11 June 1935* 434
22 – *18 June 1935* 443
23 – *18 June 1935* 447
24 – *24 June 1935* 452
25 – *24 June 1935* 457
26 – *6 July 1935* 460
27 – *9 July 1935* 463

AGNI YOGA SERIES

LEAVES OF MORYA'S GARDEN I (THE CALL)	1924
LEAVES OF MORYA'S GARDEN II (ILLUMINATION)	1925
NEW ERA COMMUNITY	1926
Signs of Agni Yoga	
AGNI YOGA	1929
INFINITY I	1930
INFINITY II	1930
HIERARCHY	1931
HEART	1932
FIERY WORLD I	1933
FIERY WORLD II	1934
FIERY WORLD III	1935
AUM	1936
BROTHERHOOD	1937
SUPERMUNDANE (IN 3 VOLUMES)	1938
LETTERS OF HELENA ROERICH, Vol. I	1929-1935
LETTERS OF HELENA ROERICH, Vol. II	1935-1939

AGNI YOGA SOCIETY
www.agniyoga.org

www.ingramcontent.com/pod-product-compliance
Lightning Source LLC
Chambersburg PA
CBHW071552080526
44588CB00010B/888